POETRY FOCUS 2019

LEAVING CERTIFICATE POEMS & NOTES FOR ENGLISH HIGHER LEVEL

MARTIN KIERAN & FRANCES ROCKS

g GILL EDUCATION

Gill Education
Hume Avenue
Park West
Dublin 12
www.gilleducation.ie

Gill Education is an imprint of M.H. Gill & Co.

ISBN: 978-0-7171-73235

Design: Tanya M. Ross, Elementic.ie
Print origination: Carole Lynch

At the time of going to press, all web addresses were active and contained information relevant to the topics in this book. Gill Education does not, however, accept responsibility for the content or views contained on these websites. Content, views and addresses may change beyond the publisher or author's control. Students should always be supervised when reviewing websites.

The authors and publisher have made every effort to trace all copyright holders, but if any have been inadvertently overlooked we would be pleased to make the necessary arrangement at the first opportunity.

For permission to reproduce photographs, the authors and publisher gratefully acknowledge the following:

© Alamy: 23, 39, 44, 110, 140, 148, 153, 162, 170, 174, 204, 209, 235, 243, 341, 352, 387, 395, 404, 409, 417, 422, 426, 447, 461, 474, 485; © The Art Archive: 435; © Bridgeman Images: 336, 372; © Collins Agency: 186, 357; © Corbis: 11, 383; © Faber & Faber Ltd: 67; © Getty Images: 5, 17, 28, 50, 57, 70, 75, 80, 94, 114, 118, 166, 230, 253, 294, 317, 323, 328, 332, 346, 362, 367, 391, 413, 443, 457, 470, 489; © Imagefile: 85, 106, 136, 144, 157, 400, 438, 466; © iStock: 191, 194, 200, 225, 239, 256, 260, 267, 275, 281, 286, 291, 292, 298, 302; © The Josef and Yaye Breitenbach Charitable Foundation, New York: 1; © National Monuments Service. Dept. of Arts, Heritage, Regional, Rural and Gaeltacht Affairs: 219; © PD Smith: 481; © Press Association: 34; © RTÉ Stills Archive: 313, 183; © Saint Patrick's Cathedral: 478; © TopFoto: 90, 98, 102, 123, 133, 451.

The authors and publisher have made every effort to trace all copyright holders, but if any have been inadvertently overlooked we would be pleased to make the necessary arrangement at the first opportunity.

The paper used in this book is made from the wood pulp of managed forests. For every tree felled, at least one tree is planted, thereby renewing natural resources.

CONTENTS

*The poems marked with an asterisk are also prescribed for the Ordinary Level course.

Introduction

Poetry Focus is a modern poetry textbook for Leaving Certificate Higher Level English. It includes all the prescribed poems for the 2019 exam as well as succinct commentaries on each one. Well-organised and easily accessible study notes provide all the necessary information to allow students to explore the poems and to develop their own individual responses and enhance their skills in critical literacy. There is no single 'correct' approach to answering the poetry question. Candidates are free to respond in any appropriate way that shows good knowledge of and engagement with the prescribed poems.

- **Concise poet biographies** provide context for the poems.
- **Initial response** questions follow the text of each poem. These allow students to consider their first impressions before any in-depth study or analysis. These questions provide a good opportunity for written and/or oral exercises.
- **Study notes** highlight the main features of the poet's subject matter and style. These discussion notes will enhance the student's own critical appreciation through focused group work and/or written exercises. Analytical skills are developed in a coherent, practical way to give students confidence in articulating their own personal responses to the poems and poets.
- **Analysis is provided using graded sample paragraphs** which aid students in fluently structuring and developing valid points, using fresh and varied expression. These model paragraphs also illustrate effective use of relevant quotations and reference.
- **Class/Homework exercises** for each poem provide focused practice in writing personal responses to examination-style questions.
- **Summary points** provide a memorable snapshot of the key aspects to remember about each poet.
- **Full sample Leaving Certificate essays** are accompanied by marking-scheme guidelines and examiners' comments. These show the student exactly what is required to achieve a successful top grade in the Leaving Cert. The examiner's comments illustrate the use of the PCLM marking scheme and are an invaluable aid for the ambitious student.
- **Sample essay plans** on each poet's work illustrate how to interpret a question and recognise the particular nuances of key words in examination questions. Student evaluation of these essay plans increase confidence in developing and organising clear response to exam questions.
- **Sample Leaving Cert questions** on each poet are given at the end of their section.
- **A glossary of common literary terms** at the back of the book provides an easy reference when answering questions.
- **A critical analysis checklist** provides hints and tips on how to show genuine engagement with the poetry.

 The FREE eBook contains:

- **Investigate Further** sections which contain **useful weblinks** should you want to learn more.
- **Pop-up key quotes** to encourage students to select their own individual combination of references from a poem and to write brief commentaries on specific quotations.
- Additional sample graded paragraphs called '**Developing your personal response**'.
- Audio of a selection of the poetry as read by the poets, including audio of all of Brendan Kennelly's poetry.

HOW IS THE PRESCRIBED POETRY QUESTION MARKED?

Marking is done (ex. 50 marks) by reference to the PCLM criteria for assessment.

- Clarity of purpose (P): 30% of the total (15 marks)
- Coherence of delivery (C): 30% of the total (15 marks)
- Efficiency of language use (L): 30% of the total (15 marks)
- Accuracy of mechanics (M): 10% of the total (5 marks)

Each answer will be in the form of a response to a specific task requiring candidates to:

- Display a clear and purposeful engagement with the set task (P)
- Sustain the response in an appropriate manner over the entire answer (C)
- Manage and control language appropriate to the task (L)
- Display levels of accuracy in spelling and grammar appropriate to the required/chosen register (M)

GENERAL

'Students at Higher Level will be required to study a representative selection from the work of eight poets: a representative selection would seek to reflect the range of a poet's themes and interests and exhibit his/her characteristic style and viewpoint. Normally the study of at least six poems by each poet would be expected.' (DES English Syllabus, 6.3)

The marking scheme guidelines from the State Examinations Commission state that in the case of each poet, the candidates have **freedom of choice** in relation to the poems studied. In addition, there is **not a finite list of any 'poet's themes and interests'**.

Note that in responding to the question set on any given poet, the candidates must refer to the poem(s) they have studied but are not required to refer to **any specific poem(s), nor are they expected to discuss or refer to all the poems they have chosen to study**.

In each of the questions in **Prescribed Poetry**, the underlying nature of the task is the invitation to the candidates to **engage with the poems themselves**.

EXAM ADVICE

- You are not expected to write about any **set number of poems** in the examination. You might decide to focus in detail on a small number of poems, or you could choose to write in a more general way on several poems.
- Most candidates write one or two well-developed **paragraphs** on each of the poems they have chosen for discussion. In other cases, a paragraph will focus on one specific aspect of the poet's work. When discussing recurring themes or features of style, appropriate cross-references to other poems may also be useful.
- Reflect on central **themes** and viewpoints in the poems you discuss. Comment also on the use of language and the poet's distinctive **style**. Examine imagery, tone, structure, rhythm and rhyme. Be careful not to simply list aspects of style, such as alliteration or repetition. There's little point in mentioning that a poet uses sound effects or metaphors without discussing the effectiveness of such characteristics.
- Focus on **the task** you have been given in the poetry question. Identify the key terms in the wording of the question and think of similar words for these terms. This will help you develop a relevant and coherent personal response in keeping with the PCLM marking scheme criteria.
- Always root your answers in the text of the poems. Support the points you make with **relevant reference and quotation**. Make sure your own expression is fresh and lively. Avoid awkward expressions, such as 'It says in the poem that ...'. Look for alternatives: 'There is a sense of ...', 'The tone seems to suggest ...', 'It's evident that ...', etc.
- Neat, **legible handwriting** will help to make a positive impression on examiners. Corrections should be made by simply drawing a line through the mistake. Scored-out words distract attention from the content of your work.
- Keep the emphasis on why particular poets **appeal to you**. Consider the continuing relevance or significance of a poet's work. Perhaps you have shared some of the feelings or experiences expressed in the poems. Avoid starting answers with prepared biographical sketches. Details of a poet's life are better used when discussing how the poems themselves were shaped by such experiences.
- Remember that the examination encourages **individual engagement** with the prescribed poems. Poetry can make us think and feel and imagine. It opens our minds to the wonderful possibilities of language and ideas. Your interaction with the poems is what matters most. Study notes and critical interpretations are all there to be challenged. Read the poems carefully and have confidence in expressing your own personal response.

ELIZABETH BISHOP

1911– 1979

'The armored cars of dreams, contrived to let us do so many a dangerous thing.'

E lizabeth Bishop was born in Worcester, Massachusetts, in 1911. During her early life she experienced a series of family tragedies. She spent part of her childhood with her Canadian grandparents following her father's death and mother's hospitalisation. She then lived with various relatives who, according to Bishop, took care of her because they felt sorry for her. These unsettling events, along with the memories of her youth, inspired her to read poetry – and eventually to write it. Like many poets and artists, Bishop was a great observer with a vivid sense of place. After studying English at university, she travelled extensively and lived in New York, Florida and, for 17 years, Brazil. She also taught at several American colleges. Throughout her life she suffered from ill health and depression. As a poet, she wrote sparingly, publishing only five slim volumes in 35 years. However, her work received high acclaim. 'I think geography comes first in my work,' she told an interviewer, 'and then animals. But I like people, too. I've written a few poems about people.' Recurring themes in her refreshing and thought-provoking poetry include childhood experiences, travel, the natural world, loneliness, detachment and the art of writing itself. Bishop died suddenly in her Boston apartment on 6 October 1979. She was 68 years old. Her poetry continues to gain widespread recognition and study.

INVESTIGATE FURTHER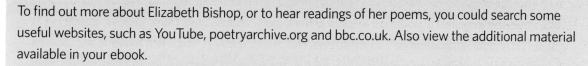

To find out more about Elizabeth Bishop, or to hear readings of her poems, you could search some useful websites, such as YouTube, poetryarchive.org and bbc.co.uk. Also view the additional material available in your ebook.

Prescribed Poems HIGHER LEVEL

* The poems marked with an asterisk are also prescribed for the Ordinary Level course.

❶   THE FISH

I caught a tremendous fish
and held him beside the boat
half out of water, with my hook
fast in a corner of his mouth.
He didn't fight.   5
He hadn't fought at all.
He hung a grunting weight,
battered and venerable
and homely. Here and there
his brown skin hung in strips   10
like ancient wallpaper,
and its pattern of darker brown
was like wallpaper:
shapes like full-blown roses
stained and lost through age.   15
He was speckled with barnacles,
fine rosettes of lime,
and infested
with tiny white sea-lice,
and underneath two or three   20
rags of green weed hung down.
While his gills were breathing in
the terrible oxygen
– the frightening gills,
fresh and crisp with blood,   25
that can cut so badly –
I thought of the coarse white flesh
packed in like feathers,
the big bones and the little bones,
the dramatic reds and blacks   30
of his shiny entrails,
and the pink swim-bladder
like a big peony.
I looked into his eyes
which were far larger than mine   35
but shallower, and yellowed,
the irises backed and packed
with tarnished tinfoil
seen through the lenses

of old scratched isinglass.   40
They shifted a little, but not
to return my stare.
– It was more like the tipping
of an object toward the light.
I admired his sullen face,   45
the mechanism of his jaw,
and then I saw
that from his lower lip
– if you could call it a lip –
grim, wet, and weaponlike,   50
hung five old pieces of fish-line,
or four and a wire leader
with the swivel still attached,
with all their five big hooks
grown firmly in his mouth.   55
A green line, frayed at the end
where he broke it, two heavier lines,
and a fine black thread
still crimped from the strain and snap
when it broke and he got away.   60
Like medals with their ribbons
frayed and wavering,
a five-haired beard of wisdom
trailing from his aching jaw.
I stared and stared   65
and victory filled up
the little rented boat,
from the pool of bilge
where oil had spread a rainbow
around the rusted engine   70
to the bailer rusted orange,
the sun-cracked thwarts,
the oarlocks on their strings,
the gunnels – until everything
was rainbow, rainbow, rainbow!   75
And I let the fish go.

'He hung a grunting weight'

Glossary

1	*tremendous*: huge, startling, fearsome.	45	*sullen*: bad-tempered, sulky.
8	*venerable*: ancient, worthy of respect.	46	*mechanism*: workings.
9	*homely*: comfortable, easy-going, unpretentious, plain.	52	*leader*: wire connecting fishhook and line.
17	*rosettes*: rose-shaped decorations made of ribbon, often awarded as prizes.	59	*crimped*: pressed into ridges.
		62	*frayed*: unravelled, worn.
19	*sea-lice*: small parasites that live on the skin of fish.	68	*bilge*: dirty water that collects in the bottom of a boat.
24	*gills*: breathing organs of fish.	71	*bailer*: bucket that scoops water out of a boat.
31	*entrails*: internal organs.	72	*thwarts*: rowers' benches.
33	*peony*: large, flamboyant flower, usually pink.	73	*oarlocks*: metal devices for holding oars.
37	*irises*: coloured parts of an eye.	74	*gunnels*: upper edges of the side of a boat.
40	*isinglass*: gelatine-like substance obtained from the bodies of fish, opaque.		

INITIAL RESPONSE

1. List two details that appealed to you in the description of the fish in lines 1–15. Why did they make an impact on you? Were they unusual or did they appeal to your senses? Support your response with quotation from the poem.

2. What is the poet's attitude towards the fish? Where does it change as the poem progresses? Give a reason for this change. Refer closely to the poem in your response.

3. Who had the 'victory' in this situation – the fish or Bishop? Why did you come to this conclusion? Support your discussion with clear references from the poem.

STUDY NOTES

'The Fish' is from Elizabeth Bishop's first published collection, North and South *(1946). She lived in Florida during the 1930s and the poem is based on her experience of catching a large jewfish at Key West. Bishop once said, 'I like painting probably better than I like poetry' and 'The Fish' is certainly a very visual poem. Bishop uses the fish as a way of exploring a 'green' awareness, the respect for nature and all living things.*

The poem's **opening line** is direct and forceful ('I caught a tremendous fish'). Bishop's use of the personal pronoun 'I' gives a sense of immediacy and intimacy. The adjective 'tremendous' reflects **the poet's breathless excitement and awe at this magnificent specimen of fish**. The act of catching the fish is described in a personal, down-to-earth way. Bishop once said, 'I always tell the truth in my poems ... that's exactly how it happened.' The fish is 'half out of water', no longer in its natural habitat.

In **line 5**, the focus shifts from the person who caught the fish to the fish itself. **It is now given a personality**: 'He didn't fight.' The onomatopoeic 'grunting' allows us to be part of this scene, as we hear the distressed noises from the gasping, ugly ('homely'), exhausted ('battered') fish. Then another facet of the fish is presented to us: it is 'venerable', ancient and worthy of reverence. Bishop the participant is giving way to Bishop the observer. While in college, Bishop met Marianne Moore, a famous American poet whose focus was on the accurate description of a particular thing. This poetic movement was known as **imagism**. We can see the similarity of style between the two poets in Bishop's description of the fish: 'Here and there/his brown skin hung in strips/like ancient wallpaper'.

The surface **detail is painstakingly and imaginatively described** ('like full-blown roses'). There seems to be an attempt to domesticate the creature, but the sordid reality of the blotches on the skin is also noted ('stained and lost through age'). The texture of the fish is described graphically, as if we were examining the skin under a microscope: 'speckled', 'infested', 'rags'. Colours ('lime', 'white' and 'green') help convey this vivid picture. The wildness of the creature is caught in the detailed phrasing 'frightening gills,/fresh and crisp with blood' (**line 24**). Its interior is also imagined ('pink swim-bladder/like a big peony'). These original and striking images appeal to both our visual and tactile senses.

Bishop's delight in catching this fine specimen soon gives way to an **emotional involvement with the fish** and his struggle for survival (**line 34**). She compares his eyes to her own ('far larger'). She notes the wear and tear from a long, hard life ('yellowed'). The irises are 'backed and packed/with tarnished tinfoil'. Here, assonance and alliteration give emphasis to the image. However, the fish's eyes are unresponsive, so there seems to be no interplay between creature and poet. This suggests both the independence and the vulnerability of the fish.

Progression in the poem is shown in the verbs: 'I caught', 'I thought', 'I looked' and, in **line 45**, 'I admired'. The **poet admires the resolute nature of the fish** ('his sullen face'). This fish has survived previous battles ('five big hooks/grown firmly in his mouth'). Precise detail emphasises the severity of these battles ('A green line, frayed at the end/where he broke it'). Military language highlights the effort the fish has made to survive: 'weaponlike', 'medals'. Bishop's sympathy is clear as she notes the fish's 'aching jaw'. For the fish, it is clear that the pain of battle remains.

Line 65 shows the poet transfixed ('I stared and stared'). Now the scene expands from a single fisher in a 'little rented boat' to something of **universal significance** ('victory' fills up the boat). Ordinary details (the 'bilge', the 'thwarts' and the 'gunnels') are transformed. The oil has 'spread a rainbow'. Everything is coloured and Bishop's relationship with the fish changes. She exercises mercy. A moment of epiphany occurs and she lets 'the fish go'. All the tension in the poem is finally released. The underlying drama contained between the opening line ('I caught a tremendous fish') and the closing line ('And I let the fish go.') has been resolved. **Victory belongs to both the poet and the fish**. The fish is free; the poet has seen and understood.

This poem is a long narrative with a clear beginning, middle and end. Bishop has chosen a suitably unrhymed form. The metre is appropriate for the speaking voice: dimeter (two stresses) and trimeter (three stresses). Short run-on lines suggest the poet excitedly examining her catch and the recurring use of dashes indicates her thought process as she moves from delight to wonder, empathy and, finally, comprehension. The concluding rhyming couplet brings a definite and satisfying resolution to the dramatic tension.

ANALYSIS

Elizabeth Bishop has been praised for her 'painterly eye'. Discuss this aspect of her style in 'The Fish'. Support your views with close reference to the poem.

Sample Paragraph

An artist looks, then sees, orders, recreates and leads both themselves and their viewers to a new insight. I think Elizabeth Bishop accomplishes all this in her poem 'The Fish'. The poet looks at the event ('I caught a tremendous fish') and then moves to describe the fish, using striking images ('brown skin hung in strips/like ancient wallpaper'). Like a camera, she pans this way and that, making us see also 'its pattern of darker brown' with 'shapes like full-blown roses'. She leads us to imagine the exotic interior of the fish, its 'coarse white flesh/packed in like feathers'. We see the order and symmetry, the 'dramatic reds and blacks'. If Bishop were painting this fish, I could imagine it in glistening oil colours. In her poem, she paints with words: 'the pink swim-bladder/like a peony'. She engages with her subject and has an emotional response to it: 'I looked into his eyes'. She acknowledges this veteran survivor, as she notes his 'medals', the 'five big hooks/grown firmly in his mouth'. They have been there so long that the skin has grown over them and she draws our attention to the fish's 'aching jaw'. Just like a painter leads us to see what they see, Bishop orders her picture so that we can see the 'five-haired beard of wisdom/trailing' from the fish. The poem concludes with a burst of colour ('rainbow, rainbow, rainbow!'). The rainbow from the oil-soaked, dirty bilge water has transformed the poet's relationship with the fish. Like Bishop, we now see the proper relationship between people and nature – one of respect. So the 'painterly eye' of Bishop has led us to see the drama of the occasion, the fish and what it really was, and finally our correct response to the earth and its creatures.

Examiner's Comment

A mature and interesting interpretation of the question. The top-grade response is very well focused and there is a sustained personal perspective throughout. Judicious use of quotations rounds off the answer. With the exception of the last sentence, expression is generally fluent and assured.

N.B. Access your ebook for additional sample paragraphs and a list of useful quotes with commentary.

CLASS/HOMEWORK EXERCISES

1. Bishop often structures her poems like a mini-drama. Examine the poem 'The Fish' and comment on how a dramatic effect is achieved. Consider setting, characterisation, conflict, the interior debate, tension building to climax, and resolution. Refer closely to the text of the poem in your response.

2. 'Elizabeth Bishop has commented that she simply tried "to see things afresh" in her poetry.' To what extent is this true of her poem, 'The Fish'? Support your answer with reference to the text.

SUMMARY POINTS

- Themes include endurance and the relationship between nature and human nature.
- Observational details, vibrant language, personification, striking comparisons.
- Engaging first person narrative voice.
- Varying tones – joyful, admiring, celebratory.
- Memorable sound effects – assonance, alliteration, sibilance, repetition.
- Dramatic development which ends in a moment of insight.

❷ THE BIGHT

On my birthday

At low tide like this how sheer the water is.
White, crumbling ribs of marl protrude and glare
and the boats are dry, the pilings dry as matches.
Absorbing, rather than being absorbed,
the water in the bight doesn't wet anything,   5
the color of the gas flame turned as low as possible.
One can smell it turning to gas; if one were Baudelaire
one could probably hear it turning to marimba music.
The little ocher dredge at work off the end of the dock
already plays the dry perfectly off-beat claves.   10
The birds are outsize. Pelicans crash
into this peculiar gas unnecessarily hard,
it seems to me, like pickaxes,
rarely coming up with anything to show for it,
and going off with humorous elbowings.   15
Black-and-white man-of-war birds soar
on impalpable drafts
and open their tails like scissors on the curves
or tense them like wishbones, till they tremble.
The frowsy sponge boats keep coming in   20
with the obliging air of retrievers,
bristling with jackstraw gaffs and hooks
and decorated with bobbles of sponges.
There is a fence of chicken wire along the dock
where, glinting like little plowshares,   25
the blue-gray shark tails are hung up to dry
for the Chinese-restaurant trade.
Some of the little white boats are still piled up
against each other, or lie on their sides, stove in,
and not yet salvaged, if they ever will be, from the last bad storm,   30
like torn-open, unanswered letters.
The bight is littered with old correspondences.
Click. Click. Goes the dredge,
and brings up a dripping jawful of marl.
All the untidy activity continues,   35
awful but cheerful.

'and the boats are dry'

Glossary

The Bight: refers to a wide bay or inlet.
2 *marl*: rich clay soil.
3 *pilings*: heavy beams supporting a jetty.
7 *Baudelaire*: Charles Baudelaire (1821–67), French symbolist poet.
8 *marimba*: wooden instrument similar to a xylophone, played by African and Central American jazz musicians.
9 *ocher*: ochre; orange-brown colour.
10 *claves*: clefs; musical keys.
17 *impalpable drafts*: slight air currents.

20 *frowsy*: shabby, foul-smelling.
21 *retrievers*: hunting dogs.
22 *bristling*: shining.
22 *jackstraw gaffs*: splinters used as hooks on fishing rods.
23 *bobbles*: trimmings.
25 *plowshares*: ploughing blades.
29 *stove in*: storm-damaged.
30 *salvaged*: repaired.
33 *dredge*: a dredger is a machine for digging underwater.

INITIAL RESPONSE

1. Using close reference to the text, describe the atmosphere in the first six lines of the poem.

2. Choose one simile that you think is particularly effective in the poem. Briefly explain your choice.

3. Although the poem is not directly personal, what does it suggest to you about Elizabeth Bishop herself? Refer to the text in your answer.

STUDY NOTES

'The Bight' showcases Elizabeth Bishop's aesthetic appreciation of the world around her. The setting for this poem is Garrison Bight in Florida. In describing the small, untidy harbour, Bishop displays a characteristically keen eye for observation and an expert use of metaphor. The subtitle, '(On my birthday)', suggests a special occasion and, perhaps, a time for reflection and reappraisal of life.

The poem begins with an introduction to the bight at 'low tide' and gradually constructs **a vivid picture of an uninviting place**: 'White, crumbling ribs of marl protrude and glare'. Grim personification and a sharp 'r' sound effect emphasise the unsettling atmosphere. There is a sense of unreality about sea water that 'doesn't wet anything'. The description in these **opening lines** is typically detailed, sensual and precise – all carefully shaped by the poet's own personal vision of the world. References to 'the pilings dry as matches' and the 'gas flame' water are rather disturbing, implying that something dangerous might be about to happen.

Bishop's mention of the French poet Charles Baudelaire (**line 7**) would suggest that she shares his belief in expressing human experience through objects and places around us. The poet imagines Baudelaire being able to 'hear' the water 'turning to marimba music'. She also finds an unexpected jazz rhythm ('perfectly off-beat claves') coming from the machine that is dredging 'off the end of the dock'. In lines **11–19**, Bishop depicts the 'outsize' birds through a series of vigorous images. They seem awkward and out of place in this busy, built-up location. **Figurative language illustrates their mechanical movements**: pelicans 'crash' into the sea 'like pickaxes', while man-of-war birds 'open their tails like scissors'. An underlying sense of disquiet can be detected in the detailed observations of these 'tense' birds as they 'tremble' in flight.

The poet's portrayal of the bight is quite realistic: 'frowsy sponge boats keep coming in' to harbour. With wry humour, she acknowledges their unlikely beauty, 'bristling with jackstraw gaffs' and 'decorated with bobbles of sponges'. The cluttered dockside is a busy working environment where 'blue-gray shark tails are hung up to dry' (**line 26**). The 'little white boats' are a reminder of the local fishing community and its dependence on the sea. Bishop compares the small fishing boats to 'torn-open, unanswered letters'. The bight suddenly reminds her of a cluttered writing-desk – her own, presumably – 'littered with old correspondences'.

This metaphor is developed in lines **33–36**. Bishop returns to sharp sounds: the 'Click. Click.' noise of the dredger (compared to an animal unearthing the wet clay) as it 'brings up a dripping jawful of marl'. The ending is highly symbolic of the poet's own impulse to dig deep into her memories. Drawing a close comparison between her own life and the 'untidy activity' of the bight, she concludes that both are 'awful but cheerful'. **The matter-of-fact tone of these closing lines is derisive but good humoured.** It reflects her realistic approach to the highs and lows of human experience – and the thoughts that are likely to have crossed her mind as she celebrated yet another birthday.

ANALYSIS

'Closely observed description and vivid imagery are striking features of Elizabeth Bishop's poems.' Discuss this statement in relation to 'The Bight'. Refer to the poem in support of your views.

Sample Paragraph

I think 'The Bight' is a good example of how Elizabeth Bishop slowly builds up a picture of a fairly inhospitable place, layer upon layer. At first, she describes the 'sheer' water and the 'crumbling ribs of marl', personifying the loose soil as an emaciated body. This is a vivid and disturbing image that suggests that the bay is bleak and unattractive. We get a sense of the sounds she hears – the 'dredge at work' pounding away in the background. Bishop uses dramatic imagery to bring the birds to life – particularly the vicious man-of-war birds whose tails are 'like scissors' and 'tense' as wishbones. We also see the poet's eye for precise detail in her imaginative description of the damaged fishing boats that lie on the shore 'like torn-open, unanswered letters'. Bishop uses colour imagery very effectively – 'blue-gray shark tails' are hanging out to dry for the local restaurant trade. But she is not restricted to visual effects. Her descriptions appeal to other senses, particularly sound. The poem ends with the rasping sound of the dredger – 'Click. Click' digging up 'a dripping jawful of marl'. This remarkable image suggests to me how the bight keeps bringing back memories to the poet, both pleasant and unpleasant. It is an impressive way of rounding off the poem, as she associates the untidy harbour with her own varied life – 'awful but cheerful'.

Examiner's Comment

A very well-focused, high-grade response, making excellent use of numerous accurate quotations. The various elements of the question are addressed and there is evidence of good personal engagement with the text. Expression throughout is also fluent and controlled.

N.B. Access your ebook for additional sample paragraphs and a list of useful quotes with commentary.

CLASS/HOMEWORK EXERCISES

1. 'Elizabeth Bishop's poetry is both sensuous and reflective.' To what extent is this true of 'The Bight'? Support the points you make with suitable reference to the text of the poem.

2. 'In many of her poems, Elizabeth Bishop begins with memorable visual and aural details which lead to moments of intense understanding.' Discuss this statement with reference to 'The Bight'.

SUMMARY POINTS

- Descriptive details give a clear picture of the littered bay at low tide.
- Enduring personal upheavals and disappointments are central themes.
- Bishop relates to the untidy location as she reappraises her own disorderly life.
- Striking metaphorical language, memorable patterns of unusual imagery.
- Contrasting tones – pessimistic, reflective, insightful, upbeat.

❸ AT THE FISHHOUSES

Although it is a cold evening,
down by one of the fishhouses
an old man sits netting,
his net, in the gloaming almost invisible,
a dark purple-brown,   5
and his shuttle worn and polished.
The air smells so strong of codfish
it makes one's nose run and one's eyes water.
The five fishhouses have steeply peaked roofs
and narrow, cleated gangplanks slant up   10
to storerooms in the gables
for the wheelbarrows to be pushed up and down on.
All is silver: the heavy surface of the sea,
swelling slowly as if considering spilling over,
is opaque, but the silver of the benches,   15
the lobster pots, and masts, scattered
among the wild jagged rocks,
is of an apparent translucence
like the small old buildings with an emerald moss
growing on their shoreward walls.   20
The big fish tubs are completely lined
with layers of beautiful herring scales
and the wheelbarrows are similarly plastered
with creamy iridescent coats of mail,
with small iridescent flies crawling on them.   25
Up on the little slope behind the houses,
set in the sparse bright sprinkle of grass,
is an ancient wooden capstan,
cracked, with two long bleached handles
and some melancholy stains, like dried blood,   30
where the ironwork has rusted.
The old man accepts a Lucky Strike.
He was a friend of my grandfather.
We talk of the decline in the population
and of codfish and herring   35
while he waits for a herring boat to come in.
There are sequins on his vest and on his thumb.
He has scraped the scales, the principal beauty,

from unnumbered fish with that black old knife,
the blade of which is almost worn away.   40

Down at the water's edge, at the place
where they haul up the boats, up the long ramp
descending into the water, thin silver
tree trunks are laid horizontally
across the gray stones, down and down   45
at intervals of four or five feet.

Cold dark deep and absolutely clear,
element bearable to no mortal,
to fish and seals . . . One seal particularly
I have seen here evening after evening.   50
He was curious about me. He was interested in music;
like me a believer in total immersion,
so I used to sing him Baptist hymns.
I also sang 'A Mighty Fortress Is Our God.'
He stood up in the water and regarded me   55
steadily, moving his head a little.
Then he would disappear, then suddenly emerge
almost in the same spot, with a sort of shrug
as if it were against his better judgment.
Cold dark deep and absolutely clear,   60
the clear gray icy water . . . Back, behind us,
the dignified tall firs begin.
Bluish, associating with their shadows,
a million Christmas trees stand
waiting for Christmas. The water seems suspended   65
above the rounded gray and blue-gray stones.
I have seen it over and over, the same sea, the same,
slightly, indifferently swinging above the stones,
icily free above the stones,
above the stones and then the world.   70
If you should dip your hand in,
your wrist would ache immediately,
your bones would begin to ache and your hand would burn
as if the water were a transmutation of fire
that feeds on stones and burns with a dark gray flame.   75
If you tasted it, it would first taste bitter,
then briny, then surely burn your tongue.

It is like what we imagine knowledge to be:
dark, salt, clear, moving, utterly free,
drawn from the cold hard mouth   80
of the world, derived from the rocky breasts
forever, flowing and drawn, and since
our knowledge is historical, flowing, and flown.

'in the gloaming'

Glossary

4	*gloaming*: twilight, evening.
6	*shuttle*: tool used for weaving and mending fishing nets.
10	*cleated*: wooden projections nailed to a ladder to prevent slipping.
10	*gangplanks*: removable ramps used for boarding or leaving boats.
15	*opaque*: murky, dark, difficult to see through.
18	*translucence*: semi-transparent, light shining partially through.
24	*iridescent*: glittering, changing colours.
24	*coats of mail*: armour made of metal rings.
28	*capstan*: round machine used for winding or hauling rope.
32	*Lucky Strike*: American cigarette.
37	*sequins*: small, shiny discs used for decorating clothes.
52	*total immersion*: completely covered in liquid; a form of baptism.
63	*associating*: linking.
74	*transmutation*: changing shape.
77	*briny*: very salty.

INITIAL RESPONSE

1. In your opinion, what role has the old fisherman in the poem? Is he a link with the past, a person in harmony with his environment or something else? Refer closely to the text in your response.

2. Bishop uses a chilling maternal image at the conclusion of the poem. What effect has this startling metaphor on the poem's tone? Support your discussion with clear references from the text.

3. Did you find 'At the Fishhouses' thought-provoking? What questions did the poem raise about the poet and her attitudes? Refer to the text in your answer.

STUDY NOTES

'At the Fishhouses' comes from Elizabeth Bishop's award-winning second collection, A Cold Spring *(1965). What Bishop sees is never quite what the rest of us see. She challenges us to look again. She gives us poetry as 'normal as sight ... as artificial as a glass eye'. An ordinary sight of an old fisherman 'in the gloaming' mending nets in Nova Scotia becomes a strange, exact hallucination examining the essence of knowledge. Bishop saw; now we see. She changes the view.*

The poem's opening section (**lines 1–40**) gives us a **detailed, sensuous description** of a scene from Nova Scotia. Bishop has an unerring sense of place. The fishhouses are described so vividly that we can almost smell the fish ('it makes one's nose run and one's eyes water'), see the fish tubs ('completely lined/with layers of beautiful herring scales') and hear the sea ('swelling slowly as if considering spilling over'). The poet draws us right into the scene with microscopic detail, making us pore over the surface of 'benches', 'lobsterpots' and 'masts'. We experience the 'apparent translucence' of the weathered, silvered wood, which matches the cold, opaque, silver sea. Musical language lends beauty to this timeless scene. The long 'o' sound in 'Although' is echoed in 'cold', 'old' and 'gloaming'. All is harmony. The colours of the fisherman's net, 'dark purple-brown', become 'almost invisible'. Nothing jars. The rhythmic work is conveyed in the pulsating phrase 'for the wheelbarrows to be pushed up and down on'. Physical effort is suggested by the assonance of 'u' and 'o'. In **lines 23–25**, the wheelbarrows are described in minute detail ('plastered/with creamy iridescent coats of mail'). The small, circular fish scales are like the metal rings on a medieval knight's coat of armour. Bishop moves in closer to show us similarly coloured little flies, also 'iridescent', moving on the scales.

The poet's eye focuses on 'the little slope behind the houses' and an 'ancient wooden capstan'. Here is a **forlorn reminder of the tough physical work** of the past. The discarded cylinder is 'cracked' and has 'melancholy stains, like dried blood'; the ironwork has also 'rusted'. In **line 32**, a human connection is made when the 'old man accepts a Lucky Strike' cigarette. The personal detail ('a friend of my grandfather') gives a surface intimacy to this chill poem. But there are hidden depths. The man is described as having 'sequins on his vest and on his thumb'. This decorative detail is more usually associated with glamorous ball gowns than an old fisherman's jersey. Does the image of the man's black knife, 'almost worn away', suggest an ebbing life?

In the poem's short second section (**lines 41–46**), we are at the water's edge and the repetition of 'down' draws us nearer the element of water as we note the 'long ramp/descending'. **The movement seems symbolic of Bishop's own descent into her subconscious mind.** As before, the graceful fish scales have transformed the wooden ramp into 'thin silver/tree trunks'.

The third section (**lines 47–83**) **changes the view**. We are now not merely looking, but seeing. We are **entering the interior**. We journey with Bishop to examine an element that is 'bearable to no mortal', yet is home 'to fish and seals'. No human can survive in the icy waters of the North Atlantic Sea: 'Cold dark deep and absolutely clear'. Another figure, a seal, appears in this bleak, surreal sequence. In this compelling episode, seal and poet are linked by a shared belief in 'total immersion'. For the seal, this is into water. Is it some form of baptism for Bishop? The poet, however, finds no comfort in religion, despite singing hymns for the seal ('A Mighty Fortress Is Our God'). Religion, like the distant fir trees, is behind her, waiting to be cut down.

The sea now takes on a nightmarish aspect as Bishop describes it 'indifferently swinging above the stones' (**line 68**). It is becoming a sea of knowledge. The poet warns us against it, telling us that we will be hurt if we delve in: wrists 'would ache immediately' and hands 'would burn'. Just as in the Garden of Eden, knowledge came with a terrible price. Knowledge gleaned from the world is hard-earned. Mother Nature is depicted with a 'cold hard mouth' and 'rocky breasts'. Here is no warm, comforting, maternal presence. Instead, Bishop's own dark life is suggested. These final lines – filled with harsh sea imagery – are insightful. Place has receded and insight is present. We, together with the poet, realise that knowledge is like water ('flowing'). It is also 'drawn', like waves are moved by the power of the moon. As we recognise that the mysterious waves pass into the past, so we realise that knowledge is 'historical' and ends up 'flown'. **All are part of the flux of nature.** In the end, Bishop seems to accept that the vast ocean – like life itself – defies understanding.

ANALYSIS

'Bishop gives us facts and minute details, sinking or sliding giddily off into the unknown.' Discuss this statement with reference to the poem 'At the Fishhouses'. Support your views with close reference to the text.

Sample Paragraph

I certainly agree that Elizabeth Bishop give us 'facts and minute details'. The 'five fishhouses' are clearly described for the reader to see, with their characteristic 'steeply peaked roofs' and their walkways, 'narrow, cleated' to enable the wheelbarrows to move smoothly. The exchange between the poet and the old man ('a friend of my grandfather') is realistically shown, with even the brand of cigarette identified ('Lucky Strike'). We not only see the fish scales, 'sequins', 'coats of mail', but we also note the 'crawling' flies on the scale-splattered wheelbarrows. Then the poem turns from this detailed scrutiny of the actual to an abstract meditation. Here, the poet is 'sliding giddily off into the unknown'. From contemplating the icy North Atlantic Sea ('Cold dark deep and absolutely clear'), Bishop starts to explore the essence of knowledge – and even of life itself. Knowing hurts, it makes you 'ache', just as the icy water 'burns'. Knowledge is not comfortable; the world is not a nice place, with its 'cold hard mouth'. Experience and knowledge come with an expensive price tag. The last two lines, for me, are dreamlike and surreal. I imagine a sea of knowledge that has been gained in the past ('historical'). This knowledge is always changing and 'flowing' as new discoveries are made. Elizabeth Bishop has brought us from a minute exploration of place to a meditation on an abstract concept.

Examiner's Comment

A precise discussion that deals directly with both aspects of the statement: 'facts and minute details' and 'sliding ... into the unknown'. Some good personal engagement and a clear understanding of the poem are evident in this top-grade response. There is also effective use of apt quotation.

N.B. Access your ebook for additional sample paragraphs and a list of useful quotes with commentary.

> CLASS/HOMEWORK EXERCISES

1. How does Bishop's style contribute to the communication of her themes? Refer to two literary techniques used by the poet in 'At the Fishhouses' and comment on their effectiveness in each case. Refer closely to the text in your response.

2. 'Elizabeth Bishop is known for her skill at creating an authentic sense of place.' To what extent is this true of her poem, 'At the Fishhouses'? Support your answer with reference to the text.

> SUMMARY POINTS

- Poet's return to her childhood home allows Bishop to reflect on her life.
- Conversational language, descriptive details and sensuous imagery add authenticity.
- Assonant effects echo the deep reflective mood.
- Alliterative and sibilant sounds evoke a realistic sense of the sea.
- Surreal, nightmarish view of nature.
- Visionary conclusion that the ocean – like life itself – is beyond understanding.

❹ THE PRODIGAL

The brown enormous odor he lived by
was too close, with its breathing and thick hair,
for him to judge. The floor was rotten; the sty
was plastered halfway up with glass-smooth dung.
Light-lashed, self-righteous, above moving snouts,   5
the pigs' eyes followed him, a cheerful stare –
even to the sow that always ate her young –
till, sickening, he leaned to scratch her head.
But sometimes mornings after drinking bouts
(he hid the pints behind a two-by-four),   10
the sunrise glazed the barnyard mud with red;
the burning puddles seemed to reassure.
And then he thought he almost might endure
his exile yet another year or more.

But evenings the first star came to warn.   15
The farmer whom he worked for came at dark
to shut the cows and horses in the barn
beneath their overhanging clouds of hay,
with pitchforks, faint forked lightnings, catching light,
safe and companionable as in the Ark.   20
The pigs stuck out their little feet and snored.
The lantern – like the sun, going away –
laid on the mud a pacing aureole.
Carrying a bucket along a slimy board,
he felt the bats' uncertain staggering flight,   25
his shuddering insights, beyond his control,
touching him. But it took him a long time
finally to make his mind up to go home.

'the pigs' eyes followed him'

Glossary

Title: The title comes from the biblical parable of the Prodigal Son, a young man who wasted his inheritance on drunkenness and ended up working as a swineherd. The word 'prodigal' refers to a spendthrift or wastrel.

1   *odor*: odour, smell.
3   *sty*: pig-shed.

5   *snouts*: pigs' noses.
9   *bouts*: sessions.
20 *companionable*: comfortable.
20 *the Ark*: Noah's Ark. In the Bible story, Noah built a boat to save animals from a great flood.
23 *aureole*: circle of light.

INITIAL RESPONSE

1. In your opinion, is Elizabeth Bishop sympathetic to the central character in this poem? Give reasons for your answer, using close reference to the text.

2. Choose two images that you found particularly memorable in the poem. Comment briefly on the effectiveness of each.

3. Write your personal response to the poem, referring to the text in your answer.

STUDY NOTES

In 'The Prodigal', published in 1951, Elizabeth Bishop returns to the well-known Bible parable of the Prodigal Son. She imagines the squalor and degradation this wayward youth endured when he was forced to live among the pigs he looked after. The poet herself had experienced depression and alcoholism in her own life and could identify with the poem's marginalised central figure. Bishop uses a double-sonnet form to trace the prodigal's struggle from wretchedness to eventual recovery.

The poem's **opening lines** present the repugnant living conditions of the exiled prodigal's everyday life: 'The brown enormous odor' engulfs him. The abhorrent stench and filth of the pig-sty is the only life he knows. Immersed in this animal-like state, he has lost all sense of judgement. Even the odour, 'with its breathing and thick hair', is beyond his notice. **Bishop's graphic imagery is typically precise**, describing the foul-smelling sty's shiny walls as 'plastered halfway up with glass-smooth dung'.

In **lines 5–8**, the 'Light-lashed' pigs are given human traits ('self-righteous', 'a cheerful stare'). The poet conveys **a disturbing sense of the young man's confused and drunken grasp on reality**. In his sub-human state, overwhelmed by nausea and isolation, he now seems almost at home among the pigs. Although he is 'sickening', he can still show odd gestures of affection towards them – 'even to the sow that always ate her young'.

Bishop delves deeper into the alcoholic's secretive world in **lines 9–14**. Ironically, the morning hangovers are not entirely without their compensations: 'burning puddles seemed to reassure'. Despite the ugliness and deprivation of his diminished existence, **he can occasionally recognise unexpected beauty in nature**, such as when 'the sunrise glazed the barnyard mud with red'. It is enough to give him hope: 'then he thought he almost might endure/his exile'. Emphatic broad vowel sounds add a further dimension of pathos to this line.

The poem's **second section** begins on a more startling note: 'But evenings the first star came to warn' (**line 15**). There is a suggestion that **the prodigal is finally confronting his personal demons**. For the first time, he seems to realise that he is out of place among the orderly routine of farm life that is going on around him. Unlike the sleeping animals ('safe and companionable as in the Ark'), the unfortunate young man is now intensely aware of his dismal alienation. He is poised on the brink of coming to his senses.

For the frustrated prodigal, a defining moment occurs when he finally disassociates himself from the snoring pigs. Yet ironically, it seems as though he almost envies their simple comfort and security 'beneath their overhanging clouds of hay'. Vivid images of routine farm life, such as 'The lantern – like the sun, going away' (**line 22**), take on a new symbolic significance for the unhappy exile. Is he finally considering the transience of life? Is there still a possibility of regaining his humanity? For an instant, **the young man seems to find a vague kind of hope** in the beautiful 'pacing aureole' of lamplight reflected on the mud.

A renewed vigour and purpose mark the poem's **final lines**. Bishop identifies exactly when the prodigal experiences 'shuddering insights'. This defining instant is symbolised by his acute awareness of 'the bats' uncertain staggering flight'. Taking his cue from nature, **he slowly accepts responsibility for his own destiny**: 'But it took him a long time/finally to make his mind up to go home'. This crucial decision to return from exile is a powerful illustration of human resilience. The poem's affirmative ending is emphasised by the importance placed on 'home' (the only unrhymed end word in the poem). Bishop's reworking of the well-known Biblical tale carries a universal message of hope, offering the prospect of recovery not just from alcoholism, but from any form of human debasement.

ANALYSIS

'Elizabeth Bishop's mood can vary greatly – from deep depression to quiet optimism.' Discuss this statement, with particular reference to 'The Prodigal'.

Sample Paragraph

Bishop's poem, 'The Prodigal', is extremely grim. The early mood, describing the 'brown enormous odor' (American spelling) is clearly meant to capture the terrible living conditions of the young alcoholic son who had left his home, partied non-stop and fallen on hard times. The description of the outhouse is extremely repulsive. Bishop's tone is one of despair. The prodigal has fallen as low as any person, living among the pigs he looks after. The images are negative – 'rotten', 'sickening', 'barnyard mud'. The stench makes him queasy. But the mood changes when the alcoholic becomes more aware of himself and dares to hope that he will get it together and return to a decent life. Images of light and beauty suggest this – 'catching light', 'a pacing aureole'. The turning point is when the prodigal stumbles on 'shuddering insights' – which refers to his belief that he can regain his dignity and humanity if he really wants to. Although this is extremely difficult and 'took him a long time', he succeeds in the end. The last line emphasises his optimistic mood – as he decides to 'make his mind up to go home'.

Examiner's Comment

A well-focused response that addresses the question. Effective use of accurate quotation throughout. The answer would have benefitted from some discussion on the restrained ('quiet') nature of the final optimism. Expression is weakened by slang and over-use of the word 'extremely', which renders it below top-grade standard.

N.B. Access your ebook for additional sample paragraphs and a list of useful quotes with commentary.

CLASS/HOMEWORK EXERCISES

1. 'Bishop's poetry often goes beyond description to reveal valuable insights about people's courage and resilience.' Discuss this statement with particular reference to 'The Prodigal'. Refer to the poem in your response.

2. 'While Elizabeth Bishop's poems can appear deceptively simple, they often contain underlying themes of universal significance.' Discuss this view with close reference to 'The Prodigal'.

SUMMARY POINTS

- Themes include the alcoholic's alienation, human determination and resilience.
- Odd glimpses of beauty exist in the most unexpected of circumstances.
- Effective descriptive details, personification and startling metaphorical language.
- Vivid picture of the prodigal's unhappy life and living conditions.
- Striking images of light and darkness.
- Varying tones, contrasting moods – despair and hope.

5 QUESTIONS OF TRAVEL

There are too many waterfalls here; the crowded streams
hurry too rapidly down to the sea,
and the pressure of so many clouds on the mountaintops
makes them spill over the sides in soft slow-motion,
turning to waterfalls under our very eyes.   5
– For if those streaks, those mile-long, shiny, tearstains,
aren't waterfalls yet,
in a quick age or so, as ages go here,
they probably will be.
But if the streams and clouds keep travelling, travelling,   10
the mountains look like the hulls of capsized ships,
slime-hung and barnacled.

Think of the long trip home.
Should we have stayed at home and thought of here?
Where should we be today?   15
Is it right to be watching strangers in a play
in this strangest of theatres?
What childishness is it that while there's a breath of life
in our bodies, we are determined to rush
to see the sun the other way around?   20
The tiniest green hummingbird in the world?
To stare at some inexplicable old stonework,
inexplicable and impenetrable,
at any view,
instantly seen and always, always delightful?   25
Oh, must we dream our dreams
and have them, too?
And have we room
for one more folded sunset, still quite warm?

But surely it would have been a pity   30
not to have seen the trees along this road,
really exaggerated in their beauty,
not to have seen them gesturing
like noble pantomimists, robed in pink.
– Not to have had to stop for gas and heard   35
the sad, two-noted, wooden tune

of disparate wooden clogs
carelessly clacking over
a grease-stained filling-station floor.
(In another country the clogs would all be tested.   40
Each pair there would have identical pitch.)
– A pity not to have heard
the other, less primitive music of the fat brown bird
who sings above the broken gasoline pump
in a bamboo church of Jesuit baroque: 45
three towers, five silver crosses.

– Yes, a pity not to have pondered,
blurr'dly and inconclusively,
on what connection can exist for centuries
between the crudest wooden footwear   50
and, careful and finicky,
the whittled fantasies of wooden cages.
– Never to have studied history in
the weak calligraphy of songbirds' cages.
– And never to have had to listen to rain   55
so much like politicians' speeches:
two hours of unrelenting oratory
and then a golden silence
in which the traveller takes a notebook, writes:

'Is it lack of imagination that makes us come   60
to imagined places, not just stay at home?
Or could Pascal have been not entirely right
about just sitting quietly in one's room?

Continent, city, country, society:
the choice is never wide and never free.   65
And here, or there ... No. Should we have stayed at home,
wherever that may be?'

'the pressure of so many clouds on the mountaintops'

Glossary

1	*here*: Brazil.
11	*hulls*: main sections of ships.
11	*capsized*: overturned in the water.
12	*barnacled*: covered with small shellfish.
20	*the sun the other way around*: the view of the sun in the southern hemisphere.
22	*inexplicable*: incomprehensible, mysterious.
34	*pantomimists*: people taking part in a pantomime, a slapstick comedy.
37	*disparate*: very different, separate.
45	*church of Jesuit baroque*: ornately decorated 17th-century churches, often found in Brazil.
51	*finicky*: excessively detailed, elaborate.
52	*whittled*: carved.
52	*fantasies*: amazing creations.
54	*calligraphy*: decorative handwriting (in this case, the swirling design of the carved birdcages).
57	*unrelenting*: never stopping, endless.
62	*Pascal*: Blaise Pascal, a 17th-century mathematician and philosopher who wrote that 'man's misfortunes spring from the single cause that he is unable to stay quietly in his room'.

INITIAL RESPONSE

1. From your reading of lines 1–12, describe Bishop's reaction to the landscape spread before her. How does she feel about this abundance of nature? Is she delighted, unhappy, awestruck? Support your response with quotation from the text.

2. Choose two examples of repetition in the poem. Briefly explain what each example contributes to Bishop's treatment of the poem's theme.

3. Would you consider the ending of the poem conclusive or inconclusive? How does Bishop really feel about travel? Refer closely to the text in your response.

STUDY NOTES

This is the title poem of Elizabeth Bishop's 1965 collection, Questions of Travel. *Bishop herself was a great traveller, aided by an inheritance from her father. In this poem, she questions the need for travel and the desire that people have to see the world for themselves. The poet provokes the reader by posing a series of questions about the ethics of travel. She places her original observations of Brazil before us and wonders whether it would be better if we simply imagined these places while sitting at home. Finally, she challenges us to consider where our 'home' is.*

The poem's **opening line** is an **irritable complaint** about Brazil: 'There are too many waterfalls here'. In the first section (**lines 1–12**), Bishop observes the luxuriant, fertile landscape spread out before her. She finds fault with the 'crowded streams' that 'hurry too rapidly' and the 'pressure of so many clouds'. The richness of the misty equatorial landscape is caught in a series of soft sibilant 's' sounds ('spill', 'sides', 'soft slow-motion'). Clouds melt into the 'mile-long, shiny, tearstains'. Everything is on the move, changing position and shape. Both Bishop and the water are 'travelling, travelling'. **Repetition emphasises this restless movement.** The circular motion suggests that neither traveller nor clouds have any real purpose or direction. An original and striking image of a mountain range ('like the hulls of capsized ships') catches our attention. The vegetation is 'slime-hung'; the outcrops of rocks are like the crustaceans of shellfish ('barnacled'). As always, the poet's interest lies in the shape and texture of the words.

A more **reflective mood is found in the poem's second section** (**lines 13–29**). Bishop presents readers with a **series of challenging questions** for consideration. In all, eight 'questions of travel' are posed. Should we remain 'at home' and imagine 'here'? Bishop is uneasy at the prying scrutiny of tourists 'watching strangers in a play'. She is aware that this is how people live; it is not a performance for public consumption. The emphasis here is on the 'childishness' of the tourists as they rush around, greedily consuming sights, viewing the sun from its other side in southern countries, such as Brazil. But as far as Bishop is concerned, historic ruins and 'old stonework' do not speak to the visitor. The repetition of 'inexplicable' stresses the inaccessibility of foreign cultures. The bland, unknowing response of tourists is captured in the conversational phrase 'always delightful'. Their selfish desire for more and more experiences is vividly shown in the image of the traveller nonchalantly packing views, as if they were clothes or souvenirs being placed in a bag at the end of a trip: 'And have we room/for one more folded sunset, still quite warm?' Perhaps Bishop is asking whether any famous sight ever actually touched the traveller, or was it skimmed over in a frenzy to pack in as much as possible?

Justification for travel is the dominant theme of the third section (**lines 30–59**): 'But surely it would have been a pity/not to have seen'; '– A pity not to have heard'; 'a pity not to have pondered'; '– Never to have studied'; 'never to have had to listen'. The repetition of 'pity' beats out a tense rhythm as the poet seeks to condone travel. Bishop's well-known 'painterly eye' provides the evidence, as she presents a series of fresh, first-hand vignettes, e.g. the trees 'gesturing/like noble pantomimists, robed in pink'. The flowing movement of the trees, their flamboyant colour and their suggestion of Brazil's mime plays would be hard to imagine if not really experienced. The sound of this easy-going, carefree society is captured in the hard 'c' sound of 'carelessly clacking', which evokes the slovenly walk of local peasants. The Brazilian love of music is evident in 'clacking', a sound usually associated with the rhythmic castanets. The difference in cultures is wryly noted: 'In another country the clogs would all be tested./ Each pair there would have identical pitch.' Elsewhere, all would be sanitised uniformity.

Are these the experiences the traveller would miss by not being in another country? The locals' cavalier attitude to functionality is shown in the contrasting images of the 'broken gasoline pump' and the intricate construction of a 'bamboo church' with 'three towers, five silver crosses'. **The spirit of the people soars in 'Jesuit baroque'.** A similar contrast is seen in wooden carving – the 'crudest wooden footwear' does not have the same importance for these free-spirited people as the 'careful and finicky ... fantasies of wooden cages' (**line 51**). Another unstoppable force, that of equatorial rainstorms, is likened to the endless rant of a politician bellowing out his 'unrelenting oratory'. Could any of this be imagined from afar?

Lines 58–67 begin in 'golden silence', as Bishop attempts to clarify her own thinking on the value of travel. In the final lines, she **wonders if we travel because we lack the imagination to visualise these places**. However, in the previous section, the poet has graphically shown that nothing can surpass a person **actually hearing and seeing** a place and its people. A reference is made to the 17th-century philosopher Blaise Pascal, who preferred to remain at home. The poet feels that he was not 'entirely right' about this, and by sharing her whimsical images of Brazil with us, she has led us to agree with her. Another interesting question is posed: How free are we to go where we wish? Bishop states that the choices are 'never wide and never free'; there are always constraints on the traveller. But an emphatic 'No' tells us that this does not take away from the authenticity of the experience.

In the poem's **concluding lines**, Bishop returns to the question of whether or not people should stay at home. She then teases the reader with the follow-up, 'wherever that may be?' (**line 67**). This is a much deeper, philosophical reflection, which reverberates in our minds. **Home is a place of belonging**, from which travellers set out and to which they return. The visited countries are not secure bases; the tourist does not belong there, but is merely a visitor en route to somewhere else. In short, the traveller's role is one of an outsider – observing, but not participating. Bishop's own life experience is revealed here. Perhaps she travelled so extensively because she never felt truly at home in any single place.

ANALYSIS

'Elizabeth Bishop's poems are not only delightful observations, but are also considered meditations on human issues.' Discuss this statement with reference to the poem 'Questions of Travel'. Support your views with close reference to the text.

Sample Paragraph

Elizabeth Bishop was a tireless traveller and in the poem 'Questions of Travel', she presents the reader with evocative images from the lush, misty equatorial landscape of Brazil, where clouds 'spill over the sides' of mountains 'in soft slow-motion'. The giant mountain ranges are imaginatively conjured up before our eyes as upturned ships, and their vegetation and rocky sections are likened to the 'slime-hung and barnacled' appearance of the bottoms of these ships. The sounds of the people intrude upon our consciousness – disparate clogs 'carelessly clacking'. The harsh alliteration mimics the sound of wood hitting floor. No detail is too minute to escape her famous 'eye': 'the broken gasoline pump', 'the whittled fantasies of wooden cages', the 'three towers' and 'five silver crosses' of the small bamboo church. These are Bishop's delightful observations. But the poet also addresses ethical questions surrounding travel, particularly relevant in our times. The reader is asked to ponder 'Questions of Travel'. What right have we to watch people's private lives, as if they were performing in public? Why should we consume experiences and squeeze them up like clothes in a suitcase ('have we room for one more folded sunset ...?'). Why are we rushing around, 'travelling, travelling'? Why do we not 'just stay at home'? These issues have a modern resonance, as we are aware nowadays of the effect of our carbon footprint on the environment when we travel. The poem concludes with a curious question on the meaning of 'home'. Bishop asks us to consider where it is ('home,/wherever that may be'). Suddenly an accepted certainty becomes as hard to define as the disintegrating clouds at the start of the poem.

Examiner's Comment

A careful top-grade examination of both parts of the statement – the poet's 'delightful observations' and her treatment of issues – is presented by the candidate. The thoughtful approach is referenced accurately with pertinent quotations from the poem.

N.B. Access your ebook for additional sample paragraphs and a list of useful quotes with commentary.

CLASS/HOMEWORK EXERCISES

1. Comment on the different tones in 'Questions of Travel'. Refer closely to the text in your response.

2. 'Elizabeth Bishop's poetry explores interesting aspects of home and belonging.' To what extent do you agree with this statement? Support your answer with suitable reference to 'Questions of Travel'.

SUMMARY POINTS

- The stunning Brazilian landscape prompts Bishop to reconsider the value of travel.
- Other themes include the natural world, home, and the creative imagination.
- Memorable onomatopoeic effects – assonance, alliteration, sibilance.
- Descriptive language, effective use of powerful metaphors and similes.
- Reflective, philosophical tone; inconclusive ending.

6 THE ARMADILLO

For Robert Lowell

This is the time of year
when almost every night
the frail, illegal fire balloons appear.
Climbing the mountain height,

rising toward a saint   5
still honored in these parts,
the paper chambers flush and fill with light
that comes and goes, like hearts.

Once up against the sky it's hard
to tell them from the stars –   10
planets, that is – the tinted ones:
Venus going down, or Mars,

or the pale green one. With a wind,
they flare and falter, wobble and toss;
but if it's still they steer between   15
the kite sticks of the Southern Cross,

receding, dwindling, solemnly
and steadily forsaking us,
or, in the downdraft from a peak,
suddenly turning dangerous.   20

Last night another big one fell.
It splattered like an egg of fire
against the cliff behind the house.
The flame ran down. We saw the pair

of owls who nest there flying up   25
and up, their whirling black-and-white
stained bright pink underneath, until
they shrieked up out of sight.

The ancient owls' nest must have burned.
Hastily, all alone,   30
a glistening armadillo left the scene,
rose-flecked, head down, tail down,

and then a baby rabbit jumped out,
short-eared, to our surprise.
So soft! – a handful of intangible ash   35
with fixed, ignited eyes.

Too pretty, dreamlike mimicry!
O falling fire and piercing cry
and panic, and a weak mailed fist
clenched ignorant against the sky!   40

'chambers flush and fill with light'

Glossary

Dedication: Elizabeth Bishop dedicated 'The Armadillo' to her friend and fellow poet, Robert Lowell. An armadillo is a nocturnal burrowing creature found mainly in South America. It rolls up into a ball to protect itself from danger.

1   *time of year*: St John's Day (24 June).
3   *fire balloons*: helium-filled balloons carrying colourful paper boxes.
5   *a saint*: St John.
6   *these parts*: Rio de Janeiro, Brazil.
7   *chambers*: hollow boxes.

11   *tinted*: shaded.
13   *the pale green one*: probably the planet Uranus.
16   *kite sticks of the Southern Cross*: cross-shaped constellation of stars.
35   *intangible*: flimsy, insubstantial.
36   *ignited*: lit up.
37   *mimicry*: imitation
39   *weak mailed fist*: the animal's bony armour (defenceless against fire).

INITIAL RESPONSE

1. Based on your reading of the first four stanzas, how does the poet present the fire balloons? Are they mysterious, beautiful, threatening? Refer to the text in your answer.

2. Comment on Bishop's use of interesting verbs in the poem.

3. In your view, is this an optimistic or pessimistic poem? Give reasons for your response.

STUDY NOTES

'The Armadillo' describes St John's Day (24 June) in Brazil, where Elizabeth Bishop lived for more than 15 years. On this annual feast day, local people would celebrate by lighting fire balloons and releasing them into the night sky. Although this custom was illegal – because of the fire hazard – it still occurred widely.

The **opening lines** introduce us to an exotic, night-time scene. The sense of drama and excitement is palpable as Bishop observes these 'illegal' balloons 'rising toward a saint'. They are also presented as fragile ('frail') but beautiful: 'the paper chambers flush and fill with light'. There is something magical and majestic about their ascent towards the heavens. **The language is simple and conversational**, reflecting the religious faith of the local people. Bishop compares the flickering light of the 'paper chambers' to 'hearts', perhaps suggesting the unpredictability of human feelings and even life itself.

Lines 9–20 associate the drifting balloons with distant planets, adding to their romantic air of mystery. The unsteady rhythm and alliterative description ('With a wind,/they flare and falter') suggest an irregular, buoyant movement. The poet is **increasingly intrigued by the fire balloons** as they 'wobble' out of sight. She notes that they sometimes 'steer between' the stars. Although she appears to be disappointed that the balloons are 'steadily forsaking us', she also worries about them 'suddenly turning dangerous' as a result of downdrafts buffeting and igniting them.

The tone changes dramatically in **line 21**, as Bishop recalls the destructive force of one exploding balloon that fell to earth near her house: 'It splattered like an egg of fire'. This characteristically stirring simile and the onomatopoeic verb highlight the sense of unexpected destruction. The shock is immediately felt by humans and animals alike. Terrified owls – desperate to escape the descending flames – 'shrieked up out of sight' (**line 28**). Contrasting **colour images emphasise the garish confusion**: the 'whirling black-and-white' bodies of the owls are 'stained bright pink underneath'.

The poet suddenly notices 'a glistening armadillo', isolated and alarmed. Determined to escape the fire, it scurries away: 'rose-flecked, head down, tail down' (**line 32**). Amid the chaos, a baby rabbit 'jumped out', its urgent movement reflecting the lethal atmosphere. Bishop expresses her intense shock at seeing its burnt ears: 'So soft! – a handful of intangible ash'. **This graphic metaphor emphasises the animal's weakness and suffering.** Its 'fixed, ignited eyes' reflect the fire falling from the sky.

Bishop's emotive voice emerges forcefully in the poem's **closing lines**. She rejects her earlier description of the elegant fire balloons as being 'Too pretty'. Having witnessed the horrifying reality of the tormented animals, she castigates all her earlier romantic notions about the colourful festivities. Such thoughts are suddenly seen as 'dreamlike mimicry'. **The final image of the trapped armadillo is highly dramatic.** Its 'piercing cry' is harrowing. Bishop imagines the terrified creature in human terms ('a weak mailed fist'). Although the armadillo's helpless body is 'clenched ignorant against the sky', it is unlikely that its coat of armour will save it from fire. The irony of this small creature's last futile act is pitiful. Despite its brave defiance, the armadillo is doomed.

Some critics have commented on the **symbolism** in the poem, seeing the victimised creatures as symbols for powerless and marginalised people everywhere. It has been said that the careless fire balloons signify warfare, mindless violence and ignorant destruction. Is Bishop indicating that people's fate is beyond their control? It has also been suggested that the fire balloons symbolise love ('that comes and goes, like hearts') or even the creative impulse itself – beautiful, elusive and sometimes tragic. As with all poems, readers must decide for themselves.

ANALYSIS

Describe the tone in 'The Armadillo'. Does it change during the course of the poem? Refer to the text in your answer.

Sample Paragraph

The opening section of 'The Armadillo' is dramatic and filled with anticipation. Bishop sets the night-time scene during the noisy Brazilian festival to honour St John. 'This is the time of year' suggests a special occasion. The tone is celebratory and excited as the local community release countless 'illegal fire balloons' which light up the skies. The poet seems in awe of the wonderful spectacle, watching the 'paper chambers flush and fill with light'. The tone changes slightly to sadness as she watches the colourful balloons rise and disappear among the stars, 'steadily forsaking us'. A more dramatic transformation occurs when the exploding balloons start 'turning dangerous'. Due to the careless human activity, fire falls from the air, causing mayhem and destruction for the vulnerable animals below. Terrified owls 'shrieked', a young rabbit is burnt to 'intangible ash' and the armadillo is reduced to 'panic'. Bishop's personal voice is filled with anger and disgust as she rages against the 'falling fire'. The italics and exclamation marks in the final stanza highlight her frustrated tone as she identifies with the unfortunate armadillo whose 'weak mailed fist/clenched ignorant against the sky' represents a useless gesture of resistance.

Examiner's Comment

A focused top-grade response that traces the development of tone in the poem. There is a real sense of well-informed engagement with the text. Short, accurate quotations are used effectively to illustrate the various changes in tone. The expression is clear, varied and controlled throughout.

N.B. Access your ebook for additional sample paragraphs and a list of useful quotes with commentary.

CLASS/HOMEWORK EXERCISES

1. 'In reading the poetry of Elizabeth Bishop, readers can discover moments of quiet reflection and shocking truth.' Discuss this statement in relation to 'The Armadillo', supporting the points you make with reference to the poem.

2. 'In her poems, Elizabeth Bishop often connects the twin themes of cruelty and vulnerability.' Discuss this view with suitable reference to 'The Armadillo'.

SUMMARY POINTS

- Both humans and animals are victims of man's thoughtless actions.
- Precise sense of place, detailed description of exotic atmospheres and experiences.
- Reflective tone reveals the poet's personal feelings and attitudes.
- Lack of judgemental comment allow us to find our own interpretation.
- Rich visual imagery, striking metaphors, onomatopoeia and end rhyme.

7   SESTINA

September rain falls on the house.
In the failing light, the old grandmother
sits in the kitchen with the child
beside the Little Marvel Stove,
reading the jokes from the almanac,   5
laughing and talking to hide her tears.

She thinks that her equinoctial tears
and the rain that beats on the roof of the house
were both foretold by the almanac,
but only known to a grandmother.   10
The iron kettle sings on the stove.
She cuts some bread and says to the child,

It's time for tea now; but the child
is watching the teakettle's small hard tears
dance like mad on the hot black stove,   15
the way the rain must dance on the house.
Tidying up, the old grandmother
hangs up the clever almanac

on its string. Birdlike, the almanac
hovers half open above the child,   20
hovers above the old grandmother
and her teacup full of dark brown tears.
She shivers and says she thinks the house
feels chilly, and puts more wood in the stove.

It was to be, says the Marvel Stove.   25
I know what I know, says the almanac.
With crayons the child draws a rigid house
and a winding pathway. Then the child
puts in a man with buttons like tears
and shows it proudly to the grandmother.   30

But secretly, while the grandmother
busies herself about the stove,
the little moons fall down like tears

from between the pages of the almanac
into the flower bed the child   35
has carefully placed in the front of the house.

Time to plant tears, says the almanac.
The grandmother sings to the marvellous stove
and the child draws another inscrutable house.

'the child draws a rigid house'

Glossary

A sestina is a traditional poetic form of six six-line
stanzas followed by a final stanza of three lines.
In Bishop's 'Sestina', the same six words recur at
the ends of lines in each stanza: tears, almanac, stove,
grandmother, house and child. The final three-line
stanza contains all six words.

4   *the Little Marvel Stove*: a heater or cooker that burns
wood or coal.

5   *almanac*: calendar giving important dates, information
and predictions.

7   *equinoctial*: the time when day and night are of equal
length (22 September, 20 March approximately).

39 *inscrutable*: secret; impossible to understand or
interpret.

INITIAL RESPONSE

1. Describe the atmosphere in the house. Is it happy, unhappy, relaxed, secretive? Support your response with quotation from the text.

2. Choose one image that you find particularly interesting and effective in the poem. Briefly explain your choice.

3. Write your personal response to the poem, supporting your views with reference to the text.

STUDY NOTES

'Sestina' was written between 1960 and 1965. For Elizabeth Bishop, the creative act of writing brought shape and order to experience. This poem is autobiographical, as it tells of a home without a mother or father. It is one of Bishop's first poems about her childhood and she was in her fifties, living in Brazil, when she wrote it. The complicated, restrictive structure of the poem can be seen as the poet's attempt to put order on her early childhood trauma.

The poem's **opening stanza** paints a domestic scene, which at first seems cosy and secure. The child and her grandmother sit in the evening light beside a stove. They are reading 'jokes from the almanac' and 'laughing and talking'. However, on closer observation, sadness is layered onto the scene with certain details: 'September rain', 'failing light' and the old grandmother hiding 'her tears'. Bishop adopts the point of view of adult reminiscence. She recollects; she is an observer of her own childhood and the poem's **tone is disturbing and challenging**. We are introduced to someone who looks, but never belongs. The six end-words echo alarmingly throughout the poem. Here is a house full of tears with a grandmother and child together, alone.

In **stanza two** the grandmother believes that her autumn tears and the rain were 'foretold by the almanac'. There is a sense of inevitability and tired resignation in the opening lines. But normality enters: 'The iron kettle sings on the stove'. Homely domesticity is seen when the grandmother cuts some bread and says to the child: 'It's time for tea now'. **Bishop suddenly switches from being an observer to being an interpreter**, as she lets the reader see the workings of the child's mind in the **third stanza**: 'but the child/is watching the teakettle's small hard tears'. The child interprets sorrow everywhere; even droplets of steam from a kettle are transformed into the unwept tears of the grandmother. The phrase 'dance like mad' strikes a poignant note as we remember that Bishop's own mother was committed to a mental asylum when Bishop was just five years old; they never met again. A cartoon-like image of the almanac ends this stanza. We view it through the child's eyes, as 'the clever almanac'.

Stanza four focuses on the almanac. It is a **sinister presence**, personified as a bird of ill-omen: 'Bird-like' it hovers, suspended 'half open'. This mood of misgiving is heightened when we are told that the grandmother's cup is not full of tea, but of 'dark brown tears'. However, normality asserts itself again – the grandmother 'shivers' and puts wood on the fire.

Stanza five opens with the eerie personification of the Marvel Stove and the almanac. A **sense of inevitability** ('It was to be') and hidden secrets ('I know what I know') is absorbed by the child. Just as the older Bishop puts order on her traumatic childhood experiences by arranging them into the tightly knit form of the sestina, the child in the poem attempts to order her experiences by drawing houses. But the house is tense, 'rigid', inflexible. The sorrow of this childhood cannot be changed; the situation was as it was. This house can only be reached by a 'winding pathway'. Does this echo Bishop's later travels, as she searches for home? The sadness of Bishop's situation focuses on the drawing now, as the child sketches a man with 'buttons like tears'.

In **stanza six**, the tears continue to fall, now 'into the flower bed' in the child's drawing. **Fantasy and reality are mixed** in the innocent perception of the child, who feels but does not understand. The **final three lines** contain all six key words as the almanac instructs that it is 'Time to plant tears'. Is the time for regret over? Is the child planting tears that will be wept in the future? Should the grandmother and child be shedding tears now? The 'child draws another inscrutable house'. The secrecy continues. Nothing is as it seems. The future looks chilling.

ANALYSIS

Elizabeth Bishop's poetry is an emotional journey. To what extent do you agree with this? Support your views with close reference to 'Sestina'.

Sample Paragraph

I agree that the reader goes on an emotional journey with Bishop in the poem 'Sestina' as Bishop struggles to come to terms with her traumatic childhood. I think we focus with her, not on her as we observe the little child valiantly drawing 'inscrutable' houses, full of tears and secrets. Our hearts go out to the small, motherless and fatherless little girl, caught in an almost nightmare scenario, as the almanac hangs 'Birdlike' above her, almost like a bird of prey. The child feels, but does not comprehend the awful tragedy in the house and Bishop allows us to see the workings of the little mind as the child blends reality and fantasy, as stoves and books talk. Everything seems to know except the child. The chaotic experiences of Bishop's childhood are strictly contained in the formal structure of the sestina, the song of sixes, with six stanzas containing six lines ending with the same six end-words: house, grandmother, child, stove, almanac and tears. This mirrors the 'rigid' house of the little girl's drawings. Both the older and the younger Bishop are trying desperately to put order and control on this overwhelming situation. The reader experiences the poignancy through the details of the 'failing light', 'the rain that beats on the roof of the house' and the teacup 'full of dark brown tears'. Finally, the reader, like Bishop, is not left comforted, but is faced with enigma as yet another 'inscrutable' house is drawn. It is interesting to note that Bishop was unable to write about her early childhood until her fifties. Was it only then that the planted tears were harvested?

Examiner's Comment

A top-grade, insightful answer focusing on the emotional journey undertaken by both the poet and reader. There is a clear sense of engagement with the poem. Quotations are used effectively throughout.

N.B. Access your ebook for additional sample paragraphs and a list of useful quotes with commentary.

CLASS/HOMEWORK EXERCISES

1. Some critics have said that 'Sestina' is a sentimental poem. Do you agree with this? Support your views with close reference to the poem.

2. 'Elizabeth Bishop's most compelling poems often address painful memories of the poet's childhood.' To what extent is this true of her poem, 'Sestina'? Support your answer with reference to the text.

SUMMARY POINTS

- Adult poet reflects on troubled childhood and the desire for security of home.
- Disturbing sinister tone, sense of inevitability.
- Ominous personification and surreal imagery blur reality.
- Tear imagery patterns emphasise sorrow-filled scene.
- Strict form of sestina contains and controls over-flowing emotions.
- Vivid imagery, powerful metaphorical language.

8 FIRST DEATH IN NOVA SCOTIA

In the cold, cold parlor
my mother laid out Arthur
beneath the chromographs:
Edward, Prince of Wales,
with Princess Alexandra,   5
and King George with Queen Mary.
Below them on the table
stood a stuffed loon
shot and stuffed by Uncle
Arthur, Arthur's father.   10

Since Uncle Arthur fired
a bullet into him,
he hadn't said a word.
He kept his own counsel
on his white, frozen lake,   15
the marble-topped table.
His breast was deep and white,
cold and caressable;
his eyes were red glass,
much to be desired.   20

'Come,' said my mother,
'Come and say good-bye
to your little cousin Arthur.'
I was lifted up and given
one lily of the valley   25
to put in Arthur's hand.
Arthur's coffin was
a little frosted cake,
and the red-eyed loon eyed it
from his white, frozen lake.   30

Arthur was very small.
He was all white, like a doll
that hadn't been painted yet.
Jack Frost had started to paint him
the way he always painted   35

the Maple Leaf (Forever).
He had just begun on his hair,
a few red strokes, and then
Jack Frost had dropped the brush
and left him white, forever.   40

The gracious royal couples
were warm in red and ermine;
their feet were well wrapped up
in the ladies' ermine trains.
They invited Arthur to be   45
the smallest page at court.
But how could Arthur go,
clutching his tiny lily,
with his eyes shut up so tight
and the roads deep in snow?   50

'the roads deep in snow'

Glossary

1	*parlor*: room set aside for entertaining guests.	8	*loon*: great crested grebe, an aquatic diving bird.
3	*chromographs*: coloured copies of pictures.	14	*counsel*: opinion.
4	*Edward*: British Royal (1841–1910).	28	*frosted*: iced.
5	*Alexandra*: Edward's wife.	36	*the Maple Leaf*: Canadian national emblem.
6	*King George*: King George V (1865–1936).	42	*ermine*: white fur.
6	*Queen Mary*: wife of King George V (1867–1953).	46	*page*: boy attendant.

INITIAL RESPONSE

1. With reference to lines 1–20 of the poem, describe the mood and atmosphere in the 'parlor'.

2. The poet uses several comparisons in this poem. Select one that you found particularly interesting and comment on its effectiveness.

3. Write your personal response to this poem, referring to the text in your answer.

STUDY NOTES

'First Death in Nova Scotia' was published when Elizabeth Bishop was in her early fifties. Written entirely in the past tense, it is an extraordinarily vivid memory of a disturbing experience. In the poem, Bishop's young narrator recounts the circumstances of an even younger cousin's death.

From the outset, we visualise Cousin Arthur's wake through a child's eyes. Characteristically, Bishop sets the scene in **stanza one** using **carefully chosen** descriptive details. It is winter in Nova Scotia. The dead child has been laid out in a 'cold, cold parlor'. Above the coffin are old photographs of two deceased royal couples. Fragmented memories of unfamiliar objects add to the dreamlike atmosphere. A stuffed loon sits on the marble-topped table. The young girl – in her desperate attempt to comprehend death – describes her cousin as 'all white, like a doll/that hadn't been painted yet'.

The dead boy and the 'dead' room soon become real for the reader, as does the dilemma faced by the **living child, who seems increasingly confused**. **Stanza two** focuses on the young narrator's fixation with the stuffed bird. By thinking hard about the death of this 'cold and caressable' loon, she is trying to find a possible explanation for death. She is fascinated by the loon – perhaps an escape mechanism from the unfamiliar atmosphere in the parlour. In any case, the bird – with its desired 'red glass' eyes – might be less threatening than the dead body in the casket. Suddenly, somewhere in the child's imagination, Cousin Arthur and the personified bird become closely associated. Both share an impenetrably cold stillness, suggested by the 'marble-topped table', which is compared to a 'white, frozen lake'.

In **stanza three** the child's mother lifts her up to the coffin so that she can place a lily of the valley in the dead boy's hand. Her mother's insistent invitation ('Come and say good-bye') is chillingly remote. We sense the young girl's vulnerability ('I was lifted up') as she is forced to place the flower in Arthur's hand. In a poignantly childlike image, she compares her cousin's white coffin to 'a little frosted cake'. **The mood turns progressively surreal** when the apprehensive narrator imagines the stuffed bird as a predator ('the red-eyed loon eyed it'). As always, Bishop's imagery is direct, brisk and to the point.

Bishop continues to explore childhood innocence in **stanza four**. Using the simplest of language, the child narrator describes her dead cousin: 'He was all white, like a doll'. In a renewed burst of imagination, she creates her own 'story' to explain what has happened to Arthur. His death must be caused by the winter frost that 'paints' the autumn leaves, including the familiar maple leaf. This thought immediately brings to mind the Canadian song 'The Maple Leaf Forever'. To the child, it seems that Jack Frost started to paint Arthur, but 'dropped the brush/and left him white, forever'. This creative **stream of consciousness highlights the child's efforts to make sense of death's mysterious reality**.

The imagery of childhood fairytales continues in **stanza five** when the narrator pictures Arthur in the company of the royal families whose pictures hang on the parlour walls. He is now 'the smallest page at court'. For the first time, the cold has disappeared and the royals are 'warm in red and ermine'. This fantasy, however, is short lived. Still shaken by the strangeness of the occasion, the young narrator questions how this could have happened – especially as Arthur could not travel anywhere 'with his eyes shut up so tight/and the roads deep in snow'. The poem's final, tender image reflects both the child's naivety and a genuine concern for her cousin. Ironically, all around are symbols of immortality – the heavenly royal images of Arthur's entrance into a new, more glorious life. But the narrator's enduring uncertainty is central to the poem.

ANALYSIS

'The unknowable nature of life and death is a central concern of Elizabeth Bishop's poetry.' Discuss this statement with reference to 'First Death in Nova Scotia'. Support the points you make by referring to the poem.

Sample Paragraph

In several poems I have studied, it's clear that Elizabeth Bishop addresses life's mysteries. Sometimes she does this through the eyes of a child, as in 'First Death in Nova Scotia'. The poem describes her first experience of a death and how she struggled to understand it. It is an elegy for her young cousin, Arthur, and Bishop's memories of his funeral are extraordinarily clear. Everything about it confuses her. The formal, domestic setting is uninviting – a 'cold, cold parlor' has strange chromographs of the British Royal Family on the walls and a stuffed loon bird on the marble table. The bird had been shot by the dead child's father. As a young girl, Bishop recalls being forced to place a lily in her dead cousin's cold hand. These objects add to her insecurity. Nothing is explained to her and she escapes into her own imaginary world, comparing Arthur's casket to 'a little frosted cake'. She tries to tell herself that 'Jack Frost' is responsible for leaving Arthur 'white forever'. In the last verse, she imagines her dead cousin in an afterlife – not in heaven, but in a magical royal castle, 'the smallest page at court'. However, the young Elizabeth is caught between make-believe and reason. Her final thoughts challenge her own fantasy about life after death. Common sense tells her that Arthur, 'with his eyes shut up so tight', could not go out into 'roads deep in snow'. I thought Bishop really captured the uncertainty of a young child's mind in this very moving poem. I also got the impression that she was making the point that life and death can never be fully understood, no matter what age a person is.

Examiner's Comment

A focused and sustained response, showing good engagement with the text. Starting with a succinct overview, the paragraph traces the progress of thought through the poem, using apt and accurate quotations effectively. Clear expression and a convincing personal approach also contribute to this top-standard response.

N.B. Access your ebook for additional sample paragraphs and a list of useful quotes with commentary.

CLASS/HOMEWORK EXERCISES

1. In your opinion, does 'First Death in Nova Scotia' present a sentimental view of death? Support your argument with reference to the text of the poem.

2. 'Elizabeth Bishop often makes effective use of simple language and childlike images to convey disturbing childhood experiences.' Discuss this statement with close reference to 'First Death in Nova Scotia'.

SUMMARY POINTS

- Cousin Arthur's death and wake is seen from the point of view of a child.
- Elegy based on vivid memories expressed in simple language.
- Surreal imagery emphasises the deathly cold atmosphere.
- Fairytale element conveys child's attempt to understand the finality of death.
- Effective use of colour, assonance, repetition.

⑨ FILLING STATION

Oh, but it is dirty!
– this little filling station,
oil-soaked, oil-permeated
to a disturbing, over-all
black translucency.   5
Be careful with that match!

Father wears a dirty,
oil-soaked monkey suit
that cuts him under the arms,
and several quick and saucy   10
and greasy sons assist him
(it's a family filling station),
all quite thoroughly dirty.

Do they live in the station?
It has a cement porch   15
behind the pumps, and on it
a set of crushed and grease-
impregnated wickerwork;
on the wicker sofa
a dirty dog, quite comfy.   20

Some comic books provide
the only note of color –
of certain color. They lie
upon a big dim doily
draping a taboret   25
(part of the set), beside
a big hirsute begonia.

Why the extraneous plant?
Why the taboret?
Why, oh why, the doily?   30
(Embroidered in daisy stitch
with marguerites, I think,
and heavy with gray crochet.)

Somebody embroidered the doily.
Somebody waters the plant,   35
or oils it, maybe. Somebody
arranges the rows of cans
so that they softly say:
ESSO–SO–SO–SO
to high-strung automobiles.   40
Somebody loves us all.

'it's a family filling station'

Glossary

3	*oil-permeated*: soaked through with oil.	27	*begonia*: house plant with large multicoloured leaves.
5	*translucency*: shine, glow.	28	*extraneous*: unnecessary, inappropriate.
8	*monkey suit*: dungarees; all-in-one working clothes.	31	*daisy stitch*: stitch pattern used in embroidery.
10	*saucy*: cheeky, insolent.	32	*marguerites*: daisies.
18	*impregnated*: saturated.	33	*crochet*: intricate knitting patterns.
24	*doily*: ornamental napkin.	39	*ESSO–SO–SO*: Esso is a brand of oil; reference to the careful arrangement of oil cans.
25	*taboret*: drum-shaped low seat; a stool.		
27	*hirsute*: hairy.		

INITIAL RESPONSE

1. In your opinion, how does Bishop make the opening of this poem dynamic and interesting? Comment on her use of punctuation, direct speech and compound words, which draw us into the world of the poem. Support your response with quotation from the text.

2. Trace the development of the poet's attitude to the filling station throughout the poem. Does it change from being critical and patronising to being more positive? Illustrate your answer with close reference to the text.

3. Comment on the effectiveness of Bishop's use of repetition in lines 34–41. Refer to the text in your response.

STUDY NOTES

Elizabeth Bishop was strongly influenced by a poetic movement called imagism, which was concerned with the accurate description of a particular thing. In this poem, she gives us an iconic description of a familiar American scene, the small-town gas station. Bishop found the new culture in 1960s California bewildering and it is noteworthy that the voice in this poem is that of an outsider trying to make sense of what is observed.

The prosaic title of the poem sets the mood for this commonplace scene. The poem opens with a **highly strung comment, disparaging the lack of hygiene** at the little station: 'Oh, but it is dirty!' The compound words ('oil-soaked', 'oil-permeated') suggest that everything is covered in a fine film of grease. This 'black translucency' has its own particular glow. Bishop's tense, dismissive tone creates a volatile, brittle atmosphere. Another voice interrupts her reverie: 'Be careful with that match!' In a few deft lines, the poet has set the scene, established the mood and introduced her characters. She uses a series of intensely descriptive lines that gives the poem a cinematic quality as we observe the details, like close-ups on a big screen.

The busy little station is captured in the **second stanza** through the poet's critical observations as she watches the family bustle about their business. The father is wearing a 'dirty,/oil-soaked monkey suit' that is too small for him ('cuts him under the arms'). The sons are described using alliteration of the letter 's', which suggests their fluid movements as well as their oily appearance ('several quick and saucy/and greasy sons assist'). Like the poet, we also become fascinated by this unremarkable place. Bishop's critical tone becomes more strident as she comments on the sons' insolence ('saucy') and their lack of hygiene ('all quite thoroughly dirty'). **We can hear the contempt in her voice.**

The **third stanza** questions, in a disbelieving tone, whether anyone could actually reside in such an awful place: 'Do they live in the station?' The poet's eye seems to pan around her surroundings **like a film camera, picking up on small details** as she tries to piece the scene into some kind of order. She lingers on the porch and its set of 'crushed and grease-/impregnated wickerwork'. Her disdain is obvious to the reader. The dog is described as a 'dirty dog' – it is almost as if it, too, has been smeared in oil. The repetition of the dead 'd' sound emphasises the unkempt appearance of everything. Then, suddenly, the poem pivots and turns on the homely word 'comfy'. The poet is surprised to note that the dog is quite content in this place. We are reminded that because of the harrowing circumstances of her own childhood, Bishop never fully knew what home was; we are left wondering if she longed to be 'comfy' too.

In **stanzas four and five**, she begins to notice evidence of a woman's hand in this place, particularly 'a big dim doily' on the 'taboret'. She notes the colourful 'comic books' and her eye is caught by the incongruous sight of 'a big hirsute begonia'. Even the plant has masculine qualities, being big and hairy. Bishop is observing the extraordinary in the ordinary; **in the most unlikely places, there is beauty and love.** We understand her bemusement as she reflects, almost in exasperation: 'Why, oh why, the doily?' We, like the narrator, have to reassess our initial view of this cluttered gas station. On closer observation, there is care and attention to detail, including artistic embroidery. We are brought right up close to examine this marvellous 'daisy stitch'. The critical, conversational tone of the poem clearly belongs to someone who is the observer, someone who does not belong. Is this the role Bishop was forced to adopt in her own life?

The poet's disturbed tone gives way in the **final stanza** to one of comfort. The lines whisper softly with sibilant 's' sounds. 'Somebody' cares for things, arranging the cans in order 'so that they softly say:/ESSO–SO–SO–SO'. Bishop commented that 'so-so-so' was a phrase used to calm highly strung horses. It is used here to calm herself, just as the oil in the cans is used to make the engines of 'high-strung automobiles' run smoothly. The tone relaxes and a touch of humour creeps in: she notes that 'Somebody waters the plant,/or oils it, maybe'. The use of repetition is also soothing as we, like Bishop, come to realise that there is 'Somebody' who cares. **The poem concludes on a quiet note of assurance that everybody gets love from somewhere: 'Somebody loves us all'.** This is a particularly poignant ending when we consider that Elizabeth Bishop's parents were both absent from her childhood. The wonderfully comforting conclusion soothes the reader, just as a mother might quieten a cranky child.

ANALYSIS

'Elizabeth Bishop's poems are often described as deceptively casual.' Discuss this view of the poet's work, with particular reference to 'Filling Station'. Support your response with close reference to the text.

Sample Paragraph

'Filling Station' deals with a central concern of all human beings, the need to feel cared for, the need to belong. Instead of a heavy, moralising tone, Bishop adopts a deceptively casual tone in this poem from the start, with its almost colloquial, conversational opening: 'Oh, but it is dirty!' However, the carefully selected compound phrases ('oil-soaked, oil-permeated') show a carefully crafted poem. The subtle use of repetition of 'why' to suggest the increasing puzzlement of the poet as she tries to make sense of this scene also convinces me that Bishop is a master craftsperson at work, whose art conceals her effort. Similarly, the repetition of 'Somebody' leaves a lasting sense of reassurance not only for the high-strung cars and their drivers, but also for us, as the poet states with deliberate calm that 'Somebody loves us all'. The tone is that of a loving parent soothing a contrary child who won't go to sleep. The word 'comfy' is also deceptively casual as, suddenly, the critical tone of the poem changes when the poet realises that the dog is content to be living there. Now the realisation dawns that even in the most outlandish places there is comfort and caring. I thought it was clever of the poet to use such a homely word as 'comfy' to totally change the mood of the poem. Finally, I think that Bishop shows her skill in the use of the sibilant 's' at the conclusion of the poem. Just as the oil stops the gears in a car from making noise and grating, the carefully arranged oil cans in the filling station send their message of comfort to the narrator and to us: 'Somebody loves us all'.

Examiner's Comment

This is a mid-grade answer, which competently addresses the question. There is some very good engagement with the poem and effective use is made of apt references. The expression is reasonably well controlled, although slightly repetitive at times, leaving this short of being a top-grade answer.

N.B. Access your ebook for additional sample paragraphs and a list of useful quotes with commentary.

CLASS/HOMEWORK EXERCISES

1. 'A sense of homelessness pervades Bishop's poetry'. Comment on this statement, referring to both the content and stylistic techniques used in 'Filling Station'. Support your discussion with reference to the poem.

2. 'Elizabeth Bishop succeeds in conveying her themes through effective use of striking visual imagery and powerful aural effects.' Discuss this view with reference to 'Filling Station'.

SUMMARY POINTS

- Bishop attempts to comprehend the significance of a run-down filling-station.
- Vivid picture of homely petrol station through closely observed visual detail.
- Cinematic techniques, conversational and colloquial language, flashes of humour.
- Contemptuous tone gives way to a concluding note of reassurance.
- Realisation that love and beauty can be found anywhere.

10 IN THE WAITING ROOM

In Worcester, Massachusetts,
I went with Aunt Consuelo
to keep her dentist's appointment
and sat and waited for her
in the dentist's waiting room.   5
It was winter. It got dark
early. The waiting room
was full of grown-up people,
arctics and overcoats,
lamps and magazines.   10
My aunt was inside
what seemed like a long time
and while I waited I read
the *National Geographic*
(I could read) and carefully   15
studied the photographs:
the inside of a volcano,
black, and full of ashes;
then it was spilling over
in rivulets of fire.   20
Osa and Martin Johnson
dressed in riding breeches,
laced boots, and pith helmets.
A dead man slung on a pole
– 'Long Pig,' the caption said.   25
Babies with pointed heads
wound round and round with string;
black, naked women with necks
wound round and round with wire
like the necks of light bulbs.   30
Their breasts were horrifying.
I read it right straight through.
I was too shy to stop.
And then I looked at the cover:
the yellow margins, the date.   35

Suddenly, from inside,
came an *oh!* of pain
– Aunt Consuelo's voice –
not very loud or long.
I wasn't at all surprised;   40
even then I knew she was
a foolish, timid woman.
I might have been embarrassed,
but wasn't. What took me
completely by surprise   45
was that it was *me*:
my voice, in my mouth.
Without thinking at all
I was my foolish aunt,
I – we – were falling, falling,   50
our eyes glued to the cover
of the *National Geographic*,
February, 1918.

I said to myself: three days
and you'll be seven years old.   55
I was saying it to stop
the sensation of falling off
the round, turning world
into cold, blue-black space.
But I felt: you are an *I*,   60
you are an *Elizabeth*,
you are one of *them*.
Why should you be one, too?
I scarcely dared to look
to see what it was I was.   65
I gave a sidelong glance
– I couldn't look any higher –
at shadowy gray knees,
trousers and skirts and boots
and different pairs of hands   70
lying under the lamps.
I knew that nothing stranger
had ever happened, that nothing
stranger could ever happen.
Why should I be my aunt,   75
or me, or anyone?

What similarities –
boots, hands, the family voice
I felt in my throat, or even
the *National Geographic*   80
and those awful hanging breasts –
held us all together
or made us all just one?
How – I didn't know any
word for it – how.'unlikely' ...   85
How had I come to be here,
like them, and overhear
a cry of pain that could have
got loud and worse but hadn't?

The waiting room was bright   90
and too hot. It was sliding
beneath a big black wave,
another, and another.

Then I was back in it.
The War was on. Outside,   95
in Worcester, Massachusetts,
were night and slush and cold,
and it was still the fifth
of February, 1918.

'then it was spilling over'

Glossary

1   *Worcester*: much of the poet's childhood was spent here.
9   *arctics*: waterproof overshoes.
14 *National Geographic*: international geography magazine.
21 *Osa and Martin Johnson*: well-known American explorers.

23 *pith helmets*: sun helmets made from dried jungle plants.
25 *'Long Pig'*: term used by Polynesian cannibals for human flesh.
61 *Elizabeth*: the poet is addressing herself.
95 *The War*: First World War (1914–18).

INITIAL RESPONSE

1. In your view, what image of women is presented in the poem? Support your answer with reference to the text.

2. Select two images that have a surreal or dreamlike impact in the poem. Comment on the effectiveness of each image.

3. Write your personal response to the poem, using textual reference.

STUDY NOTES

'In the Waiting Room' describes a defining coming-of-age experience for the poet when she was just six years old. While her aunt receives dental treatment, the child narrator browses through the pages of a National Geographic *magazine and observes what is happening around her. In the powerful and provocative moments that follow, she begins to acknowledge her individual sense of being female.*

The poem opens with a specific setting recalled in vivid detail by the child narrator. She flicks through a *National Geographic* magazine in the dentist's office while her aunt is in the patients' surgery. Familiar images of 'grown-up people,/arctics and overcoats' seem to convey a sense of well-being. It is the winter of 1918 in Worcester, Massachusetts. **The language is direct and uncomplicated, mirroring the candid observations of a young girl** as filtered through the adult poet's mature interpretation. Short sentences establish the fragmented flashback, allowing the reader to identify immediately with the narrative: 'It was winter. It got dark/early'. In addition to the unguarded tone, Bishop's short lines give the poem a visual simplicity, even though the **first stanza** is composed of 35 lines.

The mood changes from **line 18** onwards, as the young girl studies the dramatic magazine photographs of an active volcano 'spilling over/in rivulets of fire'. For the first time, **she recognises the earth's destructive force.** In contrast to the earlier feeling of security in the waiting room, the atmosphere becomes uneasy. Disturbing pictures ('A dead man slung on a pole' and 'Babies with pointed heads') are as intriguing as they are shocking. The child is drawn further into an astonishingly exotic world of cannibalism and violence. Graphic images of ornamental disfigurement seem horrifying: 'naked women with necks/wound round and round with wire'. The repetition of 'round and round' emphasises the young girl's spiralling descent into an enthralling world. Caught between fascination, repulsion and embarrassment ('too shy to stop'), she concentrates on the magazine's cover in an effort to regain control of her feelings.

The child is unexpectedly startled by a voice 'from inside' (**line 36**). At first, she presumes that the sound ('an *oh!* of pain') has been made by her aunt. But then something extraordinary happens and she realises that she has made the sound herself: 'it was *me*'. This sudden awareness that the cry has come from within herself prompts a **strange, visionary experience** in which she identifies closely with her 'foolish aunt'. The scene is dramatic and dreamlike: 'I – we – were falling, falling'.

In the surreal sequence that follows, the child focuses on her approaching birthday as she tries hard to resist the sensation of fainting: 'three days/and you'll be seven years old' (**line 54**). Ironically, it is at this crucial point (on the edge of 'cold, blue-black space') that she gains an astonishing insight into her own sense of self: 'you are an *Elizabeth*,/you are one of *them*'. The idea of sharing a common female identity with her aunt and the unfamiliar women in the magazine pictures is almost overwhelming: 'nothing stranger/had ever happened' (**line 72**). To the distraught child, it seems as though **all women have lost their individuality and have merged into a single female identity**. Although she attempts to stay calm, she is plagued by recurring questions and confusion: 'Why should I be my aunt,/or me, or anyone?' The young Elizabeth's awakening to adulthood is obviously painful. In attempting to come to terms with her destiny as both an individual and also as part of a unified female gender, she makes this hesitant statement: 'How – I didn't know any/word for it – how "unlikely" ...'.

Before she can return to everyday reality, the young girl must endure further discomfort. Her surroundings feel 'bright/and too hot' (**line 90**) and she imagines being repeatedly submerged 'beneath a big black wave', a metaphor for helplessness and disorientation. In the **final stanza**, she regains her composure in the waiting room's apparent safety, where she lists the certainties of place and time. But there is a distinct sense of life's harshness: 'The War was on' and Massachusetts is encountering 'slush and cold' (**line 97**). Such **symbols are central to our understanding of this deeply personal poem**. Just as the image of the erupting volcano seemed to signify Bishop's development, the waiting room itself is a significant location as a transition point in her self-awareness.

ANALYSIS

'An unsettling sense of not being fully in control is a central theme in the poetry of Elizabeth Bishop.' To what extent is this true of 'In the Waiting Room'? Support your answer with reference to the text of the poem.

Sample Paragraph

The theme of the trauma of growing up is central to 'In the Waiting Room'. It's unlike many nostalgic poems. They often describe childhood experiences in a sentimental way. But this one's very disturbing. It's set in a dentist's where the poet remembers waiting for 'Aunt Consuelo' who is having treatment. The atmosphere at the start is quite relaxed as the child passes the time by reading an old copy of the *National Geographic*. However, the photographs of a black volcano 'full of ashes' and of cannibals carrying a dead man ('Long Pig') are extremely upsetting. The mood becomes nervous. Photographs of African native women terrify the child as some of them wear wire necklaces. The poet compares them to 'light bulbs' – an image which immediately frightens her. The outside world is so violent and unexpected that she then goes into a trance-like state and cries out in agony. Her experience is more and more unsettled as she struggles to keep a grip on reality. Instead, she faints into 'cold, blue-black space'. The image suggests how out of control she is. However, what really unsettles her is the discovery for the very first time that she herself is a young woman and she shares this with every other female. The unusual photos of the naked African women suggest her own future and she becomes terrified. Her uneasy feelings are summed up at the end when she describes being overcome by the heat in the crowded waiting room, 'beneath a big black wave'. This leaves me feeling sympathy for this traumatised girl who is very unsure about her life and future role as a woman.

Examiner's Comment

A reasonably focused and sustained mid-grade response, which addresses the question competently. Good use is made of quotations. The expression could be more controlled in places, particularly in the opening section.

N.B. Access your ebook for additional sample paragraphs and a list of useful quotes with commentary.

CLASS/HOMEWORK EXERCISES

1. 'Bishop's reflective poems combine precise observation with striking imagery.' Discuss this view with reference to 'In the Waiting Room'. Refer to the poem in your answer.

2. 'In many of her poems, Elizabeth Bishop offers interesting insights into how children struggle to make sense of the adult world.' Discuss this statement with reference to 'In the Waiting Room'.

SUMMARY POINTS

- Themes include loss of innocence, coming-of-age experience, lack of belonging.
- Realisation of unique individuality and common female identity.
- Conversational language relays candid observations of young girl.
- Contrasting tones of alarm, dismay and disgust.
- Unnerving imagery used to explore comprehension of the wider world.
- Dreamlike atmosphere – surreal, nightmarish.

LEAVING CERT SAMPLE ESSAY

'Vivid description and intense personal reflection characterise Bishop's inquisitive poetic voice.' To what extent do you agree or disagree with the above statement? Support your answer with reference to both the themes and language found in the poetry of Elizabeth Bishop on your course.

Marking Scheme Guidelines
Reward achievement of an appropriate register, but answers must contain clear evidence of engagement with the poetry of Elizabeth Bishop on the course.

Indicative material:
- Powerful exploration of the ordinary – childhood, nature, death.
- Poet's powerful sense of people and places.
- Freshness of viewpoints; wide range of tones/moods.
- Colourful, vivid imagery, metaphors, precise description, aural effects.
- Energy and intensity of language, varied poetic forms, etc.

Sample Essay
(Vivid description and intense personal reflection characterise Bishop's inquisitive poetic voice)

1. *Elizabeth Bishop is an outsider, an observer who does not always belong. I feel this is particularly true of her poems 'Sestina' and 'Filling Station'. Both show a sense of exclusion, a feeling of insecurity and tension. She does not feel a part of where she is. She feels different – something teenagers can identify with. Bishop raises many questions in her poems and her writing style is particularly noted for its conversational tone and clear imagery.*

2. *'Filling Station' is a short dramatic poem, a small drama where the main character observes a run-down garage scene. At first, this lady driver sits criticising the 'oil-soaked, oil-permeated' filling station*

in a condescending tone, 'Oh, but it is dirty!' She continues her criticism as she describes the family, the father in his 'dirty oil-soaked money suit', and his 'several quick and saucy/and greasy sons'. The speaker's attitude towards the little station and its inhabitants is one of contemptuous superiority. Her focus is on the film of oil which permeates everything. She is revving at high speed, like the engines of the cars on the forecourt. As she smokes a cigarette, a terse voice shouts, 'Be careful with that match!' Not only does Bishop uses cinematic details allow us to see this place, but also she enables us to hear its rough sounds through the use of this conversational phrase.

3. But the driver begins to realise that this ordinary place can teach her a lesson, 'Somebody loves us all'. I found it interesting that the poet gains insights through her close observation. She notices 'a dirty dog, quite comfy'. Animals and people are happy and secure in the filling station. This humble place is a caring environment, one where people look after each other. 'Somebody embroidered the doily', 'Somebody waters the plant'. The highly-strung woman relaxes enough to even crack a joke, 'or oils it'. Just as the harsh, grating sound of the engine is lubricated to a silky purr by the oil, so the tense driver is soothed by the soft, sibilant sounds, 'ESSO-SO-SO'. Now the realisation dawns on the poet – and the reader – that love and happiness can be experienced in even the most dismal-seeming environment. For me, a shadow hangs over this ending, as I wonder whether Bishop yearned for such comfort in her own life since she experienced, at a tender age, the loss of her parents.

4. This incredible sadness is intensely felt in 'Sestina'. The poem is suffused with hidden unhappiness as the older Bishop looks back at a domestic scene, a grandmother making tea and reading to her little granddaughter. I thought it was poignant how the child tries to order her experiences by drawing 'rigid' houses, and the older poet attempts to order the chaotic experiences of her childhood by using the tightly-knit form of the sestina, the 'song of sixes'. The child's inflexible house mirrors the uncompromising form of the poem, with its six highly-charged words; 'grandmother', 'child', 'stove', 'tears', 'almanac', 'house'. These highlight the meaning of the poem, unlike the house which remains a puzzle. The older Bishop comprehends, the younger child is aware, but unknowing. The little girl does not really understand the sadness in the atmosphere, so she draws 'a man with buttons likes tears'. The evocative and vibrant image seems to be filled with sadness and the secrecy of childhood.

5. Behind the appearance of normality in this house lurks the strange. The almanac, which would be in every country home for its information on seasons and moon cycles, becomes like a prop in a mystery story. 'Birdlike it hovers' above the child. The teacup is 'full of dark brown tears'. Nothing is quite as it seems. One thing merges into another, like a nightmare. The strict six verse structure, with its never changing six-end words, all gathered together in the final three lines, hold the disturbing subject matter together. The future looks ominous, 'Time to plant tears'. At some point this sorrow will have to be

released and expressed. I found the viewpoint in this poem both original and challenging – and typical of Bishop's inquiring approach to the subjects she writes about.

6. *Many of the most deeply personal poems deal with the poet's personal travels and her reflections on exotic places. 'Questions of Travel' examines the colourful Brazilian landscape from an interesting perspective. Bishop wonders if the average traveller is just a greedy consumer, 'have we room for one more sunset?' She questions the frenzied search for new frontiers 'what childishness is it … to rush to see the sun the other way round?' Using a pleading, conversational tone, she seeks to justify this rushing around, 'But surely it would have been a pity not to have seen … not to have pondered'. Her bleak tone ('Is it lack of imagination?') seeks to know why we have to travel instead of 'just sitting quietly in one's room'. I found this intriguing and sad. She seemed to suggest that people wouldn't want to travel so much if they were already fulfilled at home. Bishop touches on this theme also in 'First Death in Nova Scotia' where she also took on the role of the perceptive observer, excluded but recording the lives of others.*

(approx. 840 words)

Examiner's Comment

This is a confident and highly impressive personal response to the question and shows close engagement with Bishop's poetry. Accurate quotes and references are used effectively to support key discussion points throughout. Expression is clear, varied, fluent and well controlled. Overall, an informed and very successful essay.

> **MARKING SCHEME**
> **GRADE: H1**
> P = 15/15
> C = 13/15
> L = 14/15
> M = 5/5
> Total = 47/50

N.B. Access your ebook for additional sample paragraphs and a list of useful quotes with commentary.

SAMPLE LEAVING CERT QUESTIONS ON BISHOP'S POETRY

(45-50 MINUTES)

1. 'Elizabeth Bishop uses close observation coupled with an objective point-of-view to examine her place in the world.' To what extent do you agree or disagree with this view? Support your answer with reference to Bishop's subject matter and writing style in her prescribed poems.

2. 'Powerful evocations of the natural world are communicated through the energy and vitality of Elizabeth Bishop's poetic language.' To what extent do you agree with this statement? Support your points with suitable reference to both the themes and language use in the poems by Bishop on your course.

3. 'Moments of discovery and a carefully controlled writing style characterise the poetry of Elizabeth Bishop.' Comment on this assessment of Bishop's poetry, supporting your answer with reference to the poems by Bishop on your course.

4. 'In her poems, Elizabeth Bishop explores issues of universal significance, using language that can be both subtle and surprising.' To what extent do you agree or disagree with this view? Support your answer with reference to Bishop's subject matter and writing style in her prescribed poems.

Sample Essay Plan (Q3)

'Moments of discovery and a carefully controlled writing style characterise the poetry of Elizabeth Bishop.' Comment on this assessment of Bishop's poetry, supporting your answer with reference to the poems by Bishop on your course.

- Intro: Bishop takes ordinary, everyday experiences and carefully reveals the insightful drama and wonder found there. Detailed, imaginative descriptions fill her poetry so that the reader journeys to self-discovery with her.

- Point 1: Based on an actual event, 'The Fish' describes a special day spent fishing. Precise similes, e.g. skin hanging 'like ancient wallpaper', allow us to examine the fish closely. The awestruck poet responds respectfully, 'rainbow, rainbow, rainbow!', reflecting her admiration and wonder.

- Point 2: 'First Death in Nova Scotia' typifies a startling first experience of death: 'Come and say good-bye/to your little cousin'. Disquieting imagery lets the reader see the event through the eyes of a child.

- Point 3: In 'The Prodigal', Bishop characteristically uses setting effectively to explore themes of degradation, alienation, resilience and redemption. Similarly, in 'The Armadillo', she discovers how defenceless animals are at risk from human carelessness.

- Point 4: The well-managed form of 'Sestina' illustrates the depth of the poet's feeling as she strains to hold chaos in order. Six key end-words in each of the six stanzas, all contained in the final rhyming triplet.

- Conclusion: Bishop's narrative and reflective poems are often journeys of discovery and realisation. The loss of innocence is a recurring theme. Her distinctive poetry is both thoughtful and thought-provoking.

Sample Essay Plan (Q3)

Develop one of the above points into a paragraph.

Sample Paragraph: Point 2

Elizabeth Bishop's poetry frequently deals with the memory of specific occurrences in her life. 'First Death in Nova Scotia' is about her little cousin's death when he was five. It is the young Bishop's first experience of death, and it is clear that she does not understand the concept. The poet enables us to see the event through the eyes of the child and also allows us to see the workings of the child's mind. She carefully sets the chilling mood at Arthur's wake. The stuffed loon 'hadn't said a word' since 'Uncle Arthur fired/a bullet into him'. The image is exact, a common feature of Bishop's writing. The 'marble-topped table' becomes 'his white, frozen lake'. The poignancy of the description of the little dead boy as a 'doll/that hadn't been painted yet' is heartbreaking, as we see the child apply a childish understanding to an adult event, death. She sustains the childlike images: 'Jack Frost had started to paint him'. This is the child referencing her nursery rhymes to try to comprehend what is happening. She continues in this way. She looks at the royal picture and imagines the 'gracious royal couples' inviting the little boy 'to be/the smallest page at court'. However, as often happens in Bishop's autobiographical poems, there is a moment of revelation – in this case, it is the painful innocence of childhood experiences, particularly of death. This is shown in the final question as the young Bishop wonders 'how could Arthur go'. The child seems obsessed with her cousin's strange appearance: 'with his eyes shut up so tight/and the roads deep in snow?' I could relate to the idea of a child learning about reality the hard way – especially in the final sad image of the little girl alone and with no one explaining what is happening.

Examiner's Comment

This top-grade paragraph makes a solid attempt to address the question in a focused manner. There is a good understanding of the poem and some personal response. References and quotes are used well to discuss the child's uncertain reaction to death. Overall, expression is varied and controlled, although slightly note-like at times.

N.B. Access your ebook for additional sample paragraphs and a list of useful quotes with commentary.

▶ LAST WORDS ❞

'Bishop was spectacular in being unspectacular.'

Marianne Moore

'Bishop disliked the swagger and visibility of literary life.'

Eavan Boland

'The sun set in the sea … and there was one of it and one of me.'

Elizabeth Bishop

model/assured

curiously
character – outside ...
atmosphere – inside ...

sitting image
occurrence ...

naked
priest like – respected / sacred ties
large social class
just a normal man

SEAMUS HEANEY

1939-2013

'Walk on air against
your better
judgement.'

Seamus Heaney was born in 1939 in Co. Derry, the eldest of nine children. He was accepted into Queen's University, Belfast in 1957 to study English Language and Literature. Heaney's poetry first came to public attention in the 1960s, when he and a number of other poets, including Michael Longley and Derek Mahon, came to prominence. They all shared the same fate of being born into a society that was deeply divided along religious grounds and was to become immersed in violence, intimidation and sectarianism. In 1966, his first poetry collection, *Death of a Naturalist*, was published. Heaney spent many years lecturing in Belfast, Dublin and America. Throughout this time, he was publishing prolifically and giving public readings. He has also written several volumes of criticism. Widely regarded as the finest poet of his generation, he was awarded the Nobel Prize for Literature in 1995 'for works of lyrical beauty and ethical depth, which exalt everyday miracles and the living past'. In accepting the award, Heaney stated that his life had been 'a journey into the wideness of language, a journey where each point of arrival … turned out to be a stepping stone rather than a destination'

INVESTIGATE FURTHER

To find out more about Seamus Heaney, or to hear readings of his poems not already available in your ebook, you could search some useful websites available, such as YouTube, poetryarchive.org or bbc.co.uk. Also view the additional material available in your ebook.

Prescribed Poems   HIGHER LEVEL

* The poems marked with an asterisk are also prescribed for the Ordinary Level course.

imposing portrait of a powerful craftsman recalls on a time where his work was respected.

1 THE FORGE 🔊 modest/assured

All I know is a door into the dark.   mystical - incites curiousity
Outside, old axles and iron hoops rusting;   disorder - outside old wasteland
Inside, the hammered anvil's short-pitched ring,   atmosphere - inside place of brilliance
The unpredictable fantail of sparks   striking image
Or hiss when a new shoe toughens in water   onomatopoeic effect, physical creativity.
The anvil must be somewhere in the centre,   core
Horned as a unicorn, at one end square,   control.
Set there immoveable: an altar   priest like - respected / sacredness of creative process.
Where he expends himself in shape and music.   lower social class
Sometimes, leather-aproned, hairs in his nose,   just a normal man -
He leans out on the jamb, recalls a clatter
Of hoofs where traffic is flashing in rows;   recalls when his work was more respected
Then grunts and goes in, with a slam and a flick   skill.   onomatopoeic effects add to
To beat real iron out, to work the bellows.   the importance of the craft.

pres magical simile

Physical, honest work

'The unpredictable fantail of sparks'

mythical role - changing everyday objects into something special

reality and legend blended together

Glossary

The Forge: refers to a blacksmith's workshop, where iron implements are made and mended (in the poem, a smith is shaping horseshoes).

2   *axles*: bars or shafts on which wheels rotate.

3   *anvil*: iron block that the smith uses as a work surface.

7   *unicorn*: mythical animal (usually a white horse) with a spiralled horn growing from its forehead.

9   *expends*: burns up, expresses.

11   *jamb*: upright door support.

14   *bellows*: instrument for drawing air into a fire

INITIAL RESPONSE

1. Describe the poet's attitude to the forge. Is he fascinated or fearful, or both? Support your answer with reference to the poem.

2. Based on your study of the poem, what is your impression of the blacksmith?

3. Comment on the effectiveness of the phrase 'The unpredictable fantail of sparks'.

STUDY NOTES

'The Forge' comes from Seamus Heaney's second collection, Door into the Dark, *which was published in 1969. The sonnet form has a clear division of an octave (the first eight lines) and a sestet (the final six lines). While the octave, apart from its initial reference to the narrator, focuses on the inanimate objects and occurrences inside and outside the forge, the sestet describes the blacksmith and his work.*

The poem's **opening line** ('All I know is a door into the dark') is both modest and assured. There is also a **mystical undertone** (a sense of otherworldliness) as Heaney revisits his childhood and his fascination with a local forge. The image, with its negative and mysterious connotations, incites our curiosity and invites us to find out what answers lie beyond. The poet recalls unwanted objects strewn outside, 'old axles and iron hoops rusting'. The irregular rhythm in **line 2** suggests the disorder of what has been discarded. He **contrasts** the lifeless exterior scene with the vigorous atmosphere ('the hammered anvil's short-pitched ring') inside the forge. The world outside is decrepit and old, a wasteland, whereas the noisy forge is a place of brilliant sparks where iron is beaten out and renewed.

Heaney's visual and aural images are characteristically striking. His vivid metaphor of 'The unpredictable fantail of sparks' (**line 4**) lets us see the glorious flurry of erratic, flashing light and hear the twang of reverberating iron.

Onomatopoeic effects add to our sense of the physical activity taking place as the blacksmith works on a new horseshoe. Suddenly, the incandescent metal begins to 'hiss when a new shoe toughens in water'. The **tone is sympathetic** and attentive as the poet reimagines the smells, sounds and tactile impressions of the blacksmith's workshop.

Lines 6–9 contain the sonnet's central image of the smith's anvil: 'an altar/Where he expends himself in shape and music'. Interestingly, the transition from the octave to the sestet is a run-on (or enjambment) based around this key metaphor. One effect of this is to enable us to experience the anvil as a **sacred or magical point of transition** between the material and immovable world of everyday life and the fluid, imaginative world of human consciousness. Heaney stresses the **mystery of the creative process**, associating it with the mythical creature of medieval fiction, 'Horned as a unicorn'. Although the simile seems somewhat strained, the comparison with a legendary beast still serves to highlight the mysterious qualities ('shape and music') of poetry.

The **final lines** focus on the blacksmith's physical characteristics. **Heaney leaves us with a down-to-earth image of a gruff, hardworking man,** 'leather-aproned, hairs in his nose'. Is the poet suggesting that art – and poetry in particular – is independent of education and social class? Seemingly wary of the world at large, the smith remembers an earlier era of horse-drawn carriages, when his skills were fully appreciated. Contrasting images of 'a clatter/Of hoofs' and modern traffic 'flashing in rows' reflect the changes he has lived through. In the end, he grudgingly accepts that he must return 'into the dark' and resume doing what he does best: 'To beat real iron out, to work the bellows'.

Heaney's poem can immediately be read as an elegy to the past and a lament for the lost tradition of the blacksmith. Readers can also interpret the anvil as a metaphor of an unreachable heritage, a traditional craft made redundant by modernisation. Many critics have seen the blacksmith figure as a **symbol or construction of the role of the poet**, one who opens the 'door into the dark', the creative artist who ritually 'expends himself in shape and music' and who 'grunts' and flicks words and language, forging his poems. As with so much of Heaney's work, the poem attests to his ability to subtly evoke resonance by making us wonder.

ANALYSIS

'Seamus Heaney's descriptive powers often endow portraits of local people with mythic qualities.' Discuss this statement with reference to 'The Forge'.

Sample Paragraph

In Heaney's elegy to the past, the disappearing tradition of the local blacksmith is brought vividly to life. Through dynamic sound effects ('ring', 'hiss') combined with the use of the compound word 'short-pitched', Heaney presents us with the imposing portrait of a powerful craftsman turning dull metal into useful farming tools. This quiet, unassuming blacksmith who 'grunts and goes in' is given another persona, one of epic quality. He becomes a High Priest at his 'altar', the anvil. We get a sense of legendary times, suggested by the image of the anvil shape, 'Horned as a unicorn'. The poet envisions the surly craftsman in a mythical role, changing one everyday substance into something special. Like Heaney himself, the priest is involved in the mysterious creative process. Yet the description of the anvil's shape is firmly rooted in physical reality – one end is shaped like a horn. The blacksmith too is exactly described, 'warts and all'. He stands, 'leather-aproned, hairs in his nose', but like the priest, he has the ability to control the constructive power of fire. Monosyllabic onomatopoeia highlights his magical skills, 'with a slam and a flick/ To beat real iron out'. Reality and legend blend seamlessly.

Examiner's Comment

This mature top-grade response focuses well on Heaney's powers of description – particularly his use of aural effects. The more challenging aspect of 'mythic qualities' is handled successfully, with clear points linking the anvil and altar. Expression is carefully controlled, using varied sentence lengths and a wide-ranging vocabulary (e.g. 'dynamic', 'persona', 'envisions'). Apt quotations are also used throughout.

N.B. Access your ebook for additional sample paragraphs and a list of useful quotes with commentary.

CLASS/HOMEWORK EXERCISES

1. 'Heaney's visual and aural imagery depict a harsh, rural life with lyrical beauty.' Discuss this statement in relation to 'The Forge'.

2. 'Many of Heaney's carefully crafted poems are populated with characters who have made a deep impression on him.' Discuss this view with reference to 'The Forge'.

SUMMARY POINTS

- Lament for and preservation of a traditional craft and rural life.
- Interesting experimental use of structure and rhyme scheme of sonnet form.
- Clever juxtaposition – exterior/interior, past/present, reality/legend.
- Striking sound effects – onomatopoeia, assonance, sibilant 's'.
- Sensuous visual images and symbols create a powerful sense of time and place.

we -the irish

② BOGLAND 🔊

for T.P. Flanagan

We have no prairies   *unlimited.*
To slice a big sun at evening –
Everywhere the eye concedes to
Encroaching horizon,

myth, legend, unknown, danger
Is wooed into the cyclops' eye   5
Of a tarn. Our unfenced country *boundless*
Is bog that keeps crusting *strates depth layer—endless*
Between the sights of the sun.

They've taken the skeleton
Of the Great Irish Elk   10
Out of the peat, set it up
An astounding crate full of air.

Butter sunk under
More than a hundred years
Was recovered salty and white. *Pure*   15
The ground itself is kind, black butter

Melting and opening underfoot,
Missing its last definition
By millions of years.
They'll never dig coal here, *never get their 20 hands on our land*   *industry*

Only the waterlogged trunks
Of great firs, soft as pulp.
Our pioneers keep striking
Inwards and downwards,

Every layer they strip   25
Seems camped on before.
The bogholes might be Atlantic seepage.
The wet centre is bottomless.

'Encroaching horizon,/Is wooed into the cyclops' eye/Of a tarn'

Glossary

1   *prairies*: a large open area of grassland (in North America).

3   *concedes*: gives way to; admits defeat.

4   *Encroaching*: advancing gradually beyond acceptable limits.

5   *wooed*: courted, enticed.

5   *cyclops' eye*: in Greek mythology, a race of one-eyed giants.

6   *tarn*: small mountain lake.

10   *Great Irish Elk*: large northern deer found preserved in Irish bogland.

18   *definition*: transformation (into coal).

23   *pioneers*: adventurers, explorers.

27   *seepage*: the slow escape of liquid through a material.

INITIAL RESPONSE

1. In your opinion, what is Heaney's central theme or point in this poem? Briefly explain your response.

2. How does Heaney employ the senses to allow the reader to share in his experience of the bogland? Refer closely to the poem in your answer.

3. Trace the poet's tone throughout the poem. Comment on where, how and why, in your opinion, the tone changes. Support your views with reference to the text.

'Bogland' (1969) is the result of a Halloween holiday Heaney spent with T.P. Flanagan (the artist to whom this poem is dedicated). Flanagan recalls that 'the bogland was burnt the colour of marmalade'. Heaney felt it was 'one of the most important poems' he had written because 'it was something like a symbol. I felt the poem was a promise of something else … it represented a free place for me'. He thought the bogland was a 'landscape that remembered everything that happened in and to it'. Heaney recalled when they were children that they were told 'not to go near the bog because there was no bottom to it'.

In the **opening stanza**, a **comparison** is drawn between the American prairies ('We have no prairies') and Ireland's bogs. Heaney said, 'At that time, I had … been reading about the frontier and the west as an important myth in the 'American consciousness, so I set up – or rather, laid down – the bog as an answering Irish myth.' The prairie in America represents the vastness of the country, its unfenced expanse a metaphor for the freedom of its people to pursue their dreams and express their beliefs. At first, Ireland's bog represents opposite values. It seems narrow, constricting and inward looking: 'the eye concedes', 'Encroaching horizon', 'cyclops' eye'. In America, the pioneers moved across the country. In Ireland, the pioneers looked 'Inwards and downwards', remembering, almost wallowing in, the past. Is the poet suggesting that Ireland is defined by the layers of its difficult history? Or is each set of pioneers on an adventure, one set discovering new places, the other set rediscovering forgotten places?

Stanza two captures **the bog's fluidity** in the onomatopoeic phrase 'keeps crusting/Between the sights of the sun'. Heaney draws the changing face of the bog, its element of mystery and danger, as it did not always remain exactly the same, but subtly fluctuates. The poet's sense of awe at this place is expressed in **stanza three** as he recounts the discovery of the Great Irish Elk as 'An astounding crate full of air'. Here the poet is referring to another aspect of the bog – its **ability to preserve the past**.

In **stanza four**, the bog's capacity to hold and preserve is emphasised when 'Butter sunk under/ More than a hundred years' was recovered fit for use, 'salty and white'. This place is 'kind'. Stanza four runs into **stanza five** in a parallel reference to the bog's fluidity. The bog never becomes hard; 'its last definition' is 'Missing', so it will never yield coal. The squidgy nature of the bog is conveyed in **stanza six** in the phrase 'soft as pulp'. The phrases of the poem are opening and melting into each other in imitation of the bog. Is this in stark contrast to the hardening prejudices of the two communities in the North of Ireland? This poem was written in 1969. **The Irish explore their past**; to them, history is important as they 'keep striking/Inwards and downwards'.

Heaney leaves us with an **open-ended conclusion** in **stanza seven**. He remembers that the bog 'seemed to have some kind of wind blowing through it that could carry on'. The boglands are feminine, nurturing, welcoming. 'The wet centre is bottomless'. The poet is aware of the depth and complexity of the national consciousness. Should we, like the bog, embrace all aspects of our national identity? Is this how we should carry on? Is there a final truth? Is it unreachable? The poem is written in seven spare, unrhymed stanzas and uses casual, almost colloquial language.

ANALYSIS

'Through the rich musicality of his poetry, Seamus Heaney evokes the difficulty of establishing a national identity.' Discuss this statement with reference to 'Bogland'.

Sample Paragraph

A collective pronoun, 'We', opens 'Bogland'. However, the poet suggests that the Irish define themselves negatively in comparison to the vast open expanse of America, 'We have no prairies'. While their pioneers move forward in their exploration of new territories, ours dig 'Inwards and downwards'. We seem to be in danger of being seduced, almost deformed by our concern with history, 'wooed into the cyclops' eye/Of a tarn'. Yet, through his visual and aural description of the bog, Heaney succeeds in creating a proud symbol of nationhood and belonging. The bog – just like our history – preserves, becoming a repository of treasures, both natural ('the Great Irish Elk') and manmade ('Butter ... recovered salty and white'). We, the Irish, are an accumulation of multiple narratives, 'Every layer they strip/Seems camped on before'. The bog symbolises a nation in a perpetual state of flux. Hard 'k' and 'c' sounds ('keeps crusting') capture the thin surface which breaks to reveal the soft interior of the bog, 'kind black butter'. Run-on lines echo the ever-changing nature of the bog and history, 'soft as pulp'. History continues forever. We embrace, but are not imprisoned by 'The wet centre' which is 'bottomless'.

Examiner's Comment

A close sensitive analysis of the poem, engaging with the subtle connections between its musical language and the theme of identity. Very good range of informed and incisive points on symbolism, sound effects and run-on lines. Expression is varied and controlled. Excellent use of reference and quotation throughout add to the quality of the discussion in this top-grade response.

N.B. Access your ebook for additional sample paragraphs and a list of useful quotes with commentary.

CLASS/HOMEWORK EXERCISES

1. 'Heaney's sensuous imagery often evokes a haunting and dramatic sense of place.' To what extent is this true of 'Bogland'? Support your answer with reference to the poem.

2. 'Through his succinct and exact use of language, Seamus Heaney enables us to make sense of the world and ourselves'. Discuss this view with reference to 'Bogland'.

SUMMARY POINTS

- Importance of history and identity expressed through the central symbol of bogland.
- Free verse, lack of rhyme and rhythm mimic the fluid nature of the bog.
- Contrasting tones of insecurity, awe and amazement turn to quiet reflection.
- Use of striking sound effects, visual imagery, personification and allusions to myth.
- Structure of poem imitates activity of digging – short lines drill down the page, while stacked stanzas reflect the layered nature of the bog.

THE TOLLUND MAN

I

Some day I will go to Aarhus
To see his peat-brown head,
The mild pods of his eyelids,
His pointed skin cap.

In the flat country near by   5
Where they dug him out,
His last gruel of winter seeds
Caked in his stomach,

Naked except for
The cap, noose and girdle,   10
I will stand a long time.
Bridegroom to the goddess,

She tightened her torc on him
And opened her fen,
Those dark juices working   15
Him to a saint's kept body,

Trove of the turfcutters'
Honeycombed workings.
Now his stained face
Reposes at Aarhus.   20

II

I could risk blasphemy,
Consecrate the cauldron bog
Our holy ground and pray
Him to make germinate

The scattered, ambushed   25
Flesh of labourers,
Stockinged corpses
Laid out in the farmyards,

Tell-tale skin and teeth
Flecking the sleepers   30
Of four young brothers, trailed
For miles along the lines.

                    III
Something of his sad freedom
As he rode the tumbril
Should come to me, driving,   35
Saying the names

Tollund, Grauballe, Nebelgard,

Watching the pointing hands
Of country people,
Not knowing their tongue.   40

Out there in Jutland
In the old man-killing parishes
I will feel lost,
Unhappy and at home.

'Something of his sad freedom'

Glossary

The Tollund Man: a reference to the well-preserved body found in 1950 by two turfcutters in Tollund, Denmark. The man had been hanged over 2,000 years earlier. One theory suggested that his death had been part of a ritualistic fertility sacrifice. The Tollund Man's head was put on display in a museum at Aarhus.

1   *Aarhus*: a city in Jutland, Denmark.
3   *pods*: dry seeds.
7   *gruel*: thin porridge.
10 *girdle*: belt.
13 *torc*: decorative metal collar.
14 *fen*: marsh or wet area.
16 *kept*: preserved.
17 *Trove*: valuable find.

18 *Honeycombed workings*: patterns made by the turfcutters on the peat.
21 *blasphemy*: irreverence.
22 *Consecrate*: declare sacred.
22 *cauldron bog*: basin-shaped bogland (some of which was associated with pagan rituals).
24 *germinate*: give new life to.
30 *sleepers*: wooden beams underneath railway lines.
31 *four young brothers*: refers to an infamous atrocity in the 1920s when four Catholic brothers were killed by the police.
34 *tumbril*: two-wheeled cart used to carry a condemned person to execution.
37 *Tollund, Grauballe, Nebelgard*: places in Jutland.

INITIAL RESPONSE

1. Comment on Heaney's tone in the first three stanzas of the poem.

2. Select one image from the poem that you find startling or disturbing and explain its effectiveness.

3. What is your understanding of the poem's final stanza? Refer closely to the text in your answer.

STUDY NOTES

Seamus Heaney was attracted to a book by P.V. Glob, The Bog People, *which dealt with preserved Iron Age bodies of people who had been ritually killed. It offered him a particular frame of reference or set of symbols he could employ to engage with Ireland's historical conflict. The martyr image of the Tollund Man blended in the poet's mind with photographs of other atrocities, past and present, in the long rites of Irish political struggles. The poem comes from Heaney's third collection,* Wintering Out *(1972).*

Part I opens quietly with **the promise of a pilgrimage**: 'Some day I will go to Aarhus'. The tone is expectant, determined. Yet there is also an element of detachment that is reinforced by the Danish place name, 'Aarhus'. Heaney's placid, almost reverential mood is matched by his economic use of language, dominated by simple monosyllables. The evocative description of the Tollund Man's 'peat-brown head' and 'The mild pods of his eyelids' conveys a sense of gentleness and passivity.

Lines 5–11 focus on the dead man's final hours in a much more realistic way. Heaney suggests that the Tollund Man's own journey begins when 'they dug him out', destroyed and elevated at the same time. The poet's meticulous observations ('His last gruel of winter seeds/Caked in his stomach') emphasise the dead man's **innocent vulnerability**. In the aftermath of a ritualistic hanging, we see him abandoned: 'Naked except for/The cap, noose and girdle'. While the poet identifies himself closely with the victim and makes a respectful promise to 'stand a long time', the action itself is passive.

Heaney imagines the natural boglands as the body of a fertility goddess. The revelation that the sacrificial victim was 'Bridegroom to the goddess' (**line 12**) conveys a more **ominous, forceful tone** as the bleak bog itself is also equated with Ireland, female and overwhelming: 'She tightened her torc on him'. Sensuous and energetic images in **lines 13–16** suggest the physical intimacy of the couple's deadly embrace. The Tollund Man becomes 'a saint's kept body', almost a surrogate Christ, buried underground so that new life would spring up. He is left to chance, 'Trove of the turfcutters', and finally resurrected so that 'his stained face/Reposes at Aarhus'. The delicate blend of sibilance and broad vowel sounds suggest tranquillity and a final peace.

Part II suddenly becomes more emphatic and is filled with references to religion. Heaney addresses the spirit of the Tollund Man, invoking him 'to make germinate' (**line 24**) and give life back to the casualties of more recent violence in Northern Ireland. Heaney acknowledges his own discomfort ('I could risk blasphemy') for suggesting that we should search for an alternative deity or religious symbol to unite people. But although it appears to be in contrast with the earlier violence, the poet's restrained style actually accentuates the horror of one infamous sectarian slaughter ('Of four young brothers'). The callous nature of their deaths – 'trailed/For miles along the lines' – is associated with the repulsive rituals in ancient Jutland. Heaney's **nightmarish images** ('Stockinged corpses') are powerful and create a surreal effect. However, the paradoxical 'survival' and repose of the Tollund Man should, the poet implies, give him the power to raise others.

Part III returns to the mellow beginning, but instead of anticipation, there is sorrow and a sense of isolation. Heaney insists that the 'sad freedom' (**line 33**) of the Tollund Man 'Should come to me'. Along with religion and a sense of history and myth, evocative language is central to Heaney's poetry, and here the idea of isolation is brought sharply to the reader through the sense of being 'lost' in a foreign land. Yet ultimately the paradoxical nature of exile is realised: the poet feels at home in a state of homelessness, and welcomes the feeling of not belonging to society which he shares with the Tollund Man, who is no longer tied to religious forces. This estrangement from society is emphasised by the list of foreign names ('Tollund, Grauballe, Nebelgard'). **The poem ends on a note of pessimistic resignation** which describes both the familiar sense of isolation and hopelessness Heaney experiences: 'I will feel lost, /Unhappy and at home'.

Heaney's imaginary pilgrimage to Aarhus has led to a **kind of revelation**. By comparing modern Ulster to the 'old man-killing parishes' (**line 42**) of remote Jutland, the poet places the Northern Irish conflict in a timeless, mythological context. It is as though the only way Heaney can fully express the horrific scenes he has seen in Ireland is to associate them with the exhumed bodies of ancient bog corpses.

ANALYSIS

'Heaney explores the ugliness of human cruelty in poems of subtle verbal melody.' Discuss this statement with reference to 'The Tollund Man'.

Sample Paragraph

Throughout his poem 'The Tollund Man', Heaney reflects on the universal experience of human cruelty. He links the ritually murdered body of the Iron Age victim sacrificed to the unnamed 'goddess' to the executions of 'four young brothers' in the Northern Ireland Troubles. A statement of quiet determination opens the poem, 'Some day I will go to Aarhus', its subtle monosyllables emphasising the poet's resolve. The vulnerability of the victim of Jutland's 'man-killing parishes' is shown in the gentle assonance of the vivid visual image, 'The mild pods of his eyelids'. The pathetic fate of the Northern Ireland victims who were dragged 'miles along lines' is also conveyed through slender assonance of the letter 'i'. Harsh 't' and 'ck' sounds suggest the unspeakable suffering of the young men, 'Tell-tale skin and teeth/Flecking the sleepers'. The barbarity of the Tollund Man's hanging is also conveyed through abrupt sounds. The terrifying goddess 'tightened her torc' around her hapless 'Bridegroom'. Through the meticulous observation of a detached observer, Heaney succeeds in engaging our sympathy for these victims. His use of powerful images and musical language increases our sense of their tragic lives.

Examiner's Comment

This is a first-rate response that shows a very close appreciation of both the poem's subject matter and style. Points are clear, succinct and successfully supported with accurate quotations. The two central elements of the question are addressed, with some particularly incisive commentary on subtle sound effects (e.g. 'subtle monosyllables' and 'gentle assonance'). Expression is also impressive ('the meticulous observation of a detached observer').

N.B. Access your ebook for additional sample paragraphs and a list of useful quotes with commentary.

CLASS/HOMEWORK EXERCISES

1. 'Heaney explores the unpalatable truth of cyclical violence and complicit acceptance through a lyrical examination of the living past.' Discuss this view, supporting your answer with reference to 'The Tollund Man'.

2. 'There is a haunting dreamlike quality to Seamus Heaney's fascination with history and mythology.' Discuss this statement, supporting your answer with reference to 'The Tollund Man'.

SUMMARY POINTS

- Examination of cyclical human violence, vulnerable victims and foreignness.
- Varying tones – resolve, reverence, detachment, uncertainty, despair, empathy.
- Use of similarity and contrast – Tollund Man/four young brothers; colloquial sound patterns/stately British rhetoric; individual human experience/universal experience.
- Lyrical and musical qualities; onomatopoeia, assonance, harsh cacophonous sounds.
- Short lines and fragmented rhythm convey the disturbing reality of death.
- List of foreign place names has intriguing, unsettling effect.

4 MOSSBAWN: SUNLIGHT 🔊

for Mary Heaney

There was a sunlit absence.
The helmeted pump in the yard
heated its iron,
water honeyed

in the slung bucket   5
and the sun stood
like a griddle cooling
against the wall

of each long afternoon.
So, her hands scuffled   10
over the bakeboard,
the reddening stove

sent its plaque of heat
against her where she stood
in a floury apron   15
by the window.

Now she dusts the board
with a goose's wing,
now sits, broad-lapped,
with whitened nails   20

and measling shins:
here is a space
again, the scone rising
to the tick of two clocks.

And here is love   25
like a tinsmith's scoop
sunk past its gleam
in the meal-bin.

'to the tick of two clocks'

Glossary

Mossbawn was Heaney's birthplace. 'Bawn' refers to the name the English planters gave to their fortified farmhouses. '*Bán*' is Gaelic for 'white'. Heaney wonders if the name could be 'white moss' and has commented, 'In the syllables of my home, I see a metaphor of the split culture of Ulster.'

Dedication: The poem is dedicated to the poet's aunt, Mary Heaney, who lived with the family throughout Heaney's childhood. He shared a special relationship with her, 'a woman with a huge well of affection and a very experienced, dry-eyed sense of the world'.

7   *griddle*: circular iron plate used for cooking food.
10   *scuffled*: moving quickly, making a scraping noise.
13   *plaque*: area of intense heat, originally a hot plate.
21   *measling*: red spots on legs made by standing close to heat.
24   *the tick of two clocks*: the two time sequences in the poem, past and present.
26   *tinsmith*: person who made pots and pans from tin.
28   *meal-bin*: a container used to hold flour, etc.

INITIAL RESPONSE

1. Describe the atmosphere in the poem 'Mossbawn', with particular reference to Heaney's treatment of time.

2. What image of Mary Heaney, the aunt, is drawn? Do you find the picture appealing or unappealing? Quote from the poem in support of your views.

3. Choose one image or phrase from the poem that you found particularly effective, and say why you found it so.

STUDY NOTES

'Sunlight' appeared in the collection North *(1975) and was the first of two poems under the title 'Mossbawn', the name of Heaney's family home. To the poet, this farm was 'the first place', an idyllic Garden of Eden, full of sunlight and feminine grace, a contrast to the brute reality of the outside world. At this time, terrible atrocities were being committed by both Catholics and Protestants in the sectarian struggle which was taking place in the North of Ireland.*

This poem opens with a **vivid, atmospheric portrayal of the silent sunlit yard**, a beautiful, tranquil scene from Heaney's boyhood in the 1940s. The pump marked the centre of this private world, which was untroubled by the activities outside. American soldiers had bases in Northern Ireland during the Second World War. For the impressionable Heaney growing up, the water pump was a symbol of purity and life. This guardian of domestic life is described as 'helmeted', a sentry soldier on duty, ready to protect. The phrase 'water honeyed' (**line 4**) emphasises this slender iron idol as an image of deep and hidden goodness, the centre of another world. The poet creates a nostalgic picture of a timeless zone of slow, deep, domestic ritual and human warmth. Here are childhood days of golden innocence and security. The repetition of 'h' (in 'helmeted', 'heated' and 'honeyed') portrays the heating process as the reader exhales breath. The sun is described in the striking simile 'like a griddle cooling/against the wall'. This homely image of the iron dish of the home-baked flat cake evokes a view of a serene place.

Line 10 moves readers from the place to the person. 'So' introduces us to a **warm, tender portrait of Heaney's beloved Aunt Mary at work**. She is a symbol of the old secure way of life, when a sense of community was firm and traditional rural values were held in high esteem. We are shown the unspectacular routine of work; she 'dusts the board' for baking. We see her domestic skill, her hands 'scuffled' as she kneads the dough. Visual detail paints this picture as if it were a Dutch still life from the artist Vermeer: 'floury apron', 'whitened nails'. There is an almost religious simplicity on the essentials of life: bread, water, love (water 'honeyed', 'scone rising', 'here is love'). The people in this scene are not glamorous. Realistic details remind us of their ordinariness: 'broad-lapped', 'measling shins'.

The **closing simile** in **lines 26–8**, 'like a tinsmith's scoop/sunk past its gleam/in the meal-bin', **shows how the ordinary is transformed into the extraordinary** by the power of love. The hidden shine of love is present in the ordinary ritual of baking. Remembering the past, the poet makes it present, 'here is love'. The two time zones of passing time and a timeless moment are held in the alliterative phrase 'to the tick of two clocks'. We are invited to listen to the steady rhythm of the repetitive 't'. As the life-giving water lies unseen beneath the cold earth, the aunt's love is hidden, but constant, ready to be drawn on, like the water in the pump. The radiant glow of love is hidden like a buried light. The change of tenses at the word 'Now' brings the moment closer as the abstract becomes concrete, and the outside becomes inside. The short four-line stanzas run on, achieving their own momentum of contained energy in this still scene, which reaches its climax in the elevating last stanza.

ANALYSIS

'Seamus Heaney often uses childhood memories to shape sensuous poetry.' Discuss this statement with reference to 'Mossbawn: Sunlight'.

Sample Paragraph

Using a tight structure of 28 lines within seven quatrains, Heaney re-creates his childhood experience through the details of the Northern Ireland countryside. In recalling his family's farm-yard, the 'helmeted pump' stands as guardian in this idyllic place. It is an icon for the hidden energies of this special setting and the people Heaney remembers. Everything Heaney writes appeals to our senses. The steady repetitive rhythm, run-on lines and assonance ('slung bucket') create a still exterior painting of a quiet landscape. Personification ('pump ... heated its iron,' 'the sun stood') adds to the magic of this extraordinary scene. The cinematic quality of the poem's opening zooms to an interior shot of his aunt baking in the kitchen. Gentle onomatopoeic sounds ('scuffled', 'dusts') barely ruffle the surface silence. The poet changes the tense from past to present ('There was', 'here is') while he and his readers enter into the living memory of Mossbawn, which resonates to the sound of the 'tick of two clocks', then and now. Love, in the person of his aunt, resides in this timeless place, concealed but present, conveyed in the beautiful simile of the final lines, like the 'tinsmith's scoop/sunk past its gleam/in the meal-bin'. Although his Mossbawn childhood has gone, the poet can still glimpse its innocence and security in his imagination.

Examiner's Comment

This is an impressive response that merits the highest grade. The focus is firmly placed on how Heaney captures significant moments from his childhood through precise sensual language ('Everything Heaney writes appeals to our senses'). Some incisive discussion of the poet's style is well supported with apt quotations. Expression is carefully controlled throughout.

N.B. Access your ebook for additional sample paragraphs and a list of useful quotes with commentary.

CLASS/HOMEWORK EXERCISES

1. The Royal Swedish Academy announced that Seamus Heaney's Nobel Prize for Literature was for 'lyrical beauty ... which brings out the miracles of the ordinary day and the living past'. Discuss this statement using reference to both the content and style of 'Mossbawn: Sunlight'.

2. 'Heaney presents readers with small domestic dramas that explore recurring themes of love and longing in his poems.' Discuss this view with particular reference to 'Mossbawn: Sunlight'.

SUMMARY POINTS

- Recurring themes of love and yearning.
- Slow-moving rhythm complements poignant childhood memories.
- Evocative tones of fondness, longing and nostalgia.
- Juxtaposition – exterior scene contrasted with gentle domestic activity within.
- Simple language, warm, homely images.
- Striking use of personification, simile, and paradox.
- Sensuous onomatopoeic effects – alliteration and assonant sounds.
- Enjambment and tense changes add to the poem's dramatic, dreamlike quality.

5   A CONSTABLE CALLS 🔊

His bicycle stood at the window-sill,
The rubber cowl of a mud-splasher
Skirting the front mudguard,
Its fat black handlegrips

Heating in sunlight, the 'spud'   5
Of the dynamo gleaming and cocked back,
The pedal treads hanging relieved
Of the boot of the law.

His cap was upside down
On the floor, next his chair.   10
The line of its pressure ran like a bevel
In his slightly sweating hair.

He had unstrapped
The heavy ledger, and my father
Was making tillage returns   15
In acres, roods, and perches.

Arithmetic and fear.
I sat staring at the polished holster
With its buttoned flap, the braid cord
Looped into the revolver butt.   20

'Any other root crops?
Mangolds? Marrowstems? Anything like that?'
'No.' But was there not a line
Of turnips where the seed ran out

In the potato field? I assumed   25
Small guilts and sat
Imagining the black hole in the barracks.
He stood up, shifted the baton-case

Further round on his belt,
Closed the domesday book,   30
Fitted his cap back with two hands,
And looked at me as he said goodbye.

A shadow bobbed in the window.
He was snapping the carrier spring
Over the ledger. His boot pushed off   35
And the bicycle ticked, ticked, ticked.

'the boot of the law'

Glossary

2   *cowl*: covering shaped like a hood.

5   *'spud'*: potato-like shape.

8   *the boot of the law*: heavy footwear of policeman;
    power and control of the law.

11 *bevel*: marked line on policeman's forehead made by
    his cap.

14 *ledger*: book containing records of farm accounts.

15 *tillage returns*: amount harvested from cultivated
    land.

19 *braid*: threads woven into a decorative band.

22 *Mangolds*: beets grown for animal feed.

22 *Marrowstems*: long green vegetables.

30 *domesday book*: William the Conqueror, the English
    king, had ordered a survey to be carried out of all
    the land and its value in England; also refers to
    Judgement Day, when all will be brought to account.

33 *bobbed*: moved up and down.

34 *carrier spring*: spiral metal coil on the back of a bike
    used to secure a bag, etc.

1. How does the poet create an atmosphere of tension in this poem? Support your response with reference to the text.

2. What type of relationship do you think the young boy has with his father? Refer closely to the text in your response.

3. Critics disagree about the ending of the poem. Some find it 'false', others 'stunning'. How would you describe the ending? Give reasons for your conclusions.

▶ STUDY NOTES

'A Constable Calls' was written in 1975 and forms the second part of the poem sequence 'Singing School'. The Heaneys were a Catholic family. The constable would have been a member of the Royal Ulster Constabulary and probably a Protestant. This poem was written when the tensions between the two communities in Northern Ireland were at their height. Heaney's 'country of community ... was a place of division'.

'A Constable Calls' is written from the **viewpoint of a young boy** caught in the epicentre of the Troubles, a time of recent sectarian violence in Northern Ireland. The poem explores fear and power from the perspective of the Nationalist community. The Catholics did not trust or like the RUC (Royal Ulster Constabulary). In the **opening stanzas**, crude strength, power and violence are all inherent in the cold, precise language used to describe the constable's bicycle. The 'handlegrips' suggest handcuffs, while the 'cocked back' dynamo hints at a gun ready to explode, its trigger ready for action. It also signifies confidence and cockiness. The oppression of the local authorities is contained in the phrase 'the boot of the law'. Heaney personifies the bicycle, which he describes as being 'relieved' of the pressure of the weight of the constable. This poem was written during the civil rights protest marches, when Nationalists were sometimes treated very severely by the RUC. This is evoked in the ugly sound of 'ow' in the word 'cowl', the assonance of the broad vowels in 'fat black' and the harsh-sounding repetition of 'ck' in the phrase 'cocked back'. Here are the observations of the child of a divided community. The character (and symbolic significance) of the constable is implicit in the description of his bicycle.

In **stanzas three** to **five**, Heaney gives us an explicit **description of the constable**. His uniform and equipment are all symbols of power, which the young boy notes in detail: 'the polished holster/ With its buttoned flap, the braid cord/Looped into the revolver butt'. Here is no friendly community police officer. The repetition of 'his' tells us that the possession of power belongs to him and what he represents. He is not a welcome visitor. His hat lies on the ground. He is not offered refreshment, although he is presumably thirsty from his work. Even the one human detail ('slightly sweating hair') revolts us. Is he as tense as the Catholic family in this time of sectarian conflict? The print of his great authority is stamped on him like a 'bevel', but does his power weigh heavily on him?

The policeman's function was to oblige the boy's father to give an account of his farm crop returns. Their terse exchange underlines the **tension in this troubled community**. The interrogation by the constable consists of four questions: 'Any other root crops?/Mangolds? Marrowstems? Anything like that?' This is met by the father's short, clipped, monosyllabic reply: 'No'. The encounter is summed up succinctly in the line 'Arithmetic and fear'. In the **seventh stanza**, the young boy becomes alarmed as he realises that his father has omitted to account for 'a line/Of turnips'. He 'assumed/Small guilts'. His Catholic inferiority is graphically shown in the reference to the 'domesday book', or 'ledger', belonging to the constable. The child imagines a day of reckoning, almost like Judgement Day, when God calls every individual to account for past sins. He imagines the immediate punishment of 'the black hole in the barracks', the notorious police cell where offenders were held. This terror of being incarcerated by the law ran deep in the Catholic psyche throughout the Troubles.

In the end, the constable takes his leave (**stanzas seven** and **eight**), formally fitting 'his cap back with two hands'. We can empathise with the young boy as he 'looked at me'. In the **final stanza**, the oppressive presence of the visitor ('A shadow') is wryly described as 'bobbed', an ironic reference to the friendly English bobby – which this particular constable was not. The verbs in this stanza continue the underlying ominous mood: 'snapping', 'pushed off'. The **poem concludes** with an intimidating reference to the sound of the departing bicycle as a slowly ticking time bomb: 'And the bicycle ticked, ticked, ticked'. Does this suggest that the tension in this divided community was always on the verge of exploding? Do you consider this an effective image or do you think the symbolism is too obvious?

ANALYSIS

'Seamus Heaney often presents moments of epiphany using autobiographical experience.' Discuss this statement in relation to 'A Constable Calls'.

Sample Paragraph

In his poem, 'A Constable Calls', a young Seamus Heaney recalls a tense incident from his childhood days in Northern Ireland during the 1950s. A local policeman calls to interview the boy's father about the taxes that are due to be paid on his farm crops. Through the attentive observant eye of the small boy, the tensions within the divided Northern community are dramatised. The focus is immediately placed on the constable's bicycle which 'stood at the window-sill' and then zooms to a close-up of the 'rubber cowl of a mud-splasher', the 'fat black handlegrips' and the 'dynamo gleaming and cocked back'. This strikingly vivid description suggests the repressive power felt by the Catholic Nationalists from the RUC. The crude metaphor, 'the boot of the law', reinforces this impression. After a tense interrogation between the officer and the boy's father ('Any other root crops? ... No'), the young boy is filled with guilt at his father's lie and fears that there might be consequences. Although he is not fully aware of the significance of the encounter, the youthful Heaney experiences a coming-of-age sense of the sectarian world around him. For the first time, he gets an intense insight into the troubled relations between the minority Nationalist community and the powerful Unionist force of law. The menacing final line describing the spokes of the constable's bicycle wheels as they 'ticked, ticked, ticked' predicts the terrible violence of bombs and explosions that will define Northern Ireland during the so-called Troubles of the 1970s and 80s.

Examiner's Comment

A top-grade response, successfully describing the setting for this dramatic confrontation between the constable and Heaney's father. There is a clear explanation of the uneasy atmosphere in which the poet gains an early awareness of sectarian conflict. Supporting quotations are integrated effectively into the commentary and the expression is excellent. The impressive final sentence succinctly sums up the poem's narrative very well.

N.B. Access your ebook for additional sample paragraphs and a list of useful quotes with commentary.

CLASS/HOMEWORK EXERCISES

1. 'The question of identity looms large in Seamus Heaney's precisely controlled poetry'. Discuss this statement with reference to 'A Constable Calls'.

2. 'Heaney frequently writes evocative poems that explore the harsh reality of ordinary life.' Discuss this view referring both to the content and style of 'A Constable Calls'.

SUMMARY POINTS

- Key themes include conflict, repressive authority and the loss of innocence.
- Engaging use of first person narrative and closely observed detail.
- Tension between divided community results in child's discomfort.
- Compelling psychological drama (threat, interrogation, lies, guilt, danger recedes).
- Dynamic cinematic movement (zooms, pans, slow motion, close-up).
- Short snappy lines juxtaposed with flowing lines and run-on quatrains.
- Ominous conclusion.

Memory — poem peppered with sensous imagery
Reliving a memory. The reader is lifted into his experience and imbibes it
immersed
Captures his experience.

6 THE SKUNK

Striking, impacting
Simile

Up, black, striped and damasked like the chasuble
At a funeral Mass, the skunk's tail
Paraded the skunk. Night after night
I expected her like a visitor.

onomatopeic sounds

The refrigerator whinnied into silence.   5
My desk light softened beyond the verandah.
Small oranges loomed in the orange tree. *soft sounds, heightened senses.*
I began to be tense as a voyeur.

misses her
After eleven years I was composing
Love-letters again, broaching the word 'wife'   10 *simile — comparing her to precous items*
Like a stored cask, as if its slender vowel
something precious
Had mutated into the night earth and air

Of California. The beautiful, useless   *useless to him as she's not there*
Tang of eucalyptus spelt your absence. *penetrating sense of loneliness*
The aftermath of a mouthful of wine   15 *although she is absent she fills*
Was like inhaling you off a cold pillow.   *his conscience.*

And there she was, the intent and glamorous,
Ordinary, mysterious skunk,
Mythologized, demythologized,
Snuffing the boards five feet beyond me.   20
onomatopeic sounds
It all came back to me last night, stirred
By the sootfall of your things at bedtime,
Your head-down, tail-up hunt in a bottom drawer
For the black plunge-line nightdress.

'the skunk's tail/Paraded the skunk'

Glossary

1	*damasked*: patterned; rich, heavy damask fabric.	12	*mutated*: changed shape or form.
1	*chasuble*: garment worn by a priest saying Mass.	14	*eucalyptus*: common tree with scented leaves found in California.
5	*whinnied*: sound a horse makes.	15	*aftermath*: consequences of an unpleasant event.
6	*verandah*: roofed platform along the outside of a house.	19	*Mythologized*: related to or found in myth.
8	*voyeur*: a person who watches others when they are being intimate.	22	*sootfall*: soft sound (like soot falling from a chimney).
10	*broaching*: raising a subject for discussion.	24	*plunge-line*: low-cut.

INITIAL RESPONSE

1. In your opinion, how effective is Heaney in creating the particular sense of place in this poem? Refer closely to the text in your answer.

2. The poet compares his wife to a skunk. Does this image work, in your view? Quote from the poem in support of your response.

3. Comment on the poem's dramatic qualities. Refer to setting, characters, action and sense of tension/climax, particularly in the first and last stanzas.

STUDY NOTES

'The Skunk' comes from Heaney's 1979 collection, Field Work. *The poet called it a 'marriage poem'. While spending an academic year (1971–2) teaching in America, he had been reading the work of Robert Lowell, an American poet. Lowell's poem, 'Skunk Hour', describes how isolation drives a man to become a voyeur of lovers in cars. Heaney's reaction to his own loneliness is very different; he rediscovers the art of writing love letters to his wife, who is living 6,000 miles away in Ireland. This separation culminated in an intimate, humorous, erotic love poem which speaks volumes for the deep love and trust between husband and wife.*

In the **opening stanza**, the reader is presented with four words describing the skunk's tail, 'Up, black, striped and damasked'. The punctuation separates the different aspects of the animal's tail for the reader's observation. An unusual simile occurs in **line 1**. In a **playfully irreverent tone**, Heaney likens the skunk's tail to the black and white vestments worn by a priest at a funeral. He then gives us an almost cartoon-like visual image of the animal's tail leading the skunk. The self-importance of the little animal is effectively captured in the verb 'Paraded'. All the ceremony of marching is evoked. The poet eagerly awaits his nightly visitor: 'Night after night/I expected her like a visitor'. Skunks are small black and white striped American mammals, capable of spraying foul-smelling liquid on attackers.

In **stanza two**, the poet's senses are heightened. The verbs 'whinnied', 'softened' and 'loomed' vividly capture **the atmosphere of the soft, exotic California night**. The bright colours of orange and green are synonymous with the Sunshine State. The anticipation of stanza one now sharpens: 'I began to be tense'. He regards himself as a 'voyeur', but here there is no violation. He is staring into darkness, getting ready to communicate with his wife. In **stanza three**, the poet, after a break of 11 years, is penning love letters to his wife again. In this separation period, he realises how much he misses her. His wife's presence, although she is absent, fills his consciousness. He is totally preoccupied with her. He uses the simile 'Like a stored cask' to show how he values her as something precious. The word 'wife' is savoured like fine wine and his affection is shown in his appreciation of 'its slender vowel', which reminds him of her feminine grace. She is present to him in the air he breathes, 'mutated into the night earth and air/Of California'.

Heaney's depth of longing is captured in the **sensuous language** of **stanza four**. The smell of the eucalyptus 'spelt your absence'. The word 'Tang' precisely notes the penetrating sensation of loneliness. Even a drink of wine, 'a mouthful of wine', does not dull this ache. Instead it intensifies his longing, 'like inhaling you off a cold pillow'. Now, the skunk, long awaited, appears. It is full of contradictions: 'glamorous', 'Ordinary'. We hear in **stanza five** the sound the little animal makes in the onomatopoeic phrase 'Snuffing the boards'. Only in **stanza six** is the comparison between the wife and the skunk finally drawn: 'It all came back to me last night'. Heaney is now back home. His wife is rummaging in the bottom drawer for a nightdress. She adopts a slightly comic pose, 'head-down, tail-up', reminding him of the skunk as she 'hunt[s]'. The sibilance of the line 'stirred/By the sootfall of your things' suggests the tender intimacy between the married couple. The word 'sootfall' conveys the gentle rustle of clothes falling. The reader's reaction is also 'stirred' to amused surprise as the realisation dawns that the adjectives 'intent and glamorous,/Ordinary, mysterious … Mythologized, demythologized' also apply to his wife. A **mature, trusting relationship** exists between the couple.

Longer lines suggest ease. The poet is relaxed and playful, his language conversational and sensuous. All our senses are 'stirred'. The light is romantic ('softened') and the colour black is alluring. The touch of the 'cold pillow' will now be replaced by the warm, shared bed. The sounds of California and the couple's bedroom echo: 'Snuffing', 'sootfall'. The smell of the eucalyptus's 'Tang' hangs in the air. The 'aftermath of a mouthful of wine' lingers on the tongue. Here is a rarity, a **successful love poem about marriage**, tender but not cosy, personal but not embarrassingly self-revealing.

ANALYSIS

'Seamus Heaney makes use of a wide range of striking images to explore experiences of people, places and events.' Discuss this statement in relation to 'The Skunk'.

Sample Paragraph

Heaney's poems are filled with memorable images. He writes about subjects that are sometimes tinged with loneliness and often filled with love, as in 'The Skunk'. Through the innovative image of the little nocturnal animal, the skunk, whose tail paraded … 'Up, black, striped and damasked', he conveys the beauty and wonder of married love. It is both mundane and mysterious. This dramatic poem appeals to our senses. Evocative personification is used along with powerful aural imagery, 'The refrigerator whinnied'. Heaney uses vivid visual detail, 'Small oranges loomed in the orange tree'. The Californian setting, with its exotic 'Tang of eucalyptus', is conjured up effectively. The lonely poet is separated from his wife and wistfully recalls her presence, 'The aftermath of a mouthful of wine/Was like inhaling you off a cold pillow'. Detailed images connect her to the skunk moving around in the yard outside the house where the poet is staying. He observes the animal's posture, 'head-down, tail-up' and the sultry lonely atmosphere is suddenly replaced by the soft, sensuous 'sootfall of your things'. The close intimacy of the married couple is highlighted in the detail of the 'black plunge-line nightdress'. By closely linking people, places and events together, Heaney presents a mysterious moment of insight about mature love.

Examiner's Comment

A close analysis of the poem, addressing the question with great confidence. Informed and focused discussion – particularly of how the poet uses sensual imagery. Expression is varied ('innovative', 'mundane and mysterious', 'close intimacy') and well controlled. Excellent use of reference and quotation throughout add to the quality of the discussion in this top-grade response.

N.B. Access your ebook for additional sample paragraphs and a list of useful quotes with commentary.

CLASS/HOMEWORK EXERCISES

1. 'Relationships, personal or otherwise, lie at the heart of Heaney's most accessible poems.' Discuss this view with reference to the poem, 'The Skunk'.

2. 'Throughout his lyrical poems, Seamus Heaney conjures up a sense of the universal, even when focusing on distinct personal experiences.' Discuss this statement with reference to both the content and style of 'The Skunk'.

SUMMARY POINTS

- Unusual, playful, intimate love poem.
- Range of tones – irreverent, reflective, wistful, emotive.
- Striking visual, aural, tactile imagery.
- Personification and onomatopoeia evoke atmosphere, people and places.
- Disconcerting juxtaposition of past/present, animal/person, loss/love, ordinary/mysterious.
- Contrasting line lengths (brief end-stopped lines, flowing run-on lines and stanzas) create urgency, tension and longing.

⑦ THE HARVEST BOW 🔊

satisfaction as the farm gear Draws to a close

As you plaited the harvest bow   *symbolises*
You implicated the mellowed silence in you   *intricate bond between father & son.*
In wheat that does not rust   *autumnal images — sense of accomplishment.*
But brightens as it tightens twist by twist   *alliteration, rhyme*
Into a knowable corona,
A throwaway love-knot of straw.

recalls the still of his father.

Hands that aged round ashplants and cane sticks   *detailed imagery to show*
And lapped the spurs on a lifetime of gamecocks   *the strength of childhood*
Harked to their gift and worked with fine intent   *memories*
Until your fingers moved somnambulant:
I tell and finger it like braille,   *The past*
Gleaning the unsaid off the palpable,

Ordinary scenes enhanced by sensory imagery

And if I spy into its golden loops   *value*
I see us walk between the railway slopes
Into an evening of long grass and midges,   15
Blue smoke straight up, old beds and ploughs in hedges,
An auction notice on an outhouse wall –
You with a harvest bow in your lapel,

relentless passing of time

Me with the fishing rod, already homesick
For the big lift of these evenings, as your stick   20
Whacking the tips off weeds and bushes
Beats out of time, and beats, but flushes   *respects the land, still.*
Nothing: that original townland
Still tongue-tied in the straw tied by your hand.

The end of art is peace   *at the end of everything*   25 *there will be peace.*
Could be the motto of this frail device
That I have pinned up on our deal dresser –
Like a drawn snare   *traps his memories*
Slipped lately by the spirit of the corn
Yet burnished by its passage, and still warm.   *Comfort*   30
still relevant.

'A throwaway love-knot of straw'

Glossary

The harvest bow, an emblem of traditional rural crafts, was made from straw and often worn in the lapel to celebrate the end of harvesting. Sometimes it was given as a love-token or kept in the farmhouse until the next year's harvest.

2   *implicated*: intertwined; revealed indirectly.

2   *mellowed*: matured, placid.

5   *corona*: circle of light, halo.

8   *lapped the spurs*: tied the back claws of fighting birds.

8   *gamecocks*: male fowl reared to take part in cock-fighting.

9   *Harked*: listened, attuned.

10   *somnambulant*: automatically, as if sleepwalking.

11   *braille*: system of reading and writing by touching raised dots.

12   *Gleaning*: gathering, grasping; understanding.

12   *palpable*: what can be handled or understood.

15   *midges*: small biting insects that usually swarm near water.

22   *flushes*: rouses, reveals.

25   *The end of art is peace*: art brings contentment (a quotation from the English poet Coventry Patmore, 1823–96). It was also used by W.B. Yeats.

26   *device*: object, artefact.

27   *deal*: pine wood.

28   *snare*: trap.

30   *burnished*: shining.

INITIAL RESPONSE

1. Based on your reading of the poem, what impression do you get of Heaney's father? Refer to the text in your answer.

2. In your view, is the harvest bow a symbol of love? Give reasons for your answer, using reference to the poem.

3. What do you understand by the line *'The end of art is peace'*? Briefly explain your answer.

STUDY NOTES

'The Harvest Bow' (from the 1972 collection Field Work*) is an elegiac poem in which Heaney pays tribute to his father and the work he did with his hands, weaving a traditional harvest emblem out of stalks of wheat. Remembering his boyhood, watching his father create the corn-dolly, he already knew that the moment could not last. The recognition of his father's artistic talents leads the poet to a consideration of his own creative work.*

The poem begins with a measured description of Heaney's reticent father as he twists stalks of wheat into decorative love-knots. The delicate phrasing in **stanza one** ('You implicated the mellowed silence in you') reflects the poet's awareness of how the **harvest bow symbolised the intricate bond between father and son**. The poet conveys a subdued but satisfied mood as another farm year draws to a close. Autumnal images ('wheat that does not rust') add to the sense of accomplishment. Heaney highlights the practised techniques involved in creating this 'throwaway love-knot of straw'. The harvest bow 'brightens as it tightens twist by twist'. Emphatic alliteration and internal rhyme enliven the image, almost becoming a metaphor for the father's expertise. The bow is likened to 'a knowable corona', a reassuring light circle representing the year's natural cycle.

In **stanza two**, the intricate beauty of the straw knot prompts Heaney to recall some of the other manual skills his father once demonstrated 'round ashplants and cane sticks'. He acknowledges the older man's 'gift' of concentration and 'fine intent' as he fashioned the harvest bow ('your fingers moved somnambulant') **without conscious effort towards artistic achievement**. Is Heaney also suggesting that poets should work that way? Carefully handling the bow 'like braille', the poet clearly values it as an expression of undeclared love: 'Gleaning the unsaid off the palpable'.

The pleasurable sentiments of Heaney's childhood memories are realised by the strength of detailed imagery in **stanza three**: 'I see us walk between the railway slopes'. Such **ordinary scenes are enhanced by sensuous details** of 1940s rural life: 'Blue smoke straight up, old beds and ploughs in hedges'. Many of the sounds have a plaintive, musical quality ('loops', 'slopes', 'midges', 'hedges'). The poet seems haunted by his father's ghost, and the silence that once seemed to define their relationship is now recognised as a secret code of mutual understanding.

Stanza four focuses on the relentless passing of time. The **tone is particularly elegaic** as Heaney recalls his father 'Whacking the tips off weeds' with his stick. In retrospect, he seems to interpret such pointless actions as evidence of how every individual 'Beats out of time' – but to no avail. The poet extends this notion of time's mystery by suggesting that it is through art alone ('the straw tied by your hand') that 'tongue-tied' communities can explore life's wonder.

At the start of **stanza five**, Heaney tries to make sense of the corn-dolly, now a treasured part of his own household 'on our deal dresser'. It mellows in its new setting and gives out heat. While 'the spirit of the corn' may have disappeared from the knot, the power of the poet's imagination can still recreate it there. So rather than being merely a nostalgic recollection of childhood, the poem takes on universal meaning in the intertwining of artistic forces. We are left with a deep sense of lost rural heritage, the unspoken joy of a shared relationship and the rich potential of the poet's art. For Heaney, **artistic achievements produce warm feelings of lasting contentment**. Whatever 'frail device' is created, be it a harvest bow or a formal elegy, 'The end of art is peace'.

ANALYSIS

'Heaney makes effective use of striking imagery to explore universal themes of love and loss.' Discuss this statement with reference to 'The Harvest Bow'.

Sample Paragraph

Heaney's nostalgic memory poem, 'The Harvest Bow', is a powerful elegy for his beloved father. Its finely crafted imagery and ingenious sound effects describe the traditional home-made straw bow which celebrates the end of the farming year when the crops are harvested. The poet recalls that his father worked with 'fine intent' to fashion the 'love-knot' from the fresh wheat 'that does not rust' because it has been transformed into a work of art. Remembering this 'frail device' allows Heaney to go back in time like a 'drawn snare', enabling him to 'spy into its golden loops' and re-experience treasured long moments between father and son. Strong aural images, broad vowels and enjambment evoke the serene mood, 'I see us walk between the railway slopes/Into an evening of long grass and midges'. Poignant memories of childhood are universal and almost everyone has special moments that symbolise family love. Heaney's father 'Beats out of time' with his stick, an image that lives forever in his memory. The phrase suggests the close bond shared by father and son, but also hints at the cruelty of time and sense of loss caused by death. For Heaney, the harvest bow is a trap which entangles his memory, yet the presence of his father escapes and lives again in the adult poet's heart, 'still warm'.

Examiner's Comment

This is a sustained high-grade response that shows close engagement with the poem. All the elements of the question (imagery, love and loss, universal significance) are addressed. Relevant quotations – referring to a range of imagery patterns – are used to support discussion points. Expression is well controlled and the critical vocabulary is very impressive.

N.B. Access your ebook for additional sample paragraphs and a list of useful quotes with commentary.

CLASS/HOMEWORK EXERCISES

1. 'Seamus Heaney frequently uses detailed observation and a lyrical style to explore close family relationships.' Discuss this view with reference to 'The Harvest Bow'.

2. 'Heaney's carefully judged language enables readers to relate to recurring themes that are often grounded in the past.' Discuss this statement with reference to both the subject matter and style of 'The Harvest Bow'.

SUMMARY POINTS

- Elegy directly addresses the poet's father.
- Warm, emotional tone, consoling perfection of the past.
- Similarity drawn between intricate artistry of the bow maker and poet.
- Contrasting aspects of his father – tough, practical, silent, tender, skilled.
- Multiple word meanings, e.g. 'implicate' = 'show', 'entrap', 'include'.
- Clever aural word-play imitates the complexity of the harvest bow.
- Concluding reassuring motto – art confronts every destructive life experience and creates order.

8 THE UNDERGROUND

There we were in the vaulted tunnel running, *— no limitations to what they can do*
You in your going-away coat speeding ahead *always ahead of him — better than him.*
And me, me then like a fleet god gaining *— mythical — Hero chasing his girl*
Upon you before you turned to a reed

intensity of situation

Or some new white flower japped with crimson   5
As the coat flapped wild and button after button *exciting.*
Sprang off and fell in a trail
Between the Underground and the Albert Hall.

Honeymooning, mooning around, late for the Proms,
Our echoes die in that corridor and now *immaturity / fruitfulness of relationship.*
I come as Hansel came on the moonlit stones
Retracing the path back, lifting the buttons *opening up memories.*

To end up in a draughty lamplit station *trusts her now — happy*
After the trains have gone, the wet track
Bared and tensed as I am, all attention   15
For your step following and damned if I look back. *true love*

love more precious over time.

'Our echoes die in that corridor' *run on lines.*

comparison to be self.

Glossary

In Greek mythology, Eurydice, the beloved wife of Orpheus, was killed by a venomous snake. Orpheus travelled to the Underworld (Hades) to retrieve her. It was granted that Eurydice could return to the world of the living, but on condition that Orpheus should walk in front of her and not look back until he had reached the upper world. In his anxiety, he broke his promise, and Eurydice vanished again – but this time forever.

1   *vaulted*: domed, arched.
2   *going-away coat*: new coat worn by the bride leaving on honeymoon.
3   *fleet*: fast; momentary.
4   *reed*: slender plant; part of a musical instrument.
5   *japped*: tinged, layered.
8   *the Albert Hall*: famous London landmark and concert venue.
9   *the Proms*: short for promenade concerts, a summer season of classical music.
11 *Hansel*: fairytale character who, along with his sister Gretel, retraced his way home using a trail of white pebbles.

INITIAL RESPONSE

1. Comment on the atmosphere created in the first two stanzas. Refer to the text in your answer.

2. From your reading of this poem, what do you learn about the relationship between the poet and his wife? Refer to the text in your answer.

3. Write a short personal response to 'The Underground', highlighting the impact it made on you.

STUDY NOTES

'The Underground' is the first poem in Station Island (1984). It recounts a memory from Heaney's honeymoon when he and his wife (like a modern Orpheus and Eurydice) were rushing through a London Underground Tube station on their way to a BBC Promenade Concert in the Albert Hall. In Dennis O'Driscoll's book, Stepping Stones, Heaney has said, 'In this version of the story, Eurydice and much else gets saved by the sheer cussedness of the poet up ahead just keeping going.'

The poem's title is infused with a piercing sense of threat. Underground journeys are shadowed with a certain menace. Not only is there a mythical association with crossing into the land of the dead, but there is also the actuality of accidents and terrorist outrages. The **first stanza** of Heaney's personal narrative uses everyday colloquial speech ('There we were in the vaulted tunnel running') to introduce his **dramatic account**. Broad vowel sounds ('vau', 'tun' and 'run') dominate the opening line with a guttural quality. The oppressively 'vaulted' setting and urgent verbs ('speeding', 'gaining') increase this sense of subterranean disquiet. For the poet, it is a psychic and mythic underground where he imagines his own heroic quest ('like a fleet god'). What he seems to dread most is the possibility of change and that, like a latter-day Orpheus, he might somehow lose his soulmate.

Cinematic images and run-on lines propel the **second stanza** forward. This **fast-paced rhythm is in keeping with the restless diction** – 'the coat flapped wild'. The poet's wife is wearing her going-away wedding outfit and in the course of her sprint, the buttons start popping off. Internal rhyme adds to the tension; 'japped' and 'flapped' play into each other, giving the impression that whatever is occurring is happening with great intensity.

The poem changes at the beginning of the **third stanza** and this is evident in the language, which is much more playful, reflecting Heaney's assessment of the occasion in hindsight. He now recognises the youthful insecurity of the time: 'Honeymooning, mooning around'. The wry reference to the fictional Hansel and Gretel hints at the immaturity of their relationship as newlyweds and emphasises the couple's initial fretfulness. But recalling how he carefully gathered up the buttons, like Hansel returning from the wilderness, **Heaney appears to have now come to terms with his uneasy past**: 'Our echoes die in that corridor'.

This latent confidence underscores the poet's recollections in the **fourth stanza**. The action and speed have now ceased. After the uncertainty of the 'draughty lamplit station', he has learned to trust his wife and his own destiny. Unlike Orpheus, the tragic Greek hero, Heaney has emerged from his personal descent into Hades, 'Bared and tense'. Although **he can never forget the desolation of being threatened with loss**, the poet has been well served by the experience, having realised that it will always be him – and not his wife – who will be damned if he dares to look back.

The ending of the poem is characteristically compelling. Commenting on it in *Stepping Stones*, Heaney has said, 'But in the end, the "damned if I look back" line takes us well beyond the honeymoon.' Although some critics feel that the final outlook is more regretful, it is difficult to miss the sheer determination that is present in the poem's last line. The **poet's stubborn tone leaves us with overwhelming evidence of his enduring devotion to love**, an emotional commitment which seems to be even more precious with the passing of time.

ANALYSIS

'Heaney's poetry operates successfully across several levels, dramatically observing and quietly reflecting.' Discuss this statement with reference to 'The Underground'.

Sample Paragraph

'The Underground' is another of Heaney's autobiographical poems in which he gives a dramatic account of a frantic dash by his young wife and himself through London's Underground train station. What is interesting is how he interweaves past and present into reality and nightmare throughout the poem. Heaney's forceful language captures the menace and threat of subterranean journeys through guttural sounds ('tunnel', 'running'). Urgent verbs ('speeding', 'gaining') and run-on lines further suggest the headlong rush. Heaney's close observations lead to deep reflection. He is aware of the carefree quality of young love – 'Honeymooning, mooning around'. Innocence is summed up in the arresting image, 'some new white flower'. The poet introduces Greek mythology into the poem – the Orpheus and Eurydice tale of tragic loss in the Underworld. Suddenly, the personal has become a universal experience. The hunting and chasing aspects of love has echoed throughout human history. Another cinematic detail – the falling buttons – are associated with the 'moonlit stones' from the fairytale of Hansel and Gretel. Heaney, like Hansel, goes back, 'retracing the path', to find a way forward. The poem's striking final phrase, 'damned if I look back', also works on two levels. Heaney is determined to keep going and put real effort into the relationship. The alternative is loss of love – a kind of damnation that he fears. Unlike the tragic myths mentioned earlier in the poem, his relationship is based on trust and will survive, 'all attention/For your step following'.

Examiner's Comment

An intelligent top-grade response that addresses both elements of this challenging question. Some focused commentary on dramatic aspects ('frantic dash', 'reality and nightmare', 'cinematic detail'). Apt quotations are successfully integrated into the discussion. Assured vocabulary ('interweaves', 'subterranean', 'alternative') is also impressive.

N.B. Access your ebook for additional sample paragraphs and a list of useful quotes with commentary.

CLASS/HOMEWORK EXERCISES

1. 'Heaney frequently invokes a vivid range of memories and mythological echoes to reveal intense feelings in his poetry.' Discuss this view with reference to 'The Underground'.

2. 'Heaney's love poems celebrate his subjects warmly, yet realistically, through the use of precise visual imagery and aural detail.' Discuss this statement with reference to both the subject matter and style of 'The Underground'.

SUMMARY POINTS

- Nostalgic love poem of a specific event infused with Greek myth and fairy story.
- Personal narrative using colloquial speech and engaging imagery.
- Dramatic atmosphere, pacy rhythm, dynamic verbs, run-on lines.
- Aural music of internal rhyme and assonance.
- Dissonant notes contrast with optimism of young love.
- Fear of loss contrasted with the poet's determined commitment to his wife.

9 POSTSCRIPT

And some time make the time to drive out west
Into County Clare, along the Flaggy Shore,
In September or October, when the wind
And the light are working off each other
So that the ocean on one side is wild   5
With foam and glitter, and inland among stones
The surface of a slate-grey lake is lit
By the earthed lightning of a flock of swans,
Their feathers roughed and ruffling, white on white,
Their fully grown headstrong-looking heads   10
Tucked or cresting or busy underwater.
Useless to think you'll park and capture it
More thoroughly. You are neither here nor there,
A hurry through which known and strange things pass
As big soft buffetings come at the car sideways   15
And catch the heart off guard and blow it open.

'along the Flaggy Shore'

Glossary

2   *the Flaggy Shore*: stretch of coastal limestone slabs in the Burren, Co. Clare.
4   *working off*: playing against.
11   *cresting*: stretching, posing.
15   *buffetings*: vibrations, shudderings.

INITIAL RESPONSE

1. Choose one image from the poem that you find particularly effective. Briefly explain your choice.

2. What is your understanding of the poem's final line?

3. In your opinion, is the advice given by Heaney in 'Postscript' relevant to our modern world? Give reasons to support your response.

STUDY NOTES

This beautiful pastoral lyric comes at the end of Seamus Heaney's 1996 collection, The Spirit Level. *The title suggests an afterthought, something that was missed out earlier. As so often in his poetry, Heaney succeeds in conveying the extraordinary by way of an everyday experience – in this case, the vivid memory of a journey westwards. The poem resonates with readers, particularly those who have also shared moments when life caught them by surprise.*

Line 1 is relaxed and conversational. The poet invites others (or promises himself, perhaps) to 'make the time to drive out west'. The phrase 'out west' has connotations both of adventurous opportunity and dismal failure. By placing 'And' at the start of the poem, Heaney indicates a link with something earlier, some unfinished business. **Keen to ensure that the journey will be worthwhile**, he recommends a definite destination ('the Flaggy Shore') and time ('September or October').

The untamed beauty of the Co. Clare coastline is described in some detail: 'when the wind/And the light are working off each other' (**lines 3–4**). The phrase 'working off' is especially striking in conveying the **tension and balance between two of nature's greatest complementary forces: wind and light**. Together, they create an effect that neither could produce singly.

Close awareness of place is a familiar feature of the poet's writing, but in this instance he includes another dimension – the notion of in-betweeness. The road Heaney describes runs between the ocean and an inland lake. Carefully chosen images **contrast** the unruly beauty of the open sea's 'foam and glitter' with the still 'slate-grey lake' (**line 7**). In both descriptions, the sounds of the words echo their sense precisely.

The introduction of the swans in **line 8** brings unexpected drama. Heaney captures their seemingly effortless movement between air and water. The poet's **vigorous skill with language** can be seen in his appreciation of the swans' transforming presence, which he highlights in the extraordinary image of 'earthed lightning'. His expertly crafted sketches are both tactile ('feathers roughed and ruffling') and visual ('white on white'). Tossed by the wind, their neck feathers resemble ruffled collars. To Heaney, these exquisite birds signify an otherworldly force that is rarely earthed or restrained. In response, he is momentarily absorbed by the swans' purposeful gestures and powerful flight.

In **line 12**, the poet cautiously accepts that such elemental beauty can never be fully grasped: 'Useless to think you'll park and capture it'. Because we are 'neither here nor there', we can only occasionally glimpse 'known and strange things'. Despite this, the poem concludes on a redemptive note, acknowledging those special times when we edge close to the miraculous. **These experiences transcend our mundane lives** and we are shaken by revelation, just as unexpected gusts of winds ('soft buffetings') can rock a car.

Heaney's journey has been both **physical and mystical**. It is brought to a crescendo in **line 16**, where it ends in the articulation of an important truth. He has found meaning between the tangible and intangible. The startling possibility of discovering the ephemeral quality of spiritual awareness is unnerving enough to 'catch the heart off guard and blow it open'. The seemingly contradictory elements of comfort and danger add to the intensity of this final image. Heaney has spoken about the illumination he felt during his visit to the Flaggy Shore as a 'glorious exultation of air and sea and swans'. For him, the experience was obviously inspirational, and the poem that it produced might well provide a similar opportunity for readers to experience life beyond the material.

ANALYSIS

'Heaney's work often addresses the wonder of poetic inspiration through the use of carefully chosen images.' Discuss this statement in relation to 'Postscript'.

Sample Paragraph

'Postscript' moves from the opening casual invitation, 'And some time make the time', building to a crescendo and concluding with a highly charged insight. The poem evokes the creative process of making and reading poetry, the ability of language to transport a person to a magical place ('when the wind/And the light are working off each other') which is just beneath the material world ('You are neither here nor there'). Heaney focuses on the sheer excitement of inspiration. The unexpected satisfaction of creativity is caught in the interaction of wind, light, ocean, lake and swans. Heaney focuses on nuances of colour ('white on white') and texture ('roughed and ruffling') to capture the enchanting moment. The less attractive aspects of the swans are also carefully noted – their arrogance ('headstrong-looking heads') and their paddling feet ('busy underwater'). Quietly, the poet cautions readers to appreciate and fully experience this moment, 'Useless to think you'll park and capture it'. The final line explodes with the emotion of being truly alive in the moment. The wind, like the poem itself, triggers uncontrollable emotion. Both come like 'big soft buffetings' to 'catch the heart off guard and blow it open'.

Examiner's Comment

An insightful response to the question. Informed discussion points focused throughout on the theme of the creative process and Heaney's use of language. Good choice of accurate quotations integrated effectively into the commentary. Expression is impressive also: varied sentence length, wide-ranging vocabulary ('crescendo', 'nuances', 'triggers uncontrollable emotion') and good control of syntax. A high-grade standard.

N.B. Access your ebook for additional sample paragraphs and a list of useful quotes with commentary.

CLASS/HOMEWORK EXERCISES

1. 'Seamus Heaney's poems are capable of capturing moments of insight in a strikingly memorable fashion.' Discuss this statement with reference to 'Postscript'.

2. 'Heaney evokes the beauty and mystery of Ireland's natural landscape through the precision of his language.' Discuss this view with reference to both the subject matter and style of 'Postscript'.

SUMMARY POINTS

- Conversational description of a car drive 'out west' into Co. Clare.
- The poem pays tribute to the sheer power of perception.
- Resonance of memory, contrasting joy at visual experience with sadness at realisation of its transience.
- Vivid visual imagery and subtle sound effects used to convey the scene.
- Cautious, reflective tone contrasts with exhilarating description.

10 A CALL

'Hold on,' she said, 'I'll just run out and get him.
The weather here's so good, he took the chance
To do a bit of weeding.'
                              So I saw him
Down on his hands and knees beside the leek rig,   5
Touching, inspecting, separating one
Stalk from the other, gently pulling up
Everything not tapered, frail and leafless,
Pleased to feel each little weed-root break,
But rueful also ...   10
                        Then found myself listening to
The amplified grave ticking of hall clocks
Where the phone lay unattended in a calm
Of mirror glass and sunstruck pendulums ...

And found myself then thinking: if it were nowadays,   15
This is how Death would summon Everyman.

Next thing he spoke and I nearly said I loved him.

'Pleased to feel each little weed-root break'

Glossary

8   *tapered*: slender; reducing in thickness towards the end.
8   *frail*: weak.
10 *rueful*: expressing regret.
12 *amplified*: increased the strength of the sound.

14 *pendulums*: weights that hang from a fixed point and swing freely, used to regulate the mechanism of a clock.
16 *Everyman*: character in 15th century morality plays.

INITIAL RESPONSE

1. How does Heaney dramatise this event? Refer to setting, mood, dialogue, action and climax in your response. Support your answer with reference to the text.

2. Describe the mood of 'A Call'. Does it change during the course of the poem? Support your answer with suitable quotations.

3. One literary critic said that the 'celebration of people and relationships in Heaney's poetry is characterised by honesty and tenderness'. To what extent do you agree or disagree with this view? Refer to the text in your response.

STUDY NOTES

'A Call' comes from Heaney's collection The Spirit Level *(1996) and deals with two of the poet's recurring themes: the father–son relationship and the passing of time. The setting is a routine domestic scene of a mother talking, a father weeding, a son calling.* The Spirit Level *refers to balance, getting the level right, measuring. It also suggests poetry, which is on another plane, free-floating above the confines of the earth. Heaney spoke about this in his Novel Prize speech, saying 'I am permitting myself the luxury of walking on air'.*

This personal narrative opens with a conversational directness, as Heaney is told to 'Hold on'. Heaney has phoned his parents' home and his mother is responding to her son's request to speak with his father. When she puts the receiver down (these were the days of the land line), the poet has time to imagine the old man at work in his garden: 'The weather here's so good, he took the chance/ To do a bit of weeding'. The rhythm of colloquial dialogue is realistically caught by the use of everyday expressions and a **simple scene of domesticity is established**. In **line 4**, the poet becomes the engrossed spectator on the fringes of the scene: 'So I saw him'. The detail of 'Down on his hands and knees beside the leek rig' invites the reader to observe for themselves.

Fragmented description shows the care and skill of the gardener's activity, 'Touching, inspecting, separating', as the father tends his vegetable patch. All farming tradition is associated with decay and growth, and the weakest is usually discarded, 'gently pulling up/Everything not tapered'. The onomatopoeia of the word 'break', with its sharp 'k' sound, suggests the snap of the root as it is pulled from the soil. The father takes pleasure ('Pleased to feel') in his work ('each little weed-root break') but he is, perhaps, regretful too ('rueful') that a form of life is ending, snapped from the nurturing earth.

In **line 11**, the **visual imagery is replaced by aural effects**. The mood in the deserted hallway indicates a significant change in the tone of the poem. Sounds are 'amplified' due to the subdued atmosphere of the location and Heaney's long wait to hear his father's voice. Time is passing, not just for the weeds but also for the man, measured by the 'grave ticking of hall clocks'. Here the poem begins to move between earthbound-reality and airiness. The image of ticking clocks in a sea ('calm') of 'mirror glass and sunstruck pendulums' is almost surreal. Broad vowel sounds create an air of serenity and otherworldliness. The word 'amplified' vividly conveys the echo of the clocks and we can imagine their loud ticking as the sound increases in intensity. The inclusion of the word 'grave' is an obvious reminder that death is edging closer – and not just for the poet's father.

In **line 15**, Heaney moves from observation to meditation, walking on air, 'And found myself then thinking'. Death is depicted as a personal communication, like a phone call from a loved one. The poet is pushing at the boundaries of what is real. His father, like the weeds, will be uprooted, spirited away to some afterlife. Here Heaney is 'seeing things'; he is mediating between states of awareness. **A keen sense of mortality informs the poem.** The last line stands apart, as Heaney is jolted out of his reverie: 'Next thing he spoke'. Family love is an important theme throughout Heaney's poetry. In this case, he considers the uncommunicated closeness of the father–son relationship and we witness the frustrating attempts at communication between them, 'and I nearly said I loved him'. Was it an awareness of his father's mortality which prompted this reaction from the poet? The careful phrasing, relaxed and casual, reflects the powerful love between these silent men and the heart-breaking tension of the impossibility of articulating their feelings. In the poem's poignant conclusion ('Next thing he spoke and I nearly said I loved him'), father and son are both united and separated.

The title of this poem is intriguing. Apart from referring to a telephone call, it also signals the final summons that 'Everyman' will receive from Death. While the dominant tone of 'A Call' celebrates the poet's father and his closeness to nature, there is an underlying elegiac quality that reveals Heaney's deep awareness of mortality and loss.

ANALYSIS

'Seamus Heaney's poetry engages the reader through his use of striking imagery and thought-provoking themes.' Discuss this statement with reference to 'A Call'.

Sample Paragraph

The poem, 'A Call', charms and challenges readers from the closely observed domestic scene to the dreamlike imagery depicting mortality and the concluding tender admission of emotion, 'I nearly said

I loved him'. We hear Heaney's mother's natural speaking voice, 'Hold on', while she rushes to get his father. Life is a matter of holding on, of endurance. We also imagine the father working quietly in his garden through a carefully punctuated list of verbs, 'Touching, inspecting, separating'. Heaney also depicts a surreal scene of passing time through the broad vowels of the 'sunstruck pendulums' which beat relentlessly. His dark humour continues through the image of Death using the modern means of communication, the telephone, to call human beings to the next world. Both man and weed will be uprooted from this earth. The tender domestic scene then gives way to serious reflections on transience. As often happens in Heaney's poems, he celebrates life while accepting the reality of death. Through his powerful associations of the multi-layered images of the telephone and the weed, Heaney teaches his readers about the significance of ordinary experiences.

Examiner's Comment

An insightful, well-informed response. Engagement with both Heaney's imagery and themes is evident throughout. Perceptive discussion of the poet's recognition of life and death is well supported by apt, accurate quotations. Expression is excellent ('carefully punctuated', 'serious reflections on transience'). A confident top-grade answer that shows close interaction with the poem.

N.B. Access your ebook for additional sample paragraphs and a list of useful quotes with commentary.

CLASS/HOMEWORK EXERCISES

1. 'Seamus Heaney's reflective poetry often reveals moments of sensitivity that can enrich our experience of life.' Discuss this statement with reference to 'A Call'.

2. 'Heaney's lyrical poems go beyond description to disclose rich insights into universal themes.' Discuss this view with reference to both the subject matter and style of 'A Call'.

SUMMARY POINTS

- Autobiographical poem expands into profound meditation.
- Colloquial, direct speech is engaging.
- Effective use of carefully observed visual detail.
- Assonance, internal rhyme and alliteration heighten the musicality of the poem.
- Personification adds an ominous note.
- Unusual line breaks highlight the poem's focus on transience.
- Final line poignantly evokes both the communication and the lack of communication between father and son.

11 TATE'S AVENUE

traditional, uninspiring — however comforting, natural, organic

Not the brown and fawn car rug, that first one
Spread on sand by the sea but breathing land-breaths, *alliteration — peaceful memory*
Its vestal folds unfolded, its comfort zone   *dream.*
Edged with a fringe of sepia-coloured wool tails.

Not the one scraggy with crusts and eggshells   5
And olive stones and cheese and salami rinds
Laid out by the torrents of the Guadalquivir
Where we got drunk before the corrida.

Instead, again, it's locked-park Sunday Belfast,
A walled back yard, the dust-bins high and silent   10
As a page is turned, a finger twirls warm hair
And nothing gives on the rug or the ground beneath it.

Places

I lay at my length and felt the lumpy earth,
Keen-sensed more than ever through discomfort,
But never shifted off the plaid square once.   15
When we moved I had your measure and you had mine.

'As a page is turned, a finger twirls warm hair'

Glossary

Tate's Avenue is located in South Belfast, a popular student area. Heaney's girlfriend (later his wife) lived there in the late 1960s.

3   *vestal*: innocent, untouched (Heaney is comparing the crumpled rug to the modest dresses of vestal virgins in ancient Rome).

4   *sepia-coloured*: faded brownish colour; old looking.
7   *Guadalquivir*: river in Andalusia, Spain.
8   *corrida*: bullfight.
9   *locked-park*: Belfast's public parks were closed on Sundays in the 1960s.
15 *plaid*: checked, tartan.

INITIAL RESPONSE

1. Comment on the poet's use of sound effects in the first two stanzas.

2. 'I had your measure and you had mine.' Briefly explain what you think Heaney means by this statement.

3. Write your own personal response to the poem.

STUDY NOTES

'Tate's Avenue' (from the 2006 collection District and Circle*) is another celebration of Heaney's love for Marie Devlin. They married in 1965 and lived off Tate's Avenue in South Belfast during the late 1960s. Here, the poet reviews their relationship by linking three separate occasions involving a collection of car rugs spread on the ground by the couple over the years.*

Stanza one invites us to eavesdrop on a seemingly mundane scene of everyday domesticity. It appears that the poet and his wife have been reminiscing – presumably about their love life over the years. Although the negative opening tone is emphatic ('Not the brown and fawn car rug'), we are left guessing about the exact nature of the couple's discussion. A few tantalising details are given about 'that first' rug, connecting it with an early seaside visit. Heaney can still recall the tension of a time when the couple **were caught between their own desire and strong social restrictions**. He describes the rug in terms of its texture and colours: 'Its vestal folds unfolded' (suggesting their youthful sexuality) contrasting with the 'sepia-coloured wool tails' (symbolising caution and old fashioned inhibitions). As usual, Heaney's tone is edged with irony as he recalls the 'comfort zone' between himself and Marie.

The repetition of 'Not' at the start of **stanza two** clearly indicates that the second rug is also rejected, even though it can be traced back to a more exotic Spanish holiday location. Sharp onomatopoeic effects ('scraggy with crusts and eggshells') and the list of Mediterranean foods ('olive stones and cheese and salami rinds') convey **a sense of freedom and indulgence**. Although the couple's hedonistic life is communicated in obviously excessive terms ('Laid out by the torrents of the

Guadalquivir'), Heaney's tone is somewhat dismissive. Is he suggesting that their relationship was mostly sensual back then?

'Instead' – the first word in **stanza three** – signals a turning point in the poet's thinking. Back in his familiar home surroundings, he recalls the rug that mattered most and should answer whatever doubts he had about the past. He has measured the development of their relationship in stages associated with special moments he and Marie shared. The line 'it's locked-park Sunday Belfast' conjures up memories of their early married life in the Tate's Avenue district. The sectarian 1960s are marked by dour Protestant domination, a time when weekend pleasures were frowned upon and even the public parks were closed. Despite such routine repression and the unromantic setting ('A walled back yard, the dust-bins high and silent'), **the atmosphere is sexually charged**.

Heaney is aware of the scene's underlying drama; the seconds tick by 'As a page is turned, a finger twirls warm hair'. The unfaltering nature of the couple's intimacy is evident in the resounding declaration: 'nothing gives on the rug or the ground beneath it'.

This notion of confidence in their relationship is carried through into **stanza four** and accentuated by the alliterative 'I lay at my length and felt the lumpy earth'. The resolute rhythm is strengthened by the robust adjectival phrase 'Keen-sensed' and the insistent statement: 'But never shifted off the plaid square once'. Heaney builds to a discreet and understated climax in the finely balanced last line: 'When we moved I had your measure and you had mine'. While there are erotic undertones throughout, the poet presents us with restrained realism in place of expansive sensuality. 'Tate's Avenue' is **a beautiful, unembarrassed poem of romantic and sexual love within a committed relationship**. Characteristically, when Heaney touches on personal relationships, he produces the most tender and passionate emotions.

ANALYSIS

'Seamus Heaney's poetry frequently explores intense relationships in a style that is fresh and innovative.' Discuss this statement with reference to 'Tate's Avenue'.

Sample Paragraph

'Tate's Avenue' is one of Heaney's most romantic poems. The poet charts the progress of his relationship with his wife through the unusual approach of recalling three rugs that mark stages in their lives together. The tentative, breathless nature of early courtship is revealed in both the colour ('sepia-coloured', reminiscent of an old photo) and texture ('vestal folds unfolded') of the first rug. Yet the strong physical attraction is revealed in aching sibilance and personification, 'Spread on sand by the sea but breathing land-breaths'. An emphatic 'Not' adds to the drama of the poem as the first two rugs are rejected. The adverb 'Instead' signals the decision to choose a 'plaid square' to truly sum up their deep feelings for each other. The focus zooms in on the sensuous detail, 'a finger twirls warm hair'. The onomatopoeic verb conveys the enticing allure of their mutual attraction. Yet no relationship runs smoothly all of the time. The 'lumpy earth' and 'discomfort' of the final stanza vividly conveys this reality to the reader. But this determined couple did not give up and the poem concludes in a wonderful moment of unity between the lovers, 'I had your measure and you had mine'. In this inventive study of important times in their relationship, Heaney conveys the drama and immediacy of their love. Overall, restrained, sensuous tension is presented in this warm study of intimacy.

Examiner's Comment

An excellent top-grade response that shows a very good understanding of this unusual love poem. Detailed examination of language use (dramatic settings, contrasting atmospheres, energetic imagery and aural effects) is supported by apt and accurate quotations. Expression is also skilfully controlled and the paragraph is well rounded off in the concise final sentence.

N.B. Access your ebook for additional sample paragraphs and a list of useful quotes with commentary.

CLASS/HOMEWORK EXERCISES

1. 'Heaney's poetry realistically depicts people and places through carefully chosen language and imagery.' Discuss this view with reference to 'Tate's Avenue'.

2. 'Seamus Heaney's poems are often filled with vivid sensuousness and evocative description.' Discuss this statement with reference to 'Tate's Avenue'.

SUMMARY POINTS

- Tender, compelling poem celebrates love in a committed relationship.
- Precise, vibrant details illustrate the various scenes.
- The headlong rush of young love is conveyed in the enjambment of the second quatrain.
- In contrast, the more measured pace of mature love is found in the final stanza.
- Compound words, onomatopoeia, alliteration and assonance create a rich aural texture.
- Compact four-quatrain structure adds to the understated quality of the poem.

12 THE PITCHFORK *an identity.*

Comparison to the freedom of poetry / the free poetic spirit

Of all implements, the pitchfork was the one
That came near to an imagined perfection: *ordinary and mundane becomes marvellous*
When he tightened his raised hand and aimed with it,
It felt like a javelin, accurate and light. *Skilled practised capability*

So whether he played the warrior or the athlete *Both require work & skill*
Or worked in earnest in the chaff and sweat, *Commitment.*
He loved its grain of tapering, dark-flecked ash *beauty of it*   *native*
Grown satiny from its own natural polish. *humble pitchfork unleashes its beauty.*

alliteration   *Lovingly depicted*

descriptive language

Riveted steel, turned timber, burnish, grain,
Smoothness, straightness, roundness, length and sheen.   *adoration of the pitchfork.*
Sweat-cured, sharpened, balanced, tested, fitted.
The springiness, the clip and dart of it.
Talked about like a work of art

ordinary to the extraordinary

And then when he thought of the probes that reached the farthest,
He would see the shaft of a pitchfork sailing past
Evenly, imperturbably through space,   *Skilled craftsman can do anything with*
Its prongs starlit and absolutely soundless – *its magical*
humble

But has learned at last to follow that simple lead
Past its own aim, out to an other side
Where perfection – or nearness to it – is imagined
Not in the aiming but the opening hand.   20

'When he tightened his raised hand and aimed with it'

Glossary

4 *javelin*: long spear thrown in a competitive sport as used as a weapon.
6 *chaff*: husks of grain separated from the seed.
7 *grain*: wheat.
7 *tapering*: reducing in thickness towards one end.
9 *Riveted*: fastened.
9 *burnish*: the shine on a polished surface.

12 *clip*: clasp; smack (colloquial).
12 *dart*: follow-on movement; small pointed missile thrown as a weapon.
13 *probes*: unmanned, exploratory spacecraft; a small measuring or testing device.
15 *imperturbably*: calmly, smoothly; unable to be upset.
16 *prongs*: two or more projecting points on a fork.

INITIAL RESPONSE

1. What is the tone of this poem? Does it change or not? Refer closely to the text in your response.

2. Select one image (or one line) that you find particularly interesting. Briefly explain your choice.

3. What do you think about the ending of this poem? Do you consider it visionary or far-fetched? Give reasons for your answer.

STUDY NOTES

'The Pitchfork' was published in Heaney's 1991 collection, Seeing Things. *These poems turn to the earlier concerns of the poet. Craft and natural skill, the innate ability to make art out of work, is seen in many of his poems, such as 'The Forge'. Heaney is going back, making 'a journey back into the heartland of the ordinary'. The poet is now both observer and visionary.*

In **stanza one**, Heaney describes a pitchfork, an ordinary farming 'implement'. Through **looking at an ordinary object with intense concentration**, the result is a fresh 'seeing', where the ordinary and mundane become marvellous, 'imagined perfection'. For Heaney, the creative impulse was held in the hand, in the skill of the labourer ('tightened his raised hand and aimed with it'). This skill was similar to the skill of the poet. They both practise and hone their particular ability. The pitchfork is now transformed into a sporting piece of equipment, 'a javelin'. The heaviness of physical work falls away as it becomes 'accurate and light' due to the practised capability of the worker. This is similar to the lightness of being and the **freeing of the poet's spirit** that Heaney allows himself to experience in this collection of poetry.

The worker is described as sometimes playing 'the warrior or the athlete' (**stanza two**). **Both professions command respect** and both occupations require courage and skill. But the worker's real work is also described realistically, 'worked in earnest in the chaff and sweat'. This is heavy manual labour, and Heaney does not shirk from its unpleasant side. However, the worker is not ground down by it because he 'loved' the beauty of the pitchfork. Here we see both the poet and the worker dazzled, as the intent observation of the humble pitchfork unleashes its beauty, its slender 'dark-flecked ash'. The shine of the handle is conveyed in the word 'satiny'. The tactile language allows the reader to feel the smooth, polished wooden handle. Now three pairs of eyes (the worker's, the poet's and our own) observe the pitchfork.

Close observation of the pitchfork in **stanza three** continues with a virtuoso display of description, as **each detail is lovingly depicted**, almost like a slow sequence of close-ups in a film. The meeting of the handle and fork is caught in the phrase 'Riveted steel'. The beauty of the wood is evoked in the alliteration of 'turned timber'. The marvellous qualities of the wood are itemised with growing wonder: its shine ('burnish'), its pattern ('grain'). It is as if the worker and the poet are twirling the pitchfork round as they exclaim over its 'Smoothness, straightness, roundness, length and sheen'. This is more like the description one would give to a work of art or a thoroughbred animal than to a farm implement. The skill that went into the making of the pitchfork is now explored in a list of verbs beginning with the compound word 'Sweat-cured'. This **graphically shows the sheer physical exertion that went into making this instrument**, as it was 'sharpened, balanced, tested, fitted'. The tactile quality of the pitchfork is praised: 'The springiness, the clip and dart of it'. The worker, just like the athlete or warrior, tests his equipment. The feel of the pitchfork in the hand is given to the reader, due to the 'Sweat-cured' poet's sensitive and accurate observation and description.

In **stanza four**, the labourer imagines space 'probes' searching the galaxy, 'reached the farthest'. The long line stretches out in imitation of space, which pushes out to infinity. The pitchfork now becomes transformed into a spaceship, 'sailing past/Evenly, imperturbably through space'. This ordinary pitchfork now shines like the metal casing of a spaceship, 'starlit', and moves, like the spaceship, through the vastness of outer space, 'absolutely soundless'. **Stanza five** shows the poet becoming a mediator between different states, actual and imagined, ordinary and fantastical. He stands on a threshold, exploring and philosophising about the nature of his observation as a familiar thing grows stranger. Together (poet, worker and reader), all follow the line of the pitchfork to 'an other side', a place where 'perfection' is 'imagined'. Perfection does not exist in our world. But it is not the 'tightened' hand, which was 'aiming' at the beginning of the poem, which will achieve this ideal state, but the 'opening hand' of the last stanza. Is the poet suggesting we must be open and ready to receive in order to achieve 'perfection'? Heaney states: '**look at the familiar things you know. Look at them with ... a quality of concentration ... you will be rewarded with insights and visions**.' The poet has become a seer.

ANALYSIS

'In celebrating traditional rural crafts in his poetry, Heaney reveals his own skills as a master craftsman of the written word.' Discuss this view with reference to 'The Pitchfork'.

Sample Paragraph

Heaney's poem 'The Pitchfork' is based on a treasured memory of his father who spent his life working on the family farm in Co. Derry. The poet has often written about farming implements in poems that celebrate traditional skills. 'The Pitchfork' begins with a dynamic image as Heaney remembers his father in an ideal way, holding the fork 'like a javelin'. In his innocent eyes, his father was god-like – 'imagined perfection'. The poet lovingly describes the pitchfork in great detail: 'Riveted steel, turned timber'. Hard 't' sounds suggest the father's strength in handling the pitchfork with confidence. The sense of deep respect for the traditional work of the farm as well as for his father is found in the tone of admiration when Heaney imagines the older man playing 'the warrior or the athlete'. He is clearly saying that his father isn't an unskilled worker, but is more of an expert craftsman. The poet moves from describing the everyday activity of gathering in the hay to a visionary level as the fork hangs in the air, 'starlit and absolutely soundless'. The skilled craft of the poet himself transforms the implement into a mysterious spacecraft. In his imagination, he has returned to childhood and is watching the fork moving 'imperturbably through space'. Through his own precise language skills, Heaney celebrates the working life of the father he idealised.

Examiner's Comment

Clear, high-grade response tackling all elements of the question and showing a good understanding of the poem. Impressive awareness of Heaney's expertise with language (particularly imagery, tone and sound effects). Focused quotations are used effectively to support key points and the expression is varied and well controlled.

N.B. Access your ebook for additional sample paragraphs and a list of useful quotes with commentary.

CLASS/HOMEWORK EXERCISES

1. 'Seamus Heaney's poetry addresses through-provoking themes in language that is both realistic and mystical.' Discuss this view with reference to 'The Pitchfork'.

2. 'In Heaney's most compelling poems, ordinary objects are lovingly and exactly described.' Discuss this statement with particular reference to 'The Pitchfork'.

- Exploration of commitment, craft and creativity.
- Focus on physical details in the first four stanzas.
- Impact of cinematic imagery and energetic rhythm.
- Sudden change of pace and mood in the last stanza.
- Compelling ending reinforces poet's devotion to generosity and acceptance.

13 LIGHTENINGS VIII 🔊

The annals say: when the monks of Clonmacnoise
Were all at prayers inside the oratory
A ship appeared above them in the air.

The anchor dragged along behind so deep
It hooked itself into the altar rails   5
And then, as the big hull rocked to a standstill,

A crewman shinned and grappled down the rope
And struggled to release it. But in vain.
'This man can't bear our life here and will drown,'

The abbot said, 'unless we help him.' So   10
They did, the freed ship sailed, and the man climbed back
Out of the marvellous as he had known it.

'Out of the marvellous'

Glossary

Lightenings: insights, transcendent experiences.

1   *annals*: monastic records.

1   *Clonmacnoise*: established in the sixth century, the monastery at Clonmacnoise was renowned as a centre of scholarship and spirituality.

2   *oratory*: place of prayer, small chapel.

7   *shinned*: climbed down, clambered.

10   *abbot*: head of the monastery.

INITIAL RESPONSE

1. How is the surreal atmosphere conveyed in this poem? Quote in support of your response.

2. Choose one striking image from the poem and comment on its effectiveness.

3. In your view, what does the air-ship symbolise? Refer to the text in your answer.

STUDY NOTES

Written in four tercets (three-line stanzas), 'Lightenings viii' (from Seamus Heaney's 1991 collection, Seeing Things), tells a legendary story of a miraculous air-ship which once appeared to the monks at Clonmacnoise, Co. Offaly. Heaney has said: 'I was devoted to this poem because the crewman who appears is situated where every poet should be situated: between the ground of everyday experience and the airier realm of an imagined world.'

Heaney's matter-of-fact approach at the start of **stanza one** leads readers to expect a straightforward retelling of an incident recorded in the 'annals' of the monastery. The story's apparently scholarly source seems highly reliable. While they were at prayers, the monks looked up: 'A ship appeared above them in the air'. We assume that the oratory is open to the sky. The simplicity of the colloquial language, restrained tone and run-through lines all ease us into a **dreamlike world** where anything can happen. But as with all good narratives, the magic ship's sudden appearance raises many questions: Why is it there? Where has it come from? Is this strange story all a dream?

Then out of the air-ship came a massive anchor, which 'dragged along behind so deep' (**stanza two**) before lodging itself in the altar rails. The poet makes **effective choices in syntax (word order) and punctuation**, e.g. placing 'so deep' at the end of the line helps to emphasise the meaning. The moment when the ship shudders to a halt is skilfully caught in a carefully wrought image: 'as the big hull rocked to a standstill'.

A crewman clambered down the rope to try to release the anchor, but he is unsuccessful. Heaney chooses his words carefully: 'shinned', 'grappled', 'struggled' (**stanza three**) are all powerful verbs, helping to create a clear picture of the sailor's physical effort. The phrase 'But in vain' is separated from the rest of the line to emphasise the man's hopelessness. The contrasting worlds of magic and reality seem incompatible. Ironically, the story's turning point is the abbot's instant recognition that the **human, earthly atmosphere will be fatal to the visitor**: 'This man can't bear our life here and will drown'.

But a solution is at hand: 'unless we help him' (**stanza four**). The unconditional generosity of the monks comes naturally to them: 'So/They did'. The word 'So' creates a pause and uncertainty before the prompt, brief opening of the next line: 'They did'. When the anchor is eventually disentangled and 'the freed ship sailed', **the crewman will surely tell his travel companions about the strange beings** he encountered after he 'climbed back out of the marvellous as he had known it'. This last line is somewhat surprising and leaves the reader wondering – marvelling, even.

Heaney's poem certainly raises interesting questions, blurring the lines between reality and illusion, and challenging our ideas about human consciousness. **The story itself can be widely interpreted**. Is the ship a symbol of inspiration while the monks represent commitment and dedication? Presumably, as chroniclers of the annals (preserving texts on paper for posterity), they were not aware of the miracle of their own labours – crossing the barrier from the oral tradition to written records – which was to astonish the world in the forthcoming centuries and help spread human knowledge.

'Lightenings viii' is a beautiful poem that highlights the fact that **the ordinary and the miraculous are categories defined only by human perception**. For many readers, the boat serves as an abstract mirror image, reversing our usual way of seeing things. In Heaney's rich text, we discover that from the outsider's perspective, the truly marvellous consists not of the visionary or mystical experience, but of the seemingly ordinary experience.

ANALYSIS

'Heaney's evocative language often makes room for everyday miracles and otherworldly wisdom.' Discuss this statement with reference to 'Lightenings viii'.

Sample Paragraph

Heaney's poem 'Lightenings' is an account of a surreal experience when the Clonmacnoise monks imagined they saw a ship appearing above them in the sky. We all think of miracles as things that are beyond explanation – and this story illustrates the power and mystery of imagination. Heaney's tone is dreamlike – particularly the wistful narrative style. The long lines and broad vowel sounds suggest an unhurried atmosphere where anything can happen – 'as the big hull rocked to a standstill'. I found the poem to have several meanings. The monks who are 'all at prayers' believe that the mysterious sailors have come out 'of the marvellous' – but the stranded sailors see the safe, earthbound monks in the same way. Indeed, their rescue is arranged by the concerned abbot. The poet seems to be saying that everything in life can be viewed as a wonder – it all depends on a person's perspective. The abbot chooses to save the desperate crewman – 'This man can't bear our life here and will drown'. For me, this is the poet's central lesson – we should help others when we can. If we do, then our lives will be filled with everyday miracles which we can transform into wise behaviour.

Examiner's Comment

This focused paragraph addresses the question effectively and shows close engagement with the poet's possible themes and language use. Discussion points are clearly expressed and aptly supported. The comments on Heaney's style (dreamlike tone, narrative approach, assonant effects,) are particularly impressive. Expression throughout this high-grade response is very well controlled.

N.B. Access your ebook for additional sample paragraphs and a list of useful quotes with commentary.

CLASS/HOMEWORK EXERCISES

1. 'Heaney's poetic world is one of wonder and mystery that is matched by the energy of his language.' Discuss this view with reference to 'Lightenings viii'.

2. 'Many of Seamus Heaney's poems communicate intense observations through thought-provoking images and symbolism.' Discuss this statement with reference to both the subject matter and style of 'Lightenings viii'.

SUMMARY POINTS

- Characteristic narrative style and use of colloquial language.
- Dramatic qualities – characters, setting, tension, dialogue, resolution.
- The poem is concerned with visionary experiences, yet rooted in the physical world.
- Effective use of vivid imagery, assonance, powerful verbs.
- Contrasting worlds – mundane monks and magical sailors.

LEAVING CERT SAMPLE ESSAY

'The subjects of Heaney's poems are treated with great love and sympathy, together with a keen eye for significant detail.' Discuss this statement, supporting your answer with reference to the poems by Seamus Heaney on your course.

Marking Scheme Guidelines
Candidates are free to agree and/or disagree wholly or in part with the statement, but they should engage with all aspects of the question. Answers should be supported by reference to the poems by Seamus Heaney on the Leaving Certificate course.

Indicative material:
- Poems populated by family members, community, local characters.
- Real and imaginary locations: Irish landscapes, bogland, cities, the natural world.
- Precise descriptive details, evocative atmospheres.
- Vividly detailed visual and aural imagery, symbolism, metaphors and similes.
- Poet's focus on memory, especially those of childhood.
- Striking love poetry linked to personal experiences, the past, etc.

Sample Essay

(Heaney's subjects treated with great love and sympathy, together with a keen eye for significant detail)

1. *Heaney is a keen observer of the world. Heaney treats the subjects of his poems with affection and compassion as he carefully observes them 'warts and all'. Poems such as 'Bogland', 'Sunlight', and 'The Forge' conjure up vivid images of people and places close to his heart. However, in 'A Constable Calls', the poet uses his impressive detail to portray the central character in an unfavourable light.*

2. *Landscape is lovingly described in 'Bogland'. Heaney compares the Irish bogland to the great open expanses of the American prairies which 'slice a big sun at evening'. But he revels in the more introverted, compact Irish scene whose 'cyclops' eye' woos the 'Encroaching horizon'. The many layers of our national heritage are also referenced, 'Every layer they strip/Seems camped on before'. He respects the bog's great capacity for preservation, recounting the store of 'Butter sunk under/More than a hundred years … salty and white' and the recovery of the 'skeleton/Of the Great Irish Elk'. The intricate tactile description of the details of the soft oozing bog, 'kind black butter/Melting and opening underfoot' is vividly captured in the flowing run-on stanza lines. The poet's compassionate eye observes and reflects on this 'bottomless' place and allows us to share the experience.*

3. *Heaney also offers us a glimpse of his tranquil, childhood sanctuary with great precision. 'Mossbawn' provides an intimate portrait of his aunt. Significant details nostalgically evoke the farm where he grew up. The 'helmeted pump' in the yard is a symbol for the contrast between this heavenly place and the brutality of conflicts in the outside world. Even the sun lazed in the backyard, captured in the run-on simile 'like a griddle cooling/against the wall/of each long afternoon'. The memory of his aunt baking bread in the family kitchen is recalled in loving detail: 'Now she dusts the board/with a goose's wing'. The long resonant vowel sounds convey the blissful peace of this enchanted place.*

4. *Heaney describes his aunt as an ordinary, homely woman. He dares to include the realistic and unflattering details of her 'broad-lapped' shape and her plain 'measling shins'. This makes his admiration of her warm affectionate nature even more poignant. She creates the peace present in the farm while she bakes and then sits 'with whitened nails'. I can see the flour caught under her nails when she had just finished kneading the griddle bread. Heaney's enduring love is evident in the simile 'here is love/like a tinsmith's scoop/sunk past its gleam/in the meal-bin'. It seems right to describe this woman by the utensil she uses. I can imagine the shining spoon buried in the meal, just like his aunt was, out of sight in the farm, yet both glowing quietly all the time.*

5. *Another realistic portrayal of a country person is found 'The Forge'. Again, the individual is elevated in the poet's eyes. The blacksmith is described as officiating like a priest who 'expends himself in shape and*

music'. The blacksmith's alienation from the modern world is shown in the contrast between his recollection of the 'clatter/Of hoofs' in comparison to 'traffic flashing in rows'. This marks the end of his traditional craft. Similar to 'Mossbawn', the poet includes raw, unflattering details in his true-to-life description of the blacksmith, 'hairs in his nose' as he 'grunts'. This creates sympathy in the reader for the 'leather-aproned' tradesman who dismisses modernity with disdain and continues to perform the age-old activity of turning iron into horse shoes. The magic of the process is described in the beautiful image of the 'fantail of sparks' unleashed by the blacksmith while working at his anvil. It is obvious that Heaney's sympathy lies with the man who beats 'real iron out'.

6. However, the picture of the central character given in 'A Constable Calls' is a very different picture. There is the usual acute eye for significant detail, but it does not convey any sympathy. Here is an ominous character who represents the enforcement of 'the boot of the law'. Even his bicycle threatens with its 'dynamo gleaming and cocked back', suggesting a gun ready to fire. The repulsive mention of his 'sweating hair' does not evoke sympathy for him, unlike the sympathetic description of the aunt's 'measling shins' or the 'grunts' of the blacksmith in the previous poems. Descriptive details of 'the polished holster' and the 'baton-case' contribute to the tense, fearful atmosphere this visiting constable has brought into Heaney's family home. He has called to show who is in charge. Harsh punishment is hinted at by the child's descriptive imaginings of 'the black hole in the barracks'. The poem ends with the menacing sound of the constable's bicycle as it 'ticked, ticked, ticked', just like an unexploded bomb ticks. The tension of the divided community in Northern Ireland which was always on the verge of exploding is captured in through the hard repetitive 't' sounds.

7. Heaney is a poet who saw and created beauty out of a local Irish background. In reading his detailed portrayals of people and places, we realise the importance of the landscape of the bogland, the importance of ordinary people like the blacksmith and his aunt, and the fear struck deep into the heart of a rural farming community by the constable. We are being invited to consider the wider issues of life which impact on us.

(approx. 890 words)

Examiner's Comment

This high-grade answer addresses both aspects of the question and shows a good understanding of Heaney's poetry. The essay is well structured, starting with a short overview followed by the main critical discussion and rounded off succinctly in the final paragraph. There is some good personal engagement in the fourth paragraph and occasional cross-references add to the quality of the response. Although there are good solid points in the sixth paragraph, expression is repetitive and awkward at times. Impressive use of accurate quotation throughout.

MARKING SCHEME
GRADE: H1
P = 15/15
C = 15/15
L = 13/15
M = 5/5
Total = 48/50

> SAMPLE LEAVING CERT QUESTIONS ON HEANEY'S POETRY

(45-50 MINUTES)

1. 'Seamus Heaney lends universal significance to his personal experiences of life through suggestive language and imagery.' Discuss this statement, supporting your answer with reference to the poems by Heaney on your course.

2. 'Heaney disturbs our complacent distinctions between reality and the visionary through a combination of colloquial and mystical language.' Discuss this view, supporting your answer with reference to the poetry of Seamus Heaney on your course.

3. 'In many of Heaney's poems, autobiographical drama reveals moments of great insight.' Discuss this statement, supporting your answer with reference to the poetry of Seamus Heaney on your course.

Sample Essay Plan (Q1)

'Seamus Heaney lends universal significance to his personal experiences of life through suggestive language and evocative imagery.' Discuss this statement, supporting your answer with reference to the poems by Heaney on your course.

- Intro: Heaney, master storyteller with a 'wonderful gift of eye and ear' gives accurate, detailed images of a feisty blacksmith, a silent, morose, father and a sacrificial martyr. Poems explain, console and force the reader to consider universal themes through an examination of local subjects. Engaging, accessible style in poems of lyrical beauty.

- Point 1: 'The Forge' – universal theme, something new unsettles, explored through local activity of blacksmith. Feelings of anxiety about stepping into unknown contained in first line, humility in opening word 'All', mystery in alliteration, 'door into dark'. Visual imagery ('fantail of sparks', 'Horned as a unicorn') and sound effects (onomatopoeia, assonance) conjure up authentic atmosphere of the forge.

- Point 2: 'The Harvest Bow' – deep satisfaction with traditional values and evolving relationships. Symbol of 'bow', sensuous language. Passing of time and importance of memories, universal concerns. Lyrical writing matches the positive conclusion.

- Point 3: 'The Tollund Man' – common experience of death explored through sacrificial martyr from 2,000 years ago, juxtaposed with more recent victims of Northern Troubles. Poet's empathy shown in details. Tollund Man's innocence portrayed through precise images – 'mild pods' of eyelids, vulnerability through 'naked except for cap, noose and girdle'. Portrayal of exiles, list of foreign names ('Tollund, Grauballe, Nebelgard'), feeling of not belonging ('Watching the pointing hands'). Widespread human brutality, 'old man-killing parishes'.

- Point 4: 'A Constable Calls' – general fear of repressive authority. Detailed description of unwelcome constable, ('His cap was upside down', 'The line of its pressure ran like a bevel', 'A shadow'). Focus on his equipment ('fat, black handlegrips', 'boot of the law', 'heavy ledger', 'polished holster') and movements ('unstrapped', 'Fitted', 'snapping').

- Conclusion: Poet transforms basic intuitions into universal insights. Evocative language and imagery transport reader to dark Troubles of Northern Ireland, sunny countryside of his childhood, violent past of Jutland and magical interior of blacksmith's forge. Heaney engages readers through accessible, lyrical poetry.

Sample Essay Plan (Q1)

Develop one of the above points into a paragraph.

Sample Paragraph: Point 2

Traditional values and relationships are conveyed through evocative language and imagery in 'The Harvest Bow' which opens with a beautiful description of 'wheat that does not rust' making up a decorative harvest bow. The bow becomes a symbol of enlightenment for Heaney, brightening into 'a knowable corona'. Heaney uses this bow to relate to his own father. The poet's observance of his father at work is pensive – 'your fingers moved somnambulent'. As Heaney touches the bow, he can read it 'like braille' and it helps him understand what is left 'unsaid' between father and son. Many people experience this lack of communication with their parents. The 'love-knot' of straw bridges the barrier between father and son. The understanding between them is poignant. Details of old, rural Irish life are sensuously evoked, 'Blue smoke straight up, old beds and ploughs in hedges'. I found this poem inspirational, 'The end of art is peace'. The poet has learned from his father that he needs to work 'with fine intent' on his poems, just like his father 'plaited the harvest bow' with such care. Time slips by mysteriously unnoticed. Heaney, like all of us, will be left with his memories, 'I see us walk between the railway slopes'.

Examiner's Comment

As part of the full essay answer to Q1, this is an impressive top-grade response that shows very good engagement with the central theme of 'The Harvest Bow'. The discussion on symbolism is well rooted in the text and accurate quotations are effectively used throughout. Overall, a very confident and focused treatment of the poem.

N.B. Access your ebook for additional sample paragraphs and a list of useful quotes with commentary.

LAST WORDS

'A poet for whom sound is crucial, who relishes the way words and consonants knock around together.'

Tim Nolan

'Heaney has achieved a hard-won clarity of vision.'

Heather Clark

'The best moments are those when your mind seems to implode and words and images rush of their own accord into the vortex.'

Seamus Heaney

GERARD MANLEY HOPKINS

1844- 1889

'Every poet must be original.'

Gerard Manley Hopkins, a priest and poet, was born in Stratford, outside London, in 1844. Throughout his youth, Hopkins demonstrated excellent academic and artistic talent. In 1863 he began studying classics at Balliol College, Oxford, where he wrote a great deal of poetry. Hopkins converted to Catholicism and was later ordained a Jesuit priest in 1877. It was while studying for the priesthood that he wrote some of his best-known religious and nature poems, including 'The Windhover' and 'Pied Beauty'. His compressed style of writing, especially his experimental use of language, sound effects and inventive rhythms, combined to produce distinctive and startling poetry. In 1884 Hopkins was appointed Professor of Greek at University College, Dublin. He disliked living in Ireland, where he experienced failing health and severe depression. A devout and ascetic Jesuit, he was caught between his religious obligations and his poetic talent. In 1885 he wrote a number of the so-called 'terrible sonnets', including 'No worst, there is none', which have desolation at their core. Hopkins died of typhoid fever in June 1889 without ever publishing any of his major poems. He is buried in Glasnevin Cemetery.

INVESTIGATE FURTHER

To find out more about Gerard Manley Hopkins, or to hear readings of his poems, you could search some useful websites available such as YouTube, poetryarchive.org and bbc.co.uk. Also view the additional material available in your ebook.

Prescribed Poems

* The poems marked with an asterisk are also prescribed for the Ordinary Level course.

❶ GOD'S GRANDEUR

The world is charged with the grandeur of God.
  It will flame out, like shining from shook foil;
  It gathers to a greatness, like the ooze of oil
Crushed. Why do men then now not reck his rod?
Generations have trod, have trod, have trod;   5
  And all is seared with trade; bleared, smeared with toil;
  And wears man's smudge and shares man's smell: the soil
Is bare now, nor can foot feel, being shod.

And for all this, nature is never spent;
  There lives the dearest freshness deep down things;   10
And though the last lights off the black West went
  Oh, morning, at the brown brink eastward, springs –
Because the Holy Ghost over the bent
  World broods with warm breast and with ah! bright wings.

'nature is never spent'

Glossary

Hopkins' philosophy emphasised the uniqueness of every natural thing, which he called inscape. He believed that there was a special connection between the world of nature and an individual's consciousness Hopkins viewed the world as an integrated network created by God. The sensation of inscape (which the poet termed instress) is the appreciation that everything has its own unique identity. The concept is similar to that of epiphanies in James Joyce's writing.

1 *charged*: powered; made responsible.
2 *foil*: shimmering gold or silver.
4 *Crushed*: compressed from olives or linseed.
4 *reck his rod*: pay heed to God's power.
6 *seared*: scorched; ruined.
6 *bleared*: blurred.
6 *toil*: industrialisation.
8 *shod*: covered; protected.
9 *spent*: exhausted.
11 *last lights*: the setting sun.

INITIAL RESPONSE

1. Describe Hopkins' tone in the first four lines of this poem. Refer closely to the text in your answer.

2. How are human beings portrayed in the poem? Support your points with reference.

3. Select two unusual images the poet uses. Comment on the effectiveness of each.

STUDY NOTES

Hopkins wrote many Italian (or Petrarchan) sonnets (consisting of an octave and a sestet). The form suited the stages in the argumentative direction of his themes. Like many other Christian poets, he 'found' God in nature. His poetry is also notable for its use of sprung rhythm (an irregular movement or pace which echoed ordinary conversation). 'God's Grandeur' is typical of Hopkins in both its subject matter and style. The condensed language, elaborate wordplay and unusual syntax – sometimes like a tongue twister – can be challenging.

The poem's **opening quatrain** (four-line section) is characteristically dynamic. The **metaphor ('charged') compares God's greatness to electric power**, brilliant but hazardous. The visual effect of 'flame out' and 'shook foil' develops this representation of God's constant presence in the world. This image of oozing oil signifies a natural richness. The reference to electricity makes a subtle reappearance in **line 4**, where the 'rod' of an angry Creator is likened to a lightning bolt. The tone is one of energised celebration, but there is also a growing frustration: 'Why do men then now not reck his rod?' Hopkins seems mystified at human indifference to God's greatness.

The second quatrain is much more critical. We can sense the poet's own weariness with the numberless generations who have abandoned their spiritual salvation for the flawed material benefits of 'trade' and 'toil'. Hopkin's laboured repetition of 'have trod' is purposely heavy-handed. The internal rhymes of the negative verbs ('seared', 'bleared' and 'smeared') in **line 6** convey his deep sense of disgust at a world blighted by industry and urbanisation. **Man's neglect of the natural environment is closely linked to the drift away from God.** Hopkins symbolises this spiritual alienation through the image of the 'shod' foot out of touch with nature and its Creator.

However, in response to his depression, the mood changes in the **sestet** (the final six lines of the sonnet). Hopkins' tone softens considerably and is aided by the gentle, sibilant effect in **line 10**: 'There lives the dearest freshness deep down things'. As in many of his religious poems, he takes comfort in conventional Christian belief. For him, 'nature is never spent'. The world is filled with 'freshness' that confirms God's presence. This **power of renewal** is exemplified in the way morning never fails to follow the 'last lights' of dark night.

The reassuring image in the **last line** is one of God guarding the world and promising rebirth and salvation. The source of this constant regeneration is 'the Holy Ghost' (God's grace) who 'broods' over a dependent world with the patient devotion of a bird protecting its young. In expressing his faith and surrendering himself to divine will, the poet can truly appreciate the grandeur of God. The final exclamations ('Oh, morning' and 'ah! bright wings') echo Hopkins' **sense of euphoria**.

ANALYSIS

'Hopkins' original voice explores God's presence in this weary world.' Discuss this statement, with particular reference to the poem 'God's Grandeur'.

Sample Paragraph

Gerard Manley Hopkins uses the Petrarchan sonnet form to examine man's lack of awareness of the beauty of God's world. A dynamic alliterative metaphor dramatically opens the poem, 'The world is charged with the grandeur of God'. His power and brilliance are conveyed through condensed references to electricity, 'It will flame out, like shining from shook foil'. Yet man remains unconcerned at God's lightning bolt and does 'not reck his rod'. The tone in the second quatrain suggests the drudgery of man's mechanical world. The blight of industrialisation has 'smeared' God's glorious creation. The heavy repetition of the phrase 'have trod' coupled with the internally rhymed verbs ('seared' and 'bleared') show the horrendous effects of factories and urbanisation on both man and landscape. Hopkins, in an innovative image, suggests that man is no longer in touch with his natural environment, the 'shod' foot can no longer feel the earth. A gentler tone emerges in the sestet. Hopkins realises the power of nature to regenerate itself, 'nature is never spent'. Unusual word order and a gentle sibilant effect stresses this ability to renew, 'There lives the dearest freshness deep down things'. I was impressed with Hopkins' religious belief expressed in the lovely natural image of the bird protecting its young, 'the Holy Ghost over the bent/World broods with warm breast'. The cold man-made world which humans have created has now been replaced by the deeply satisfying awareness of God's glowing grace expressed in the final exclamation, 'ah! bright wings'.

Examiner's Comment

A very solid discussion on Hopkins' twin themes of God's power and man's indifference. There is a keen awareness of Hopkins' innovative use of language: 'A dynamic alliterative metaphor dramatically opens the poem'. Varied expressive language and accurate use of quotation also contribute to this top grade.

N.B. Access your ebook for additional sample paragraphs and a list of useful quotes with commentary.

CLASS/HOMEWORK EXERCISES

1. Comment on Hopkins' use of sound in this poem. Refer closely to the text in your answer.

2. Hopkins is a poet of intense emotion, ecstasy and distress. Trace his expression of these emotions in your response. Support your answer with reference to the text.

SUMMARY POINTS

- Combination of conflicting emotions, ecstasy and distress.
- Natural world enlivened by God's presence.
- Assonance and alliteration emphasise despondency, man's neglect of natural environment associated with drift away from God.
- Belief in nature's ability to regenerate.
- Sonnet concludes with a benevolent image of Holy Ghost as benevolent mother bird.
- Tone becomes more reassuring in the sestet.

② SPRING

Nothing is so beautiful as Spring –
    When weeds, in wheels, shoot long and lovely and lush;
    Thrush's eggs look little low heavens, and thrush
Through the echoing timber does so rinse and wring
The ear, it strikes like lightnings to hear him sing;   5
    The glassy peartree leaves and blooms, they brush
    The descending blue; that blue is all in a rush
With richness; the racing lambs too have fair their fling.

What is all this juice and all this joy?
    A strain of the earth's sweet being in the beginning   10
In Eden garden. – Have, get, before it cloy,
    Before it cloud, Christ, lord, and sour with sinning,
Innocent mind and Mayday in girl and boy,
    Most, O maid's child, thy choice and worthy the winning.

'that blue is all in a rush/With richness'

Glossary

2 *in wheels*: radiating out like spokes; rampant; pivoting movement.
2 *lush*: growing thickly, luxuriantly.
3 *Thrush's eggs*: songbird's eggs, which are light blue.
4 *rinse*: wash out with fresh water.
4 *wring*: to twist or squeeze; drain off excess water.

8 *have fair their fling*: the lambs are enjoying their freedom.
10 *strain*: a trace; streak; a segment of melody.
12 *cloud*: darken; depress.
13 *Mayday*: innocence of the young.
14 *Most:* the best choice.
14 *maid's child*: Jesus, son of Mary.

INITIAL RESPONSE

1. This poem opens with a confident statement. In your opinion, does the first section of the poem do justice to this declaration? Refer both to the style and content of the octet in your answer.

2. What is the mood in the second section of the poem? What reasons would you give for this change in the sestet? Use reference or quotation to support your point of view.

3. Hopkins preferred movement to stopping. What evidence for this statement is contained in the poem? Illustrate your response by referring to the expression and subject matter of the poem.

STUDY NOTES

'Spring' was written in May 1877. Hopkins had a special devotion to Mary, Queen of Heaven, and May is the month that is devoted to her. The poem was written after a holiday spent walking and writing poetry in Wales. He captures the exuberance of nature bursting into life.

The simple **opening sentence** in the first section, 'Nothing is so beautiful as spring', is a deliberately exaggerated statement (hyperbole) used to emphasise a feeling. This Petrarchan sonnet's **octet** starts with an **ecstatic account of the blooming of nature in spring**. As we examine the poet's use of language, we can understand why it should be heard rather than read. Here in the second line – 'When weeds, in wheels, shoot long and lovely and lush' – the alliteration of 'w' and 'l', the assonance of 'ee' and the slow, broad vowels 'o' and 'u' add to this description of abundant growth. We can easily imagine the wild flowers growing before our eyes, as if caught by a slow-motion camera, uncurling and straightening to reach the heavens.

The **energy of the new plants** is contained in the verb 'shoot'. Just as the plants are shooting from the fertile earth, so one word seems to sprout out of another in the poem, e.g. 'thrush' springing from 'lush'. Now we are looking down, carefully examining a delicately beautiful sight among the long grasses: 'Thrush's eggs look little low heavens'. Note the speckled appearance of the eggs, similar to the dappling of blue and white in the sky. The oval shape is like the dome of the heavens.

The poet's **breathless excitement** at the sight of Heaven on earth is caught by the omission of the word 'like'. Now we hear the song of the bird as the assonance of 'rinse' and 'wring' sings purely, cleansing our human ears with heavenly sounds. It has a powerful effect, like a bolt of lightning. The focus shifts to the gleam on the leaves of the pear tree, as its 'glassy' appearance is observed. Hopkins looked closely at objects to try to capture their essence (inscape). He once said, 'What you look hard at seems to look hard at you'.

Hopkins **pushes language** to its boundaries as nouns become verbs ('leaves' and 'blooms'). His unique style empowered modern poets to experiment to explore their own individuality. The sky seems to bend down to reach the growing trees: 'they brush/The descending blue'. The blueness of the sky is captured in the alliteration of 'all in a rush/With richness'. Meanwhile, newborn lambs are bounding happily, 'fair their fling'. This octet is a joyous exploration of a kaleidoscope of the colours, sounds and movement of spring. The poet's imagination soars as he strains language to encapsulate the immediacy of the moment.

In the **sestet, the mood becomes reflective** as the poet considers the significance of nature: 'What is all this juice and all this joy?' As he meditates, he decides it is 'A strain of the earth's sweet being', a fleeting snatch of melody from a perfect world 'In Eden garden', before it was sullied with sin. Hopkins **had a deep love of God**, especially as the Creator. His tone becomes insistent as he urges God to grasp the world in order to preserve it in its perfect state. The hard 'c' sound of 'cloy' and 'cloud' shows how the beauty will become stained and imperfect if Christ does not act swiftly. Hopkins desires virtue and purity: 'innocence', 'Mayday in girl and boy'. He refers to Christ as Mary's child ('O maid's child') as he attempts to persuade God that this world is worth the effort ('worthy the winning').

The regular rhyme scheme, cdcdcd, adds to the music of the poem as well as emphasising key words: 'joy', 'cloy', 'boy', 'beginning', 'Sinning', 'winning'. The poet was influenced by reading the medieval theologian Duns Scotus, who said that the material world was an incarnation of God. Thus Hopkins felt justified in his preoccupation with the material world, as it had a sacramental value.

ANALYSIS

'Hopkins uses poetry to speak of the glory of God.' Write a paragraph in response to this statement, using reference or quotation from 'Spring' to support your views.

Sample paragraph

Hopkins had felt uneasy loving the natural world or a friend in case it distracted him from loving God, which was the main focus of his life. But after reading the theologian Duns Scotus, who maintained that the material world was a representation of God, Hopkins felt if he loved nature, he was loving its creator. This had swayed his 'spirits to peace'. So in giving us the glorious octet of this poem 'Spring', with the weeds spiralling 'long and lovely and lush', the blue of the sky in 'a rush/With richness', the thrush's eggs like 'little low heavens', Hopkins is worshipping God. In the sestet he becomes more reflective as he more closely links the poem to the glory of God as he meditates on the meaning of all this 'juice' and 'joy'. He thinks we have seen a glimpse, 'A strain', of the earth before the Fall of Adam and Eve. He asks God to preserve the world in its sinless state. We also see his devotion to the Mother of God, Our Lady in this poem. The references to 'O maid's child' and 'Mayday' confirm this. May is the month associated with the worship of Mary, Queen of Heaven. Never since the 17th century has a poet given a deeper poetic expression to religious belief than Hopkins as he celebrates the abundant world of nature. I agree that 'nothing is so beautiful as spring'.

Examiner's Comment

This confident answer has noted some of the key influences on Hopkins (Duns Scotus) in his decision to glorify God in his poetry. Personal engagement with the poem is evident in the lively language, e.g. 'in giving us the glorious octet of this poem'. Expression throughout is clear and assured: 'He asks God to preserve the world in its sinless state'. The effective use of accurate quotation is central to this successful top-grade response.

N.B. Access your ebook for additional sample paragraphs and a list of useful quotes with commentary.

CLASS/HOMEWORK EXERCISES

1. Hopkins employs language in an energetic, intense and religious way. Do you agree? Use reference to the poem 'Spring' in your answer.

2. Hopkins is fascinated by the uniqueness of things. How does Hopkins convey the wonder of the individuality of an object through his use of language in this poem?

SUMMARY POINTS

- Euphoric declaration of beauty of nature.
- Jubilant tone, rush of energy, one word sprouts from another.
- Rich visual detail and stunning sound effects.
- Religious impulse, reflection on innocence, God's beauty in nature and man.
- Sonnet form – descriptive octet and reflective sestet.

❸ AS KINGFISHERS CATCH FIRE, DRAGONFLIES DRAW FLAME

As kingfishers catch fire, dragonflies draw flame;
  As tumbled over rim in roundy wells
  Stones ring; like each tucked string tells, each hung bell's
Bow swung finds tongue to fling out broad its name;
Each mortal thing does one thing and the same: 5
  Deals out that being indoors each one dwells;
  Selves – goes itself; myself it speaks and spells,
Crying *What I do is me: for that I came.*

I say more: the just man justices;
  Keeps grace: that keeps all his goings graces;   10
Acts in God's eye what in God's eye he is –
  Christ. For Christ plays in ten thousand places,
Lovely in limbs, and lovely in eyes not his
  To the Father through the features of men's faces.

'dragonflies draw flame'

Glossary

1	*kingfishers*: brilliantly coloured birds that hunt small fish.
1	*dragonflies*: brightly coloured insects with transparent wings.
3	*tucked*: plucked.

4	*Bow*: rim of bell that makes a sound when struck.
7	*Selves*: (used as a verb) defining or expressing its distinctiveness.
9	*justices*: (as a verb) acting justly.
10	*Keeps grace*: obeys God's will.

INITIAL RESPONSE

1. Comment on the nature images in the poem's opening line.

2. Select two interesting sound effects from the poem and briefly explain the effectiveness of each.

3. 'Celebration is the central theme in this poem.' Write your response to this statement, supporting your answer with reference to the text.

STUDY NOTES

This sonnet is often cited as an example of Hopkins' theory of inscape, the uniqueness of every created thing as a reflection of God's glory. The poet believed that human beings had the uniqueness to recognise the divine presence in everything around us. This sonnet is written in an irregular ('sprung') rhythm that gives it a more concentrated quality.

The poem begins with two strikingly vivid images as Hopkins describes some of nature's most dazzling creatures. In **line 1**, he observes their vivid colour and dynamic movement (note the sharp alliteration and fast-paced rhythm) in the brilliant sunlight. The poet associates both the kingfisher and the dragonflies with fire. Aural images dominate **lines 2-4**. He takes great **delight in the uniqueness of existence** by listing a variety of everyday sounds: the tinkling noise of pebbles ('Stones ring') tossed down wells, the plucking of a stringed instrument and the loud ringing of a bell are all defined through their own distinctive sounds.

Hopkins is certain that the same quality applies to humans – 'Each mortal thing'. **We all express our unique inner selves**. Every individual does the same by presenting their inner essence (that dwells 'indoors'). The poet invents his own verb to convey how each of us 'Selves' (or expresses) our individual identity. The didactic tone of **lines 7-8** clearly reflects his depth of feeling, summed up by his emphatic illustration about our god-given purpose on earth: 'What I do is me: for that I came'.

Hopkins' enthusiasm ('I say more') intensifies at the start of the **sestet**. His central argument is that **people should fulfil their destiny by being themselves**. Again, he invents a new verb to illustrate his point: 'the just man justices' (good people behave in a godly way). Acting 'in God's eye' and availing of God's grace is our purpose on earth. The poet focuses on his belief that human beings are made in God's image and have the capacity to become like the omnipresent Christ.

Hopkins' **final lines** are filled with the devout Christian faith that **God will redeem everyone who 'Keeps grace'**. The poet repeatedly reminds us of the 'Lovely' personal relationship between God and mankind. It is Christ's presence within every human being that makes 'the features of men's faces' lovely in God's sight. Typically, Hopkins is convinced of the reality of Christ and the existence of the spirit world. He sees his own role as a 'kingfisher' catching fire – reeling in souls with his mystical poems of hope and spirituality.

Some critics have commented that the poem is too instructive and that Hopkins was overly concerned with getting across his message at the expense of method. The poet himself did not consider it a success. Yet there is no denying the poetic language of feeling and excitement in every line of the poem.

ANALYSIS

What aspects of this poem are typical of Hopkins' distinctive poetic style? Refer closely to the text in your answer.

Sample Paragraph

It seems to me that Hopkins the priest is the key speaker in 'As kingfishers catch fire'. To me, the poem is not as typical as 'Pied Beauty' or 'The Windhover'. However, his writing is unique. It is full of energy and unusual language patterns. It starts with lively images drawn from nature – 'As kingfishers catch fire, dragonflies draw flame'. In my opinion, no other poet on our course could write as precisely as this. There is an immediacy about his images that simply demands attention. The alliteration of 'f' and 'd' sounds suggest blinding flashes of colour, darting flames and dramatic movements – exactly what fish and insects do in their natural habitats. Hopkins uses very effective personification to show the vitality of the natural world – 'Stones ring'. He makes up new words of his own, such as 'justices'. Again, this is typical of his vibrant style. Hopkins does not bother with strict grammar either. He reduces sentences to childlike phrases to show his joy in being aware of the mystery of creation – 'For Christ plays in ten thousand places'. Even here, the alliteration adds energy to the rush of language. This is typical of so much of his poetry.

Examiner's Comment

This answer is somewhat narrowly focused, lacking development of points raised, e.g. 'Hopkins does not bother with strict grammar either'. More thorough engagement with the body of the poem is expected for a top grade. This note-like response, listing significant elements of Hopkins' style, comes short of the highest grade.

N.B. Access your ebook for additional sample paragraphs and a list of useful quotes with commentary.

CLASS/HOMEWORK EXERCISES

1. Hopkins admitted that his poetry had an 'oddness' about it. Comment on his management of language in this poem. Refer closely to the text in your answer.

2. Hopkins uses the Petrarchan sonnet form of an octet (eight lines) and sestet (six lines) in this poem. How does the poet's treatment of his theme of wonder change in these two sections? Support your answer with close reference to the text.

SUMMARY POINTS

- Distinctive quality of everything in the natural world.
- Invents verb, 'selves', to suggest unique quality of nature and man.
- Aural imagery, onomatopoeia, use of everyday sounds, sprung rhythm.
- Compliance with God's will.

4 THE WINDHOVER

To Christ our Lord

I caught this morning morning's minion, kingdom
  of daylight's dauphin, dapple-dawn-drawn Falcon, in his riding
  Of the rolling level underneath him steady air, and striding
High there, how he rung upon the rein of a wimpling wing
In his ecstasy! then off, off forth on swing,   5
  As a skate's heel sweeps smooth on a bow-bend: the hurl and gliding
  Rebuffed the big wind. My heart in hiding
Stirred for a bird, – the achieve of, the mastery of the thing!

Brute beauty and valour and act, oh air, pride, plume here
  Buckle! AND the fire that breaks from thee then, a billion   10
Times told lovelier, more dangerous, O my chevalier!

  No wonder of it: sheer plod makes plough down sillion
Shine, and blue-bleak embers, ah my dear,
  Fall, gall themselves, and gash gold-vermilion.

'how he rung upon the rein of a wimpling wing'

Glossary

Windhover: a kestrel or small falcon; resembles a cross in flight.

1   *minion*: favourite; darling.

2   *dauphin*: prince, heir to French throne.

2   *dapple-dawn-drawn*: the bird is outlined in patches of colour by the dawn light, an example of Hopkins' use of compression.

4   *rung upon the rein*: circling movement of a horse at the end of a long rein held by a trainer; the sound of the bird pealing like a bell as it wheels in the sky.

4   *wimpling*: pleated.

6   *bow-bend*: a wide arc.

7   *Rebuffed*: pushed back; mastered.

7   *My heart in hiding*: the poet is afraid, unlike the bird.

10   *Buckle*: pull together; clasp; fall apart.

11   *chevalier*: medieval knight; Hopkins regards God as a knight who will defend him against evil.

12   *sheer plod*: back-breaking drudgery of hard work, similar to Hopkins' work as a priest.

13   *ah my dear*: intimate address to God.

14   *Fall, gall ... gash*: a reference to the Crucifixion of Christ as He fell on the way to Cavalry, was offered vinegar and gashed by a spear on the cross.

14   *gold-vermilion*: gold and red, the colours of Christ the Saviour and also of the Eucharist, the Body and Blood of Christ which offers redemption.

INITIAL RESPONSE

1. In your opinion, has the poet been as daring in his use of language as the bird has been in its flight? Support your view by referring closely to the poem.

2. The sonnet moves from description to reflection. What does the poet meditate on in the sestet? Support your response by reference to the text.

3. Write your own personal response to the poem, referring closely to the text in your answer.

STUDY NOTES

'The Windhover' was Hopkins' favourite poem, 'the best thing I ever wrote'. It is dedicated to Christ – Hopkins wrote it in 1877, when he was thirty-three years old, the same age as Christ when he died. This is also the age at which Jesuits are ordained. The poet celebrates the uniqueness of the bird and his own deep relationship with God the Creator.

The name of the bird comes from its custom of hovering in the air, facing the wind, as it views the ground for its prey. The opening lines of the **octet** are **joyful and celebratory** as Hopkins rejoices in the sight of the bird, 'daylight's dauphin'. The verb 'caught' suggests not just that the poet caught sight of the bird, but also that he 'caught' the essence of the bird on the page with words. This is an example of Hopkins' compression of language where he edges two meanings into one word or phrase. ▼

Hopkins shaped language by omitting articles, conjunctions and verbs to express the energy of the bird, 'off forth on swing'. **Movement fascinated the poet**. The bird is sketched by the phrase 'dapple-dawn-drawn'. A vivid image of the flecks of colour on his wings (as the dawn light catches him) is graphically drawn here.

The **momentary freshness** is conveyed by 'this morning', with the bird in flight beautifully captured by the simile 'As a skate's heel sweeps smooth on a bow-bend'. The 's' sound mimics the swish of the skater as a large arc is traced on the ice. This curve is similar to the strong but graceful bend of a bow stretched to loose its arrow, with all its connotations of beauty of line and deadly strength.

In the **octet**, there is typical **energetic language**: 'how he rung upon the rein of a wimpling wing/ In his ecstasy!' This carries us along in its breathless description. It is not necessary for the reader to comprehend every word in order to appreciate the phrase's meaning. The word 'wimpling' refers to the beautiful, seemingly pleated pattern of the arrangement of the outstretched wings of the bird. The capital 'F' used for 'Falcon' hints at its symbolism for Christ. This very personal poem uses 'I' in the octet and 'my' in the sestet. Hopkins lavishes praise on the bird: 'dauphin' (young prince, heir) and 'minion' (darling). Run-on lines add to the poet's excitement. He acknowledges that the bird has what he does not possess: power, self-belief and grace ('My heart in hiding'). The lively rhyme, such as 'riding'/'striding', never becomes repetitive because of the varying line breaks. The octet concludes with Hopkins' admiration of 'the thing', which broadens the focus from the particular to the general. All of creation is magnificent.

This leads to the **sestet**, where **God the Creator becomes central to the poem**. The essence (inscape) of the bird is exposed: 'air, pride, plume here'. The bird is strong, brave, predatory, graceful and beautiful. The word 'Buckle' is paradoxical, as it contains two contradictory meanings: clasp together and fall apart. The bird is holding the line when it rides the rolling wind and falls apart as it swoops down on its prey. Capital letters for the conjunction 'AND' signal a moment of insight: 'the fire that breaks from thee'. The pronoun refers to God, whose magnificence is shown by 'fire'. The Holy Spirit is often depicted as a bird descending with tongues of flame. A soft tone of intimacy is then revealed: 'O my chevalier!' It is as if Hopkins wants God to act as the honourable knight of old, to take up his cause and fight on his behalf against his enemy. God will be Hopkins' defender against evil.

The **sestet** concludes with **two exceptional images**, both breaking apart to release their hidden brilliance. The ploughed furrow and the 'bluebleak embers' of coal both reveal their beauty in destruction: 'sillion/Shine', 'gash gold-vermilion'. Christ endured Calvary and crucifixion, 'Fall, gall … gash', and through his sacrifice, the 'Fall', achieved redemption for us. So too the priest embracing the drudgery of his service embraces his destiny by submitting to the will of God. In doing so, he reflects the greatness of God. Earthly glory is crushed to release heavenly glory. The phrase 'ah my dear' makes known the dominant force of Hopkins' life: to love God. The colours of gold and red are the colours of Christ the Saviour as well as the colours associated with the Eucharist, the Body and Blood of Christ. When Christians receive the sacrament of Holy Communion, they are redeemed. So, as the poem begins, 'dapple-dawn-drawn Falcon', it ends with 'gold-vermilion' in a triumph of glorious colour.

ANALYSIS

'Hopkins' intense reflections on Christ in his poetry are always conveyed with visual energy.' Discuss this statement, with particular reference to 'The Windhover'.

Sample Paragraph

In 'The Windhover', Hopkins uses the image of the falcon, which hovers in a cross-shape on the wind, as an emblem of Christ. Using strong images, the poet describes the bird's magnificent beauty, 'dapple-dawn-drawn', and its strength, 'rebuffed the big wind'. In the sestet, Hopkins calls God 'O my chevalier'. This gives me a vivid picture of a highly moral individual who was both strong-willed and who fought against evil. The verb 'Buckle' reminds me of the knight putting on his armour and stumbling in fierce battle. Christ also fell on the way to Cavalry where he was crucified – out of which a great glory was given to man, 'the fire that breaks from thee'. This sacrifice won our salvation. Hopkins felt it was right to focus on nature as it is a manifestation of the power and beauty of God. He believed that his vocation in life was to love God. In glorifying Him through the dramatic emblem of the windhover, he is glorifying divine creation, and therefore God Himself. The flash of red and gold, with which this visually powerful poem ends, 'gash gold-vermilion', reminds me that the lowly priest carrying out his ordinary duties is also revealing the beauty of God's creation. I think Hopkins' reflections on Christ add a real spiritual dimension to his poetry.

Examiner's Comment

Close reading of the poem is evident in this top-grade personal response: 'The verb "Buckle" reminds me of the knight putting on his armour'. Quotations are very well used here to highlight Hopkins' commitment to his Christian faith, 'The flash of red and gold, with which the poem ends, "gash-gold-vermilion", reminds me that the lowly priest carrying out his ordinary duties is also revealing the beauty of God's creation'. Well-controlled language use throughout.

N.B. Access your ebook for additional sample paragraphs and a list of useful quotes with commentary.

CLASS/HOMEWORK EXERCISES

1. How does Hopkins adapt the Petrarchan sonnet for his own purposes in 'The Windhover'? Use reference to the poem in your answer.

2. This profoundly personal poem commemorates the inimitable nature of the bird and the poet's intense relationship with God. For each of these aspects, pick an image from the poem which you considered particularly effective and explain why you have chosen that image.

SUMMARY POINTS

- Deeply personal poem, engaging opening.
- Relationship with God accentuated by poet's ability to see the divine in nature.
- Medieval chivalric imagery.
- Bird's movement depicted by alliteration and assonance.
- Optimistic ending, illustrated by 'blue-black' becoming 'gold-vermilion'.

5 PIED BEAUTY

Glory be to God for dappled things –
  For skies of couple-colour as a brinded cow;
    For rose-moles all in stipple upon trout that swim;
Fresh-firecoal chestnut-falls; finches' wings;
  Landscape plotted and pieced – fold, fallow, and plough;   5
    And all trades, their gear and tackle and trim.

All things counter, original, spare, strange;
  Whatever is fickle, freckled (who knows how?)
    With swift, slow; sweet, sour; adazzle, dim;
He fathers-forth whose beauty is past change: 10
           Praise him.

'skies of couple-colour'

Glossary

	Pied: varied.		6	*trades*: farmwork.
1	*dappled*: speckled, spotted.		6	*gear*: equipment.
2	*brinded*: streaked.		6	*tackle*: implements.
3	*rose-moles*: red-pink spots.		6	*trim*: fittings.
3	*stipple*: dotted.		7	*counter*: contrasting.
4	*Fresh-firecoal chestnut falls*: open chestnuts bright as		7	*spare*: special.
	burning coals.		8	*fickle*: changeable.
5	*pieced*: enclosed.		10	*He*: God.
5	*fold*: sheep enclosure.		10	*fathers-forth*: creates.
5	*fallow*: unused.			

INITIAL RESPONSE

1. In your view, what is the central theme in this poem? Refer to the text in your answer.

2. Discuss the poet's use of sound effects in the poem. Support your answer with quotations.

3. Choose two striking images from the poem and comment on the effectiveness of each.

STUDY NOTES

'Pied Beauty' is one of Hopkins' 'curtal' (or curtailed) sonnets, in which he condenses the traditional sonnet form. It was written in the so-called sprung rhythm that he evolved, based on the irregular rhythms of traditional Welsh verse. The poem's energetic language – particularly its sound effects – reflects Hopkins' view of the rich, abundant diversity evident within God's coherent creation.

The simplicity of the prayer-like **opening line** ('Glory be to God') is reminiscent of Biblical language and sets the poem's devotional tone. From the start, Hopkins displays a **childlike wonder** for all the 'dappled things' around him, illustrating his central belief with a series of vivid examples from the natural world.

Included in his panoramic sweep of nature's vibrant delights are the dominant blues and whites of the sky, which he compares to the streaked ('brinded') patterns of cowhide. The world is teeming with contrasting colours and textures, captured in **detailed images**, such as 'rose-moles all in stipple upon trout' and 'Fresh-firecoal chestnut-falls'.

For the exhilarated poet, everything in nature is linked. It is ironic, of course, that what all things share is their god-given individuality. In **line 4**, he associates broken chestnuts with burning coals in a fire, black on the outside and glowing underneath. In turn, the wings of finches have similar colours. Condensed imagery and compound words add even greater energy to the description.

Hopkins turns his attention to human nature in **lines 5–6**. The farmland features he describes reflect hard work and efficiency: 'Landscape plotted and pieced – fold, fallow, and plough'. The range of man's impact on the natural world is also worth celebrating, and this is reinforced by the **orderly syntax and insistent rhythm**. Human activity in tune with nature also glorifies God.

Hopkins' **final four lines** focus on the **unexpected beauty of creation** and further reveal the poet's passionate Christianity. As though overcome by the scale and variety of God's works – 'who knows how?' – the poet meditates on a range of contrasting adjectives ('swift, slow; sweet, sour; adazzle, dim'), all of which indicate the wonderful diversity of creation. As always, the alliteration gives an increased dynamism to this image of abundance and variety in nature.

The poem ends as it began – with a shortened version of the two mottoes of St Ignatius of Loyola, founder of the Jesuits: *Ad majorem Dei gloriam* (to the greater glory of God) and *Laus Deo semper* (praise be to God always). For Hopkins, **God is beyond change**. The Creator ('He fathers-forth') and all the 'dappled' opposites that enrich our ever-changing world inspire us all to 'Praise him'.

ANALYSIS

'Hopkins' appreciation of the energy present in the world is vividly expressed in his unique poetry.' Discuss this statement, with particular reference to 'Pied Beauty'.

Sample Paragraph

It seems to me that 'Pied Beauty' is more like a heartfelt prayer than an ordinary poem. It begins with the phrase 'Glory be to God' and continues to the final words 'Praise him'. In between, Hopkins lists a whole litany of examples of the variety of the 'dappled' natural environment, the 'brinded' patterns of cowhide, 'landscape plotted and pieced'. The pace of the poem is rapid as though he is in a rush to explain his astonishment: 'Fresh-firecoal chestnut-falls'. There is an overwhelming sense of God's mystery and greatness. This is partly due to the compound phrases, such as 'couple-colour' and 'rose-moles' which make us more aware of the varied appearances of natural things. The energetic rhythm builds to a climax in the last line. This is short, direct and almost breathless – just one simple monosyllabic phrase that sums up Hopkins' awareness of God's creation: 'Praise him'. From start to finish, I can easily appreciate Hopkins' personal sense of the overpoweringly beautiful world around him.

Examiner's Comment

A short, focused response that ranges over a number of interesting features of Hopkins' style, particularly his description of nature's energy: 'The pace of the poem is rapid, as though he is in a rush to explain his astonishment'. The rapidity of Hopkins' verse is effectively explored, particularly in the reference to the lead-up to the 'climax in the poem's final line'. A successful top-grade answer.

N.B. Access your ebook for additional sample paragraphs and a list of useful quotes with commentary.

CLASS/HOMEWORK EXERCISES

1. Compare and contrast the views expressed in 'Pied Beauty' with any other 'religious' poem by Hopkins from your course. Support your answer with reference to both poems.

2. In your opinion, how does Hopkins express his attitude towards God in this poem? Refer to his use of imagery and pay particular attention to the concluding four lines.

SUMMARY POINTS

- Condensed version (ten and a half lines) of traditional sonnet form (fourteen lines).
- Anthem of praise to God for nature's variety.
- Catalogue of vibrant examples of 'dappled beauty'. Effective use of compound words.
- Alliteration conveys how man's activities are in harmony with God's design.

6 FELIX RANDAL

Felix Randal the farrier, O he is dead then? my duty all ended,
Who have watched his mould of man, big-boned and hardy-handsome
Pining, pining, till time when reason rambled in it, and some
Fatal four disorders, fleshed there, all contended?

Sickness broke him. Impatient he cursed at first, but mended   5
Being anointed and all; though a heavenlier heart began some
Months earlier, since I had our sweet reprieve and ransom
Tendered to him. Ah well, God rest him all road ever he offended!

This seeing the sick endears them to us, us too it endears.
My tongue had taught thee comfort, touch had quenched thy tears   10
Thy tears that touched my heart, child, Felix, poor Felix Randal;

How far from then forethought of, all thy more boisterous years,
When thou at the random grim forge, powerful amidst peers,
Didst fettle for the great grey drayhorse his bright and battering sandal!

'at the random grim forge'

Glossary

Felix Randal: the parishioner's name was Felix Spenser. 'Felix' in Latin means 'happy'. Randal can also mean a lowly, humble thing or trodden on.

1   *farrier*: blacksmith.

1   *O he is dead then*: reaction of priest at Felix's death.

2   *hardy-handsome*: compound word describing the fine physical appearance of the blacksmith.

4   *disorders*: diseases.

4   *contended*: competitively fought over Felix.

6   *anointed*: sacraments administered to the sick by a priest.

7   *reprieve and ransom*: confession; penance; communion; redemption from sin.

8   *Tendered*: offered.

8   *all road ever*: in whatever way (local dialect).

13   *random*: casual; irregular.

14   *fettle*: prepare.

14   *drayhorse*: big horse used to pull heavy carts.

14   *sandal*: type of horseshoe.

INITIAL RESPONSE

1. 'Hopkins is a poet who celebrates unique identities and experiences, their meaning and their value.' Discuss this statement with reference to the poem, illustrating your answer with quotations.

2. How does the octet differ from the sestet in this Petrarchan sonnet? Refer to theme and style in your response. Use quotations in support of your views.

3. Choose two aural images that you found interesting and give reasons for their effectiveness.

STUDY NOTES

'Felix Randal' was written in Liverpool in 1880. The poem contrasts with others such as 'Spring'. Hopkins had been placed as a curate to the city slums of Liverpool, 'a most unhappy and miserable spot', in his opinion. He didn't communicate successfully with his parishioners and he didn't write much poetry, except this one poem about the blacksmith who died of tuberculosis, aged thirty-one.

The opening of the **octet** identifies the man with his name and occupation, 'Felix Randal the farrier'. Then the poet shocks us with the priest's reaction: 'O he is dead then? my duty all ended'. On first reading, this sounds both dismissive and cold. However, when we consider that the death was expected and that the priest had seen all this many times, we realise that the line rings with authenticity and professional detachment. Also, in the face of the big events of life, we articulate our feelings with thoughtless, numbed remarks. For Hopkins, 'duty' was a sacred office. **The farrier is recalled in his physical prime**, using the alliteration of 'm', 'b' and 'h' in the phrase 'mould of man, big-boned and hardy-handsome'. The repetition of 'Pining, pining' marks his decline in health. His illness is graphically conveyed as his mental health deteriorated ('reason rambled') and the diseases attacked his body ('Fatal four disorders, fleshed there, all cotended'). The **illnesses took possession of the body** and waged a horrific battle to win supremacy, eventually killing Felix. The use of the word 'broke' is suitable in this context, as in the world of horses it refers to being trained. Is Felix trained ('broke') through suffering? His realistic reaction to the news – 'he cursed' – changes when he receives the sacraments ('being anointed'). Felix was broken but is now restored by 'our sweet reprieve and ransom', the healing sacraments. **The tone changes** with the personal pronoun. The priest–patient relationship is acknowledged: we, both priest and layperson, are saved by God. A note of resigned acceptance, almost an anti-climax, is evident in the line 'Ah well, God rest him all road ever he offended!' The use of the Lancashire dialect ('all road') by the priest shows a developing relationship between the two men.

The detached priest's voice resurfaces in the **sestet**: 'This seeing the sick'. This section of the sonnet focuses on **the reality of sickness** and its effects. Both the sick man and the priest received something from the experience. We respond to the sick with sympathy ('the sick endears them to us'), but we also appreciate ourselves and our own health more ('us too it endears') as we face another's mortality. The priest comforted the sick man with words ('My tongue') and the Last Sacraments, anointing by 'touch'. The priest becomes a father figure to 'child' Felix. Is there a suggestion that one must become like an innocent child to enter the kingdom of Heaven? The **tercet** (three-line segment) is intimate: 'thee', 'thy', 'Thy tears', 'my heart'. The **last tercet** explodes in a **dramatic flashback** to the energy of the young blacksmith in his prime, when there was little thought of death: 'How far from then forethought'. Onomatopoeia and alliteration convey the lifeforce (inscapes) of the young Felix, 'boisterous' and 'powerful amidst peers'.

Sprung rhythm adds to the force of the poem as the six main stresses are interspersed with an irregular number of unstressed syllables. Felix did a man's job at the 'grim forge' when he made the 'bright and battering sandal' for the powerful carthorse, magnificently captured in the assonance of 'great grey drayhorse'. The poem ends not with Felix in heavenly glory, but in his former earthly glory: 'thou … Didst fettle'. God has fashioned Felix through his suffering just as Felix had fashioned the horseshoe. Both required force and effort to bend them to the shape in which they can function properly. The poem is a celebration of God's creation of the man.

ANALYSIS

'Hopkins is a poet who celebrates unique identities and individual experiences, exploring their meaning and worth.' Discuss this statement in relation to one or more of the poems on your course, quoting in support of your points.

Sample Paragraph

In 'Felix Randal', Hopkins captures the unique essence of the man and his inscape, a great big strong man struck down by illness. He was 'big-boned and hardy-handsome', and the alliteration emphasises the magnificence of his physique. His understandable reaction to his own misfortune is caught in 'he cursed at first', the assonance echoing the deep guttural oaths. The repeated 'f' of 'Fatal four disorders, fleshed there' conveys the impossible odds stacked against the man. Here Hopkins has given us the unique identity of the man and his individual experience. He also gives us the rather dismissive voice of the weary priest: 'O he is dead then? my duty all ended'. Here is a man who has seen too much suffering. His use of the Lancashire dialect 'all road' shows how he has tried to enter the world of his parishioners, but he quickly reverts back to his professional capacity: 'This seeing the sick'. He has a strong belief that the sacraments he is offering will help: 'sweet reprieve and ransom'. So Hopkins also gives us the individual essence of the weary priest trying his best for the sick in his care. The poem leaves us feeling that the priest has received as much from the sick man as the sick man has received from the priest: 'Thy tears that touched my heart'. The experience broke through the cold exterior of the priest to reveal his human capacity for compassion. Felix's acceptance of his lot and the priest's acceptance of his lot both show the value of the experience.

Examiner's Comment

As part of a full essay answer, this paragraph has dealt comprehensively with the various elements of the question. The close attention to the poet's use of language, assonance and alliteration, enhances the answer. Real personal engagement with the poem is evident in the in-depth discussion of the priest's transition from tiredness to his regained 'professional capacity'. A highly successful answer which merits the top grade.

N.B. Access your ebook for additional sample paragraphs and a list of useful quotes with commentary.

CLASS/HOMEWORK EXERCISES

1. Hopkins deals with suffering in his poetry. Has this any relevance to the modern reader? Use reference to 'Felix Randal' in your answer.

2. Hopkins gives a vivid portrait of the farrier. Discuss how his changing tone conveys his view of Felix Randal. Support your answer with close reference to the text.

SUMMARY POINTS

- Inscape (essence captured) of blacksmith in this Petrarchan Sonnet.
- 'Randal' suggests man's insignificance; glory only achieved through Christian faith.
- Sprung rhythm (many unstressed syllables) add to poem's energy.
- Simple everyday speech and colloquialisms root poem firmly in North of England.
- Final image is positive; 'b' sound accentuates energy.

⑦ INVERSNAID

This darksome burn, horseback brown,
His rollrock highroad roaring down,
In coop and in comb the fleece of his foam
Flutes and low to the lake falls home.

A windpuff-bonnet of fawn-froth   5
Turns and twindles over the broth
Of a pool so pitchblack, fell-frowning,
It rounds and rounds Despair to drowning.

Degged with dew, dappled with dew
Are the groins of the braes that the brook treads through,   10
Wiry heathpacks, flitches of fern,
And the beadbonny ash that sits over the burn.

What would the world be, once bereft
Of wet and of wildness? Let them be left,
O let them be left, wildness and wet;   15
Long live the weeds and the wilderness yet.

'the fleece of his foam'

Glossary

Inversnaid is a remote area located near Loch Lomond in the Scottish Highlands.

1	*burn*: stream.	7	*fell*: fiercely.
3	*coop*: hollow.	9	*Degged*: sprinkled about.
3	*comb*: moving freely.	10	*groins of the braes*: sides of hills.
4	*Flutes*: grooves; whistles.	11	*heathpacks*: heather outcrops.
6	*twindles*: spins.	11	*flitches*: ragged tufts.
		12	*beadbonny*: mountain ash tree with bright berries.
		13	*bereft*: deprived.

INITIAL RESPONSE

1. From your reading of the first stanza, explain how the poet conveys the stream's energy.

2. Sound effects play a key part in the second and third stanzas. Choose two aural images that convey Hopkins' excited reaction to the mountain stream. Comment on the effectiveness of each.

3. Write your own personal response to the poem, referring closely to the text in your answer.

STUDY NOTES

'Inversnaid' was written in 1881 after Hopkins visited the remote hillsides around Loch Lomond. He disliked being in cities and much preferred the sights and sounds of the wilderness. The poem is unusual for Hopkins in that there is no direct mention of God as the source of all this natural beauty.

The **opening lines** of **stanza one** are dramatic. Hopkins compares the brown, rippling stream ('This darksome burn') to a wild horse's back. The forceful alliteration – 'rollrock highroad roaring' – emphasises the power of this small and dismal stream as it rushes downhill, its course directed by confining rocks. A sense of immediacy and energy is echoed in the **vigorous onomatopoeic effects**, including end rhyme ('brown', 'down'), repetition and internal rhyme ('comb', 'foam'). This is characteristic of Hopkins, as is his use of descriptive details, likening the foamy 'fleece' of the water to the fluted surface ('Flutes') of a Greek or Roman column.

Stanza two begins with another effective metaphor. The poet compares the yellow-brown froth to a windblown bonnet (hat) as the water swirls into a dark pool on the riverbed. The **atmosphere is light and airy**. Run-on lines reflect the lively pace of the noisy stream. However, the tone suddenly darkens with the disturbing image of the 'pitchblack' whirlpool which Hopkins sees as capable of drowning all in 'Despair'. The sluggish rhythm in **lines 7–8** reinforces this menacing mood.

Nature seems much more benign in **stanza three**. The language is softer sounding – 'Degged with dew, dappled with dew' – as Hopkins describes the **steady movement of the water** through 'the groins of the braes'. Enclosed by the sharp banks, the stream sprinkles nearby branches of mountain ash, aflame with their vivid scarlet berries. As always, Hopkins delights in the unspoiled landscape: 'Wiry heathpacks, flitches of fern,/And the beadbonny ash'. Throughout the poem, he has also used traditional Scottish expressions ('burn', 'braes') to reflect the lively sounds of the Highlands.

The language in **stanza four** is rhetorical. Hopkins wonders what the world would be like without its wild qualities. The tone is personal and plaintive: 'O let them be left, wildness and wet'. While repetition and the use of the exclamation add a sense of urgency, his plea is simple: let nature remain as it is. The final appeal – 'Long live the weeds and the wilderness yet' – is reminiscent of his poem 'Spring'. Once again, there is no doubting Hopkins' **enthusiasm for the natural beauty of remote places** and the sentiments he expresses are clearly heartfelt. Although written in 1881, the poem has obvious relevance for today's generation.

ANALYSIS

'Hopkins' deep appreciation of nature is a central feature of his striking poetry.' Discuss this statement, with particular reference to 'Inversnaid'.

Sample Paragraph

The most immediate thing that emerges about Hopkins is his extraordinary closeness to nature. This is evident in all his poems. He seems to have a heightened awareness of the sights and sounds of the remote mountain 'burn' in 'Inversnaid'. He details the colours of the water. It is 'darksome', 'horseback brown' and 'fawn-froth'. Hopkins is always excited by his natural environment. To him, the river is alive. It is 'roaring down'. He describes the Scottish rowan trees as 'the beadbonny ash', referring to their attractive red berries. Everything he says suggests his love for the natural world. In the last section of the poem, Hopkins openly states his fears for nature. He begs us to preserve the 'wildness and wet'. For him, all of nature deserves respect. He ends the poem with his own slogan, 'Long live the weeds and the wilderness'. Hopkins strikes me as being a lonely man who preferred the secluded Scottish hills where he could appreciate the natural world rather than being in a crowded city. Nature obviously inspired him and he seems to be deeply moved by the beauty of places such as Inversnaid. He repeats the words 'wet' and 'wildness' a number of times in the final lines, leaving us in no doubt about how much the natural landscape meant to him.

Examiner's Comment

Hopkins' awareness of the unruly aspects of nature is effectively explored: 'He details the colours of the water. It is "darksome"'. There is a convincing sense of close engagement with the body of the poem: 'Hopkins is always excited by his natural environment'. Accurate textual references and impressive, fluent expression ensure the top grade.

N.B. Access your ebook for additional sample paragraphs and a list of useful quotes with commentary.

CLASS/HOMEWORK EXERCISES

1. In your opinion, does the poem 'Inversnaid' have relevance to our modern world? Support the points you make with reference to the text.

2. How does Hopkins reveal his intense love of nature in this poem? Refer to his subject matter and stylistic techniques in your response.

SUMMARY POINTS

- Celebration of nature's unruly beauty; unusually no reference to God.
- Colloquial Scots-English language locates poem in Scottish Highlands.
- Steady movement of water conveyed through onomatopoeic effects.
- Plea on behalf of unspoilt natural scenes.

8 I WAKE AND FEEL THE FELL OF DARK, NOT DAY

I wake and feel the fell of dark, not day.
What hours, O what black hours we have spent
This night! what sights you, heart, saw; ways you went!
And more must, in yet longer light's delay.
    With witness I speak this. But where I say   5
Hours I mean years, mean life. And my lament
Is cries countless, cries like dead letters sent
To dearest him that lives alas! away.

    I am gall. I am heartburn. God's most deep decree
Bitter would have me taste: my taste was me;   10
Bones built in me, flesh filled, blood brimmed the curse.
    Selfyeast of spirit a dull dough sours. I see
The lost are like this, and their scourge to be
As I am mine, their sweating selves; but worse.

'I wake and feel the fell of dark, not day'

Glossary

1   *fell*: threat; blow; knocked down; past tense of fall (fall of Adam and Eve cast into darkness); also refers to the mountain.

7–8 *dead letters sent /To dearest him*: communication which is of no use, didn't elicit a response.

9   *gall*: bitterness; anger; acidity; vinegar.

9   *deep decree*: command that cannot easily be understood.

11 *Bones built in me, flesh filled, blood brimmed the curse*: the passive tense of the verb might suggest how God created Man, yet Man has sinned.

12 *Selfyeast of spirit a dull dough sours*: yeast makes bread rise; Hopkins feels he cannot become good or wholesome.

13 *The lost*: those condemned to serve eternity in Hell with no hope of redemption, unlike the poet.

INITIAL RESPONSE

1. How is the oppressive atmosphere conveyed in this sonnet? Quote in support of your response.

2. How does the poem conclude, on a note of hope or despair? Illustrate your answer by referring closely to the text.

3. Comment on the use of alliteration to convey Hopkins' sense of dejection. Mention at least three examples.

STUDY NOTES

'I wake and feel the fell of dark, not day' was written in Dublin, where Hopkins was teaching at UCD and was burdened by a massive workload of examination papers. He was there for six years and had over 1,300 scripts a year to correct. After a long silence, he wrote the 'terrible sonnets'. Hopkins said of these, 'If ever anything was written in blood, these were.' This sonnet was discovered among his papers after his death.

The last three sonnets on the course are called the 'terrible sonnets'. They are similar to Frost's 'Acquainted with the Night'. Here Hopkins reaches the **darkest depths of bleak despair**. The sonnet opens in darkness and the only mention of light in the whole poem is 'light's delay' in **line 4**, as it is postponed. He wakes to the oppressive blow of the dark ('the fell of dark'), not to the brightness of daylight. The heaviness of depression is being described, the oppressive darkness which Adam woke to after his expulsion from the Garden of Eden. Hopkins and his soul have shared these 'black hours' and they will experience 'more'. It is not just hours they have spent in darkness, but 'years', 'life'.

The formal, almost Biblical phrase 'With witness I speak this' emphasises that what he has said is true. The hard 'c' sounds in 'cries countless' and the repetition of 'cries' keenly describe the **fruitless attempts at communication** ('dead letters'). There is no response: he 'lives alas! away'. We can imagine the poet in the deep dark of the night attempting to gain solace from his prayers to God ('dearest him'), but they go unanswered.

Hopkins feels this deep depression intensely. **Note the repetition of 'I'**: 'I wake', 'I speak', 'I say', 'I mean', 'I am gall', 'I am heartburn', 'I see', 'I am'. He is in physical pain, bitter and burning. The language might well refer to Christ's Crucifixion, when he was offered a sponge soaked in vinegar to drink, and pierced through his side. However, the poet recognises that it is God's unfathomable decision that this is the way it should be: 'God's most deep decree'. **The poet is reviled by himself** in **line 10**: 'my taste was me'. He describes how he was fashioned: 'Bones built in me, flesh filled, blood brimmed'. The alliteration shows the careful construction of the body by the Creator, but Hopkins is full of 'the curse'.

Could this sense of revulsion be related to original sin emanating from the fall of Adam and Eve? The deadening 'd' sound of 'dull dough' shows that there is no hope of rising. The body is tainted, soured. It does not have the capacity to 'Selfyeast', to resurrect or renew. Is it being suggested that Hopkins needs divine intervention? Is there an overtone of the bread of Communion, the wholesome Body of Christ? The scope of the poem broadens out at the end as the poet gains an **insight into the plight of others**. All those condemned to Hell are like this and in fact are worse off: 'but worse'. The horrific atmosphere of Hell is fixed in the phrase 'sweating selves'. For those 'lost', it is permanent. For Hopkins, perhaps it is just 'longer light's delay'. Some day **he will be redeemed**.

ANALYSIS

'Hopkins' poetry displays a deeply personal and passionate response to the human condition.' Discuss with reference to the poems on your course, illustrating your answer with relevant quotations.

Sample Paragraph

I was fascinated when reading about Hopkins' life to learn that he had to examine hundreds of scripts five or six times a year, and that his college lectures were conducted in uproar. He writes of a 'daily anxiety about work to be done', 'All impulse fails me'. Everyone can identify with this man suffering from depression. This is evident in 'I wake and feel the fell of dark, not day'. To me he is describing waking over and over again at night. The long vowel sounds in 'O what black hours' give an idea of the man tossing and turning, trying to sleep, his head in a whirl. Hopkins' personal and passionate relationship with God was the focus of his life. His passionate pleas to God, 'To dearest him', are useless, 'dead letters'. Usually God is written with a capital letter. I wonder if Hopkins is telling us that he doesn't even know how to address his Lord? So he is devastated and he uses the language of the Crucifixion to express that 'I am gall'. He, like all depressives, despises himself: 'the curse', 'dull dough'. The poem seethes with self-disgust. The only slight glimmer for the poet is that those condemned to Hell are in a worse situation 'and their scourge to be ... their sweating selves; but worse'. Hopkins writes passionately about being human and the feeling of unworthiness. Sometimes people would say Hopkins is out of fashion, with his emphasis on sin and religion, but when I read of all the suicides today, I realise that Hopkins is describing a universal human condition, 'the deep night of the soul'.

Examiner's Comment

This is a mature personal response to the assertion that Hopkins reacts deeply and passionately to the human condition: 'The poem seethes with self-disgust'. There is also in-depth exploration of the poem's sound effects: 'The long vowel sounds in "O what black hours" give an idea of the man tossing and turning'. Vocabulary and expression are impressive, adding to a highly successful, top-grade paragraph.

N.B. Access your ebook for additional sample paragraphs and a list of useful quotes with commentary.

CLASS/HOMEWORK EXERCISES

1. 'Hopkins charts an extraordinary mental journey in the "terrible sonnets".' Give a personal response to this statement, quoting in support of your opinions.

2. Hopkins graphically explores his deep feeling of despair through light and dark imagery in 'I wake and feel the fell of dark, not day'. Pick one image of brightness and one of darkness which you considered effective and explain your choice.

SUMMARY POINTS

- Feeling of abandonment by God; spiritual suffering.
- Depressive's experience of waking into night vividly conveyed by imagery.
- Long vowel sounds and dragging repetition emphasise the prevailing darkness.
- Sense of self-disgust balanced by the poet's concluding empathy.

⑨ NO WORST, THERE IS NONE

No worst, there is none. Pitched past pitch of grief,
More pangs will, schooled at forepangs, wilder wring.
Comforter, where, where is your comforting?
Mary, mother of us, where is your relief?
My cries heave, herds-long; huddle in a main, a chief   5
Woe, world-sorrow; on an age-old anvil wince and sing –
Then lull, then leave off. Fury had shrieked 'No ling-
ering! Let me be fell: force I must be brief.'

    O the mind, mind has mountains; cliffs of fall
Frightful, sheer, no-man-fathomed. Hold them cheap   10
May who ne'er hung there. Nor does long our small
Durance deal with that steep or deep. Here! creep,
Wretch, under a comfort serves in a whirlwind: all
Life death does end and each day dies with sleep.

'frightful, sheer, no-man-fathomed'

Glossary

1	*Pitched past pitch*: pushed beyond.	8	*fell*: harsh; cruel.
2	*pangs*: sudden pains.	8	*force*: perforce; therefore.
2	*schooled at forepangs*: prepared by earlier sorrows.	12	*Durance*: endurance; determination.
3	*Comforter*: the Holy Spirit.	13	*whirlwind*: turmoil.
5	*main*: crowd.		

INITIAL RESPONSE

1. Comment on how Hopkins creates a sense of suffering and pessimism in the first four lines of the poem.

2. Discuss the effectiveness of the mountain images in lines 9–12.

3. In your opinion, is this a completely negative poem? Support your response by referring closely to the text.

STUDY NOTES

This Petrarchan sonnet was written in Hopkins' final years, at a time when he suffered increasingly from ill health and depression. It was one of a short series of sonnets of desolation, now known as the 'terrible sonnets' or 'dark sonnets'. In 'No worst, there is none', we see a man experiencing deep psychological suffering and struggling with his religious faith. The poem reveals a raw honesty from someone close to despair.

The **opening** is curt and dramatic, revealing the intensity of Hopkins' suffering: 'No worst, there is none'. He is unable to imagine any greater agony. The emphatic use of monosyllables in **line 1** reflects his **angry frustration**. Having reached what seems the threshold of torment, 'Pitched past pitch of grief', the poet dreads what lies ahead and the horrifying possibility that his pain ('schooled at forepangs') is likely to increase. The explosive force of the verb 'Pitched', combined with the harsh onomatopoeic and alliterative effects, heighten the sense of uncontrollable anguish. Both 'pitch' and 'pangs' are repeated, suggesting darkness and violent movement.

The rhythm changes in **line 3**. The three syllables of 'Comforter' slow the pace considerably. This is also a much softer word (in contrast to the harshness of the earlier sounds) and is echoed at the end of the line by 'comforting'. Hopkins' desolate plea to the Holy Spirit and the Virgin Mary emphasises **his hopelessness**: 'where, where is your comforting?' The tone, reminiscent of Christ's words on the Cross ('My God, why hast thou forsaken me?'), is both desperate and accusatory.

The poet likens his hollow cries for help to a herd of cattle in **line 5**. The metaphor highlights his lack of self-worth – his hopeless prayers 'heave' and 'huddle in a main'. He feels that his own suffering is part of a **wider universal 'world-sorrow'**. There is an indication here that Hopkins recognises that experiencing a crisis of faith can affect any Christian from time to time. This possibility is supported by the memorable image of the anvil being struck in **line 6**. He realises that the Christian experience involves suffering the guilt of sin and doubt to achieve spiritual happiness: 'on an age-old anvil wince and sing'.

But for the poet, any relief ('lull') from suffering is short lived. His unavoidable feelings of shame and the pain of remorse are hauntingly personified: 'Fury had shrieked'. Once again, the severe sounds and the stretching of the phrase 'No lingering!' over two lines reinforce the relentlessness of Hopkins' troubled conscience.

This tormented tone is replaced by a more reflective one in the opening lines of the **sestet**, where Hopkins moves from the physical world of his 'cries' into the metaphorical landscape of towering mountains, with their dark, unknown depths. This **dramatic wasteland**, with its 'no-man-fathomed' cliffs, is terrifyingly portrayed. The poet reminds us that the terror of depression and separation from God cannot be appreciated by those 'who ne'er hung there'. The terror of being stranded on the 'steep or deep' rock face cannot be endured for long.

In the **last two lines**, Hopkins resigns himself to the **grim consolation** that all the depression and pain of this world will end with death, just as everyday troubles are eased by sleep. The final, chilling image of the wretched individual taking refuge from the exhausting whirlwind is less than optimistic. There is no relief from the terrible desolation and Hopkins' distracted prayers have yet to be answered.

ANALYSIS

'Hopkins' deep despair is evident in the 'terrible sonnets'. Discuss this statement, with particular reference to 'No worst, there is none'.

Sample Paragraph

At the start of 'No worst, there is none', the tone is totally despondent. The first sentence is short and snappy, emphasising that Hopkins has reached rock bottom. Hopkins was a manic depressive and obsessed with religion. He also had issues with sexuality. In many ways he was caught between his role as a Jesuit priest and his human desires. Rhetorical questions highlight his dependence on his religious faith – 'Comforter, where, where is your comforting?' This gives a heartfelt tone. Hopkins uses effective images which always make us feel sympathy for him, for example 'My cries heave, herds-long'. His tone is sorrowful and this is emphasised by the way he uses comparisons. The prayers he offers to Heaven are just useless words which he intones: 'My cries heave, herds-long'. He goes on to compare his sense of desperate danger from sin with being trapped on a steep mountain – 'O the mind, mind has mountains'. The use of the 'O' punctuation mark emphasises the tone of desperation. The end of the poem is even more negative. Hopkins obviously had issues with his own faith in God. He uses a strong tone of despair as he compares himself to a stranded wanderer finding shelter from a 'whirlwind'. His only comfort is sleep and eventually death, which will silence his inner pain. The last line emphasises his feelings of being tired with life – 'each day dies with sleep'. The tone is of complete hopelessness.

Examiner's Comment

This response includes a number of relevant examples of the varying tones throughout. Accurate quotations are effectively used in support and there is some good engagement with the poem. The expression was slightly awkward in places: 'This gives a heartfelt tone', and there is overuse of the verb 'emphasises'. Although hard-working, the answer does not merit the highest grade.

N.B. Access your ebook for additional sample paragraphs and a list of useful quotes with commentary.

CLASS/HOMEWORK EXERCISES

1. Write your own personal response to 'No worst, there is none'. Refer closely to the text in your answer.

2. The poet feels utterly abandoned by God in this poem. Trace the development of thought in 'No worst, there is none' and discuss how Hopkins uses vivid description to explore his negative feelings. Support your answer with close reference to the text.

SUMMARY POINTS

- Most despairing and bleakest of 'terrible sonnets'.
- Alarming metaphors and powerful sound effects reveal inner suffering.
- Ups and downs of man's spiritual journey suggested by mountain imagery.
- Slightly optimistic end, death brings end to suffering for man.

⑩ THOU ART INDEED JUST, LORD, IF I CONTEND

*Justus quidem tu es, Domine, si disputem tecum: verumtamen
justa loquar ad te: Quare via imporium prosperatur? &c.*

Thou art indeed just, Lord, if I contend
With thee; but, sir, so what I plead is just.
Why do sinners' ways prosper? And why must
  Disappointment all I endeavour end?
    Wert thou my enemy, O thou my friend,   5
  How wouldst thou worse, I wonder, than thou dost
Defeat, thwart me? Oh, the sots and thralls of lust
Do in spare hours more thrive than I that spend,
Sir, life upon thy cause. See, banks and brakes
Now leaved how thick! laced they are again   10
With fretty chervil, look, and fresh wind shakes
Them; birds build – but not I build; no, but strain,
Time's eunuch, and not breed one work that wakes.
Mine, O thou lord of life, send my roots rain.

'laced they are again/With fretty chervil, look'

Glossary

Latin quotation: Indeed you are just, O Lord, if I dispute with you; yet I would plead my case before you. Why do the wicked prosper?

1   The first lines of the poem are a version of a Latin quotation that is taken from the Bible.

1   *contend*: dispute; argue; challenge.

7   *sots*: drunkards.

7   *thralls*: slaves.

9   *brakes*: thickets; groves of trees.

11   *fretty*: fretted; interlaced; the herb chervil has lacy leaves.

11   *chervil*: garden herb; the 'rejoicing leaf'.

13   *Time's eunuch*: a castrated male, incapable of reproducing.

INITIAL RESPONSE

1. List the questions put to God. What tone is evident in each – anger, rebelliousness, reverence, resentment, trust, despair, etc.?

2. Is there a real sense of pain in the poem? At what point is it most deeply felt? How does the abrupt, jerky movement of the poem contribute to this sense of pain? Quote in support of your points.

3. Is the image of God in the poem stern or not? Do you think that Hopkins had a good or bad relationship with God? Illustrate your answer with reference to this poem.

STUDY NOTES

'Thou art indeed just, Lord, if I contend' was written in 1889 at a time of great unhappiness for Hopkins in Dublin. He had written in a letter that 'all my undertakings miscarry'. This poem is a pessimistic yet powerful plea for help from God. It was written three months before he died.

This sonnet opens with the **formal language of the courtroom** as the poet, in clipped tones, poses three questions in the **octet**. With growing frustration, he asks God to explain why sinners seem to prosper. Why is he, the poet, continually disappointed? If God was his enemy instead of his friend, how could he be any worse off? God, he allows, is just, but he contends that his own cause is also just. The language is that of a coherent, measured argument: 'sir', 'I plead'. This is a contrast to the twisted, tortured grammar of the 'terrible sonnets', which echoes the deep, dark despair of the poet.

However, in **lines 3–4**, 'and why must/Disappointment all I endeavour end?', the inversion of the natural order makes the reader concentrate on the salient point that 'Disappointment' is the 'end' result of all the work the poet has done. But **the tone remains rational**, as he points out to 'sir' that the worst doing their worse 'more thrive' than he does. But his frustration at his plight makes the line of the octet spill over into the sestet, as Hopkins complains that he has spent his life doing God's will ('life upon thy cause').

The **sestet** has the ring of the real voice breaking through as he urgently requests God to 'See', 'look'. Here is **nature busily thriving**, producing, building, breeding, growing. The movement and pace of continuing growth and regrowth is caught in the line 'Now leaved how thick! laced they are again'. The **alliteration** of 'banks and brakes', 'birds build' vividly portrays the abundance of nature, as does the **assonance** of 'fretty' and 'fresh'. **Flowing run-on lines** describe the surge of growing nature. Hopkins is the exception in this fertile scene. The negatives 'not', 'no', the punctuation of semi-colon and comma and the inversion of the phrase 'but not I build; no, but strain' depict the **fruitless efforts of the poet to create**. The terrible, dramatic, sterile image of 'Time's eunuch', the castrated male, contrasts the poet's unhappy state of unsuccessful effort with the ease of fruitful nature. Time is kind to nature, enabling it to renew, but the poet cannot beget one work: 'not breed one work that wakes'.

The **last line** of the poem pleads for help and rescue. An image of a drought-stricken plant looking for life-giving water is used to describe the poet's plight of unsuccessful poetic creativity. **He looks to the 'lord of life' for release**. Hopkins had written in one of his final letters, 'If I could produce work ... but it kills me to be time's eunuch and never to beget'. It is intriguing that someone of such great faith can argue ('contend') so vehemently with God. Hopkins stretches the disciplined structure of the sonnet form to echo his frustration as he strains to create. He died unknown as a poet, his body of work not even mentioned in his obituary. But the irony is that he did create 'work that wakes'.

His friend, Robert Bridges, submitted some of his poems for an anthology of 19th century poetry and it attracted a favourable review which commented on how it possessed a 'poignant, even a passionate sincerity'. Thus, Hopkins finally found his place in the early 20th century, a time of innovation and technical experimentation. His 'roots' had been sent 'rain'.

ANALYSIS

'Hopkins' poetry deals with the theme that God's will is a mystery to us.' Discuss this statement, illustrating your response with relevant quotation from 'Thou art indeed just, Lord, if I contend'.

Sample Paragraph

How interesting to hear a man of great faith, a Jesuit priest, argue so openly and directly with God! As we see all the man-made and natural tragedies in the world, which of us has not thought, why has God allowed this to happen? Using the highly disciplined form of the sonnet, Hopkins charges

God with accusations in the form of questions. How is it that sinners 'prosper'? Why 'must/ Disappointment all I endeavour end?' The poet is frustrated, as we sometimes are; he does not know what is going on. God's will is a mystery to us. The tension at the centre of this sonnet is conveyed by Hopkins spilling the concerns of justice and morality into the sestet. He cannot contain himself. The mood of puzzlement continues in the sestet as he urgently points out ('See', 'look') how nature is thriving ('fretty chervil', 'birds build'). But he, in contrast, is not. He concludes with the striking image of himself as the sterile 'Time's eunuch', a castrated slave unable to produce. He makes one final plea to God to nourish his parched 'roots' with 'rain'. The alliteration of 'roots rain' aligns him with the fertile world of nature, 'banks and brakes'. God is the 'lord of life', his divine plan a mystery to us, but we have the capacity to pray to Him.

Examiner's Comment

Close reading of the text is evident here, particularly in the use of the rhetorical question, 'which of us has not thought, why has God allowed this to happen?' Assured use of language and accurate quotation: 'The mood of puzzlement continues in the sestet as he urgently points out ("See", "look") how nature is thriving ("fretty chervil", "birds build")'. This guarantees an impressive top grade.

N.B. Access your ebook for additional sample paragraphs and a list of useful quotes with commentary.

CLASS/HOMEWORK EXERCISES

1. Hopkins' innovative stylistic techniques make his work accessible to the modern reader. How true is this of 'Thou art indeed just, Lord, if I contend'? Use reference to the poem in your answer.

2. Hopkins complains and questions throughout this poem. What conclusion does he reach in the end? Did you find this ending satisfactory or not? Give reasons for your opinion.

SUMMARY POINTS

- Deeply personal and direct address to God.
- Hurt and frustration as poet wrestles with his religious faith.
- Struggle to control anger and frustration.
- Effective use of alliteration and vivid imagery.
- Contrast between abundance of nature and man's infertility.
- Concluding prayer to enable creativity to blossom.

LEAVING CERT SAMPLE ESSAY

'The poetry of Gerard Manley Hopkins explores twin themes of nature and religion in an innovative and dramatic fashion.' Discuss this statement, supporting your answer with suitable reference to the poetry of Hopkins on your course.

Marking Scheme Guidelines

Candidates are free to agree and/or disagree with the statement. However, the key terms, 'themes of nature and religion' and 'innovative and dramatic fashion' should be addressed implicitly or explicitly. Reward responses that show clear evidence of personal engagement with the poems.

Indicative material:

- Provocative personal views on religion, the natural world, life.
- Experimental language – sound, imagery, symbolism, sprung rhythm.
- Christian themes – finding God in nature.
- Varying tones/moods; development of traditional poetic forms.
- Fresh approaches and originality, dramatic/descriptive power, etc.

Sample Essay

(Hopkins' exploration of nature and religion in innovative, dramatic fashion)

1. *In my opinion, Hopkins is by far the most interesting and inventive of the poets I studied. As a Jesuit priest, it is hardly surprising that his personal faith in Catholicism is central to his poetry. He honestly and openly expressed himself through his poetry and that is an admirable quality. For much of the time, Hopkins focused on nature and the beauty of God's creation. His work raises questions about the Christian experience. We may not share his beliefs, but there is no doubting their sincerity. On a personal level, he openly confessed his own weaknesses. He is easy to identify with when he feels unworthy and hurt by God. His nature poems – always written in a distinctive dramatic style – are beautifully descriptive and give a great sense of the wonder of the natural world.*

2. *In the sonnet, 'Spring', Hopkins states his awe and admiration at the season of renewal. He begins with a confident arresting sentence which instantly grabs our attention. 'Nothing is so beautiful as spring'. This sense of immediacy lets us know that this is what Hopkins really believes. The urgent tone reflects his closeness to the growth that is taking place everywhere around him. Even the 'weeds in wheels shoot long and lovely and lush'. For Hopkins, all of nature is alive. This energy is echoed in the vigorous alliteration, suggesting the great range of wild plants growing untamed. Hopkins' fresh and condensed imagery seems to range over every aspect of nature – 'Thrush's eggs look little low heavens'. The simile*

associating the common shape and colour is filled with intensity, and introduces an early association between nature and the divine power responsible for creation. The octave continues with vibrant descriptions of springtime – 'The glassy peartree', 'descending blue', 'the racing lambs'. For this poet, spring is overwhelming.

3. The sestet is typical of Hopkins in that he responds to the sights and sounds that he has just outlined, making sense of the world through his Christian beliefs. It is God who created 'all this juice and all this joy. Religious references dominate as he imagines his surroundings as 'Eden garden'. The tone becomes worshipful, almost prayer-like. He urges God to maintain this natural world in all its mystery and beauty – 'before it cloy'. Like other sonnets, 'Spring' concludes in a strong declaration of Hopkins's own faith, expressing the importance of virtue and purity – 'Innocent Mind and Mayday in girl and boy'. I found the ending visionary, as though the poet truly has a religious experience – and this was one of the most compelling aspects of Hopkins' poetry.

4. 'The Windhover' also addresses the themes of God and nature. Hopkins takes delight in the bird's dramatic flight amid 'the rolling level underneath him steady air'. The childlike syntax and powerful rhythm capture the kestrel's majestic movement. As usual, the poet's sound effects reinforce the bird's immense strength – 'morning's minion', 'daylight's dauphin', 'wimpling wing'. I was very impressed by the sheer control of such intensive language. The run-through lines in the octave emphasise the 'mastery' of the falcon and Hopkins' admiration for it. As with 'Pied Beauty' and 'God's Grandeur', the poet celebrates the unique beauty and wonder of existence. The final lines of 'The Windhover' recognise the birds as Hopkins' personal 'chevalier' – or champion – a dramatic symbol of God as a medieval knight who will save him.

5. While most of the Hopkins poems I have read are notable for the poet's unique use of language, 'Felix Randal' is a more biographical account of a hard-working Christian man who was a friend and a parishioner. Yet in telling the moving dramatic story of a simple blacksmith's life and death, the poet gets to the heart of what it means to be a good Christian. The farrier's anger when faced with serious illness – 'Impatient, he cursed at first' – is soon replaced by God's 'sweet reprieve and ransom'. Hopkins uses the poem as a parable, showing how every human being must come to terms with death. Another aspect of Christian life addressed in the poem is the priest's role bringing spiritual 'comfort'. But for me, what I liked most about 'Felix Randal' was the image of Hopkins himself as a sympathetic man who combined his official clerical duties with generous friendship towards the dying blacksmith – 'seeing the sick endears them to us'.

6. Religion and nature are very closely linked in Hopkins' poetry. Although the 'terrible sonnets' reveal the poet's doubts about his faith, he is always intent on strengthening his belief in God. For the most

part, though, he clearly finds evidence of God's existence in the beauty and wonder of everyday natural surroundings. 'Inversnaid' – describing a remote area of the Scottish Highlands characterises his great love for 'the weeds and the wilderness'. In many ways, as an outdoor enthusiast, I can relate to this. Hopkins has always reminded me of the freedom and beauty of rural landscapes – and that is one of the main reasons why his poems are so enjoyable.

(approx. 825 words)

Examiner's Comment

A very solid and impressive essay, showing some close personal interaction with Hopkins' poetry. Both aspects of the question (subject matter and writing style) were tackled confidently. The overview set out in the opening paragraph, combined with occasional cross references indicated a broad knowledge of key poems. Effective used of reference and accurate quotation throughout.

MARKING SCHEME GRADE: H1
P = 14/15
C = 13/15
L = 14/15
M = 5/5
Total = 46/50

N.B. Access your ebook for additional sample paragraphs and a list of useful quotes with commentary.

SAMPLE LEAVING CERT QUESTIONS ON HOPKINS' POETRY

(45–50 MINUTES)

1. 'Hopkins uses language in a startling and unique way.' Would you agree? Discuss this view, with reference to both the subject matter and language use in the poems by Hopkins on your course.

2. 'Hopkins' innovative poetry can range from delight to despair.' Discuss this statement with reference to both the themes and language use in the poems by Hopkins on your course.

3. 'The intensity of Hopkins' complex relationship with God is often reflected in the power of his poetic voice.' Discuss this view, with reference to both the subject matter and language use in the poems by Hopkins on your course.

Sample Essay Plan (Q1)

'Hopkins uses language in a startling and unique way.' Would you agree? Discuss this view, with reference to both the subject matter and language use in the poems by Hopkins on your course.

- Intro: A personal examination is required of the imaginative, innovative techniques used by the poet, and also a reference to their purpose. These include sound effects, vivid imagery, bending words, coining new ones.

- Point 1: 'Spring' – sound effects, alliteration, assonance, onomatopoeia, run-on lines, all reflect the exuberance of springtime.

- Point 2: 'Pied Beauty' – compound words suggest dappling effect and ecstatic elation. Similarly, 'Inversnaid' also uses compound phrases to convey euphoric expressions of joy in nature.

- Point 3: 'No worst, there is none' – repetition recreates the fear of the poet as he descends into desolation as he feels abandoned by God.

- Point 4: 'The Windhover' – sprung rhythm, pushing many unstressed syllables into the line, creates a childlike enthusiasm. His patent sincerity moves us.

- Point 5: 'Felix Randal' – Contrasting views of the blacksmith and the priest suggested through alliteration, repetition, sprung rhythm, use of dialect and flashback.

- Conclusion: Like the Impressionists with paint, Hopkins with words bent his raw material into new shapes and textures so that the reader can experience the world from a unique and starling perspective.

Sample Essay Plan (Q1)

Develop one of the above points into a paragraph.

Sample Paragraph: Point 2

Hopkins loved movement rather than rest. This is evident from the poem 'Pied Beauty'. Alliteration – 'Fresh-firecoal', 'plotted and pieced', 'Fold, fallow'; assonance – 'finches' wings'; and compound words 'chestnut-falls' all celebrate the diversity of God's creation. This poem in particular reminds me of the Impressionist painters as they dabbed and speckled paint to recreate the varying light effects in nature. Hopkins uses his compound words in a similar way, 'couple-colour', 'rose-moles'. We sweep across the great patterns in nature which are 'adazzle', 'adim'. We see man working in harmony with nature, 'And all trades, their gear and tackle and trim.' There is a glorious orderly disorder, 'counter, original, spare, strange', in this 'dappled' place of God's creation, 'he fathers-forth'. Hopkins was a Jesuit and it was the custom for the Jesuit schools to start and finish their written work with praise to God. 'For the greater glory of God' is 'Glory be to God' while the ending 'Praise God always' is shortened to a more emphatic 'Praise Him'. Hopkins succeeds, in my opinion, in capturing the mystery, 'who knows what?' and the wonder, 'whose beauty is past change', of God's creation through his innovative techniques.

Examiner's Comment

As part of a full essay answer, this is a good personal response to Hopkins' techniques focusing on one of his trademarks, his use of compound words. An in-depth exploration is well supported with quotation. A top-grade answer.

N.B. Access your ebook for additional sample paragraphs and a list of useful quotes with commentary.

LAST WORDS

'What you look hard at seems to look hard at you.'

G. M. Hopkins

Hopkins is more concerned with 'putting across his perceptions than with fulfilling customary expectations of grammar'.

Robert Bernard Martin

'Design, pattern, or what I am in the habit of calling inscape is what I above all aim at in poetry.'

G. M. Hopkins

BRENDAN KENNELLY

1936–

‘Everything has a voice. The poet is used only to let the voices speak.’

Brendan Kennelly is one of Ireland's most important and popular contemporary poets. His prolific output extends to over twenty books of poetry (as well as plays, novels and literary criticism) since the publication of his first collection in 1959. His critically acclaimed collections include *Cromwell*, *The Book of Judas*, *The Man Made of Rain* and *Guff*.

He was born in Ballylongford, Co. Kerry, on 17th April 1936. He studied at the local national school and then at St Ita's College in Tarbert before reading English and French at Trinity College, Dublin. Among his early influences were Patrick Kavanagh and the American 'Beat poets', particularly Allen Ginsberg.

For more than forty years, Kennelly taught English at Trinity College, Dublin where he was Professor of Modern Literature. As writer, teacher and social commentator, he has produced work that explores the legacy of Ireland's colonial past, the place of religion in contemporary culture and politics, gender, language and the role of poets and artists.

Kennelly's poetry is densely peopled with 'voices' – a cast of named characters and personae (including inanimate objects) whose stories are told in a variety of forms from strict ballad and epic sequences to free verse and comic narrative. The poems range from warm-hearted lyricism to the bleakest desolation. At its best, Kennelly's work reflects the complexity of Irish life and provides a wonderful model for addressing it with curiosity, creativity and compassion.

INVESTIGATE FURTHER

To find out more about Brendan Kennelly, you could search some useful websites, such as YouTube, poetryarchive.org and bbc.co.uk. Also view the additional material available in your ebook, where you'll also be able to access audio of the poet reading his poems.

Prescribed Poems HIGHER LEVEL

* The poems marked with an asterisk are also prescribed for the Ordinary Level course.

[Handwritten annotations:]

Praise the simple 'joys/sights/sounds
observations
memory-present
reflection
Routine

Humans
Cherish life
+
Resiliance

1 BEGIN 🔊

Begin again to the summoning birds
to the sight of light at the window,
begin to the roar of morning traffic — *aggressive*
all along Pembroke Road.
Every beginning is a promise   5
born in light and dying in dark
determination and exaltation of springtime *resiliance.*
Positive - optimistic
flowering the way to work.
Begin to the pageant of queuing girls — *queueing to cross - patience - ritual*
beauty...semi exotic   something fresh, life goes on the same everyday.
the arrogant loneliness of swans in the canal   10
darkness
bridges linking the past and future
old friends passing though with us still.
Begin to the loneliness that cannot end
since it perhaps is what makes us begin,
begin to wonder at unknown faces   15
at crying birds in the sudden rain
at branches stark in the willing sunlight
at seagulls foraging for bread — *working-workers for money - trying to make some*
at couples sharing a sunny secret   *'dough' - homelessness.*
alone together while making good.   20
Though we live in a world that dreams of ending
that always seems about to give in
something that will not acknowledge conclusion
insists that we forever begin.

Forceful - obligation.   *resiliance*
Perseverence

'linking the past and future'

INITIAL RESPONSE

1. Briefly trace the development of thought throughout the poem. Support your answer with suitable reference to the text.

2. Comment on the effectiveness of the poet's use of repetition in the poem.

3. Write a short paragraph (at least 100 words) contrasting the images Kennelly uses of sunlight and intimacy with those of darkness and loneliness. Support your answer with suitable reference to the poem.

STUDY NOTES

Kennelly wrote 'Begin' in his fifties while recovering from heart surgery. He had radically changed his lifestyle after a series of health and personal problems. His renewed enthusiasm to live every moment to the full is evident in the poem's celebratory tone, which makes singing sense out of life's confusing experiences. Through sound, rhyme and contrast, the music of the language expresses not only actual reality but also possible reality.

The emphatic verb 'Begin' introduces an immediate uplifting movement. Nature calls through birdsong, 'the summoning birds', and sunrise, 'the sight of the light'. The adverb 'again' suggests that this need to start afresh must happen repeatedly. Kennelly skilfully employs characteristics of old Gaelic verse to add a **jaunty lilt** to the rhythm. The ecstatic **opening four lines** are filled with playful half rhyme, 'begin again', and internal rhyme (rhyming of words not at the end of the line), 'the sight of the light', to announce the wonder of the morning. This co-exists with the rush of the traffic as commuters speed to work, captured through the onomatopoeic verb 'roar'. Four steady beats mark the ballad's rhythm as the early morning rush strives headlong 'all along Pembroke Road' in Dublin.

Description gives way to reflection in **lines 5-8**: 'Every beginning is a promise'. The poet is setting out what might be, the opportunity for something better in our lives. The optimism is 'born in light' but its failure is signalled by the deadening alliteration: 'dying in dark/determination'. The mood recovers, however, rising again in acknowledgement of the new season – 'exaltation of springtime'. Kennelly was educated in a formal Roman Catholic ethos. The religious connotations of this echoes in his use of 'exaltation' to express such high praise. It is further amplified by the personification of spring, 'flowering' the route to work. The energy and dynamism of the new year blooms. The city workers no longer trudge along on their daily routine, but move through an avenue of spring blossom. Run-on lines convey the forward movement of the young season, the rush towards hope. Through his intent gaze, **the ordinary has become extraordinary**. The overwhelming sense of delight pays homage to another Irish poet, Patrick Kavanagh, who had also written about celebrating the wonder of creation through innocent eyes.

Line 9 invites the reader once more to start again. Literal observation captures the **familiar images** of early morning Dublin. The common sight of female workers queuing for buses is re-defined by the descriptive noun 'pageant'. Their beauty is transformed into something elaborate and dramatic. It's as though a public entertainment is taking place, an elegant procession in elaborate costume. This theatrical image is matched by nature, 'the arrogant loneliness of swans' – the broad vowel assonance highlighting the aloof character of the birds as they glide under canal bridges. For a moment, the intense stillness reminds Kennelly of the sad 'passing' of 'old friends'. This adult experience of death and loss now replaces the joyful wonder of earlier lines. Yet the poet feels these friends remain 'with us still' in memory. Kennelly has said: 'When we write of loneliness, even of what might feel like despair, we discover that there is in language a kind of resilience, a surging hopeful energy that is redemptive and reassuring'.

In **line 13**, the poet advises: 'Begin to the loneliness that cannot end/since it perhaps is what makes us begin'. The run-through **lines 15-20** convey the spiritual excitement that stimulates and intensifies this sense of wonder. It resurges in a series of urgent images that 'makes us begin'. Subtle internal rhyme ('wonder' and 'unknown') heralds the process of looking at strangers and guessing their story. **Contrast is used to convey the harshness and optimism** of the new season. Harsh-sounding discordant consonants ('crying birds', 'sudden rain', 'branches stark', 'foraging seagulls') evoke the stridency and competitiveness of nature. Yet these co-exist with images of warmth, expressed through musical language and soft alliteration ('willing sunlight', 'sharing a sunny secret'). Playfully, the poet acknowledges the presence of human nature – 'couples sharing a sunny secret' completely at ease in their own world.

The **last four lines** conclude with the mature awareness of inevitable endings, 'give in', 'conclusion'. But this dark mood is challenged by the statement 'something ... insists that we forever begin'. The assonance of the slender vowel 'i' draws attention to the idea that there is some unknown force that encourages people to keep going. This poem ends as it starts – with the word 'Begin'. To a great extent, Kennelly has addressed the mystery of time itself. All beginnings and endings can be seen as metaphors for birth and death. By its very nature, life is transitional, yet human beings have an innate urge to be resilient and to cherish life.

ANALYSIS

'Kennelly's poems shape and articulate our most joyous and troubling moments.' To what extent is this true of 'Begin'? Support your answer with reference to the poem.

Sample Paragraph

Brendan Kennelly believes 'Poetry discovers, protects and celebrates the deepest values of the heart'. In 'Begin', he voices our strongest fears of loneliness, partings and death. However, he places these beside the optimism of nature. Despite its harsh aspects, 'seagulls foraging for bread', nature is always ready to 'begin', 'summoning birds'. In this carefully crafted poem, Kennelly asks us to acknowledge the reality of life, 'old friends passing', 'a world that dreams of ending'. The dull alliterative phrase 'dying in dark/determination' conveys life's sorrow. Yet run-on lines capture the unstoppable force of life. Personification lifts the ordinary sight of girls queuing for a bus into participants in a spectacular 'pageant'. Using the old Gaelic poetic techniques, Kennelly creates a poem that almost sings with joy through the assonance of slender vowels, 'the sight of the light at the window', the repetition of the broad vowel sounds, 'wonder at the unknown faces'. I particularly liked the final lines, which close with the cruel truth of mortal life, 'ending', 'give in' and 'conclusion'. But Kennelly shatters such dark thoughts with the little verb 'begin'. Indeed, the repetition of this verb throughout the poem and the steady four beat rhythm of the ballad echo the beat of life in this life-affirming poem.

Examiner's Comment

A clear, focused response that shows a very close understanding of the poem. Impressive awareness of the poet's language use (particularly sound effects) throughout. Quotations are used to support key points and the expression is varied and well controlled. While some further analysis of contrast would have been useful, this is a very confident top-grade answer.

N.B. Access your ebook for additional sample paragraphs and a list of useful quotes with commentary.

CLASS/HOMEWORK EXERCISES

1. 'Kennelly's tender lyric poetry evokes a sense of wonder in his reader through his use of imagery and sound.' Discuss this statement with particular reference to 'Begin'.

2. 'Kennelly's adventure in words and rhythms effectively conveys light and dark, hope and despair.' Discuss this view, with reference to the poem, 'Begin'.

SUMMARY POINTS

- Kennelly often addresses the essential mystery of existence.
- Human resilience and the refusal to give up are central themes.
- Natural images carry the poem's contrasting views of life.
- Effective use of simple language, everyday sights, intricate sound effects.
- Variety of tones – optimistic, realistic, exciting, inspiring, etc.

craftsmanship - skill
Passion,

Personified the bread
Give it a voice - living, breathing
vital relationship.

2 BREAD 🔊

Wheat - brutal necessity:

value -

Someone else cut off my head   timeless
In a golden field. beauty.   mutual dependence
Now I am re-created - growth   & gentleness.
energy - intimacy   breathing - creating the bread.
individuality. ritualistic.
By her fingers. This
Moulding is more delicate tender.   5
Than a first kiss, ritualistic sacred.
remember it - joy - rush of blood

More deliberate than her own purpose.
Rising up   commitment, devoted   ritual
And lying down.

I am fine quality worth   10
As anything in
This legendary garden. plentiful, scope of possibilities
epic

Yet I am nothing till lives b. it
She runs her fingers through me fluid.   moulding life
And shapes me with her skill. recognition admiration   15
Passionate

The form that I shall bear organic development.
Grows round and white. Pure.
It seems I comfort her fulfilment, reassurance.

Even as she slits my face   cruel to be kind - like his Mother.
And stabs my chest.   20
Her feeling for perfection is will not fail.

Absolute. completion, undisputed, unwavering.
So I am glad to go through fire sacrifice, will do anything to please them.
And come out belief.

Shaped like her dream.   25
In my way
I am all that can happen to men.
I came to life at her finger-ends.
I will go back into her again.

Cycle of life
influence of people - h shape

ANALYSIS

It has been said that Kennelly's poetry 'moves from the here-and-now to the mystical'. To what extent is this evident in his poem 'Bread'?

Sample Paragraph

The setting in Kennelly's poem 'Bread' is not in the least out of the ordinary. Remembering his grandmother at work in the kitchen would suggest a simple nostalgic poem, but this is not how the poet presents the scene. By giving the bread its own 'voice', Kennelly transcends the ordinary, making it extraordinary. He gives the wheat a consciousness as though it were a living person – 'Now I am re-created'. The poet develops this intriguing idea of 'permanent beginning' when the voice of the dough-mix takes over the narration, reacting to the woman's touch as she 'shapes me'. It seems that everything and every person has a spiritual life and that there is a constant state of change in this 'legendary garden' or heavenly existence. The bread will 'go through fire' to reach 'perfection'. Kennelly's memory of bread-making becomes a mystical exploration of the mysteries of the universe. Just as the wheat 'suffered' to become bread, human souls must endure pain on earth for spiritual fulfilment. The ending of the poem is optimistic. 'I will go back into her again' suggests the soul's progress as part of the natural cycle.

Examiner's Comment

This is a very good top-grade attempt at tackling a challenging question, focusing well on how Kennelly uses the domestic scene to explore a spiritual theme. The notion of development and 'permanent beginning' is a very effective point. Commentary is effectively supported by apt (and accurate) quotations. Expression is clear and very well controlled throughout.

N.B. Access your ebook for additional sample paragraphs and a list of useful quotes with commentary.

CLASS/HOMEWORK EXERCISES

1. 'Brendan Kennelly uses evocative language to create poems that are deeply reflective.' To what extent is this true of 'Bread'? Support your answer with reference to the poem.

2. Comment on the use of contrasts in this poem, referring closely to the text in your answer.

SUMMARY POINTS

- Simple family theme – a woman is making bread and the bread is 'speaking'.
- Other themes include: time, change, the natural cycle, creativity and continuity.
- Contrasting moods, everyday imagery, use of extended metaphor.
- Resonant narrative voice creates a dreamlike atmosphere.

[handwritten top annotations:]
besotted
inspired
enchanted /under her spell
obsessed.
muses over her.
captivates.

bewitched
fascinated.
mesmerised.
worship
engulfed.
in awe.

enthralled.
ensnared.
hypnotised.

3 'DEAR AUTUMN GIRL' 🔊

[handwritten:] Diary quote? cherishing memory. why autumn? ~~cher~~ beauty, crisp, fleeting. temporary, ~~regretting~~

(*from* Love Cry)

[handwritten:] Delight - spontaneous, fun-fair, untamed

Dear Autumn girl, these helter-skelter days,

[handwritten:] insane, senseless, intoxicated, over-whelmed.

When mad leaf-argosies drive at my head,

[handwritten:] words are inadequate

I try but fail to give you proper praise

For the excitement you've created

In my world: an islander at sea,   5

[handwritten left margin:] a story to unfold.

A girl with child, a fool, a simple king,

Garrulous masters of true mockery *[handwritten:]* -superfluous

My hugest world becomes the littlest thing

[handwritten:] Simplifies life - Basic - makes everything small.

Whenever you walk smiling through a room

[handwritten:] fresh, unpolished

And your flung golden hair is still wet *[handwritten:]* goddess, worship. 10 seductive.

Ready for September's homaged rays;

I see what is, I wonder what's to come,

I bless what you remember or forget

And recognise the poverty of praise. *[handwritten:]* trite - too superficial, cant express what he feels

'Ready for September's homaged rays'

Glossary

1 *helter-skelter*: chaotic, hurriedly.

2 *leaf-argosies*: leaves like a fleet of rich merchant ships.

7 *Garrulous*: talkative, long-winded.

INITIAL RESPONSE

1. In your opinion, is the 'Autumn girl' an effective symbol for poetic inspiration? Briefly explain your answer, referencing the text.

2. Choose two images from the poem that appeal to you and comment on their effectiveness.

3. Write your own personal response to the poem, referring closely to the text in your answer.

STUDY NOTES

Brendan Kennelly's poetry collection Love Cry: The Kerry Sonnets *(1971) contains forty-eight beautifully composed, affirmative love sonnets, including '"Dear Autumn Girl"'. Kennelly has commented that at the time, the sonnet form got so deeply embedded inside his head that for around three years, he could write nothing but sonnets. In this poem, he addresses the subject of poetic inspiration – something that is very close to his heart.*

A buoyant tone is immediately struck in the **opening lines** with the tender address to 'Dear Autumn girl', the representation of Kennelly's poetic muse. The **chaotic rush** of golden, tumbling autumn leaves is vividly evoked in the run-on lines, 'these helter-skelter days/When mad leaf-argosies drive at my head'. The use of the vibrant compound word, 'helter-skelter', reinforces the glorious, 'mad', haphazard nature of the season. For Kennelly, the falling leaves are as precious as rich merchant ships bearing priceless cargo, spinning rapidly towards the poet's mind. The monosyllabic verb 'drive' catches their relentless descent. Is this the force, the delight, that gives rise to poetry?

In a confessional **third line**, the poet admits his futile attempt to do justice to the inspiration: 'I try but fail'. While the monosyllabic verb 'try' suggests his effort, the disconsolate word 'fail' trails weakly. Kennelly is aware that mortal man is prone to failure in his attempts to give 'proper praise' to his muse. The alliterative, explosive 'p' effect forces the reader to exert effort in pronouncing the phrase, thereby **mimicking the poet's own struggle to write**. Use of the adjective 'proper' reveals Kennelly's attempts to celebrate his beautiful 'Autumn girl' in an appropriate ladylike fashion. He believes that literature is something to be celebrated rather than criticised and he is grateful for the gift of 'excitement', the thrill and pleasure that literature has produced in his world. Elsewhere, he has described his poetic talent as 'a gift that took me unawares/And I accepted it'.

Lines 5-6 list some of the **characters and personae** brought into existence by Kennelly's poetic muse. First, there is the outsider ('an islander at sea') with whom he shares that experience. As a very young child, Kennelly was sent to live with his aunt for eighteen months. He later commented,

'I do think that an experience like that leaves you feeling a bit of an outsider'. The follow-up image of Our Lady is equally resonant: 'A girl with child'. In his poetry, Kennelly often adopts the critical stance of the jester of barbed jibes, 'a fool'. Such a persona is similar to the bitter-sweet Fool in Shakespeare's *King Lear*, someone who speaks the truth by questioning and challenging. Kennelly's poetry also examines 'a simple king', one who does not consider the consequences of his actions.

In **line 7**, he even **pokes fun at himself** through the onomatopoeic adjective, 'Garrulous'. Kennelly had a reputation as a raconteur and has admitted: 'I want to write poetry that is capable of containing … this kind of self-critical laughter'. He believed that there was too much self-importance in the world. The comic sense forbids us from taking ourselves too seriously, but it also unleashes scathing utterances against pomp, falsehood and self-regarding ego. It's not surprising that so much of his poetry (which he refers to elsewhere as a 'house of voices') states, pleads, commentates and confesses.

The **octet** flows seamlessly into the sestet. Kennelly loosens the restricting order of the Petrarchan sonnet in the same way as the flurry of autumn leaves were unleashed by the wind. His 'Autumn girl' has flung her 'golden hair'. Now, when she gifts him with creativity ('Whenever you walk smiling through a room'), he becomes intensely aware, sensitised to 'the littlest thing'. His muse has provided the inspiration and awaits his praise, 'September's homaged rays'. The poet now understands something of the mystery that has occurred, 'I see what is', but even more importantly for the artist, **his sense of astonishment has been stirred**, 'I wonder what's to come'. He is happy to accept any inspiration that might come his way and he is keen to show gratitude for the creative impulse – which he acknowledges in religious terms: 'I bless what you remember or forget'.

In the **concluding lines** Kennelly comments wryly on his poetic efforts. Although he wished to be more appreciated, he has only been able to achieve 'poverty of praise'. He is deeply self-critical of his inadequate attempts to glorify his 'Dear Autumn girl'. Autumn is the season of maturity and abundance. She has provided plentiful well-developed ideas and stimulus. Yet there is **one final irony**: the romantic outsider has succeeded in creating a tender lyric poem of rhythmical elegance. The poet has displayed his craft in combining its flowing iambic pentameter and abab, cdcd rhyme scheme from the sonnets of Shakespeare, the octet/sestet form of the Petrarchan sonnet and his own unique rhyme scheme in the sestet, efg, efg. His original compound word, 'leaf-argosies' and the image of his dream woman (the 'Autumn girl') all add to the originality of his affectionate tribute to poetic inspiration.

ANALYSIS

'Brendan Kennelly's poetry is distinctive, memorable and powerful.' To what extent is this true of '"Dear Autumn Girl"'? Support your answer with reference to the poem.

Sample Paragraph

'"Dear Autumn Girl"' is a distinctive sonnet addressed to Kennelly's muse or source of artistic inspiration. His distinct combination of various elements from the sonnet creates a new and fresh take on the 14-line classic form. He divides his poem on the Petrarchan model of an octet and sestet, yet he allows one to flow into the other, 'My hugest world becomes the littlest thing/Whenever you walk smiling through a room'. Inspiration can strike at any time, it is not confined. He uses the Shakespearean octet rhyme scheme, yet adds Gaelic half-rhyme 'head', 'created'. His original rhyme scheme for the sestet adds to his unique version of the sonnet form. However, it is the poem's imagery that makes it so memorable. The swirl of dancing autumn leaves, 'mad leaf-argosies', are echoed in the 'flung golden hair … still wet' of the 'Autumn girl'. In my opinion, Kennelly does create a poem of 'proper praise' for her. The poem's power lies in the ability of the poet to be self-critical, 'I try but fail', 'Garrulous', 'I … recognise the poverty of praise'. We can easily empathise with his self-deprecation because we all wish we could have done better in meeting life's challenges. Through his viewpoint, style and content, Kennelly has created a distinctive, memorable and powerful poem that reveals the inner vitality of his words.

Examiner's Comment

A successful top-grade response that explores interesting aspects of a challenging poem, with some well-focused discussion about Kennelly's 'unique version' of the sonnet form. Other effective points deal with imagery and the poet's self-criticism. Some good use of quotation reflects a close knowledge of the poem. Expression is impressive throughout.

N.B. Access your ebook for additional sample paragraphs and a list of useful quotes with commentary.

CLASS/HOMEWORK EXERCISES

1. Comment on the effectiveness of Kennelly's use of rhyme in this poem, referring closely to the text in your answer.

2. 'Kennelly's poetry has been described as an adventure in words and rhythms, in images and dreams.' In your opinion, how true is that view in relation to the poem, '"Dear Autumn Girl"'? Support your response with reference to the text.

SUMMARY POINTS

- Innovative adaptation of the sonnet form.
- The mysterious power of artistic inspiration is a central theme.
- Startling visual imagery and use of an extended metaphor.
- Rhythmic iambic pentameter and distinctive rhyme patterns.
- Varied tones: upbeat, reflective, self-critical, appreciative, etc.

4 POEM FROM A THREE YEAR OLD 🔊

And will the flowers die?

And will the people die?

And every day do you grow old, do I
grow old, no I'm not old, do
flowers grow old?   5

Old things – do you throw them out?

Do you throw old people out?

And how you know a flower that's old?

The petals fall, the petals fall from flowers,
and do the petals fall from people too,   10
every day more petals fall until the
floor where I would like to play I
want to play is covered with old
flowers and people all the same
together lying there with petals fallen   15
on the dirty floor I want to play
the floor you come and sweep
with the huge broom.

The dirt you sweep, what happens that,
what happens all the dirt you sweep   20
from flowers and people, what
happens all the dirt? Is all the
dirt what's left of flowers and
people, all the dirt there in a
heap under the huge broom that   25
sweeps everything away?

Why you work so hard, why brush
and sweep to make a heap of dirt?
And who will bring new flowers?
And who will bring new people? Who will   30
bring new flowers to put in water

where no petals fall on to the
floor where I would like to
play? Who will bring new flowers
that will not hang their heads   35
like tired old people wanting sleep?
Who will bring new flowers that
do not split and shrivel every
day? And if we have new flowers,
will we have new people too to   40
keep the flowers alive and give
them water?

And will the new young flowers die?

And will the new young people die?

And why?   45

'the petals fall'

Glossary

25 *broom*: sweeping brush.   38 *shrivel*: wither and shrink.

INITIAL RESPONSE

1. Choose one visual image from the poem and briefly comment on its effectiveness.

2. From your reading of the poem, what do you learn about the relationship between the poet and his young daughter? Refer to the text in your response.

3. In your opinion, is this an optimistic poem? Support your answer with reference to the text.

STUDY NOTES

Kennelly's love of the sense of newness and his enthusiasm for the essential strangeness of people and things are central to 'Poem from a Three Year Old' in which he paraphrases a child's intimations of mortality. He has commented: 'One night, my three-year-old daughter was noisily refusing to sleep, screaming her little head off, in fact. I brought her downstairs to the living-room and tried to have a chat with her. A vase of flowers stood on the table. Petals were falling from the flowers. She said, "What are these?" "Petals," I replied. "Why are they falling?" she asked. "Because the flowers are dying," I answered. She was quiet for a while and then the questions began to pour out of her.'

This poem begins in the voice and language of a very young child: 'And will the flowers die?' While the direct simplicity of the stand-alone **first line** is characteristic of **childhood wonder**, the follow-up question strikes a more startling note: 'And will the people die?' The line-break with its in-built pause emphasises the actual thought process. This is the moment when the infant is coming into contact with the grown-up world, raising a universal reality that is likely to be more disquieting to her adult father than it is to her.

The directness of the child's language seems to fascinate Kennelly. Her additional series of questions in **lines 3-5** are couched in a highly animated personal tone: 'do you grow old, do I/ grow old, no I'm not old'. The **broken syntax and insistent rhythm** reflect the intense activity of her young mind, eagerly trying to make sense of the real world. Three further questions (**lines 6-8**) indicate a new train of thought about what happens to 'Old things' and – even more puzzling for her – 'old people'. Innocence and reason come together in the impatient pursuit of answers: 'And how do you know a flower that's old?'

Lines 9-18 dramatise the spirit of play, the incessant questioning, and the moments of wonder intrinsic to childhood. The infant's innately chaotic thoughts and feelings are expressed in a **dreamlike internal monologue** characterised by an absence of regular punctuation. In the middle of the torrential questioning about decaying flowers, the child suddenly returns to her natural state of cheerfulness. Random syntax and diction ('flowers and people all the same/together lying there') create a surreal mood. Yet the central idea is repeatedly stated: 'I want to play'.

The **exuberant interrogative tone** continues through lines 19-26 – but with the focus on 'all the dirt'. In exploring childhood consciousness, Kennelly reminds us that the strangeness of everyday life is usually taken for granted by adults. Unlike children, our curiosity is destroyed by familiarity and experience. While his daughter's concerns might seem foolish at first, she is much more aware of what is going on around her, regardless of how trivial her observations might appear.

Throughout **lines 27-42**, the child turns her attention to the future: 'And who will bring new flowers?' She reveals an **intuitive compassion** not just for the vulnerability of nature, but for human nature: 'And who will bring new people?' In her engaging vision of an ideal existence, she imagines being able to play forever in a timeless world where flowers 'will not hang their heads/ like tired old people wanting sleep'. Such an ingenuous dream unleashes her profound vitality with its emphasis on freshness – 'new flowers', 'new people'.

Despite her instinctive optimism, the child is still aware that she has touched on more serious aspects concerning life and death. The resonant tone of the **last three lines** makes it clear that she retains some of her earlier unease about the cycle of life: 'And will the new young people die?' The poem ends as it began – with a much more general, **fundamental question** ('And why?') that gets straight to the heart of the mystery and wonder of creation.

Many of Kennelly's early poems address **the strange sensation of being alive** and an awareness of being part of a universal spirit. The poet has stated: 'I like to write about children, especially about their talk because they say very wise things and ask very strange and wonderful questions. And also they love to play in the middle of it all frequently. So asking questions and loving to play – I sometimes think that's what education should be about'.

ANALYSIS

In your opinion, how successful is Brendan Kennelly in conveying the authentic voice of a young child in this poem? Support your answer with reference to the text.

Sample Paragraph

The child's innocent voice dominates this poem. The simple diction and haphazard word order is exactly the way young children speak. It's not just the endless questions, but the language itself that is so true to life – 'Why you work so hard'. The poet presents readers with the disorganised thoughts of the young child who mixes up various topics – age, flowers, waste, playing, work, etc. What better way of expressing the child's sense of wonder? Kennelly also structures the poem effectively to capture the hectic rhythms of the child's voice. Using run-on lines and omitting punctuation marks allows the voice to be heard without interruption.

Everything is a mystery for small children who are discovering new things all the time. I found it interesting that the child kept comparing flowers with people. She has an understanding of the beauty and fragility of flowers – and is saddened when 'petals fall on to/ the floor'. I liked the concluding line, 'And why?', as it summed up every little child's natural inquisitiveness. There was even a sense that she knew she was now the centre of attention and was playfully testing her father's knowledge of the world.

Examiner's Comment

This is an assured top-grade response that tackles the question directly by examining both what the child says and how Kennelly uses language to convey her 'voice'. Succinct, supported points highlighting syntax and diction are particularly effective. Expression is confident throughout and the paragraph ends on an interesting note.

N.B. Access your ebook for additional sample paragraphs and a list of useful quotes with commentary.

CLASS/HOMEWORK EXERCISES

1. Trace the changing tones throughout the poem, supporting your answer with close reference to the text.

2. 'Kennelly's poems can sometimes appear simple, but they often have layers of underlying meaning.' Discuss this view, with particular reference to 'Poem from a Three Year Old'.

SUMMARY POINTS

- Key themes include time, the natural cycle and essential mystery of life.
- Effective use of simple language, rhythm, repetition and vivid imagery.
- Conveys the authentic 'voice' of the child throughout.
- Variety of tones – inquisitive, concerned, reflective, playful, bitter-sweet, etc.

Private/Personal
+
The public Role

5 OLIVER TO HIS BROTHER 🔊 *Faith*

Loving brother, I am glad to hear of your welfare
And that our children have so much leisure
They can travel far to eat cherries.
This is most excusable in my daughter
Who loves that fruit and whom I bless.   5
Tell her I expect she writes often to me
And that she be kept in some exercise.
Cherries and exercise go well together.
I have delivered my son up to you. *Biblical overtone, religious overtone.*
I hope you counsel him; he will need it;   10
I choose to believe he believes what you say.
I send my affection to all your family.
Let sons and daughters be serious; the age requires it. *need to be tough*
I have things to do, all in my own way.
For example, I take not kindly to rebels.   15
Today, in Burford Churchyard, Cornet Thompson
Was led to the place of execution.
He asked for prayers, got them, died well.
After him, a Corporal, brought to the same place
Set his back against the wall and died. *minimalistic*   20
A third chose to look death in the face,
merciless. Stood straight, showed no fear, chilled into his pride. *resent him*
Men die their different ways
And girls eat cherries
In the Christblessed fields of England.   25
Some weep. Some have cause. Let weep who will. *distancing himself from it all*
Whole floods of brine are at their beck and call.
I have work to do in Ireland.

'I have work to do in Ireland'

Glossary

1   *Loving brother:* Extract from letter sent by Oliver Cromwell to his brother, Richard Mayor, Bristol, 19th July, 1649.

... I am very glad to hear of your welfare, and that our children have so good leisure to make a journey to eat cherries: it's very excusable in my Daughter; I hope she may have a very good pretence for it. I assure you, Sir, I wish her very well; and I believe she knows it. I pray you tell her from me I expect she writes often to me; by which I shall understand how all your Family doth, and she will be kept in some exercise. I have delivered my Son up to you; and I hope you will counsel him: he will need it; and indeed I believe he likes well what you say, and will be advised by you. I wish he may be serious; the times require it. I hope my sister is in health; to whom I desire my very hearty affections and service may be presented; as also to my cousin Ann, to whom I wish a good husband. I desire my affections may be presented to all your Family, to which I wish a blessing from the Lord. I hope I shall have your prayers in the Business to which I am called ...

1   *welfare*: well-being.

9   *delivered*: entrusted.

10   *counsel*: advise.

16   *Burford Churchyard, Cornet Thompson*: Three leaders of the rebel soldiers known as the 'Levellers' (including Captain Cornet Thompson) were executed on the orders of Cromwell. Extract from contemporary book, *The Works of Thomas Carlyle*:

This day in Burford Churchyard, Cornet Thompson ... was brought to the place of execution, and expressed himself to this purpose: That it was just what did befall him; that God did own the ways he went; that he had offended the General: he desired the prayers of the people; and told the soldiers who were appointed to shoot him, that when he held out his hands, they should do their duty.

28   *work to do in Ireland*: The Cromwellian conquest of Ireland, or Cromwellian war in Ireland (1649–53), refers to the conquest of Ireland by the forces of the English Parliament, led by Oliver Cromwell, in order to crush the Royalists who wished to restore an English monarchy and who were allied with the Irish Catholic Confederation. Cromwell landed in Ireland with his New Model Army on 15th August, 1649, promising to carry on 'the great work against the barbarous and blood-thirsty Irish'.

INITIAL RESPONSE

1. In your opinion, what kind of impact does the poet achieve by using so much of Cromwell's actual correspondence in the poem? Support your answer with close reference to the text.

2. Based on your reading of the poem, were you surprised by any aspects of Cromwell's character? Briefly explain your response.

3. Write a short personal response to the poem, referring closely to the text in your answer.

Brendan Kennelly's comic-grotesque epic, Cromwell (published in 1983) is a book-length poem comprised of many smaller poems, in various discursive modes (letter, newspaper article, history, legend, folktale and fantasy). Yet all share an angry focus on the nature of human brutality. Kennelly reimagines the complex persona of Cromwell, a man blamed for barbaric violence against the people of Ireland. The poet taunts the reader with the story of the realist statesman against whom hopeless visionaries strike. This bold attempt to dramatise the savage complications of Irish history delighted and scandalised readers. Seamus Heaney chose it as his book of the year (1983), speaking of a 'sense of outbreak' – something that is difficult to pin down.

Brendan Kennelly's poetry often gives a voice to others and otherness. In this poem, closely based on Oliver Cromwell's original letter to his brother, Kennelly reinvents one of Ireland's most reviled figures of hate. Cromwell's affectionate address to his 'Loving brother' seems somewhat unexpected. The poet broadens the traditional Irish view of Cromwell the monster into a multi-dimensional figure – a concerned parent and courteous brother. Indeed, the tone throughout the **opening section** portrays **a warm and generous character**, 'I am glad to hear of your welfare'. Run-on lines convey the fond father, 'our children have so much leisure/They can travel far to eat cherries'. He is softly indulgent of his young daughter and concerned that she keeps in contact with him, 'Tell her I expect she writes often to me'. Like most fathers, he dotes on his child and is worried about her happiness.

A slightly **sterner tone emerges** (**line 9**) in discussing his son's welfare. Cromwell asks his brother to advise his son, whom he clearly thinks is in need of instruction: 'I choose to believe he believes what you say'. But he is also considerate in wishing his brother's family well: 'I send my affection to all your family'. At this point, the narrative voice changes even more as Cromwell begins to focus on English society at large: 'Let sons and daughters be serious; the age requires it'. These were certainly changing times. The flamboyant and artistic monarch, Charles I, had just been defeated by Cromwell and his Model Army.

Over the course of the next sixteen lines, however, a different Cromwell emerges. Here is the methodical, calculating politician and assured leader, 'I have things to do, all in my own way'. The plain monosyllabic line reflects his blunt Protestant mindset. Cromwell had ordered the execution in Burford Churchyard of several leaders of the Levellers movement in 1649: 'I take not kindly to rebels'. The short staccato statement shows his lack of compassion with one of these, Cornet Thompson, the only officer to be named in the poem. Yet Cromwell's detached sense of **military honour** is evident in his obvious regard for an enemy soldier who 'died well'.

The anonymous 'Corporal' mentioned in **line 19** also faced death bravely: 'Set his back against the wall and died'. A third rebel was equally prepared to 'look death in the face'. The alliterative phrase, 'Stood straight', emphasises his fearlessness while the verb, 'chilled', reflects his steely composure. We are left in no doubt about Cromwell's cold professionalism when dealing with the rebels. In **line 23**, he explains his handiwork, 'Men die their different ways'. The pounding alliterative 'd' effect suggests the sound of the executed men falling to the ground.

But Kennelly is realistic about the fleeting nature of military history, reminding us that people get on with their everyday lives, 'And girls eat cherries'. The rich rolling 'r' contrasts the warm pulse of life with the cold finality of death. There is more than a little **irony** in the deeply religious Cromwell's reference to his new English society. The bland compound description, 'Christblessed fields', conveniently glosses over the suffering Cromwell has caused. Apart from the token acknowledgement – 'Some weep. Some have cause', the sense of expediency dominates: 'Let weep who will', and the tears of his countless victims are dismissed as 'floods of brine'. Kennelly makes it clear that the pragmatic Cromwell was intent on solving the problem of his restless military force by distracting them with a campaign in Ireland that would allow them to acquire wealth and land for resettlement, 'I have work to do in Ireland'.

The detached military leader's unsettling statement in the **final line** is in marked contrast with the loving father's earlier humanity. Throughout this poem, the varied rhythms and tones of Cromwell's voice insinuate themselves into the mind and psyche of readers, so that we are forced to question assumed perceptions of this complex man. As always, Kennelly is the bardic puppet-master controlling not only the performance of his characters onstage, but also the reactions of his audience. He challenges us to question, but provides few answers.

ANALYSIS

Brendan Kennelly's poetry gives expression to 'voices out of history' to 'deepen and extend the self'. To what extent is this evident in his poem, 'Oliver to His Brother'? Support your answer with reference to the text.

Sample Paragraph

Kennelly often speaks even from the mind of hate-filled figures from history such as the reviled Oliver Cromwell who was responsible for so much bloodshed and suffering in Ireland. The poet captures his authoritative voice, 'I have things to do in my own way'. His lack of empathy is seen in his account of the executions of the leaders of the failed revolt against him, 'Men die their different ways'. His capacity to unnerve is evident in his dismissal of suffering in the clipped line, 'Some weep. Some have cause. Let weep who will.' But Kennelly also asserts the humanity of this man whom so many regarded as a cold-blooded monster. The loving father of the private Cromwell is developed in the tender run-on lines, 'This is most excusable in my daughter/Who loves that fruit and whom I bless'. Through the picture that develops of an anxious father and a polite brother, 'I send my affections to all your family', Kennelly forces us to have a plural response to history. He challenges our complacency of a received image and compels us to consider the wider human condition. Cromwell can speak of 'Christblessed lands' and also still remark, 'Whole floods of brine are at their beck and call'. Cromwell's mature formal register is repellant, but his warm human tones engage.

Examiner's Comment

A very assured high-grade response to a challenging question. Focused points address the way in which Kennelly's presentation of Cromwell forces readers to reassess their views and 'have a plural response'. Despite some errors in the quotations, the paragraph included effective analysis of language use.

N.B. Access your ebook for additional sample paragraphs and a list of useful quotes with commentary.

CLASS/HOMEWORK EXERCISES

1. 'Kennelly is an investigative poet who wishes to understand the complexity of historical characters.' Discuss this view, with particular reference to the poem, 'Oliver to His Brother'.

2. 'Brendan Kennelly's evocative use of language is ideally suited to his disturbing subject matter.' To what extent is this true of 'Oliver to His Brother'? Support your argument with reference to the text.

SUMMARY POINTS

- Private letter format – hearing Cromwell's actual words creates intimacy between reader and subject.
- Repetition of first person highlights self-regarding assurance of Cromwell.
- Contrasting tones (warm, human, cold, methodical, pragmatic, dismissive) develop the image of this multi-dimensional character.
- Reliance on real documentation brings an air of authenticity to this bold endeavour.

- essence of a memory, captured in simple, unadorned effective language
- Truth is captured in accessible language, reflecting the value of the memory
- The sentiment is simple: affection, fondness. The simple language is fitting.

Brendan Kennelly 209

* use of enjambement
fluid
* present tense

6 I SEE YOU DANCING, FATHER 🔊

No sooner downstairs after the night's rest
And in the door
Than you started to dance a step
In the middle of the kitchen floor.   Centre of the house for himself

And as you danced
You whistled.   making your own music, inner content/own identity
You made your own music
Always in tune with yourself.

Well, nearly always, anyway.   10 Stark acceptance of Mortality
You're buried now   simplicity   loss
In Lislaughtin Abbey   Sharp juxtaposition / contrast
And whenever I think of you

I go back beyond the old man   another stark contrast
Mind and body broken   15
To find the unbroken man.   former youthful self
It is the moment before the dance begins,   preparation, anticipation

Your lips are enjoying themselves
Whistling an air.   realising the past and whats gone
Whatever happens or cannot happen
In the time I have to spare   reflects, keeping 20 him close, sentimental.
I see you dancing, father.

Lislaughtin Abbey

Conversational
intimate
warm
familiar
at ease
wholesome.

INITIAL RESPONSE

1. What is your impression of the poet's relationship with his father? Support your answer with suitable reference to the poem.

2. Select one visual image from the poem that shows Kennelly's eye for close observation. Comment briefly on the effect of your chosen image.

3. Write a short personal response to the poem, explaining its impact on you.

STUDY NOTES

Brendan Kennelly's parents owned a pub at the village crossroads in Ballylongford, where he and his six siblings sang, told stories and exchanged banter with the local men and women. Unsurprisingly, North Kerry resurfaces in many of his most compelling poems. Indeed, the family kitchen – the primal place of familial relationships – was also the home of Kennelly's poetic imagination. 'I See You Dancing, Father' centres around the fragment of the poet's fondest memory of his father. To a great extent, however, this bittersweet tribute is essentially about how we choose to remember the dead.

The poem's title introduces an immediate **sense of celebration**. Kennelly chooses to set aside all morbid thoughts of death and insists on remembering his father in his prime. This note of defiance is developed in the **opening stanza** as he recalls his extrovert father at his happiest – the centre of attention – 'dancing in the middle of the kitchen floor'. The run-on lines and lively rhythm create a relaxed, playful mood. Kennelly's use of the present tense allows him relive the past. He addresses his father directly: 'You started to dance'. There is little doubt that the poet has made a decision to highlight the positive aspects of his father's happy-go-lucky nature rather than criticise him for sleeping late or behaving irresponsibly. The slightly petulant tone ('No sooner downstairs ...') suggests that Kennelly's father had a habit of behaving like a mischievous child.

The energetic vocabulary of **stanza two** ('danced', 'whistled', 'music', 'tune') adds to the exuberant atmosphere and helps to define the father's carefree personality. Kennelly's unmistakable sense of awe is present in the easy image of his father naturally breaking into a traditional solo dance (*damhsa ar an sean nós*) and stepping out to his own whistling. The poet cannot hide his feelings of admiration for someone who clearly lived life on his own terms – 'Always in tune with yourself'. The pun seems ideally suited to such a colourful character.

Yet Kennelly is realistic about his father – 'Well, nearly always, anyway' – and checks himself from idealising him as a man without faults. The tone changes in **stanza three** with the **stark** acceptance of mortality and loss: 'You're buried now/In Lislaughtin Abbey'. In contrast with the earlier lines, the pace becomes sluggish, slowed by the use of commas and half-rhymes. This creates an unsettling sense of pathos. Short lines and broad vowel assonant sounds match the sombre mood, quietly conveying the son's unspoken grief.

But the air of sorrow is soon replaced with an emphatic pledge to acknowledge his father's happy life: 'I go back beyond the old man'. **Stanza four** reveals the poet's crucial choice to focus on preserving his memory of 'the unbroken man'. Kennelly's determination in catching the timeless image of 'the moment before the dance begins' challenges death and mourning. In this ecstatic instant of anticipation, neither father nor son can ever grow old. Even if it is illusory, it marks a **momentary triumph**, celebrating their close relationship.

Stanza five illustrates the beauty and simplicity of the reminiscence as the poet delights in imagining his father's presence again: 'Your lips are enjoying themselves'. The **detailed personification** has a surreal quality that is both uplifting and unnerving. For Kennelly, all that he can still hold dear is this curious image of his father whistling. The poet communicates his feelings subtly, by suggesting his love for his father rather than stating it directly. In the **final three lines**, he returns to the present and accepts the poignant reality of coping and grieving 'In the time I have to spare'. Faced with the inevitability of death, he prefers to make the most of life – just as his father did.

Dance is a central motif in this heartfelt love poem – with its distinct echoes of Patrick Kavanagh's elegies. From the start, Kennelly makes characteristic use of a crisp, pared-down language – a distinctive style that is always a model of melodious clarity. The rhythmical elegance of expression captures the movement into dance when the poet's father truly became himself. Throughout 'I See You Dancing, Father', the **uninhibited nostalgia and tender lyricism** typify Brendan Kennelly's extraordinary enthusiasm for life.

ANALYSIS

'Kennelly's most personal poems are filled with deeply felt sentiment which never lapses into sentimentality.' To what extent is this true of 'I See You Dancing, Father'? Support your answer with reference to the poem

Sample Paragraph

The respectful title, 'I See You Dancing, Father', sets the tone of this compassionate poem. Kennelly takes a narrative theme to remember the fondest memory he has of his late father and how he must move on after his death. The initial picture of the poet's father is not all positive – as a man who preferred dancing to hard work 'after a night's rest'. But Kennelly's true feelings are seen in his appreciation: 'You made your own music'. There is nothing false about the poet's feelings. Without being over-emotional, he makes a conscious decision to remember a loved one who celebrated the bright side of life. While the son feels unconditional love, he refuses to become sentimental about his father's good behaviour – which was only 'nearly always'. Kennelly does not shy away from the fact that the old man became sick – 'Mind and body broken' – but he will always recall the good times – 'the moment before the dance begins'. The poem is caring, but it is also rooted in the real world. The way the memory was mixed with reality impressed me and showed that Kennelly can be sincere.

Examiner's Comment

This is a reasonably focused response that maintains a focus on the poet's attitude and feelings. Quotations are used to support points and the expression is generally controlled. More detailed analysis of tone and language use would have improved the standard from a solid middle grade.

N.B. Access your ebook for additional sample paragraphs and a list of useful quotes with commentary.

CLASS/HOMEWORK EXERCISES

1. 'Brendan Kennelly's most heart-rending poems often highlight the twin themes of love and loss.' Discuss this statement with reference to 'I See You Dancing, Father'.

2. 'Kennelly's deceptively simple language in "I See You Dancing, Father" is ideally suited to his emotional subject matter.' Discuss this view, with reference to the poem.

SUMMARY POINTS

- Memory, family love and the celebration of life are central themes.
- Dancing used as a symbol of the father's life and the poet's enduring love.
- Effective use of simple language, energetic verbs and vivid imagery.
- Variety of tones – nostalgic, realistic, reflective, loving, etc.

7 A CRY FOR ART O'LEARY 🔊

(from the Irish of Eibhlín Dubh Ní Chonaill)

My love
The first time I saw you
From the top of the market
My eyes covered you
My heart went out to you   5
I left my friends for you
Threw away my home for you

What else could I do?

You got the best rooms for me
All in order for me   10
Ovens burning for me
Fresh trout caught for me
Choice meat for me

In the best of beds I stretched
Till milking-time hummed for me   15

You made the whole world
Pleasing to me

White rider of love!

I love your silver-hilted sword
How your beaver hat became you   20
With its band of gold
Your friendly homespun suit
Revealed your body
Your pin of glinting silver
Glittered in your shirt   25

On your horse in style
You were sensitive pale-faced
Having journeyed overseas
The English respected you
Bowing to the ground   30
Not because they loved you
But true to their hearts' hate

They're the ones who killed you
Darling of my heart

My lover   35
My love's creature
Pride of Immokelly
To me you were not dead
Till your great mare came to me
Her bridle dragging ground   40
Her head with your startling blood
Your blood upon the saddle
You rode in your prime
I didn't wait to clean it
I leaped across my bed   45
I leaped then to the gate
I leaped upon your mare
I clapped my hands in frenzy
I followed every sign
With all the skill I knew   50
Until I found you lying
Dead near a furze brush
Without pope or bishop
Or cleric or priest
To say a prayer for you   55

Only a crooked wasted hag
Throwing her cloak across you

I could do nothing then
In the sight of God
But go on my knees   60
And kiss your face
And drink your free blood

My man!
Going out the gate
You turned back again   65
Kissed the two children
Threw a kiss at me
Saying 'Eileen, woman, try

To get this house in order,
Do your best for us   70
I must be going now
I'll not be home again.'
I thought that you were joking
You my laughing man

My man!   75
My Art O'Leary
Up on your horse now
Ride out to Macroom
And then to Inchigeela
Take a bottle of wine   80
Like your people before you
Rise up
My Art O'Leary
Of the sword of love

Put on your clothes   85
Your black beaver
Your black gloves
Take down your whip
Your mare is waiting
Go east by the thin road   90
Every bush will salute you
Every stream will speak to you
Men and women acknowledge you

They know a great man
When they set eyes on him   95

God's curse on you Morris,
God's curse on your treachery
You swept my man from me
The man of my children
Two children play in the house   100
A third lives in me

He won't come alive from me

My heart's wound
Why was I not with you
When you were shot   105
That I might take the bullet
In my own body?
Then you'd have gone free
Rider of the grey eye
And followed them   110
Who'd murdered me

My man!
I look at you now
All I know of a hero
True man with true heart   115
Stuck in a coffin
You fished the clean streams
Drank nightlong in halls
Among frank-breasted women

I miss you   120

My man!
I am crying for you
In far Derrynane
In yellow-appled Carren
Where many a horseman   125
And vigilant woman
Would be quick to join
In crying for you
Art O'Leary
My laughing man   130

O crying women
Long live your crying
Till Art O'Leary
Goes back to school
On a fateful day   135
Not for books and music

But for stones and clay

My man!
The corn is stacked
The cows are milking   140
My heart is a lump of grief
I will never be healed
Till Art O'Leary
Comes back to me

I am a locked trunk   145
The key is lost
I must wait till rust
Devours the screw

O my best friend
Art O'Leary   150
Son of Conor
Son of Cadach
Son of Lewis
East from wooded glens
West from girlish hills   155
Where rowanberries grow
Yellow nuts budge from branches
Apples laugh like small suns
As once they laughed
Throughout my girlhood   160
It is no cause for wonder
If bonfires lit O'Leary country
Close to Ballingeary
Or holy Gougane Barra
After the clean-gripping rider   165
The robust hunter
Panting towards the kill
Your own hounds lagged behind you
O horseman of the summoning eyes
What happened you last night?   170
My only whole belief
Was that you could not die
For I was your protection

My heart! My grief!

My man! My darling!   175

In Cork
I had this vision
Lying in my bed:
A glen of withered trees
A home heart-broken   180
Strangled hunting-hounds
Choked birds
And you
Dying on a hillside
Art O'Leary   185
My one man
Your blood running crazily
Over earth and stone

Jesus Christ knows well
I'll wear no cap   190
No mourning dress
No solemn shoes
No bridle on my horse
No grief-signs in my house
But test instead   195
The wisdom of the law
I'll cross the sea
To speak to the King
If he ignores me
I'll come back home   200
To find the man
Who murdered my man

Morris, because of you
My man is dead

Is there a man in Ireland   205
To put a bullet through your head

Women, white women of the mill
I give my love to you
For the poetry you made
For Art O'Leary   210
Rider of the brown mare
Deep women-rhythms of blood
The fiercest and the sweetest
Since time began
Singing of this cry I womanmake   215
For my man

'I miss you'

Glossary

Art O'Leary (1746-73) from Irish Roman Catholic gentry, captain in Hungarian Hussars regiment of Empress Maria Theresa of Austria.

Eibhlín Dubh Ní Chonaill (Eileen O'Connell) was the Irish noblewoman wife of Art O'Leary. She was born in 1743 and died in 1800.

1   *My love*: lament was composed extempore (as an impromptu lament) by Eibhlín, mourning her young husband's death and calling for revenge.

7   *Threw away my home for you*: her parents were opposed to the marriage.

20   *beaver hat*: fur hat; Penal laws demanded payment to the British Crown for wearing a gentleman's hat.

22   *homespun*: plain, unpretentious.

37   *Immokelly*: reference to Art O'Leary's lineage from lords of Athenry.

40   *bridle*: buckled straps used to control horse.

48   *frenzy*: turmoil, passion.

78   *Macroom*: Rattleigh House near Macroom, Co. Cork was O'Leary's home.

79   *Inchigeela*: small Co. Cork village with beautiful landscapes.

96   *Morris*: Abraham Morris, Protestant sheriff of Cork.

101   *A third lives in me*: Eibhlín is pregnant with their third child.

123   *Derrynane*: Co. Kerry village named after Daniel O'Connell ('Liberator of Irish people') and nephew of Eibhlín Dubh Ní Chonaill.

124   *Carren*: Small region near the Burren, Co. Clare.

131   *crying women*: professional keeners who wept at funerals.

156   *rowanberries*: red berries from rowan trees.

163   *Ballingeary*: village in the Co. Cork mountains.

206   *bullet through your head*: Morris was eventually shot by Art O'Leary's brother.

INITIAL RESPONSE

1. Based on your reading of the poem, what impression do you get of Art O'Leary? Support your answer with reference to the text.

2. Choose one image from the poem that you found particularly interesting and briefly explain your choice.

3. Write your own personal response to the poem, highlighting the impact it made on you.

BACK STORY

The hot-tempered Art O'Leary became involved in a feud with an arrogant Englishman, Abraham Morris of Hanover Hall, Macroom, Co. Cork. The Englishman demanded that Art sell to him a beautiful brown mare that he had brought back with him from Austria. The Penal Laws stated that no Catholic could own a horse worth more than five pounds and so could be forced to sell it at that price to any Protestant. When Art refused to sell, Morris used his position as magistrate to proclaim O'Leary an outlaw who could then, legally, be shot on sight. On 4th May, 1773, he tracked O'Leary to Carraig an Ime where one of Morris's soldiers shot and killed Art.

STUDY NOTES

'A Cry for Art O' Leary' is a translation by Brendan Kennelly of the Irish lament, 'Caoineadh Airt Uí Laoghaire', which was published in his collection Love of Ireland *(1989). Kennelly, a native Irish speaker, believed that a good verse translation 'is also a completely new, autonomous poem in English'. The purpose of translation, he felt, was to deconstruct and reconstruct. He regarded himself as a version-maker rather than translator. Frank O'Connor, Thomas Kinsella and Eilis Dillon, among others, have also translated this famous Irish elegy.*

This poem has been called the 'greatest poem written in these islands in the whole of the eighteenth century' by Peter Levi, Professor of Poetry at Oxford University. It was composed by Art O'Leary's wife (Eileen of the Raven Hair) and recited on the spot where he lay murdered. This lament for her dashing young husband of twenty-six is a traditional **caoineadh** or keen from the oral tradition of Irish literature, a song of the dead performed by women at a wake. It is divided into three parts: the salutation calls upon the deceased with affection ('My love'); the dirge or keen praises the character ('sensitive'), virtues ('great man'), achievements ('hero'), lineage ('Son of Conor') and dreams ('vision'); and the third section focuses on the declaration of an enemy ('Morris').

The **language** of the keen is clear, direct and plain, 'I miss you'. It is people's poetry. This poem explores one individual's personal loss of a loved one. The young widow's passionate feelings for her flamboyant husband ring with a haunting, time-defying force. The poem's momentum is unimpeded by punctuation marks, except for those conveying her grievous sense of loss, 'My heart! My grief!'

Eibhlín speaks directly to the reader (**lines 1-7**) reciting her **thrilling first encounter** with her good-looking husband, 'My eyes covered you/My heart went out to you'. It was certainly love at first sight. She refers to the price she paid for this love, forsaking friends and family, but a wistful rhetorical question intones: 'What else could I do?' The young woman was so intoxicated with the handsome Hussar that she had no will of her own. Their idyllic romance is evoked through **lines 9-18**. The gentle repetitive 'm' sound in 'Till milking-time hummed for me' recalls the harmony of their life together. She obviously worships her young husband, 'White rider of love'.

Lines 19-25 portray in a series of telling details **Art O'Leary in his prime** with his 'silver-hilted sword' and 'beaver hat' with its 'band of gold'. At this time, under Penal Laws, a gentleman's hat could only be worn if a payment was made to the ruling British Crown. Eibhlín refers to Art's impressive army service, 'having journeyed overseas'. The first inclination that the young woman had of her husband's murder was the arrival of his blood-stained horse. This riderless horse is not only a messenger of death, but also an emblem of the political vacuum in a country without a true leader. Her anguished reaction is caught in the explosive verb 'leaped'. From this point onwards, the poem's form is one headlong rush encompassing a single breathless thought – her husband's murder. Tragically, she finds Art 'Dead near a furze bush' without having had any proper funeral rites. Burial in monastic ground was forbidden under Penal Law. Alone and agitated, she performs her own personal funeral rites.

Lines 63-74 poignantly relate the couple's **final meeting**. Art has asked Eibhlín to get 'this house in order', prophetically remarking, 'I'll not be home again'. Ironically, she believed that her 'laughing man' was only joking. In her distress, she now exhorts her dead husband to return to life and ride out where all may greet him: 'Men and women acknowledge you' (**line 93**). This memory of how great a man he had been causes her to explode with anger and she utters a curse against his enemy, Abraham Morris, who ordered the killing. The brutal finality of Art's death is highlighted in **line 98**, 'You swept my man from me'. Equally upsetting is the heartbreaking picture of their two children innocently playing, still unaware that they are fatherless. A further tragic consequence is to follow – the loss of their unborn child.

The frantic widow berates herself for not being with Art so that she could have been killed instead of him. Then she would most certainly have been avenged by her husband. But now she has to deal with his murder, its stark reality related in the cacophonous phrase, 'Stuck in a coffin' (**line 116**). This **dreadful sight** contrasts sharply with what he had once been, 'True man with true heart', someone who lived life to the full. Eibhlín's simple admission, 'I miss you', reaches across the ages to touch the reader. She urges the keeners to mourn Art in the alliterative 'Long live your crying' and she recounts with pride how she has kept their house in order, 'The corn is stacked/ The cows are milking' (**line 139**). But she remains overcome by unhappiness and the powerful metaphor, 'My heart is a lump of grief' palpably communicates her profound sorrow. A second comparison emphasises the sense of resignation, 'I am a locked trunk' – which will heal only through the passing of time, 'I must wait till rust/Devours the screw'.

Lines 150-153 describe Art O'Leary's fine lineage, 'Son of Conor'. The fertile Irish landscape is detailed through internal rhyme of the broad 'ow' ('rowanberries grow') and alliteration ('Yellow nuts budge from branches'). Personification enlivens the simile, 'Apples laugh like small suns'. In the meantime, bonfires continue to mourn Art's passing. Eibhlín still cannot fully understand what has happened. She shares a **nightmare vision** that she had of 'withered trees'. Graphic description transmits the horrific violence and devastation: 'Strangled', 'Choked', 'crazily'. Yet she refuses to mourn, preferring to seek justice, 'I'll cross the sea/To speak to the King'.

This determined widow decides that if she gets no satisfaction, then she alone will hunt whoever 'murdered my man' (**line 202**). Her desire for vengeance could hardly be clearer as she imagines the single bullet that will end Morris' life. A more formal, dignified tone emerges as she thanks the keening women ('I give my love to you') for their protestations. She reverts to the **strong force within women** that enables them to withstand terrible sorrows, communicated through original compound words, 'women-rhythms' and 'womanmake'. Through this impressive plaintive lament, Eibhlín herself has just created a tremendous elegy for her dead husband.

In translating the work of other writers, Kennelly illuminates people and events by absorbing them and allowing the language of his sources to pass through him to his readers. He offers up these stories for us to interpret and in so doing preserves them for posterity. In this poem, the raw grief and frustration of a young wife is caught in the **tonal complexity**, which ranges widely from misty-eyed remembrances to vivid accounts of action and anger, to scenes of heart-rending sorrow, deep curses and quiet dignity.

Kennelly's version of this 18th-century lament presents all the torment of one woman's personal heartache after the sudden death of the man she loves and whose name continually haunts her. Aching tenderness, a furious wish for retribution, pleas for justice, pride and reassurance in the continuities of family are all expressed through remarkable imagery. The poet has listened to the **voice of the young widow** and conveys her reactions to human cruelty in the subtle interwoven harmonies of alliteration and internal rhyme.

The strength of Eibhlín's feeling is shown by the perfection of the poetic technique. This narrative epic confirms not only confidence in the essential dignity and greatness of man but also **celebrates the feminine ability to love** in all its sublime blossoming, vigour and maturing. The poem succeeds in communicating what it means to grieve over loss in all its sadness and rage. It also proves the ability of woman to suffer and survive, to 'womanmake' and endure.

ANALYSIS

'Brendan Kennelly's translations encompass the spirit of the original work to let it sing.' Discuss this view, with particular reference to 'A Cry for Art O'Leary'.

Sample Paragraph

In this traditional ballad, 'A Cry for Art O'Leary', Kennelly describes the harrowing consequences of Art's brutal murder. We see the heroic husband, the beautiful Irish landscape, the warm love between Eibhlín and Art, and a wife's powerful feelings. Through the use of the aural poetic techniques of old Gaelic poetry and the traditional keening chant rhythm, Kennelly's translation really lets the poem sing. The couple's idyllic marriage is conveyed through assonance, 'You made the whole world/Pleasing to me'. The style and vitality of the handsome husband is found in the slender vowels, 'Your pin of glinting silver/Glittered in your shirt'. Sweeping rhythm adds to the choral effect of the old keening voices expressing grief at a funeral. Harsh consonants contrast sharply with the detailed description of the Irish landscape in the alliterative line, 'Yellow nuts budge from branches'. The explosive 'b' sounds echo the new year's fresh growth. Kennelly's use of compound words ('womanmake') shows how women have always survived sorrow and concludes the poem with musical language.

Examiner's Comment

An impressive top-grade response that shows close engagement with the poem. The introductory overview is clearly developed with well-supported discussion points. These include some incisive comments on various poetic techniques, such as rhythm, sound effects and the use of compound words. Reference and quotation are highly effective throughout. Expression is particularly good – varied, lively and controlled.

N.B. Access your ebook for additional sample paragraphs and a list of useful quotes with commentary.

CLASS/HOMEWORK EXERCISES

1. 'The ferocity of people's feelings is coupled with an awesome control of language in Kennelly's poetry.' Discuss this view, with particular reference to 'A Cry for Art O'Leary'.

2. 'Kennelly's poetry raises disturbing perspectives about the human condition in ways that challenge readers.' To what extent is this true of 'A Cry for Art O'Leary'? Support your answer with reference to the poem.

SUMMARY POINTS

- Central themes include love, loss, grieving, relationships, memory, anger and acceptance.
- Simple direct language, vivid imagery, lack of punctuation.
- Hypnotic tone and keening rhythm add to the sense of pathos.
- Poem's structure based on the traditional form of the Irish lament.
- Varied moods and tones: shock, tenderness, nostalgic reverie, personal outrage, vengeance concluding in immense dignity.

8 THINGS I MIGHT DO 🔊

I thought of things I might do with my heart.
Should I make it into a month like October,
A chalice for the sad madness of leaves
That I might raise in homage to the year's end?

Should I make it into a small white church in   5
A country-place where bells are childhood prayers?
Or a backroom of a brothel in Dublin
Where the trade of somethinglikelove endures?

Should I make it a judge to judge itself?
Or a caring face in a memory-storm?   10
Or a bed

For Judas dreaming of the tree:
     'There now, there now, rest as best you can,
     Darling, rest your treacherous head
     And when you've rested, come home to me.'   15

'the sad madness of leaves'

Glossary

3   *chalice*: wine cup used in religious ceremonies.   14   *treacherous*: false, deceptive.
4   *homage*: honour, praise.

INITIAL RESPONSE

1. Over the course of the poem, Kennelly explores emotions through a series of metaphors. Choose the metaphor that you think is most interesting. Give at least one reason for your choice.

2. Describe the mood in the last three lines of the poem. Refer to the text to support your answer.

3. In your opinion, what is the central theme or message in this poem? Support your answer with suitable reference to the text.

STUDY NOTES

Brendan Kennelly's The Book of Judas *(published in 1991) explores the theme of betrayal at various levels. Many of the poems bring Judas' story to life in a modern context by addressing the failings of Irish society. The central character is an elusive figure who takes numerous forms.*

In the poem's **opening lines**, the unnamed speaker is initially concerned with the 'heart' and finding ways of expressing emotion. The plaintive question: 'Should I make it into a month like October?' has a poignant quality. The month marks the transition from autumn into winter's bitter weather. Kennelly introduces another metaphor for feelings in **line 3**, using the religious image of lifting up a chalice to give thanks for another year. **The narrative voice is downbeat**, however, focusing on 'the sad madness of leaves'. The wistful description is filled with onomatopoeic effects: internal rhymes echo the chaos in nature while sibilant 's' sounds accentuate the narrator's tone of quiet dejection. Does the 'year's end' offer any good reason for celebration?

Lines 5-9 present a stark contrast between the simple fulfilment of youthful Christian faith (symbolised by 'a small white church') and the loss of innocence in later adult life. The seedy image, 'a backroom of a brothel in Dublin', illustrates the loneliness of people seeking a substitute for genuine human connection. To highlight the irony, Kennelly **experiments with the layout** of the poem. The self-created compound word, 'somethinglikelove', makes an immediate visual impact on the page, simulating the close physical contact of the anonymous sexual encounters endured in 'the trade'.

The efforts to come to terms with the speaker's entangled emotional life continue in **line 9** with another pertinent suggestion: 'Should I make it a judge to judge itself?' The **self-critical tone** challenges the 'heart'. Can an individual's own feelings be fully trusted? Are they sometimes selfish or false – even based on self-betrayal? This disturbing possibility is immediately countered with a much more consoling interpretation of human emotions: 'a caring face in a memory storm'.

The poem's **final lines** envision a disturbing scene featuring **conflicting experiences of guilt and compassion**. The speaker imagines the outcast Judas recalling his crucial role in bringing about Christ's death on the cross. The self-destructive deceiver is 'dreaming of the tree' while another tender voice tries to console him: 'there now, rest as best you can'. Shame, regret, forgiveness and concern amalgamate in the well-worn words of comfort – but the startling inclusion of 'rest your treacherous head' is an unnerving reminder of the consequences of betrayal.

Throughout this reflective poem, moments of tender lyricism have been undermined by Kennelly's bleak vision of modern life. The **bitterly articulate narrative voice** presents readers with a disturbing irony. Just like Judas, every human being is capable of a variety of feelings – both sympathetic and destructive. In the end, individuals have to face up to the reality of their emotional behaviour – 'and when you've rested, come home to me'. They must then live with themselves and the truth about all their relationships. The poem's conclusion offers no hint of salvation, leaving the original question about what to 'do with my heart' almost entirely unresolved.

ANALYSIS

'Brendan Kennelly writes hauntingly powerful poems that make an immediate impact on readers.' Discuss this statement, with particular reference to 'Things I Might Do'.

Sample Paragraph

I thought the mood in 'Things I Might Do' was tense and edgy, especially at the end where it seems that Judas, the apostle who betrayed his friend Jesus, is being pampered by someone in his family. The idea of somebody close to Judas being so supportive is disturbing. I was surprised by the paradox, 'Darling, rest your treacherous head'. The whole poem has the sense of a dying person's bucket list. At the start, the imagery is mainly about death, 'madness of leaves' in October and 'the year's end'. Kennelly struggles with his feelings as if he fears the future and is sorry about the past. He suggests making his heart into a judge 'to judge itself'. This is another alarming thought as if he is feeling self-loathing. Everyone experiences remorse at times, a feeling of sadness about something said or about a serious mistake that you have made. Overall, this was a very thought-provoking poem that made me ask questions about how we can hurt other people's feelings.

Examiner's Comment

A solid middle-grade response that includes some close personal engagement and good points on imagery. Effective use is made of accurate quotations. More analysis of the poet's use of language (memorable comparisons, introspective tone, etc.) would have raised the standard.

N.B. Access your ebook for additional sample paragraphs and a list of useful quotes with commentary.

CLASS/HOMEWORK EXERCISES

1. 'Soul-searching and existential anguish are recurring features of the poetry of Brendan Kennelly.' Discuss this view, with particular reference to the poem, 'Things I Might Do'.

2. 'The casual force that energises Kennelly's language use is a key characteristic of his poetry.' To what extent is this true of 'Things I Might Do'? Support your answer with reference to the poem.

SUMMARY POINTS

- Kennelly raises incisive questions about people's emotional lives and relationships.
- Effective use of metaphors, rhetorical questions, contrasts and layout.
- Dreamlike atmosphere and sense of timelessness.
- Range of tones: inquisitive, reflective, self-critical, confessional, etc.

Simple, accessible, conversational tone.

⑨ A GREAT DAY 🔊

She was all in white.

An uninterrupted flow of thoughts and feelings through the poets mind

Snow
Suggests itself as metaphor

But since this has been so often said
I may be justified in considering it dead.   5
Something about snow is not quite right.

memory.

Therefore, she was all in white.   *Purity innocence*

He was most elegant too
All dickied up in dignified blue.

alliteration + internal rhyme   sum up his appearance

They came together, as is habitual   10
In that part of the world,
Through a grave ritual,

Listening
With at least a modicum of wonder –
What God has joined together   15
Let no man put asunder.

Man in woman, woman in man.
Soon afterwards, the fun began.

*false faces,
temporary.*

It was a great day –
Long hours of Dionysiac festivity.   20

Songs poured out like wine.
Praises flowed as they had never done.

The people there
Seemed to see each other in a new way.
This added to the distinction of the day.

attention is drawn to the extraordinary significance of the reception through alliteration

And all the time she was all in white
Enjoying every song and speech
Enjoying every sip and bite.

Use of repetition.

not true

Such whiteness seems both beautiful and true
He thought, all dickied up in dignified blue.   30

He looks so good in blue *role reversal*
(This warmed her mind) *Commenting on him.*
Blue suits him *chosen for him*
Down to the ground.

At the table where they sat   35
Things seemed to fit.

losing touch with reality
dont want to return to life *Will see the emptness & vulnerability*
And the loud crowd sang and danced   *Suspended reality*
The whole day long, the whole night long. *afraid to stop*
There could never be anything but dance and song. *dragging out.*

hesitation --regret
needs to change- I must change, she whispered,   40
dosent want to I must change my dress. *amidst all noise*
not comfortable *She whispers*
He never saw the white dress again. —*stark shift*

In the train, the trees wore their rainy veils
With a reticent air.

daily life.
It's good to get away, she whispered, *small talk*   45
Touching her beautiful hair.

think/escape/relax/holding onto it
She closed her eyes, the trees were silent guests,
A tide of thoughts flowed in her head,
In his head.

reassuring them both
'Darling, it was a great day,' she said. *Convincing*   50
'beautiful and true' *herself*

Pathetic Fallacy - When a poet describes a persons mood through weather/landscape.

Glossary

3   *metaphor*: describing somebody or something using a vivid comparison.
9   *dickied up*: well dressed.
10 *habitual*: usual, expected, customary.
12 *grave*: solemn, ominous.
12 *ritual*: ceremony, sacrament.
14 *modicum*: small amount.

14 *wonder*: surprise, doubt.
16 *asunder*: apart, in bits.
20 *Dionysiac*: relating to Dionysus, Greek god of wine and fertility.
25 *distinction*: special importance, excellence.
44 *reticent*: silent, uncommunicative.

INITIAL RESPONSE

1. In your opinion, what expectations does the poet raise in the reader by the use of the title, 'A Great Day', and are these expectations fulfilled? Support your answer with close reference to the poem.

2. Choose one image from the poem that appealed to you and comment on its effectiveness.

3. Write a short personal response to the poem, referring closely to the text in your answer.

STUDY NOTES

'A Great Day' forms part of Brendan Kennelly's collection, Familiar Strangers: New and Collected Poems (1960–2004). *The poet himself arranged this 'collection of voices' into thematic, rather than chronological, sections. 'Looking back over the poems I've tried to write, they all seemed to be moments, or stabs of memory, or sudden images, and seemed independent of chronological time,' he observed.*

Kennelly offers a thought-provoking **portrait of a wedding** in his poem, 'A Great Day'. It takes the form of a stream of consciousness (an uninterrupted flow of thoughts and feelings through the poet's mind). The poem begins with a familiar visual image, 'She was all in white'. White is traditionally worn by brides and suggests purity, innocence, a new beginning. The poet dismisses the familiar cliché of snow as a metaphor to describe this colour, 'since this has been so often said/I may be justified in considering it dead'. Run-on lines and a banal rhyme scheme ('said', 'dead') emphasise the hackneyed reference. 'Poetry,' according to Kennelly, 'is an attempt to cut through the deadening familiarity and repeated mechanical usage' of language.

Suddenly an unrhymed line produces an air of mystery, 'Something about snow is not quite right' (**line 6**). The poet challenges the reader to consider what is not quite right about the comparison. In a stand-alone line, he chooses to record his simplified solution to the dilemma,

'Therefore, she was all in white'. In **line 8**, attention turns to the groom. Alliteration, internal rhyme and a rhyming couplet sum up his appearance, 'He was most elegant too/All dickied up in dignified blue'. The syntax is as carefully arranged as the groom is scrupulously turned out. But the colloquial expression 'dickied up' strikes an almost **comical note**, particularly when linked through assonance with 'dignified'. It would seem as though the groom is not accustomed to being so formally dressed.

The official marriage ceremony is presented as a **connecting experience**, 'They came together'. The bride and groom have embraced tradition, 'as is habitual/In that part of the world,/Through a grave ritual'. The adjective 'grave' (**line 12**) suggests a solemn occasion, echoing an earlier reference to 'dead'. This casts a shadow on the happy event. The steady rhyme ('habitual' and 'ritual') point to the importance of keeping up appearances. A further unsettling note from the wedding liturgy is introduced in **line 15**, 'What God has joined together/Let no man put asunder'. The ominous adverb 'asunder' reminds the reader of what happens when a marriage breaks down – everything joyous is left smashed into pieces. The newlyweds appear to be slightly bemused by all the formalities but listen intently, 'With at least a modicum of wonder'. Is there a suggestion of last minute doubts? If so, they are soon forgotten and the prospect of forging two separate individuals into one is cleverly summed up in the well-balanced line, 'Man in woman, woman in man'. The couple's acceptance of their newly wedded state calls for celebration, 'Soon afterwards, the fun began'.

Everyone **rejoices in the marriage ceremony** because it ensures the continuation of society, so it truly is 'a great day' (**line 19**). Broad vowelled assonance, 'Long hours', echo the lengthy celebrations, so full of over-indulgence and lack of inhibition that the poet describes the festivities as 'Dionysiac', referring to the Greek god of wine and fertility. The lavishness and excess is conveyed in the simile, 'Songs poured out like wine' and in the assonance, 'Praises flowed as they had never done'. All the wedding guests reach new levels of perception, 'The people there/Seemed to see each other in a new way'. Attention is drawn to the extraordinary significance of the reception through the alliterative phrase, 'distinction of the day'. For Kennelly, love is the impetus that demands and enables the self to express and receive. The bride's beautiful appearance, 'And all the time she was all in white', appears to be the catalyst for the outpouring of joy. Repetition and alliteration in the run-on lines draw attention to her willing participation, 'Enjoying every song and speech/Enjoying every sip and every bite' (**line 27**).

The groom's thoughts are also recorded – and he is enchanted by his lovely bride, 'Such whiteness seems both beautiful and true'. In turn, she is delighted with her new husband, 'He looks so good in blue'. The couple sit together and 'Things seemed to fit'. Yet the **reader is left feeling increasingly uneasy**. Short lines contain glib comments ('Blue suits him'). The couplet in **lines 35-36** obviously does not rhyme, ('sat', 'fit'). But once again, the reader is distracted by the noise of the party, 'And the loud crowd sang and danced/The whole day long, the whole night long'. Caught up in the excitement, they lose all touch with reality: 'There could never be anything but dance and song' (**line 39**).

The **mood alters dramatically** when the bride changes her dress. In a simple stand-alone line, the groom states: 'He never saw the white dress again.' Did the magic also go out of the relationship? Was the fairytale over so soon? Pathetic fallacy accentuates the strangely subdued mood, 'the trees wore their rainy veils/ With a reticent air' (**line 43**). An atmosphere of diffidence, secrecy and reserve replaces the boisterous wedding party. The bride's personality also changes, no longer delighted to enjoy 'every sip and every bite', but instead becoming more self-obsessed, 'It's good to get away, she whispered,/Touching her beautiful hair'.

In **line 47**, she retreats even more, 'She closed her eyes'. There is an underlying sense that the couple have been actors who have just played their parts in a **public performance**. But at least the noisy party-goers are now replaced by the contrasting trees as 'silent guests'. The newly-weds retreat into their own private worlds, 'A tide of thoughts'. She appears to reach out to her new husband in the **concluding line**, '"Darling, it was a great day," she said'. Is the tone enthusiastic or half-hearted? Is the new bride simply saying what she is expected to say? Might there be an ironic acceptance that the future will not be quite so wonderful?

The poet has succeeded in challenging readers to consider the difficulty facing two people, two separate entities actually becoming one. As always, **Kennelly's poetry examines and questions the world we live in**, confronting personal weaknesses in human behaviour. He feels 'almost everyone needs a cover', but when masks and costumes are left aside, is there only emptiness and a sense of disconnectedness? Is happiness only momentarily attainable on 'a great day', but impossible to sustain in ordinary life? Kennelly has presented a familiar event and made it strangely disquieting.

ANALYSIS

'Kennelly's poetry stimulates and intensifies the reader's sense of wonder.' Discuss this statement, supporting your answer with particular reference to the poem, 'A Great Day'.

Sample Paragraph

'A Great Day' opens with the traditional image of the bride, 'She was all in white'. Kennelly succeeds in making us look at the familiar wedding ritual again through his subtle use of suggestion. He stimulates our admiration and doubt. The emphasis is on appearance, both bride and groom are 'most elegant'. All, on the surface, is as it should have been, the wedding was indeed a 'great day', full of 'dance and song'. However, through the poem is threaded the feeling that 'something is not quite right'. The repetition of 'Seemed' and 'seems' strikes an uneasy note. 'Things seemed to fit', but when the bride changes her clothes, the mood suddenly changes too. The dynamic pulse falters, and with a clever use of personification the trees adopt a 'reticent air'. The connection between the couple is already coming 'asunder': the bride breaks off communication, 'She closed her eyes', and they each become locked in their own thoughts, 'A tide of thoughts flowed in her head,/In his head'. Although a note of affection concludes the poem, the reader is left with 'a modicum of wonder' that the joining together of two individuals, 'Man in woman, woman in man', is not so easy. Kennelly raises the question and leaves it to us to search for the answer or to ask another question.

Examiner's Comment

An impressive high-grade response that includes several good discussion points, such as the poet's successful use of suggestion. Good sense of engagement with the text and effective use of apt reference. Accurate quotations are well integrated into critical commentary. Clarity of expression throughout (e.g. 'threaded', 'dynamic pulse falters').

N.B. Access your ebook for additional sample paragraphs and a list of useful quotes with commentary.

CLASS/HOMEWORK EXERCISES

1. 'Kennelly has remarked that poetry remains a bewildering and enlightening adventure in language.' Discuss this view, with particular reference to the poem, 'A Great Day'.

2. 'Brendan Kennelly's evocative use of language displays resilience and hope in a troubling world.' To what extent is this true of 'A Great Day'? Support your argument with reference to the text.

SUMMARY POINTS

- Stream of consciousness format allows readers to share intimately Kennelly's reflections on the 'great day'.
- Subtle suggestion and repetition create an unsettling atmosphere.
- Colloquial language lends an air of informality.
- Rhyme and assonance used to link and contrast ideas and moods.
- Ambivalent, thought-provoking ending.

[handwritten: jigsaw of thought / Shards of memory.]　　*[handwritten: Personal]*

10 FRAGMENTS 🔊 *[handwritten: Shattered / Broken]*　　*[handwritten: What do we remember / How do we remember?]*

[handwritten: 3rd person]

What had he to say to her now? *[handwritten: processing thought.]*
Where was the woman he believed he had known *[handwritten: Failed relationship]*
In a street, out walking, by the sea, *[handwritten: once familiar scenes are pitiful now]*
In bed, working, dancing, loving the sun *[handwritten: enjambement]*
[handwritten: fluid, energetic.]

And saying so, always for the first time?　　5
Who was this stranger with the graven face? *[handwritten: alienation. – could be about himself.]*
What led to the dreaming-up of a home?
And what was he, at sixty? Who was *[handwritten: reflection, was he fulfilled, loss of identity doesn't know himself.]*

That man lifting the blackthorn stick *[handwritten: traditional image]*
With the knobbed top from its place　　10
At the side of the fire, quietly dying?

He listened to his own steps in the walk *[handwritten: feeling of isolation]*
Past the reedy mud where plover rose *[handwritten: recognition of timeless natural beauty]*
And scattered, black fragments, crying.

'where plover rose'

Glossary

6	*graven*: death-like, etched.	13	*plover*: short-legged wading birds.
9	*blackthorn stick*: shillelagh, knotty Irish stick.	14	*fragments*: remnants, scraps.
13	*reedy*: marshy, rush-filled.		

INITIAL RESPONSE

1. Identify and briefly comment on the changing tones through the poem, supporting your answer with close reference to the text.

2. What is your impression of the woman referred to in line 2? Support your answer with reference to the poem.

3. Write your own personal response to the poem, highlighting the impact it made on you.

STUDY NOTES

Throughout much of his poetry, Brendan Kennelly emphasises that the world cannot be understood easily. Knowledge (and particularly self-knowledge) is an ongoing process of questioning and reformulations of the same questions, in order to find a more appreciative angle of what they seek to clarify. 'Fragments' is a poignant, reflective poem that can be interpreted in several ways, exploring the individual's attempts to understand the past while at the same time facing an uncertain future. Kennelly's method has been to combine apparently disparate perspectives in service to universal themes – often addressing the essential meaning of life itself.

From the outset of this sonnet, questions dominate. The speaker's deep sense of disillusionment and separation is signalled in the **half-hearted tone** of voice in **line 1**: 'What had he to say to her now?' Still struggling to come to terms with the unnamed 'woman he believed he had known', the narrator wonders where she might be at present and imagines her 'out walking, by the sea' or 'working'. The glimpses of these once familiar scenes appear pitiful now, suggesting the bitter-sweet nature of a failed relationship. Perhaps the true response to the opening question is that there really is nothing left to say – even if she were to return. Has the couple's initial closeness and spontaneity ('always for the first time') been irreparably lost?

The mood darkens further in **stanza two** with the startling description of 'this stranger with the graven face'. The speaker's tone is detached and he seems **alienated** from others – as well as from himself. Mention of the woman's 'graven' expression counters the happier memories of their lives together ('dancing, loving the sun'). The feelings of incredulity increase as he challenges the romantic notion of earlier times when they were planning a future together: 'What led to the dreaming-up of a home?' Both the dismissive tone and underlying irony reflect a deeply felt cynicism about the possibility of enduring love. It's the cue for the narrator to reflect on the fleeting nature of human experiences, relationships and his own achievements: 'And what was he, at sixty?'

The question is pursued through **stanza three** as the poem **moves from the here-and-now to the mystical** with deceptive ease. In imagining – or remembering – 'That man lifting the blackthorn stick', he transcends ordinary time and place. The speaker's thoughts become fixated on a traditional Irish image – the elderly man sitting close to the fire, 'quietly dying'. In describing 'That man', the narrator associates his own life with the persona of his father and forefathers. Were their lives as uncertain as his? And were they a constant source of wonder to themselves?

Detailed imagery from the Irish countryside creates the subdued setting and elegiac mood in **stanza four**. Acutely aware of his place among the generations, the speaker 'listened to his own steps' as he passed 'the reedy mud where the plover rose'. Despite the pervading feeling of isolation and despondency, there is a recognition of the **timeless natural beauty** that marks Kennelly's sense of place. The run-through lines, broad assonant effects and sibilant 's' sounds add a delicate, musical quality. Above all, the final image of the plover – 'black fragments, crying' – is particularly evocative, symbolising the remnant memories of a forsaken life.

The conclusion is undoubtedly bleak, but not entirely tragic. Even though the speaker is still unable to realise the full extent of his regret, the **eloquent linguistic expression** of the poet's narrative has somehow humanised him. There is an acknowledgment that people find short-lived moments of happiness where they can while enduring the attrition of ordinary day-to-day living.

Kennelly has written elsewhere about the betrayal that underlines human relationships: 'I wonder if many people feel as I do – that in the society we have created it is very difficult to give your full, sustained attention to anything or anybody for long, that we are compelled to half-do a lot of things, to half-live our lives, half-dream our dreams, half-love our loves'.

ANALYSIS

'By confronting life's uncertainties in his poetry, Kennelly finds a way out of that pain.' Discuss this view, with particular reference to 'Fragments'.

Sample Paragraph

In 'Fragments', Kennelly tackles the difficult subject of how to deal with the past. He does not refer directly to himself, but the painful breakdown of his marriage has been well documented. By distancing himself, he makes the theme universal so that others can relate to it. I found the phrase 'the woman he believed he had known' very revealing because it is impossible to know another person completely. The poet admits to still being unsure about his ex, 'What had he to say to her now?' and these anguished questions are never really resolved as he remembers her, 'this stranger'. He is even more confused about himself, 'what was he at sixty?' Kennelly pictures himself as an old man beside an open coal fire 'quietly dying'. The image is as much about him fading away as the dying cinders. In the last stanza, he finds comfort in nature, watching the plover rising like 'scattered black fragments, crying'. I believe Kennelly is saying that it is perfectly natural to feel sorrow and to be unsure about life. The poem might not cancel out his pain, but in the end, he seems to come to terms with it.

Examiner's Comment

A good, personal high-grade response that shows close engagement with the poem. The paragraph includes some very incisive discussion, effectively supported by apt quotation – sometimes well integrated into the commentary. Overall expression is lively and varied.

N.B. Access your ebook for additional sample paragraphs and a list of useful quotes with commentary.

CLASS/HOMEWORK EXERCISES

1. 'A disturbing sense of underlying sadness is frequently found in Brendan Kennelly's poems.' In your opinion, how true is this of 'Fragments'? Support your answer with reference to the poem.

2. 'Kennelly's poetry often has a universal significance that raises interesting questions about the human condition.' To what extent is this true of 'Fragments'? Support your answer with reference to the poem.

SUMMARY POINTS

- Central themes include relationships, memory and the passing of time.
- Characteristic use of simple language, imagery and natural speech rhythms.
- Poem's structure based around a series of rhetorical questions.
- Varied moods and tones: introspective, nostalgic, cynical, despondent, realistic, etc.

Search within
Search for purpose
Pursuit of happiness
spiritual
emotional

depths of self
emptiness

11 THE SOUL'S LONELINESS 🔊

it's nothing to go on about
but when I hear it
in the ticking of the clock

Despite the wealth - loneliness
Self deprecating
almost dismissive of himself + his entitlement to think + express it.

beside the books and photographs
or see it in the shine
of an Eason's plastic bag at midnight   5

Soft language
worthless / common sight / everyday

or touch it in the tree I call
Christ there outside my window
swaying in the day's afterglow

tangible

I shiver a little at the strangeness
of my flesh, the swell of sweat,
the child's poem I'll never forget   10

Purification.
doesn't know his own flesh
Letting go of who he was
dehumanisation
stranger to himself.

and find my eyes searching the floor
for a definition of grace
or a trace of yourself I've never noticed before.   15

wants to find himself.

reassurance / hopeful conclusion.

'touch it in the tree'

Glossary

6   *Eason's*: popular book store.

INITIAL RESPONSE

1. Based on your reading of the poem, what is your impression of the speaker? Support your answer with reference to the text.

2. Choose one aural image from the poem that appeals to you and comment briefly on its effectiveness.

3. Write your own personal response to the poem, highlighting the impact it made on you.

STUDY NOTES

Brendan Kennelly believes that poetry is a constant search for an answer never found: 'There is objectivity and there is the voices. I think they are connected. You are objective as well as being open to absorbing another identity; the identity of the floor or the roof or the light.' This poem considers what goes on in the 'shadowlands' of the poet's mind when he is in a state of loneliness, of mesmerised emptiness. The mystery of creation finds dramatic expression in its simple structure and awestruck lyricism.

Kennelly begins his exploration of his own spiritual awareness with a dismissive line, 'it's nothing to go on about'. At one level, soul-searching might seems unnecessary. The deliberate use of the lowercase 'i' in **line 1** highlights the brushing aside of the issue. Yet through ten run-on lines and three run-through stanzas, the poem records the rush of the poet's **mystical imagination** in full flow. The reader shares in this heightened sense of consciousness as the wonder of ordinary things is revealed.

The poet experiences awakening, purification, illumination and transformation. An everyday domestic sound, 'the ticking of the clock' (**stanza one**) and a common sight, 'an Eason's plastic bag' (**stanza two**) are reimagined through repetition ('it'), careful patterning of the slender vowel 'i' ('ticking', 'beside', 'midnight') and soft alliteration ('see', shine'). Both poet and reader encounter **the sensation of being alive** with greater intensity and sensitivity.

In **stanza three**, Kennelly moves from experience of sound and sight to touch. The repeated letter 't' emphasises the tactile sensation, 'touch it in the tree'. Again, the poet is enjoying a **fleeting glimpse of the miraculous quality of nature** – his senses are leading him to the divine spark that ignites only in the loneliness of the soul. Illumination occurs when the mind is no longer clouded by familiarity, and becomes lucid, awake, able to 'see into the life of things' when sensitised. The mystic poet searches for beauty, goodness and truth – all of which he finds 'in the tree I call/Christ there outside my window'. The gentle movement of the tree in the evening sunset, 'swaying in the day's afterglow', is beautifully suggested through resonant broad-vowel assonance.

The **fourth stanza** details another stage of the mystical experience, purification, **the letting go of one's ego**, 'I shiver a little at the strangeness/of my flesh'. Sibilance accentuates this inexplicable feeling. The alliterative phrase, 'swell of sweat', captures the physicality of the self while the distant memory of 'the child's poem' evokes Kennelly's enduring emotional life. All are left aside for a moment as he suddenly becomes alert to the sacredness of matter: 'my eyes searching the floor/for a definition of grace'. He is willing to open up, to look beyond himself and discover 'a trace of yourself I've never noticed before'.

The eager anticipation of transcendence becomes tangible. Kennelly has spoken of his belief in otherness, other ways of being at one with the world. Throughout the poem, **he has sought spiritual fulfilment** by battling against cosy familiarities and inviting new presences ('Christ', 'grace') into the abject loneliness of his own inner consciousness.

As in so many of Kennelly's poems, his dreamlike world is infused with animistic presence. This underlying sense of being **part of a universal spirit** is pervasive and the 'yourself' he addresses in **line 15** could refer to anyone and everyone – including himself, of course. Such a surging, hopeful conclusion is both redemptive and reassuring. The price for loving life's miracles is isolation.

Kennelly has observed: 'Poetry is a singing art of natural and magical connection because, though it is born out of one person's solitude, it has the ability to reach out and touch in a humane and warmly illuminating way the solitude, even the loneliness of others ... Poetry is one of the most vital treasures that humanity possesses; it is a bridge between separated souls'.

ANALYSIS

'By confronting loneliness in his poetry, Kennelly gains a new level of awareness in his life.' Discuss this view, with particular reference to 'The soul's loneliness'.

Sample Paragraph

Kennelly, like so many poets, both hates and delights in solitude. The actual title, 'The soul's loneliness' and the touching image of 'the ticking of the clock' acknowledge this deep awareness from the start. Every single thing excites his imagination, even 'the shine/of an Eason's plastic bag at midnight'. His eyes become unsealed as he begins to recognise the extraordinary in the ordinary. The poet begins to see the divine 'in the tree I call/Christ there'. But the poet does not hold onto this mystic awareness for himself. He also brings us on this journey of awakening leading to an intense realisation or understanding of his own place in

God's creation. Through the skilful use of powerful sound effects – both emphatic alliteration ('see it in the shine') and assonance ('Eason's plastic bag'), he enables readers to look again, to leave aside life's complacency and to become aware. The soothing movement of the tree ('swaying in the day's afterglow') is re-enacted through the slow progress of broad vowels. As readers, we also experience Kennelly's dazzling vision of the world when he gains a deeper understanding of the loneliness of the soul, its stillness and capacity for openness.

Examiner's Comment

This focused high-grade response addresses the question effectively and shows close interaction with the poem. Ideas are considered, organised, clearly expressed and aptly supported. The detailed and sustained focus on sound effects is particularly impressive. Language use throughout is also well controlled.

N.B. Access your ebook for additional sample paragraphs and a list of useful quotes with commentary.

CLASS/HOMEWORK EXERCISES

1. 'Through his distinctive use of language, Brendan Kennelly is able to shape and articulate both joyous and troubling moments.' In your opinion, how true is this of 'The soul's loneliness'? Support your answer with reference to the poem.

2. 'Kennelly's poetry discovers, protects and celebrates the deepest values of the heart.' To what extent is this true of 'The soul's loneliness'? Support your answer with reference to the poem.

SUMMARY POINTS

- Central themes include loneliness, spiritual awareness and connection.
- Aural effects – alliteration, assonance and run-on lines – all capture the mystic experience.
- Poem's dreamlike, serene mood embodies the delight to be found in solitude.
- Effective use of structure, simple diction, rhythm, etc.

12 SAINT BRIGID'S PRAYER 🔊

(from the Irish)

I'd like to give a lake of beer to God.
    I'd love the Heavenly
Host to be tippling there
    for all eternity.

I'd love the men of Heaven to live with me,   5
    to dance and sing.
If they wanted, I'd put at their disposal
    vats of suffering.

White cups of love I'd give them
    with a heart and a half;   10
sweet pitchers of mercy I'd offer
    to every man.

I'd make Heaven a cheerful spot
    because the happy heart is true.
I'd make the men contented for their own sake.   15
    I'd like Jesus to love me too.

I'd like the people of Heaven to gather
    from all the parishes around.
I'd give a special welcome to the women,
    the three Marys of great renown.   20

I'd sit with the men, the women and God
    there by the lake of beer.
We'd be drinking good health forever
    and every drop would be a prayer.

St Brigid's cross

Glossary

3	*Host*: multitude of angels.	11	*pitchers*: jugs, containers.
3	*tippling*: imbibing, drinking.	20	*the three Marys*: pious women mentioned in the
8	*vats*: casks, tanks.		Bible.

INITIAL RESPONSE

1. In your opinion, is this a serious or comic poem? Refer to the text in your answer.

2. Kennelly's use of language throughout this poem is vibrant and energetic. Do you agree? Support your answer with reference to the text.

3. Write your own personal response to the poem, referring closely to the text in your answer.

STUDY NOTES

Saint Brigid is the patron saint of poetry in Ireland. Down through the centuries, old pagan rituals and new Christian celebrations became associated with her feast day, 1st February. Her fabled love of beer is perfectly summed up in this 10th-century poem which is attributed to her, but adapted by Kennelly and narrated in her voice.

Saint Brigid's reputation for hospitality is evident in the celebratory tone of the **opening lines**. Her mischievous dream to join the 'tippling' angels in Heaven clearly suggests that she would like to see more joy in the world. Her personal enthusiasm – 'I'd like', 'I'd love' – is equally evident. The whimsical image of 'a lake of beer' typifies Irish people's fondness for exaggeration – and sometimes for glorifying alcohol. From the outset, Kennelly establishes a relaxed, **good-humoured atmosphere**. Neither the saint's unusual sentiments nor the colloquial language are characteristic of a formal conventional 'prayer'.

Brigid turns her attention to 'the men of Heaven' in **lines 5-12**, inviting them to 'live with me'. The request is a reminder of Ireland's conservative, male-dominated society. As a nun working with impoverished families, she would have seen the effects of patriarchal behaviour and drunkenness. The mood of the poem changes significantly when she offers to provide 'vats of suffering', suggesting that it's time for men to understand the harsh reality so many women have experienced. The critical voice grows **increasingly moralistic**, proposing that Irishmen should swap their self-indulgent 'vats' of beer for kinder 'cups of love'. As a sign of forgiveness to 'every man', Brigid will whole-heartedly give them 'sweet pitchers of mercy' – to encourage them to act more compassionately.

The assertive feminist perspective continues in **lines 13-16**, but within a positive Christian context. Looking forward to the prospect of Heaven as 'a cheerful spot', Brigid's self-confidence is emphasised through repetition ('I'd make') and by the **mischievous tone** of her promise to keep the men happy 'for their own sake'. The casual expression and jaunty rhythm of everyday speech reveal her good-natured personality which is based primarily on her unreserved religious faith: 'I'd like Jesus to love me too'.

Lines 17-20 focus on Ireland's traditional rural communities – often defined by shared religious links. While Brigid is keen to re-unite 'all the parishes around', once again she singles out the countless women she admires for 'special welcome'. In her eyes, they are all unsung heroines like 'the three Marys of great renown'. The poem's **last lines** present an **idyllic picture** of Heaven where men and women are equally treated alongside God. The emphasis is firmly placed on enjoyment and 'drinking good health' for all eternity, reflecting Brigid's theology. This final image – which grows out of the central comparison between drinking and glorifying God in prayer – leaves readers in no doubt about the poet's own enthusiasm for life.

Like so many of the personae in Kennelly's poems, Saint Brigid represents the search for unity and meaning in a world of division and suffering. In her femininity, she inclusively embodies several kinds of cross currents, some of them apparently contradictory – male and female, pagan and Christian, ancient and modern. Brigid was also a woman who believed in celebrating **the wonder of being alive** – something that made her particularly appealing to the poet – so that her life itself inspired unity and reconciliation.

ANALYSIS

'Brendan Kennelly creates living poetry without ever resorting to overly convoluted or pretentious language.' To what extent is this true of the poem, 'Saint Brigid's Prayer'? Support your answer with reference to the text.

Sample Paragraph

The language used throughout 'Saint Brigid's Prayer' is simple and even childlike at times. The chanting of 'I'd like' or 'I'd make' is more nursery rhyme than formal prayer. This gives energy and vitality to what she says. Lines are short and the images Kennelly creates, such as 'the lake of beer', are vivid and have universal appeal. The poem reads very easily, with a singalong beat. The poet avoids complex or long drawn-out descriptions. Instead, he uses common expressions, 'a heart and a half', 'the happy heart is true'. This is how ordinary Irish people speak, especially older people in some country areas. The themes in this poem are clearly expressed with the minimum of fuss. Kennelly gets to the point that St Brigid was a woman well ahead of her time. She doesn't take men too seriously and believes everyone should make the most of life. The poem ends on an upbeat note that shows Paradise as a happy place with 'everyone drinking good health' equally, just as Brigid imagined that 'cheerful spot'. The message is simple and easy to understand, and this is typical of Kennelly's poetry.

Examiner's Comment

This succinct top-grade paragraph manages to cover a wide range of aspects very successfully. Effective points are made regarding the poet's themes, diction and rhythm. Accurate quotations provide good support and the expression throughout is confident and controlled.

N.B. Access your ebook for additional sample paragraphs and a list of useful quotes with commentary.

CLASS/HOMEWORK EXERCISES

1. 'Brendan Kennelly's poetic style can be strikingly spirited and playful.' To what extent is this true of 'Saint Brigid's Prayer'? Support your answer with reference to the text.

2. In your opinion, does the poem 'Saint Brigid's Prayer' have relevance to our modern world? Support the points you make with close reference to the text.

SUMMARY POINTS

- Brigid envisions Heaven as being a place of infinite hospitality.
- Realistic views about Irish society, gender and Christianity.
- Advocates the positive aspects of religion to bring love and joy.
- Addresses issues about abusing alcohol and its detrimental effects.
- Use of colloquial language and natural rhythms of ordinary speech.
- Variety of tones: animated, comic, critical feminist, positive, etc.

> LEAVING CERT SAMPLE ESSAY

'Brendan Kennelly uses language in innovative ways to explore experiences of love and hate.' Discuss this view, supporting your answer with suitable reference to the poems by Kennelly on your course.

Marking Scheme Guidelines

Responses to the question should contain clear evidence of engagement with the poetry by Kennelly on the course. Expect a wide variety of approaches in the candidates' answering, but they should focus on the poet's innovative language use in exploring experiences of love and hate.

Indicative material:

- Themes range widely from love and idealism to hatred and hopelessness.
- Repetition, rhetorical questions, unusual punctuation, intricate sound effects.
- Varied images – nature, romance, characters, religion, mysticism, dance, violence.
- Contrasting moods/tones – tender, reflective, nostalgic, transcendent, sorrowful, angry.
- Inventive use of different writing forms, letter, lament, sonnet, etc.

Sample Essay

(Kennelly's innovative exploration of love and hate)

1. *Brendan Kennelly believes poetry can 'shape and articulate our most joyous and troubling moments'. He offers us poetry that 'makes a kind of singing sense out of confusing experience' from the inspirational poem 'Begin' to the surprising 'Oliver to His Brother' and the reflective 'Fragments' to the heart-rending 'A Cry for Art O'Leary'. All four poems bring the reader on a thrilling, unsettling journey through life's moments of love and hate.*

2. *After a series of health problems, Kennelly falls back in love with life in the celebratory poem, 'Begin'. An ecstatic opening announces the tranquil wonder of a spring morning through playful half-rhyme ('Begin again') and the elaborate use of assonance ('sight of light at the window'). Kennelly believed a poem 'protects and celebrates the heart's deepest values'. I found this poem to be quite inspirational. We are given a comforting message of love in the midst of loss, 'old friends passing though with us still'. We are being reassured that we never really lose those we love because they continue to live in our memory.*

3. *Through vivid imagery and rich sound effects, the poet enables us to see 'branches stark in the willing sunlight'. We are encouraged through the broad vowel 'a', to slow down and become aware of the beauty of branches silhouetted by the eager sun. His optimistic conclusion stimulates our realisation that the essence of this world is not only sadness and ending, but endurance and resilience; 'something that will not acknowledge conclusion insists that we forever begin'.*

4. *Kennelly's adventure in language continues in 'Oliver to His Brother'. The name 'Cromwell' can conjure up a deep hatred of England, but this poet dares to present another view of the man – the loving concerned father, the courteous brother. In presenting such a complex character, Kennelly imaginatively uses the actual words of Cromwell from a letter he once wrote. This gives an air of both authenticity and authority to the poem. A gentle address ('Loving brother') and warm wishes ('I send my affection to all your family') provide a startling contrast to the stereotypical image of Cromwell as the bloody butcher of the Irish.*

5. *Kennelly dares to juxtapose Cromwell's tender side with the stern pragmatism of the military leader, 'I have things to do all in my own way'. His chilling comment after the execution of the three rebel soldiers, 'Men die their different ways', is matter-of-fact and realistic. The deceptively simple last line, 'I have work to do in Ireland', can be seen with the benefit of hindsight, knowing the horrific hatred and bloodshed that he caused. The poet has now disturbed and challenged us to look at the complexity of the human condition, where good and evil co-exist. He places the coldly repellent formal rhetoric ('Let weep who will') beside the warmth of his private rich rolling comment, 'And girls eat cherries'. Through his fresh control of different registers and tones, Kennelly has provided a deeply troubling experience from history.*

6. *Kennelly shows skill in using many different poetic forms, including the sonnet. There is another reflection on the past in 'Fragments'. The poet asks a series of rhetorical questions to engage the reader. He uses an effective image of the plover as 'black fragments' to suggest that people eventually lose love in their lives and must face up to loss.*

7. *In 'A Cry for Art O'Leary', a translation of the great Irish elegy from 1773, Kennelly makes good use of the technique of the stand-alone line to describe the feelings that the bereaved wife goes through. The use of the stand-alone line to narrate different stages of emotion is also evident in his poem, 'A Great Day'. Here the poet wishes to highlight the beauty and magic of the young bride, 'She was all in white'. He uses it again later in the poem to stress the disappointment of the young husband, 'He never saw that white dress again'.*

8. *Such sadness is present throughout 'A Cry for Art O'Leary', where the young wife's helpless love for her husband is recorded in the rhetorical, 'What else could I do?' Her simple declaration, 'I miss you' connects on a universal level with everyone who has experienced the loss of a loved one. Evocative use of the ugly metaphor, 'My heart is a lump of grief' suggests both the widow's swollen eyes and the immovability of her sorrow. The poem covers extremes of love and hatred. Art's young widow despises Morris, her husband's killer, and is filled with vengeance. Yet the poem concludes with the dignity of this woman reasserting itself in the unique expression 'womanmake'. When a woman is faced with loss and sorrow, often at the hands of man, she has to carry on and endure. Art's young widow created a fitting lament for her dead husband.*

9. Brendan Kennelly believes poetry should 'restore and reveal the miraculous character of language'. Bringing his readers on an exciting, daring and unusual series of experiences in the poems 'Begin', 'Oliver to His Brother', 'Fragments' and 'A Cry for Art O'Leary', the poet has considered the best and worst of human nature, showing that good and evil can often co-exist. Through his great skills with language – especially sound effects, different poetic forms, wide-ranging imagery and tones – Kennelly has surprised and excited his readers into 'a sense of wonder' at this world.

(approx. 880 words)

Examiner's Comment

This is a sustained and informed response that shows close engagement with Kennelly's poetry. The opening paragraph provides a clear overview and both elements of the question (themes and style) are addressed effectively. Terms such as 'imaginatively', 'fresh' and 'unique' maintain the focus on the poet's innovative language use – particularly sound effects, stand-alone lines, varying forms and tones. Paragraph 6 is short and includes a worthwhile point that required more development. Good use is made of a brief cross-reference in paragraph 7. Overall, a top-grade essay.

MARKING SCHEME GRADE: H1
P = 15/15
C = 12/15
L = 13/15
M = 5/5
Total = 45/50

N.B. Access your ebook for additional sample paragraphs and a list of useful quotes with commentary.

SAMPLE LEAVING CERT QUESTIONS ON KENNELLY'S POETRY

(45–50 MINUTES)

1. 'Brendan Kennelly discusses both loneliness and connectivity through direct language and complex word play.' To what extent do you agree with this assessment of his poetry? Your answer should focus on his themes and the way he expresses them. Support the points you make with suitable reference to the poems of Kennelly on your course.

2. 'Kennelly's clarity of self-knowledge engages readers through his distinctive style.' Discuss this statement. In your answer you should refer to both style and subject matter. Support your answer with suitable references to the poetry of Kennelly on your course.

3. 'The poetry of Brendan Kennelly explores the tensions of modern life in an inventive and insightful fashion.' Discuss this view, supporting your answer with reference to the poems by Kennelly on your course.

Sample Essay Plan (Q1)

'Brendan Kennelly discusses both loneliness and connectivity through direct language and complex word play.' To what extent do you agree or disagree with this assessment of his poetry? Your answer should focus on his themes and the way he expresses them. Support the points you make with suitable reference to the poems of Kennelly on your course.

- Intro: Identify the elements of the question to be addressed (<u>both</u> 'loneliness and connectivity', 'direct language', 'complex word play'). Relationships or the lack of relationships between people, or towards places, events, society or self are studied in simple words, yet the poet uses complex sound effects and registers. The language of the heart is shaped and ordered through his discerning choices.

- Point 1: 'Dear Autumn Girl', tender lyric address. Common writer's experience, inability to connect with poetic muse ('Autumn girl') given fresh treatment through original blending of Petrarchan and Shakespearean sonnet forms, unique rhyme scheme (efg, efg in sestet) and original compound word ('leaf-argosies').

- Point 2: Universal themes of loneliness ('arrogant loneliness of swans') and death ('old friends passing') scrutinised in 'Begin'. Poem optimistically breaks through boundaries of human existence using images from nature of the struggle for life ('crying birds', 'branches stark', 'seagulls foraging'). Irrepressible nature 'insists that we forever begin' too. The dynamic pulse of life is caught in the steady four-beat ballad metre.

- Point 3: Loneliness is again considered in 'Things I Might Do'. The alliterative phrase 'backroom of a brothel' stresses the empty substitution of anonymous sexual encounters for genuine human affection. A unique compound word 'somethinglikelove' challenges the false appearance of love by mimicking its unreality. Natural imagery is used again, as in 'Begin'. Here it is used to describe death, ('madness of leaves', 'year's end').

- Point 4: 'Saint Brigid's Prayer' explores the importance of connectivity between male/female, pagan/Christian, ancient/modern through simple, childlike phrases ('I'd like', 'I'd make'), a singalong beat and universal imagery ('lake of beer', 'cups of love'). Colloquial expressions ('a heart and a half') and exaggeration ('drinking good health forever') communicate the Irish saint's merry attitude towards an inclusive life for all.

- Point 5: Contrasting treatment of solitude and union in 'The soul's loneliness' and 'A Great Day'. Advantages and disadvantages of these two states studied through explicit imagery and word play.

- Conclusion: The candid poet, Kennelly, expresses the contradictory experiences of seclusion and association that humans experience through his exactness of observation, rhythmic energy and innovative style. Through his connection with self, he invites the reader to undertake the same exciting journey by embracing aloneness.

Sample Essay Plan (Q1)

Develop one of the above points into a paragraph.

Sample Paragraph: Point 5

Loneliness and connectivity are treated in a contrasting manner in the poems 'The soul's loneliness' and 'A Great Day'. Kennelly believes that solitude is essential in order to become aware of the sensation of being alive. He transforms two common, familiar occurrences, the sound of a clock and the sight of a plastic bag, through skilful patterning of the slender vowel 'i' into a mosaic of assonance, 'ticking', 'beside', 'it', 'shine', 'plastic', 'midnight'. Not only is the poet becoming sensitised through associating strongly with these objects, he enables the reader to become lucid too, to see, as he does, 'into the life of things'. The tactile alliteration of 'touch it in the tree' transforms the sight of a tree outside his window into a mystical experience. The tree then becomes transformed into 'Christ there outside my window/swaying in the day's afterglow'. However, loneliness is not seen as a positive experience in 'A Great Day'. The union of 'Man in woman, woman in man' is cruelly severed. When the bride decides she 'must change' her white dress, the magic of the noisy, happy wedding party evaporates too. The singing guests are replaced by trees who are 'silent guests'. Once the bride, who 'all the time she was all in white' was 'Enjoying every song and speech', changed her dress, her attitude changed too, she was 'glad to get away'. She no longer communicates with her new husband, 'Closed her eyes'. Each retreats into their own thoughts. He, sadly, 'never saw the white dress again'. 'What God has joined together' is unravelling. Two separate individuals can find this close unity difficult to negotiate in the real world.

Examiner's Comment

As part of a complete essay, this is an impressive high-grade paragraph that shows clear understanding of both poems. Discussion points are well focused on the key elements of the question. The poet's style is illustrated with particularly incisive comments on 'intricate sound effects'. The assured cross-referencing between the two poems reflects good personal appreciation and engagement. Expression is controlled and relevant quotations are integrated effectively into the commentary.

N.B. Access your ebook for additional sample paragraphs and a list of useful quotes with commentary.

LAST WORDS

'With considerable honesty and bravery Kennelly enters and becomes others in order to perceive, understand and suffer.'

Aidan Murphy

'What emerges from Kennelly's entire body of work is a relationship with his subjects that is based on curiosity and mischievous respect.'

Katleyn Ferguson

'A writer is not interested in explaining reality, he's only interested in capturing it.'

Brendan Kennelly

D. H. LAWRENCE

1885–1930

'Ours is an excessively conscious age.
We know so much, we feel so little.'

David Herbert Lawrence was born in Nottinghamshire, England, on 11th September, 1885. A miner's son, he was to become a rebellious and polemical writer with radical views. Though better known as a novelist (*The Rainbow, Women in Love, Lady Chatterley's Lover*), Lawrence was also a prolific poet.

His collected writings represent an extended reflection on the dehumanising effects of modernity and industrialisation. In them, Lawrence confronts issues relating to emotional health and happiness, spontaneity, human sexuality and instinct. He believed in writing poetry that was stark and true to the mysterious creative force that motivated it.

Some of his best-loved poems address the physical and inner life of plants and animals; others are bitterly satirical and express outrage at the hypocrisy of conventional society. In much of his later poetry, he attempted to capture emotion through free verse.

D. H. Lawrence travelled extensively and spent many years in Italy. A lifelong sufferer from tuberculosis, he died on 2nd March, 1930 in the South of France. He is now widely regarded as one of the most influential writers of the 20th century.

INVESTIGATE FURTHER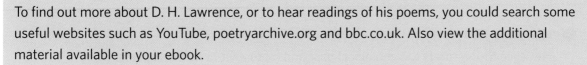

To find out more about D. H. Lawrence, or to hear readings of his poems, you could search some useful websites such as YouTube, poetryarchive.org and bbc.co.uk. Also view the additional material available in your ebook.

Prescribed Poems

* The poems marked with an asterisk are also prescribed for the Ordinary Level course.

1 CALL INTO DEATH

Since I lost you, my darling, the sky has come near,
And I am of it, the small sharp stars are quite near,
The white moon going among them like a white bird among snow-berries,
And the sound of her gently rustling in heaven like a bird I hear.

And I am willing to come to you now, my dear,   5
As a pigeon lets itself off from a cathedral dome
To be lost in the haze of the sky; I would like to come
And be lost out of sight with you, like a melting foam.

For I am tired, my dear, and if I could lift my feet,
My tenacious feet, from off the dome of the earth   10
To fall like a breath within the breathing wind
Where you are lost, what rest, my love, what rest!

'among snow-berries'

Glossary

3 *snow-berries*: round white berries eaten by birds, but poisonous to humans.

6 *dome*: round roof.

7 *haze*: mist, cloud.

10 *tenacious*: clinging, firmly held.

INITIAL RESPONSE

1. Lawrence's poems explore difficult subject matter. In your opinion, what is the main theme or message of 'Call into Death'? Support your answer with reference to the text.

2. Lawrence uses several similes in this poem. Choose one that appeals to you and comment briefly on its effectiveness.

3. Write your own personal response to the poem, highlighting the impact it made on you.

STUDY NOTES

'Call into Death' is part of D. H. Lawrence's two-volume Collected Poems *(1928). He divided the collection into 'Rhyming Poems' and 'UnRhyming Poems' (to which this particular poem belongs). Lawrence wrote this poem in 1910, the year his mother died of cancer, confessing 'in that year, for me, everything collapsed, save the mystery of death, and the haunting of death in life. I was twenty-five and from the death of my mother, the world began to dissolve around me, beautiful, iridescent, but passing away substanceless. Till I almost dissolved away myself and was very ill ...'*

This tender 12-line elegy has the poet crying out in the direction of death like a mystic in the desert, attempting to get attention. Lawrence's relationship with his mother was close, 'so sensitive to each other that we never needed words'. The poet had also suffered several relationship break-ups in the year prior to his mother's death. Genuine emotion is caught in the plain, honest conversational expression: 'Since I lost you, my darling' (**line 1**). Lawrence turns his back on traditional poetry that elaborated and decorated poetic verse for effect, not feeling. He believes that the experiences of loss have given him a **new insight into life**, the oneness of the ordered universe, 'the sky has come near'. He feels part of it now: 'I am of it'. The sibilant alliteration, 'small, sharp stars', accentuates the pinpoint light radiating from these planets.

Lawrence's vivid **observational skill** is displayed in the beautiful simile of the moon moving among them like 'a white bird among snow-berries' (**line 3**). A haunting sense of the unity of all creation is conveyed in the imagery pattern. The long irregular line length mirrors the moon's majestic journey through the heavens while insistent rhyme ('near', 'hear') adapts to the idea of the oneness of the universe and man. Onomatopoeia ('rustling') conveys the soft sound of the mother bird searching for food. Lawrence fully acknowledges the natural inclusion of death in life, just as the 'white moon' shines in the dark sky – though it is not always visible to the human eye – and the 'white bird' is camouflaged among the white berries.

The **second verse** opens with a warm term of endearment, 'my dear', as the poet wishes to immediately and voluntarily join his loved one, 'I am willing to come to you now'. Using another simile, Lawrence expresses his wish to launch himself into oblivion, 'As a pigeon lets itself off from a cathedral dome/To be lost in the haze of the sky' (**line 6**). The bird disappears from view of the human world, lost in the mist and clouds, yet it still lives. **Death and life are not separate events**, but part of the whole human experience. Like the bird, Lawrence needs to become invisible to the human eye and join his beloved, 'like a melting foam'. Irregular rhyme ('dome', 'come', 'foam') adds a subtle quality to the harmonious mood. The repetition of the suffix 'ing' in the first and last lines of the two verses knits them closely together ('darling'/'rustling', 'willing'/'melting').

The **lethargic mood** in the **third verse** is in contrast to the previous two. Lawrence admits the reason for his wish to leave this world, 'For I am tired'. But his feet cling stubbornly to the earth, 'tenacious'. The repetition of 'feet' suggests the sheer physical effort the poet is making in his attempt to escape, not like the bird from the dome of a cathedral, but from the 'dome of the earth' (**line 10**). However, there is a final sense of resurgence as he imagines the effortless flight into the realm of his loved one. Lawrence sees himself easing into death with the grace of a breath joining the wind. The gentle repetition and affectionate tone of 'what rest, my love, what rest' brings the poem to a serene conclusion.

The poet has succeeded in **confronting one of the great taboos** of society, the terrifying reality that death comes to all. He has even emphasised its advantages. Characteristically, his honest poetry confronts one of life's bitterest experiences, death and loss. In the final poignant verse, Lawrence changes his linking mechanism, joining the verb 'lift' in the first line with 'lost' in its concluding line, and unlike the previous two verses, there is no rhyme. His wish is not granted. He cannot yet escape the earth.

ANALYSIS

'D. H. Lawrence's poetry addresses complex ideas in fresh, vivid yet controlled language.' Discuss this statement in relation to 'Call into Death'.

Sample Paragraph

The complex concept of death in the midst of life is explored successfully by Lawrence in 'Call into Death'. One of his beliefs was that death is not an end, but is part of the cycle of life. If something is not seen by humans, that does not mean it is not there. It is still there. The human eye may not always be able to see the moon or a high flying bird, but they are still there. Using precisely observed details from the natural world, Lawrence puts forward his intricate view of life and death. Repetition and the comparison of 'a white bird among snow-berries' illustrates the difficulty of seeing what is actually there. The ease of the descent into oblivion is vividly captured by another simile, 'a pigeon lifts itself off from a cathedral dome'. Bodily substance disappears into another simile, 'melting foam'. But the wish and the reality conflict. Hard 't' sounds show the strong pull of the earth on the living, 'tired', 'lift', 'feet', 'tenacious'. Yet the poem ends with the wish of entering another level of consciousness, spontaneously falling into easeful death, as naturally as 'a breath' joins 'the breathing wind'. Life is not final any more than the dead are totally disconnected from the living; they exist in our memory.

Examiner's Comment

Shows close engagement with the poem. Overall, a high-grade standard that focuses well on the two elements of the question – ideas and style. Despite some slight awkwardness of expression, there are some supported discussion points that effectively explore Lawrence's beliefs in the natural life cycle and his innovative use of sound effects.

N.B. Access your ebook for additional sample paragraphs and a list of useful quotes with commentary.

CLASS/HOMEWORK EXERCISES

1. 'Lawrence's poems are spontaneous and fresh, but they often investigate dark and disturbing subjects.' Discuss this view with reference to the poem 'Call into Death'.

2. 'Lawrence's personal poetry engages readers through carefully composed language and imagery.' To what extent is this true of 'Call into Death'? Support your answer with reference to the poem.

SUMMARY POINTS

- Central themes include death, loss, longing, grief, escape, peace.
- Poetic techniques – irregular line length, rhyme and linking devices, sound effects.
- Effective use of imagery drawn from the natural world.
- Varied tones – affection, sorrow, longing, tiredness, sense of achievement, etc.

❷ PIANO

Softly, in the dusk, a woman is singing to me;
Taking me back down the vista of years, till I see
A child sitting under the piano, in the boom of the tingling strings
And pressing the small, poised feet of a mother who smiles as she sings.

In spite of myself, the insidious mastery of song   5
Betrays me back, till the heart of me weeps to belong
To the old Sunday evenings at home, with winter outside
And hymns in the cosy parlour, the tinkling piano our guide.

So now it is vain for the singer to burst into clamour
With the great black piano appassionato. The glamour   10
Of childish days is upon me, my manhood is cast
Down in the flood of remembrance, I weep like a child for the past.

'great black piano appassionato'

Glossary

2	*vista*: scenic view, panorama.	9	*clamour*: loud noise, racket.
4	*poised*: perched, composed.	10	*appassionato*: impassionate performance.
5	*insidious*: subtle, deceptive.	10	*glamour*: charm, mystique.
6	*Betrays*: tricks, compels.		

INITIAL RESPONSE

1. Based on your reading of the poem, do you agree that memory can be both fascinating and troubling? Support your answer with reference to the text.

2. Choose one aural image from the poem that appeals to you and comment briefly on its effectiveness.

3. Write your own personal response to the poem, highlighting the impact it made on you.

STUDY NOTES

'Piano' is one of D. H. Lawrence's earliest and best known lyrical poems. It was published in 1918 when he was 33 years old. In this candid record of controlled emotion, Lawrence reminisces about his happy childhood and his conflicted desire to return to its warmth and security. He believed in the 'rich, piercing rhythm of recollection, the perfected past'.

Lyrical poetry expresses strong emotion, typically from a first person point-of-view. Lawrence's title has multiple aspects. While 'Piano' refers to the concert that the adult poet is attending in the present, it is also a reference to Lawrence's childhood memory of listening to his mother playing. Interestingly, the word 'piano' itself is the Italian musical direction to play softly.

Aptly, the poem begins with the adverb, 'Softly'. Immediately, a **gentle mood** is being created, 'in the dusk', just between evening and night-time. The atmosphere is entirely appropriate for a poem exploring connections and disconnections between past and present. Lawrence describes a somewhat anonymous event: 'a woman is singing', the atmospheric 's' sounds similar to that of a whisper. The absence of detail initially suggests a lack of engagement on his part but it also releases him to travel down the 'vista of years'. This metaphor of such a panoramic view evokes the wide expanse of the past which poet and reader alike must journey through to reach child-hood again. Each has to travel 'back down' from the heights of maturity and adulthood.

The recollections of the past are sharp and detailed in contrast to the bland opening scene in the present. The **descriptive flashback** reveals a tender image of a young child sitting 'under the piano', pressing his mother's feet while she plays and sings. In **line 3**, the viewpoint suddenly changes to the third person ('A child') as the poet realises that he is no longer that little boy. The use of tactile imagery and the present tense ('sitting', 'pressing') conjures up a vivid sensual memory. Indeed, the scene is one of familiar comfort and childlike innocence, of intimacy and security.

Lawrence makes full use of **aural techniques**, particularly assonance ('boom', 'tingling strings') to convey the contrasting deep and high piano notes. The mother's grace and skill are highlighted in the detail 'small, poised feet'. Simple language has established a nostalgic, happy serenity throughout the **first stanza**. Sibilant 's' and slender vowel sounds ('smiles', 'sings') evoke an ideal picture of a relaxed family scene.

In the more sombre **second quatrain**, the poet indulges in self-analysis. The focus on how the flashback makes him feel brings the outlook back to the first person. Lawrence recalls his childhood days with reluctance ('In spite of myself'). Knowing that he is being sentimentally nostalgic, he is unwilling to return to the past – as many people are – because sometimes it is simply too sad to remember happy times and to realise that they are gone for good. A run-on line features the subtle, **treacherous allure of earlier times**, 'the insidious mastery of song/Betrays me back'. The explosive 'b' in the alliterative phrase delivers the message that he feels he has been cheated. As an adult, Lawrence is now aware of the gap between his idealised childhood perceptions and the reality of loss.

Yet he has been inveigled into the past by the singing and he is overwhelmed ('the heart of me weeps'). The disjointed syntax reflects his obvious distress. Lawrence desperately **longs for his old identity** back in the comforting family home. His romantic feelings flow, unstoppable for 'the old Sunday evenings at home', 'And hymns in the cosy parlour'. The cold 'winter outside' provides a fitting contrast to this warm sanctuary. Ironically, the 'tinkling piano' still acts as a moral compass. In childhood, it represented the close connection ('our guide') between mother and child. Now it counsels the poet about the gulf between childhood and adulthood.

The **third stanza** opens with the conjunction, 'So', indicating the effects of revisiting the past. Lawrence is now no longer interested in the present. He feels it is both useless and arrogant ('vain') of the musician at the concert to display vocal artistry. His wry dismissal is expressed in the negative phrase, 'burst into clamour'. The heavily stressed 'great black piano appassionato' contrasts starkly with the appealing 'tinkling piano' and its broad vowels mimic the melodramatic artistic display of emotion. The **poet admits that he has been seduced** by 'The glamour/Of childish days'. Even the unusual juxtaposition of the more adult noun 'glamour' alongside 'childish' suggests the superficial deception of memory. Lawrence accepts that he is looking at the past through rose-tinted glasses.

In the end, the **power of remembrance breaks him**, 'my manhood is cast/Down'. He has been led from the beginning ('Taking me back', 'Betrays me back') although he is fighting what he sees as a sentimental response. Placing the adverb 'Down' at the beginning of the line emphasises the conflict Lawrence is experiencing by being lured back in time. He reverts to behaving in the frank, open manner of a child, publicly displaying his feelings, 'I weep like a child'. The gentle sounds of his mother on a Sunday evening have surpassed the sophisticated dramatic performance of the singer in the present. More than anything, he now wants 'the past'.

Although the poem explores the floodgates unleashed by random memories, its **form is tightly controlled**. Three quatrains (four-line stanzas) trace the progress of thought in the poem, alternating present and past with inner and outer feelings. The couplet rhyme scheme (aa-bb-cc-dd-ee-ff) is reminiscent of a simple hymn or nursery rhyme. The sprung rhythm (irregular metrical stress on key words) reflects ordinary speech ('Softly', 'Taking', 'Betrays', 'Down'). However, the long, irregular line lengths at the conclusion of each stanza and the frequent use of enjambment suggest the uncontrolled 'flood of remembrance' that can sweep away restraint.

Throughout this beautiful and haunting poem, Lawrence is writing from the perspective of a middle-aged man. But in his subconscious mind, his childhood and adulthood are almost one, as he weeps 'like a child for the past'. In this there is a duality and a contrast. As in so much of his poetry, he portrays the complex workings and dealings of the human heart in a characteristically refined and elegant manner.

ANALYSIS

'D. H. Lawrence's poems often explore the devastating consequences of memory in carefully composed lines.' Discuss this view, with particular reference to 'Piano'.

Sample Paragraph

Lawrence carefully crafts his lyric poem, 'Piano', into three quatrains which move seamlessly from present to past and back again. Using rhyming couplets ('me'/'see', 'strings'/'sings', 'song'/'belong'), the poet seeks to control the overpowering 'flood of remembrance' activated by the spark, 'in the dusk, a woman is singing to me'. The secretive, underhand way memory works soon overcomes him emotionally. The adult Lawrence is 'cast /Down', broken and weeping for what can never be, a return to the happy security of childhood days. The poem itself works just as 'insidiously' on the readers, pulling them back through the rhythms and rhymes reminiscent of simple childhood songs. Lawrence's memories will not be contained neatly into the three quatrains, but break through in frequent enjambment ('The glamour/Of childish days') and irregular line lengths, particular in the last two lines of the first stanza when he describes his memory of sitting as a child under the piano. The poet's careful juxtaposition of the appealing 'glamour' of childhood with the discordant 'clamour' of the singer clearly shows how memory has conquered him. The poem concludes with the realisation of his paradoxical position, openly expressing his distress and nostalgia for the past while still feeling guilty at his betrayal of the present.

Examiner's Comment

A well-written response that focuses effectively on the poet's use of language techniques in treating the theme of memory. Informed discussion points on structure, rhyme, enjambment and contrast are aptly illustrated. Assured expression (using varied sentence length and impressive vocabulary) throughout contributes greatly to the top-grade standard.

N.B. Access your ebook for additional sample paragraphs and a list of useful quotes with commentary.

CLASS/HOMEWORK EXERCISES

1. 'Lawrence's poetry often struggles to record immature experience faithfully and yet at the same time escape from it.' In your opinion, how true is this of 'Piano'? Support your answer with reference to the poem.

2. 'D. H. Lawrence explores the country of the heart in intricate, sensual poetry.' To what extent is this evident in 'Piano'? Support your answer with reference to the poem.

SUMMARY POINTS

- Central themes include recollection, loneliness, self-awareness.
- The opening stanza juxtaposes the present with childhood recollections.
- Aural effects – repetition, assonance and onomatopoeia – vividly recreate the past.
- The poem's structure reflects the poet's struggle with memory.
- Conflicting moods of nostalgia, regret, longing and pragmatism vie in this lyric.

3   THE MOSQUITO

When did you start your tricks,
Monsieur?

What do you stand on such high legs for?
Why this length of shredded shank,
You exaltation?   5

Is it so that you shall lift your centre of gravity upwards
And weigh no more than air as you alight upon me,
Stand upon me weightless, you phantom?

I heard a woman call you the Winged Victory
In sluggish Venice.   10
You turn your head towards your tail, and smile.

How can you put so much devilry
Into that translucent phantom shred
Of a frail corpus?

Queer, with your thin wings and your streaming legs,   15
How you sail like a heron, or a dull clot of air,
A nothingness.

Yet what an aura surrounds you;
Your evil little aura, prowling, and casting a numbness on my mind.

That is your trick, your bit of filthy magic: 20
Invisibility, and the anaesthetic power
To deaden my attention in your direction.

But I know your game now, streaky sorcerer.
Queer, how you stalk and prowl the air
In circles and evasions, enveloping me,   25
Ghoul on wings
Winged Victory.

Settle, and stand on long thin shanks
Eyeing me sideways, and cunningly conscious that I am aware,
You speck.   30

I hate the way you lurch off sideways into air
Having read my thoughts against you.

Come then, let us play at unawares,
And see who wins in this sly game of bluff.
Man or mosquito.   35

You don't know that I exist, and I don't know that you exist.
Now then!

It is your trump,
It is your hateful little trump,
You pointed fiend,   40
Which shakes my sudden blood to hatred of you:
It is your small, high, hateful bugle in my ear.

Why do you do it?
Surely it is bad policy.

They say you can't help it.   45

If that is so, then I believe a little in Providence protecting the innocent.
But it sounds so amazingly like a slogan
A yell of triumph as you snatch my scalp.

Blood, red blood
Super-magical   50
Forbidden liquor.

I behold you stand
For a second enspasmed in oblivion,
Obscenely ecstasied
Sucking live blood,   55
My blood.

Such silence, such suspended transport,
Such gorging,
Such obscenity of trespass.

You stagger 60
As well as you may.
Only your accursed hairy frailty,
Your own imponderable weightlessness
Saves you, wafts you away on the very draught my anger makes in its snatching.

Away with a paean of derision, 65
You winged blood-drop.

Can I not overtake you?
Are you one too many for me,
Winged Victory?
Am I not mosquito enough to out-mosquito you? 70

Queer, what a big stain my sucked blood makes
Beside the infinitesimal faint smear of you!
Queer, what a dim dark smudge you have disappeared into!

Siracusa

'I know your game now, streaky sorcerer'

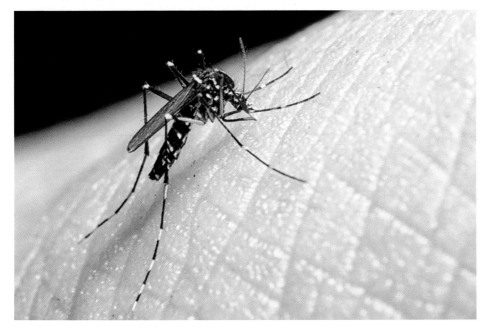

Glossary

Mosquito: Spanish word meaning 'little fly'. This small midge-like insect feeds on blood and is a transmitter of harmful diseases.

1   *tricks*: mischievous, deceitful actions.
2   *Monsieur*: formal address to a Frenchman ('sir').
4   *shredded shank*: ragged lower legs.
5   *exaltation*: joy.
9   *Winged Victory*: statue of Nike, Greek Goddess of Victory.
10 *sluggish*: listless, slow-moving.
13 *translucent*: glowing, radiant.
13 *phantom*: ghost, spirit.
14 *corpus*: body, mass.
16 *heron*: long-legged fish-eating bird.
16 *clot*: lump.
17 *aura*: force, glow.
21 *anaesthetic*: deadening, numbing.
23 *sorcerer*: magician, wizard.
25 *evasions*: avoidances, equivocations.

26 *Ghoul*: ghost, spirit.
30 *speck*: spot, scrap.
31 *lurch*: stagger, sway.
34 *game of bluff*: contest, scam.
38 *trump*: winner, decider.
40 *fiend*: villain, devil.
46 *Providence*: destiny, wisdom.
53 *enspasmed*: suddenly caught.
53 *oblivion*: unconsciousness, nothingness.
59 *obscenity*: indecency.
59 *trespass*: invasion.
63 *imponderable*: unknown.
64 *wafts*: blows.
64 *draught*: breeze.
65 *paean*: rapturous expression.
65 *derision*: contempt, mockery.
72 *infinitesimal*: tiny, insignificant.
72 *smear*: mark, splodge.
73 *smudge*: spot, scrap.

INITIAL RESPONSE

1. Based on your reading of the poem, describe the encounter between man and creature. In your opinion, is it fascinating or disturbing, or both? Support your answer with reference to the text.

2. Choose one example of repetition used in the poem that appeals to you and comment briefly on its effectiveness.

3. Write your own personal response to the poem, highlighting the impact it made on you.

STUDY NOTES

D. H. Lawrence's 1923 poetry collection, Birds, Beasts and Flowers, *was named after a Victorian hymn and included 'The Mosquito'. Lawrence reflects on the 'otherness' of the non-human world in this visualisation of the animal kingdom. He wrote 'The Mosquito' on 17th May, 1920 while staying at the Grand Hotel in Syracuse, Sicily. In his memoirs, Lawrence recalls it as 'a rather dreary hotel – and many bloodstains of squashed mosquitos on the bedroom walls'. He exclaimed, 'Ah, vile mosquitos!' This inspired his confident, witty poem.*

'The Mosquito' is an odd, contradictory poem in the form of an imagined **one-sided dialogue** on the occasion when man confronts insect. The narrative voice is presented in verse paragraphs and the spaces between are occupied by the presence of the mosquito whose internal responses are interpreted by the poet.

The mosquito is a small midge-like fly that lives by piercing human skin and sucking blood. This can cause a nasty rash. The mosquito, while not dangerous itself, can be the carrier of diseases, such as malaria and the Zika virus.

At first, the speaker is slightly condescending, **adopting a superior attitude to the little insect** by addressing it sarcastically with extravagant titles ('Monsieur', 'You exaltation') and wondering about its deceptive 'tricks' (**line 1**). The poet poses a series of questions: 'What do you stand on such high legs for?' Alliteration suggests the insect's threadlike thinness, 'shredded shank' (**line 4**). Yet, while physically insignificant, the creature has the ability to defy the forces of nature – and is able to 'lift your centre of gravity upwards' – unlike human beings. Its flimsy buoyancy fools the poet who can barely feel it, 'Stand upon me weightless'. Lawrence remains focused on the insect's insubstantiality – like a spirit or 'phantom' (**line 8**). It reminds him of how a woman he once knew described the mosquito as 'the Winged Victory', a famous statue in the Louvre Museum honouring Nike, the Greek goddess of Victory. Both insect and statue inhabit moments where action and stillness meet. The ominous irony is that the malaria-transmitting mosquito, winged itself, can boast its own past conquests of mankind. The poet notes that the creature's flowing movement and action of alighting contrasts sharply with the stagnant canals of Venice.

In **line 11**, Lawrence describes the mosquito's threatening action in the alliterative phrase, 'You turn your head towards your tail'. It is almost as if **the creature is aware of its own power**. He even imagines it beginning to 'smile', turning the tables on him and gaining control. In response, Lawrence's own attitude also changes. He no longer regards the insect with patronising amusement, but becomes puzzled and afraid. The poet recognises the insect's slightness ('translucent phantom shred/Of a frail corpus') as bizarre, 'Queer' (**line 15**). He attempts to rationalise the flimsiness of what he sees, 'thin wings and streaming legs' by using the simile, 'like a heron', the long-legged wading bird. Yet the mosquito still has a forceful quality. Lawrence becomes fascinated by its 'evil little aura'. He sees it as a 'prowling' predator stalking its prey. It has assumed the position of authority and the poet is reduced to the paralysis of a victim, 'casting a numbness on my mind'. The extended line winds slowly – just like the encircling insect.

By **line 20**, Lawrence finally has the answer to the question he initially posed regarding the mosquito's 'tricks'. He accepts that it can cast a spell ('filthy magic') - the undetected creature has the power to sedate or freeze its prey. He even suggests the hypnotic effect of the insect through internal half-rhymes ('attention', 'direction'). However, in **line 23** the poet suddenly becomes hyper-aware, 'I know your game now'. **The battle between nature and human nature is on.** The striated insect's mesmerising quality is conveyed in the soft sibilant description, 'streaky sorcerer'. Lawrence regards its ability to inhabit the air as unsettling and eerie. Broad vowels capture the lazy circling of the hunter-insect ('stalk', 'prowl') while the poet continues to feel increasingly trapped. In frustration, he resorts to name-calling, 'Ghoul on wings', but then he remembers the statue to Victory. Is the insect about to get its victory by alighting on the poet? The tension rises.

Once again, **the insect out-manoeuvres the man**. Not only does the mosquito use its ace card, but it also sounds its 'high, hateful bugle' in the poet's ear. He analyses the mosquito's behaviour, using formal business language to criticise its tactics, 'Surely it is bad policy'. But the creature does not operate in this way, surviving instead on instinct. A single, stand-alone line announces, 'They say you can't help it'. For a moment, Lawrence relaxes because he believes that 'Providence' is protecting the blameless, 'the innocent'. But he becomes aware of the insect's mantra ('slogan') and the climax of the poem is reached in insert space **line 48** when the mosquito finally strikes ('snatch my scalp'). Sinister sibilance underlines the the insect's deceit.

A striking incantatory passage draws attention to **the goal of the mosquito**, 'Blood, red blood'. Its sole quest was always for something 'Super-magical/Forbidden liquor'. The insect is consumed into total ecstasy as it gorges on the poet's blood, 'enspasmed in oblivion'. Lawrence is outraged because it has invaded his blood-being, ('My blood') and has grossly violated their separateness by crossing a forbidden frontier, 'Such obscenity of trespass' (**line 59**). The exaggerated effect of the mosquito's action on the poet is conveyed in the repetition of 'Such'.

Lawrence is satisfied at witnessing the insect 'stagger', commenting wryly, 'As well as you may'. He now treats it as one who has become intoxicated. But once more, it is the mosquito's weightlessness that lifts it out of harm and past the poet's exhaling breath. The **insect's escape is caricatured** by the very long line, 'Saves you, wafts you away on the very draught my anger makes in its snatching'. We can sense Lawrence's extreme frustration in his futile attempts to catch the annoying creature.

Not for the first time, the **mosquito reigns supreme**, emitting a 'paean of derision', a joyful expression of disdain. And once again, Lawrence is reduced to impotent abuse: 'You winged blood-drop' (**line 66**). Three rapid quick-fire questions simulate the poet's breathless dash as he rushes around the room attempting to catch the tiny creature, culminating in the pathetic, convoluted 'Am I not mosquito enough to out-mosquito you?' The poet is now less important than his enemy. He has fallen very far from his opening position of the condescending man patronising the little insect. The mosquito is 'Winged Victory'. Yet, while Lawrence reluctantly admits to some admiration for its cleverness and strategy, it is not enough to prevent him from swatting it, reducing the creature to a 'dim dark smudge'.

So **the man eventually kills**. Is this how humans react when confronted by something beyond their understanding? Lawrence comments on how remarkably big the 'stain' of his own blood is in contrast to the tiny 'infinitesimal faint smear' (**line 72**) of the insect. Is he attempting to reassert his earlier dominance? We are left to consider whether man has really won by this act of annihilation. Or has the insect actually reduced man to the animal status, persuading him to follow the law of the jungle, kill or be killed?

As in so much of his narrative poetry, Lawrence writes in **free verse**. Certain repeated phrases ('Queer', 'Such', 'Winged Victory'), spacing between the verse paragraphs, and the internal pattern of sounds ('shredded shank', 'attention', 'direction') all create rhythm and structure. The carefully chosen vocabulary ('devil', 'evil', 'filthy', 'evasions', 'sideways', 'cunningly', 'fiend', 'obscenity of trespass', 'accursed') adds to the association of the insect with wickedness in the poet's mind.

Lawrence believed that free verse was appropriate for poetry of the 'immediate present'. Through this form, he involves the reader in his account of a random clash between man and nature. The poem follows the rhythm of **a hostile exchange**, tracing the outraged thoughts and almost manic tussle of wills between human and creature from the opening threat and ensuing contest to bloodshed and closing death.

ANALYSIS

'D. H. Lawrence's poems capture the raw physical world with intensity and vigour.' Discuss this view, with particular reference to 'The Mosquito'.

Sample Paragraph

'The Mosquito' opens with a direct address from the patronising speaker who is quick to mock the mosquito – 'When did you start your tricks, Monsieur?' Lawrence immediately creates the vividly individualised presence of the insect with its 'shredded shanks' as it confronts the human. Through the poet's skill, we nervously follow the angry human as he observes the increasingly annoying insect. His growing irritation is conveyed in vindictive references to the insect's perceived personality, 'pointed fiend'. The mosquito never stops moving, it preys, it will 'stalk and prowl the air;' and manoeuvre in 'circles and evasions'. The creature is gradually challenging the human's supremacy by its 'anaesthetic power'. The man's helplessness is graphically conveyed through forceful language, 'deaden my attention in your direction'. The predator succeeds in 'enveloping', sealing the man. But it is the act of sucking blood from the outraged victim that is most intensely and vigorously highlighted. Short, abrupt lines conjure up the power of the mosquito as it gorges on 'Blood, red blood', 'My blood'. Its intense action is emphasised through repetition ('Such gorging'), which almost leaves it helpless, 'You stagger'.

Reading the poem, I get a strong sense of how the insect is only following the rules of the natural world, obeying its instinct for survival.

Examiner's Comment

Very good confident response that focuses on the raw physicality of nature. Discussion points are suitably supported with suitable references. Expression is impressive, with a strong, varied vocabulary ('individualised presence', 'perceived personality', 'manoeuvre', 'mystical transcedence'). Overall, a top-grade response, well rounded off with the concluding sentence.

N.B. Access your ebook for additional sample paragraphs and a list of useful quotes with commentary.

CLASS/HOMEWORK EXERCISES

1. 'D. H. Lawrence strips away sentimentality and consolation through his free verse poems.' In your opinion, how true is this of 'The Mosquito'? Support your answer with reference to the poem.

2. 'Conflict and drama are recurring features in Lawrence's poems.' Discuss this statement, with particular reference to 'The Mosquito'.

SUMMARY POINTS

- Man's relationship with nature and the animal world is a central theme.
- Powerful aural effects – repetition, alliteration, sibilant 's'.
- Satanic and magical terms, unusual similes and metaphors.
- Long sweeping lines interspersed with short one/two word lines.
- Range of attitudes, e.g. arrogance, uneasiness, derision, frustration, fulfilment, aggression, etc.

4 SNAKE

A snake came to my water-trough
On a hot, hot day, and I in pyjamas for the heat,
To drink there.

In the deep, strange-scented shade of the great dark carob-tree
I came down the steps with my pitcher   5
And must wait, must stand and wait, for there he was at the trough before me.

He reached down from a fissure in the earth-wall in the gloom
And trailed his yellow-brown slackness soft-bellied down, over the edge of the stone trough
And rested his throat upon the stone bottom,
And where the water had dripped from the tap, in a small clearness,   10
He sipped with his straight mouth,
Softly drank through his straight gums, into his slack long body,
Silently.

Someone was before me at my water-trough,
And I, like a second-comer, waiting.   15

He lifted his head from his drinking, as cattle do,
And looked at me vaguely, as drinking cattle do,
And flickered his two-forked tongue from his lips, and mused a moment,
And stooped and drank a little more,
Being earth-brown, earth-golden from the burning bowels of the earth   20
On the day of Sicilian July, with Etna smoking.

The voice of my education said to me
He must be killed,
For in Sicily the black, black snakes are innocent, the gold are venomous.

And voices in me said, If you were a man   25
You would take a stick and break him now, and finish him off.

But must I confess how I liked him,
How glad I was he had come like a guest in quiet, to drink at my water-trough
And depart peaceful, pacified, and thankless,
Into the burning bowels of this earth?   30

Was it cowardice, that I dared not kill him?
Was it perversity, that I longed to talk to him?
Was it humility, to feel so honoured?
I felt so honoured.

And yet those voices: 35
If you were not afraid, you would kill him!

And truly I was afraid, I was most afraid,
But even so, honoured still more
That he should seek my hospitality
From out the dark door of the secret earth.   40

He drank enough
And lifted his head, dreamily, as one who has drunken,
And flickered his tongue like a forked night on the air, so black,
Seeming to lick his lips,
And looked around like a god, unseeing, into the air,   45
And slowly turned his head,
And slowly, very slowly, as if thrice adream,
Proceeded to draw his slow length curving round
And climb again the broken bank of my wall-face.

And as he put his head into that dreadful hole,   50
And as he slowly drew up, snake-easing his shoulders, and entered farther,
A sort of horror, a sort of protest against his withdrawing into that horrid black hole,
Deliberately going into the blackness, and slowly drawing himself after,
Overcame me now his back was turned.

I looked round, I put down my pitcher,   55
I picked up a clumsy log
And threw it at the water-trough with a clatter.

I think it did not hit him,
But suddenly that part of him that was left behind convulsed in undignified haste.
Writhed like lightning, and was gone   60
Into the black hole, the earth-lipped fissure in the wall-front,
At which, in the intense still noon, I stared with fascination.

And immediately I regretted it.
I thought how paltry, how vulgar, what a mean act!
I despised myself and the voices of my accursed human education.   65

And I thought of the albatross,
And I wished he would come back, my snake.

For he seemed to me again like a king,
Like a king in exile, uncrowned in the underworld,
Now due to be crowned again.   70

And so, I missed my chance with one of the lords
Of life.
And I have something to expiate;
A pettiness.

Taormina

'like a guest in quiet'

Glossary

1	*snake*: limbless reptile; some are poisonous.	32	*perversity*: obstinacy, contrariness.
1	*trough*: container.	47	*thrice adream*: in deep unconsciousness.
4	*carob-tree*: Mediterranean red-flowered tree.	57	*clatter*: crashing sound.
5	*pitcher*: container, small bucket.	59	*convulsed*: shuddered, collapsed.
7	*fissure*: crevice, opening.	60	*Writhed*: thrashed, struggled.
9	*slackness*: looseness, sagging.	64	*paltry*: low, contemptible.
15	*second-comer*: late arrival.	66	*albatross*: white ocean bird; a metaphor for worry or guilt. In Coleridge's poem, 'The Rime of the Ancient Mariner', an albatross was the bird that a sailor repented killing.
18	*mused*: reflected, wondered.		
20	*bowels*: *depths*, underground.		
21	*Etna*: Mount Etna, an active volcano in Sicily.	73	*expiate*: correct, redress.
24	*venomous*: poisonous, deadly.	74	*pettiness*: spitefulness, small-mindedness.

INITIAL RESPONSE

1. In your own words, describe the mood and atmosphere that Lawrence creates in lines 1-13.

2. Choose two vivid images from the poem and comment briefly on the effectiveness of each.

3. In your view, what is the central theme or message of 'Snake'? Support your answer with reference to the poem.

STUDY NOTES

'Snake' was written when D. H. Lawrence was living in Taormina, a hilltop town on the east coast of Sicily, in 1920–1921, and is probably his best-known poem. It dramatises a confrontation between the refined human mind and the native forces of the earth, embodied by a snake that appears one morning at the narrator's water-trough. The experience is transformed by Lawrence and invested with mythical grandeur. The poem can be examined not only as a prime example of Lawrence's free verse technique, but as one in which the 'immediate present' comes to life on the page and in the mind of the reader.

The poem's **opening lines** establish the sweltering Mediterranean setting. 'On a hot, hot day', Lawrence's narrator takes his pitcher to the water-trough. Repetition – a prominent feature of this free verse poem – initiates the **hypnotic rhythm**. Lawrence's style is simple, the diction colloquial, and the word order that of common speech. But the effect is reserved and dignified. Domestic and exotic images are combined as the pyjama-clad human observes the snake 'In the deep, strange-scented shade of the great dark carob-tree'. At first, the presumptuous speaker views the snake as an intruder forcing him to 'stand and wait'.

Light and dark are contrasted in the snake's vivid golden colour and the surrounding gloom. Lawrence conveys the creature's physicality with emphasis on his 'straight mouth', 'slack long body' and flickering 'two-forked tongue'. Run-through lines and emphatic sibilant sounds suggest the snake's **slow, subtle movement**. The poet stretches his sentences, using multiple adjectives in lines such as 'yellow-brown slackness' and 'soft-bellied down' (**line 8**). Many phrases such as these use hyphenation, so that several words are elongated. Lawrence also hooks his sentence-long stanzas together by beginning lines with conjunctions: 'And must wait', 'And trailed'. When we trace the visual structure of the lines on the page, it seems almost as if the snake has swallowed the poem's form.

Lines 7-13 provide a **sensual description** of the animal's precise behaviour. Unlike the human observer, it acts entirely on instinct. Yet Lawrence personifies the reptile: 'He reached down', 'sipped with his straight mouth'. The snake's natural ease within this timeless primal setting creates a strong sense of harmony. It is completely unaware of the human intruder, clearly out of place in this wilderness. There is something slightly ridiculous about the speaker's immediate reaction. Coming from the civilised world, he accepts that he is now the 'second-comer' in an orderly queue – but with begrudging resentment.

The tense stand-off between the human and natural worlds continues through **lines 16-26**. Compelled by an inherent reverence, the narrator watches closely as the snake drinks. He focuses on its graceful movements, comparing it to domesticated farm animals, 'drinking cattle'. Slow, deliberate rhythms suggest the intense heat and languor of the **sultry Mediterranean atmosphere**. But this is where the snake is in its true element: 'earth-golden from the burning bowels of the earth'. Meanwhile, distant volcanic smoke from Mount Etna testifies to the inner earth's hidden powers.

Both fear and fascination are evident in the speaker's **internal struggle** between rational and natural feelings. His 'education' has always warned him that the snake is dangerous: 'in Sicily the black, black snakes are innocent, the gold are venomous'.

Although he has been taught to destroy these creatures, he cannot bring himself to harm the snake because he 'liked him' and was glad 'he had come like a guest in quiet' (**line 28**). This tense scene can also be interpreted on a symbolic level. Associated with evil, the snake assumes a more ominous meaning. Emerging from the 'burning bowels of this earth', it is particularly suggestive of the biblical serpent.

The narrator continues to struggle with the two conflicting 'voices' he hears: one insists that the snake should be killed while the other maintains that it deserves respect and must therefore be spared. In his **conflicted, deepening consciousness**, the speaker moves from casual description to insightful confession. An urgent series of rhetorical questions reflects this intense inner debate: 'Was it cowardice, that I dared not kill him?' Increasingly conscious that he does not belong in the underworld of the snake, he wavers between an uncomfortable sense of 'perversity' and feeling 'honoured' (**line 32**). But the expectations of his masculine conditioning persist: 'If you were a man', '*If you were not afraid, you would kill him!*'

The powerfully crafted syntax and unbroken rhythm of **lines 41-49** work together to produce a **mesmerising effect**. Repeated references to the snake's dreamlike and unhurried presence add to the wistful tone. The narrator envisions this majestic creature as a mythical lord of the underworld ('like a god, unseeing'), an embodiment of all those mysterious forces of nature that man fears and neglects. Lawrence's detailed imagery is characteristically compelling. The snake's black tongue flickers 'like a forked night on the air', the dramatic simile suggesting a lightning flash plunging the noon-day scene into momentary night. It seems as though dark powers inhabit the 'door of the secret earth': Mount Etna might erupt, the deadly snake might strike. Suddenly the tone becomes harsh and ugly as the speaker reverts to the conditioned reflex of a rationalistic culture.

Faced with the snake's withdrawal into a fissure ('the blackness'), the narrator's **fearful imagination takes over** and he almost becomes incoherent. His disgust expresses itself in hysterical terms – 'dreadful', 'horrid'. He is overcome by 'a sort of protest' that causes him to act: 'I picked up a clumsy log/And threw it at the water-trough' (**line 56**). This cowardly action has an instant effect; the snake loses its former dignity and becomes 'convulsed', an obscene writhing thing that the speaker's education tells him it is, a reptile of the mind.

It's interesting that the narrator expresses neither triumph nor relief, but **deep revulsion** and self-disgust at causing such pointless violence: 'immediately I regretted it' (**line 63**). He regards his behaviour as 'mean' and 'vulgar', likening himself to the fictional Ancient Mariner who killed the albatross and was then compelled to acknowledge his offence. The speaker's 'paltry' action leads him to reverse the usual hierarchy. It is his 'human education' that is 'accursed', while in its majestic naturalness, the snake remains 'one of the lords /Of life' (**line 71**). The snake has recoiled into the underground and now appears to be like 'a king in exile' whereas in the open air it was a powerful sovereign. The ending fades away on a note of self-loathing as the narrator comes to terms with the 'pettiness' of what he has done.

Lawrence's 'Snake' is a typically resonant discourse between the teachings of reason and natural intuition. The poet presents us with a triumph of style and idiom, a highly memorable example of free verse where perception is embodied in rhythms that are an essential part of the poem's meaning. Religious terminology – of atoning for sin – would indicate that Lawrence is using the snake as a symbol of the battle between good and evil. Perhaps its real significance lies in the wider questions it raises about how human beings face up to the moral challenges of the natural world.

ANALYSIS

'Drama and tension are recurring features of Lawrence's poems.' Discuss this statement, with particular reference to 'Snake'.

Sample Paragraph

D. H. Lawrence's poem 'Snake' has many dramatic elements, particularly conflict. The poet sets the scene on a 'hot day' in Sicily where the central character is in his pyjamas beside a water-trough. The atmosphere is edgy with intense heat. He is immediately challenged by the 'yellow-brown' snake seeking water and a stalemate occurs. In the background, a volcanic mountain adds to the tension – 'Etna smoking'. I thought that the real conflict was taking place within the man's mind, saying 'take a stick and break him now'. This internal debate is agonising. Several rhetorical questions show how conflicted the man is – 'Was it cowardice?' His upbringing and 'education' tells him to kill but he feels 'so honoured' that the snake is seeking 'hospitality'. This drama continues throughout the poem. Lawrence also uses striking, dramatic images of darkness and light to illustrate the conflict between good and evil. The snake has come from 'the dark door of the secret earth'. When the drama reaches a climax and the man throws the stick at the snake, it retreats back into the 'horrid black hole'. In a way, the conflict has been resolved and the man is left with his guilt – an anti-climax.

Examiner's Comment

Informed discussion focusing well on aspects of drama (setting, conflict, tension, climax, contrasting images). Ranges over a variety of points, e.g. 'internal debate is agonising'. Supporting quotations are integrated successfully into the commentary. Expression is clear, but slightly pedestrian, e.g. the second last sentence. Overall, a good, solid response that just falls short of the top grade.

N.B. Access your ebook for additional sample paragraphs and a list of useful quotes with commentary.

CLASS/HOMEWORK EXERCISES

1. 'D. H. Lawrence makes effective use of rhythm and repetition to convey meaning in his poems.' To what extent is this true of 'Snake'? Support your answer with reference to the poem.

2. 'Lawrence's poetry often addresses themes that have a universal significance.' To what extent do you agree with this view? Support your answer with reference to 'Snake'.

SUMMARY POINTS

- Key themes include the natural world, human culture, nature, sin and guilt.
- Conflicting 'voices' within him represent natural instinct and cultural conditioning.
- Dramatic tension created by the confrontation between man and nature.
- Effective use of precise description, vivid imagery, contrasting tones and moods.
- The rhythm of the loose verse often suggests the snake's movement.

reflections on us Perspective.
not ^just about a bird.

5 HUMMING-BIRD

I can imagine, in some otherworld
Primeval-dumb, far back   *no personality*
                                  eerie nature, stagnant, emotionless
In that most awful stillness, that only gasped and hummed,
Humming-birds raced down the avenues. *energised, dynamic*

Before anything had a soul, *spirit, conscience*   5
While life was a heave of Matter, half inanimate,
This little bit chipped off in brilliance
And went whizzing through the slow, vast, succulent stems.

I believe there were no flowers, then,
In the world where the humming-bird flashed ahead of creation.   10
I believe he pierced the slow vegetable veins with his long beak.

Probably he was big
As mosses, and little lizards, they say, were once big.   *room for thought &*
Probably he was a jabbing, terrifying monster.   *speculation*
                  irritant
We look at him through the wrong end of the long telescope of Time, 15
Luckily for us. *inappropriate scale*
                underestimate   *Española*   *exaggerated sense*
                                                       of self-importance.

'ahead of creation'

Glossary

There are over 300 species of humming-birds. All are small and brilliantly coloured. They get their name from the humming sound created by their rapidly beating wings. They can fly backwards, and are the only group of birds able to do so.

2   *Primeval-dumb*: pre-historic, elemental, primordial.
6   *Matter*: substance.
6   *inanimate*: lifeless.
7   *succulent stems*: luscious stalks.

INITIAL RESPONSE

1. From your reading of lines 1-4, what image do you get of the prehistoric world? Support your answer with reference to the text.

2. Choose two aural images from the poem that appeal to you and comment briefly on their effectiveness.

3. In your opinion, what point is Lawrence making in line 15: 'We look at him through the wrong end of the long telescope of Time'?

STUDY NOTES

Like so many of the poems in Lawrence's Birds, Beasts and Flowers *collection (published in 1923), 'Humming-Bird' has a fresh, modern feel and spontaneity. It is thought that Lawrence wrote this short poem after reading several vivid descriptions of humming-birds, so it is probably not a record of immediate experience. Instead, the poet reinterprets the geological past and restores it to its own special sense of excitement. Through his poetic imagination, he creates a timeless image of the humming-bird whose life force evokes the hidden power of its evolution.*

The poem travels 'far back' in geological time to the origin and predominance of the humming-bird. Lawrence sets the chilling scene: 'some otherworld/Primeval-dumb'. He imagines the 'most awful stillness' of a strange pre-historic setting. When the humming-bird appears, it flashes through the poem: 'raced down the avenues'. The ecstatic **opening four lines** include playful internal rhyme ('dumb', 'some') and sibilant effects ('stillness', 'gasped') that suggest the **unexpected presence** of these primal creatures.

Dynamic verbs ('chipped off', 'whizzing') capture the life force and energy of the humming-bird, highlighting the 'awful stillness' of the surrounding 'half inanimate' natural environment where sprawling plants leave only 'avenues' between them. **Lawrence controls the pace of the poem** beautifully – contrasting the lumbering 'heave of Matter' with the agility and darting pace of the humming-bird, which is 'a little bit chipped off in brilliance' (**line 7**). In this unfamilar primeval location, these small birds provide an unexpected striking flash of colour.

The poet is filled with enthusiasm and a childlike sense of wonder about pre-human times, 'Before anything had a soul'. He sees the humming-bird as the first independent entity to evolve from undifferentiated matter – the original isolated soul. Lawrence is also **a master of free verse and informal language**. Throughout 'Humming-Bird', the pace alternates between the shorter curt lines and the longer free-winging descriptions associated with the bird in flight: 'And went whizzing through the slow, vast succulent stems' (**line 8**). Throughout the poem, this jaunty lilt to the rhythm mirrors the bird's swift movement.

In imagining the long distant past, Lawrence considers how the earliest birds would have survived in a flowerless environment by living off the sap of plants ('pierced the slow vegetable veins'). A range of song-like **auditory techniques** – the onomatopoeic verb, slender vowels and the alliterative 'v' effect – echoes the determined efforts to survive within the prehistoric habitat.

Reiteration and recapitulation are features of Lawrence's train of thought, which is propelled forward and held together by such repeated phrasing as 'in some otherworld', 'In that most awful stillness' and 'I believe', 'I believe'. Such repetition continues into the poem's final lines where the poet speculates on the likely size of the first humming-bird: 'Probably he was big' and 'Probably he was a jabbing, terrifying monster' (**line 14**). The emphasis on the humming-bird's monstrous antecedents is disturbingly realistic. But although this is a somewhat bizarre vision, Lawrence clearly rejoices at the nightmare image he has created.

He concludes on **an ironic note**, personifying the bird and showing it appropriate respect. The thought that the prehistoric creature was 'once big' – and indeed monstrous – should make us revise our attitude to his smaller, contemporary counterpart 'through the long telescope of Time'. The poet might well be reminding readers that humans were not always masters of creation. Is he warning us against complacency and that there will also be something new to displace the old?

The 'long telescope of Time' – the image magnified by the capitalised 'T' – occupies a long line whereas the succinct **line 16** startles us with the implication of **human limitation**. Today's humming-birds are small and – as the telescope metaphor indicates – we see them in inappropriate scale. The colloquial final line, 'Luckily for us', half-humorously leaves the reader to decide how a proper perspective might challenge our own human status and exaggerated sense of self-importance.

Lawrence's **witty poem quivers with energy**, mirroring the alternating order and chaos inherent in creation. It typifies many of the poet's hallmarks – the lightness of touch, the immediacy of the voice and quicksilver language – all of which are the perfect embodiment of the wondrous humming-bird.

ANALYSIS

'D. H. Lawrence's most memorable poems have a spontaneity and sense of drama that make an immediate impact on readers.'

Sample Paragraph

'Humming-Bird' is an exotic, highly imaginative poem in which the poet envisions the bird in a primeval-dumb world, in an 'awful stillness' before 'anything had a soul,/While life was a heave of Matter'. Lawrence begins with the words 'I imagine' and then takes us on a dreamlike journey to when life was starting to evolve on Earth. It's a very dramatic scene. Then suddenly out of the great void, the humming-bird is seen as flashing 'ahead of creation', piercing 'the slow vegetable veins with his long beak'. The images of nature are vivid and cinematic. The sense of immediacy is evident in the conversational language and everyday speech rhythms used by the poet – 'This little bit chipped off in brilliance' for example, referring to how the colourful bird accidentally evolved into life. Some of the expressions are youthful – 'Probably he was big' and 'Luckily for us'. The poet's tone is always one of excitement and wonder. I liked Lawrence's personal enthusiasm and his fascination with these tiny birds. The poem was both thoughtful and playful – almost like a song in its lively rhythm – the kind of spontaneous poetry that I enjoy.

Examiner's Comment

A good personal response to the question. The focus on spontaneity is sustained throughout and includes interesting points on Lawrence's dreamlike poetic vision and informal language use. There is also some impressive discussion on key aspects of dramatic style (imagery, rhythm and tone). Overall, a confident high-grade standard.

N.B. Access your ebook for additional sample paragraphs and a list of useful quotes with commentary.

CLASS/HOMEWORK EXERCISES

1. 'Lawrence often makes imaginative use of evocative sound effects to convey meaning in his poetry.' Discuss this statement with particular reference to 'Humming-Bird'.

2. 'Throughout much of his poetry, D. H. Lawrence is primarily interested in making discoveries.' Discuss this view, with particular reference to 'Humming-Bird'.

SUMMARY POINTS

- Free verse achieves greater emotional intensity than simple fragmented prose.
- Lawrence articulates the essence of the humming-bird.
- He also challenges us to re-evaluate our views on evolution.
- Effective use of varying line lengths and informal tone.
- Wide-ranging aural effects – repetition, sibilance, assonance and alliteration.

Private, closeness, seduction, quiet still.

6 INTIMATES

Dominant figure
Sense of conflict
Don't you care for my love? she said bitterly. *argumentative*
direct, blunt

casual
I handed her the mirror, and said: *- passed on*
Please address these questions to the proper person! *bureaucratic*
mocking Please make all requests to head-quarters! *ridiculing her* 5
formal. In all matters of emotional importance
please approach the supreme authority direct! *clinical tone*
So I handed her the mirror.

volatile/violent
And she would have broken it over my head,
ego
but she caught sight of her own reflection *unpredictable*
and that held her spellbound for two seconds *-fickle* 10
while I fled. *mesmerised* *inconsistent*

'spellbound'

INITIAL RESPONSE

1. Based on your reading of the poem, describe the relationship between the speaker and his female companion. Support your answer with reference to the text.

2. Lawrence uses several poetic techniques in the poem, including direct speech, repetition, alliteration and run-on lines Choose one technique that particularly appeals to you and comment briefly on its effectiveness.

3. Write your own personal response to the poem, highlighting the impact it made on you.

STUDY NOTES

'Intimates' is a short, witty poem from Lawrence's collection, More Pansie, *published in 1932 after his death from tuberculosis. In his introduction, the poet wrote: 'This little bunch of fragments is offered as a bunch of pensées ... handful of thoughts'. They were based on 'Pensées' by the French philosopher Blaise Pascal, fragments of thoughts and theology, such as, 'Do you believe people to wish good of you? Don't speak'. Lawrence also refers to the French word 'panser', to dress or bandage a wound. He regarded these verses as medicinal, administering them to the emotional wounds we suffer in modern civilisation. He regarded 'Each little piece' as a thought which comes from the heart, 'with its own blood and instinct running in it ... if you hold my pansies properly to the light, they may show a running vein of fire.'*

The title, 'Intimates', if used as a noun suggests a loving relationship, but if as a verb, it can mean 'insinuates' or 'hints'. Lawrence sets up the expectation that this couple really understand each other. However, the poem begins with jolting directness and readers are placed, without warning, in the middle of a **spiteful argument** between the couple. A woman's acerbic question plaintively intones, 'Don't you care for my love?' (**line 1**). She is complaining about a lack of concern for her happiness and the welfare of their relationship. The use of the verb 'said' indicates that this is more a statement than a plea. Her tone is harsh: 'bitterly'. The implication is clearly that the man is not particularly interested.

But he is stung into action and hands her 'the mirror'. The definite article suggests that she used this mirror frequently. In a clipped detached tone, he issues a list of formal requests. The repeated use of the word 'Please', usually found in polite conversation, seems not only absurd but sardonic and cold. The alliteration of the hard 'p' sound, ('Please', 'proper person') conveys an anger barely concealed. The adjective 'proper' (**line 3**) not only refers to the correct person to whom the questions should be addressed, but also indicates a prudish one. Meanwhile, he continues to reprimand her, 'Please make all requests to head-quarters'. The **sarcastic inference** of this odd remark suggests that the fraught relationship is being controlled by a third party or some other outside influence.

The speaker feels increasingly **frustrated**, as it appears that the woman is not even listening to him. Paradoxically, in stilted language that is anything but sensitive, he directs that 'all matters of emotional importance', should be with the person who has the unnamed official power that can enforce obedience, 'please approach the supreme authority direct' (**line 6**). He then concludes his terse argument with the conjunction 'So'. It is left to the reader to decide whether the section concludes as 'and then' he handed her the mirror or 'therefore' he handed her the mirror. If the latter is the case, it would signify that he thinks he has won the argument. Lawrence places a creative pause at this stage to allow us to imagine the woman's feelings of anger rising.

Line 8 discloses that the speaker knew precisely what he was doing all along and is also able to predict the outcome of his actions. He has given his companion the mirror to look at her reflection because, in his opinion, she feels that she is the 'the proper person', the 'head-quarters', 'the supreme authority'. This implies a certain smugness in the woman's attitude; she is always right. We are left with the impression that **this is not the first hurtful exchange** between the couple. These 'intimates' know each other very well and so can deliver cruel blows in a quarrel. The conditional 'she would have broken it over my head' infers that their rows often descend into physical violence.

However, the mood changes on the conjunction 'but'. Wryly, the speaker recounts how the woman sees herself in the mirror and becomes mesmerised by 'her own reflection'. The use of the pronoun 'own' and the emphatic verb 'spellbound' paint a picture of an extremely **self-interested person**. Run-on lines capture the 'two seconds' she spends gazing at herself. They hint at the vanity of the fairytale Wicked Queen who asks 'Mirror, mirror on the wall, who is the fairest of them all?' **Line 11** heralds the man's last evasive action, 'while I fled'. Fearing the worst, he makes a hasty escape while his companion is preoccupied. The monosyllabic verb 'fled' has a finality that suggests a victory of sorts in this particular skirmish. The man has escaped the stifling constraints of the woman's demands – for the moment.

While the female character in this poem has been exposed as domineering and self-obsessed, the man's behaviour throughout has not exactly been admirable. Is the poet suggesting that while the couple know each other well, they are by no means 'Intimates'? The only victim of their feud is the relationship itself. This unsettling poem challenges readers. The poet has **presented this small domestic drama through quoted conversation and actions**, but has refrained from commenting directly. Is the poem simply holding up a reflective surface allowing the reader to look at personal relationships and the lack of successful communication? Lawrence believed that poetry makes us more aware of ourselves. 'Intimates' provides an opportunity to examine the conflict between frustration and fulfilment in relationships and in ourselves.

ANALYSIS

'D. H. Lawrence believed that all poems should be personal sentiments with a sense of spontaneity.' Discuss this statement in relation to the poem 'Intimates'.

Sample Paragraph

In this elegant, bitter poem, Lawrence parachutes unsuspecting readers into the midst of the swirling emotions of a squabbling couple. The poem opens on the jarring note of a complaining woman, 'Don't you care for my love?' The spontaneous combustion of frustration and lack of fulfilment is conveyed through reported conversations and the behaviour of the woman and her partner. I felt as though I was actually eaves-dropping on a private moment. The man's spontaneous action in handing the mirror to the self-obsessed woman and his list of deeply wounding orders suggests a dysfunctional couple. Genuine personal sentiments are disclosed – the woman does not feel appreciated while he feels harangued by 'the supreme authority'. At the same time, the reader's sympathy sways towards the rather vain woman who is subjected to such derision. She also has to contend with a man who runs away – another unexpected development. He, however, feels stifled by her superiority, 'the proper person'. An insistent jabbing rhyme adds to the man's growing feeling of claustrophobia, 'said', 'head', 'fled'. Through capturing the spontaneity of the fight, Lawrence reveals the truth to all couples, the irony that scoring points in an argument is not genuine contact and only succeeds in destroying the relationship.

Examiner's Comment

Good, intelligent high-grade response that engages closely with the poem. The idea of spontaneity is addressed effectively through specific expressions, (such as 'parachutes', 'spontaneous', 'unexpected' and 'growing'). Apt quotations are successfully integrated into the discussion and assured vocabulary ('derision', 'harangued by', 'contend with', 'feeling of claustrophobia', etc.) is impressive.

N.B. Access your ebook for additional sample paragraphs and a list of useful quotes with commentary.

CLASS/HOMEWORK EXERCISES

1. 'Lawrence's poetry often uses particular everyday scenes to explore issues that have much wider universal significance.' Discuss this view with reference to the poem 'Intimates'.

2. 'D. H. Lawrence's carefully crafted poetry frequently challenges social constraints.' To what extent is this true of 'Intimates'? Support your answer with reference to the poem.

SUMMARY POINTS

- Central themes include conflict, lack of communication, vanity, deception.
- Poetic techniques – direct speech, contrast between personal and formal language, alliteration, repetition, run-on lines, creative pause, paradox.
- Varied tones – disappointment, hurt, anger, sarcasm, mockery, etc.

(Handwritten annotations around the top:)

unexpected - surprised
delight - mood of deep satisfaction
ecstasy contentment

Can't reflect, pause, observe in the clutter of life.

. H. Lawrence 291

absolute
uncontaminated
sheer - unadulterated
pure

unapologetic confession

delicious - taste
savour
sweetness of the experience
envelops him.

authentic

7 DELIGHT OF BEING ALONE

I know no greater delight than the sheer delight of being alone.
It makes me realise the delicious pleasure of the moon
that she has in travelling by herself: throughout time,
or the splendid growing of an ash-tree
alone, on a hill-side in the north, humming in the wind.   5

travelling - voluntary exploration

soft
cold

'humming'

moon - constant fixed point

STUDY NOTES

This is one of Lawrence's most conventional and beautiful poems. It was published after his death in Last Poems (1932). It expresses the poet's romantic attitudes about the pleasures of being alone and reflects his closeness to nature.

The simple directness and sincerity of the opening line shows Lawrence's enthusiasm for 'the sheer delight of being alone'. His emphasis on 'delight' establishes the mood of deep satisfaction. The poet's acknowledgment of the 'delicious pleasure of the moon' is enhanced by the use of **richly sibilant sounds**. As always, Lawrence's appreciation of nature is beyond doubt. The moon has long been a traditional symbol of solitude and self-sufficiency – and the poet now senses its mysterious power 'throughout time'.

To some extent, **line 2** reads like an excerpt from the diary of a man who is seriously ill and close to death. This would explain Lawrence's desire to take up a form outside of his human body, that of the night-wandering moon. He is also drawn to the 'splendid growing of an ash-tree … humming in the wind', described with characteristically precise eloquence. The poem takes on **a mystical quality** with the final suggestion that Lawrence's soul may return to become part of the greater spirit of the timeless natural world. Lawrence's attraction to the moon and the lonely tree on a hillside is the refuge of his poetic imagination – the last refuge.

8 ABSOLUTE REVERENCE

I feel absolute reverence to nobody and to nothing human,
neither to persons nor things nor ideas, ideals nor religions nor institutions,
to these things I feel only respect, and a tinge of reverence
when I see the fluttering of pure life in them.

But to something unseen, unknown, creative
from which I feel I am a derivative
I feel absolute reverence. Say no more!

'fluttering of pure life'

Glossary

1	*reverence*: devotion, worship.		3	*institutions*: organisations, establishments.
2	*ideals*: dreams, principles.		7	*derivative*: product, result.
4	*tinge*: touch, hint.			

INITIAL RESPONSE

D. H. Lawrence always maintained that he was 'a profoundly religious man'. His religion was certainly real enough, but unorthodox and informal. For Lawrence, it was essentially mystical, similar to other visionary poets, such as Shelley and Yeats.

The poem's emphatic opening establishes Lawrence's belief that all of reality is identical with divinity. His passionate tone ('I feel absolute reverence to nobody and to nothing human') can be understood positively as the view that nothing exists outside of God. He goes on to clarify his deeply felt opposition to conventional doctrines and organised religions.

The poet's sympathies lie entirely with what he calls 'the fluttering of pure life', an image that immediately evokes the vitality and beauty of nature. His God is the transcendent reality of which the material universe and human beings are mere manifestations. Characteristically uncompromising, he concludes his personal philosophy on a dismissive note: 'Say no more!'

D. H. Lawrence's poetry is a long and rich exploration of reverence towards the mystery of embodied life: 'something unseen unknown, creative/from which I feel I am derivative'. There is no logic in such lines, but they sum up Lawrence's pantheistic, mystical, unswerving and wholly sincere worship of life and the life force that lies at the root of all his thinking.

9 WHAT HAVE THEY DONE TO YOU?

What have they done to you, men of the masses, creeping back and forth to work?

What have they done to you, the saviours of the people, oh what have they saved you from
    while they pocketed the money?

Alas, they have saved you from yourself, from your own frail dangers
and devoured you from the machine, the vast maw of iron.

They saved you from your squalid cottages and poverty of hand to mouth   5
and embedded you in workmen's dwellings, where your wage is the dole of work, and the
    dole is your wage of nullity.

They took away, oh they took away your man's native instincts and intuitions
and gave you a board-school education, newspapers, and the cinema.

They stole your body from you, and left you an animated carcass
to work with, and nothing else: 10
unless goggling eyes, to goggle at the film
and a board-school brain, stuffed up with the ha'penny press.

Your instincts gone, your intuitions gone, your passions dead
Oh carcass with a board-school mind and a ha'penny newspaper intelligence,
what have they done to you, what have they done to you, Oh what have they done to you?   15

Oh look at my fellow-men, oh look at them
the masses! Oh, what has been done to them?

'the vast maw of iron'

Glossary

1   *the masses*: the working classes.
2   *saviours*: redeemers, protectors.

INITIAL RESPONSE

1. In your opinion, what is the dominant tone of this poem? Is it angry, powerful, ironic, sentimental, uncontrolled, etc.? Support your answer with reference to the text.

2. Choose one memorable image (visual or aural) from the poem and comment on its effectiveness.

3. Based on your reading of the poem, what impression do you get of the poet, D. H. Lawrence? Support your answer with reference to the text.

STUDY NOTES

D. H. Lawrence did not profess to be a socialist, but there can be no doubt that he possessed strong ideas about what he believed was wrong with the money-wages-profit system and what sort of society would be best for humans to live in. Lawrence describes his aversion to modernity in 'What Have They Done To You?'. The poem is thought to have been written during the poet's visits to Majorca and Tuscany in 1929.

Throughout his literary work and poetry, D. H. Lawrence expressed his criticism of modernisation as reflected in urban poverty, steel-mills factory work. The poem opens with an **impassioned rhetorical question** that directly challenges uncontrolled materialism: 'What have they done to you, men of the masses, creeping back and forth to work?' The alliterative 'm' sound suggests the countless numbers of industrialised employees who are diminished by their adverse working conditions. Lawrence's choice of the emotive verb, 'creeping', emphasises the notion of suppression and dependency.

The impassioned rhetorical tone and emotive language, which will dominate the entire poem, continues in **line 2** as the poet mocks the so-called 'saviours of the people'. In accusing the wealthy employers of exploitation ('they pocketed the money'), Lawrence points out the obvious irony that this was the only saving involved. But the poet's anger is moderated with expressions of **regretful frustration** ('Alas'). However, his compassion for the poor and their 'frail dangers' is quickly replaced by fury at what he sees as their victimisation. The new industrial age has: 'devoured you with the machine, the vast maw of iron'. Lawrence's choice of violent metaphorical language symbolises the monstrous dehumanising effect of mass mechanisation.

Lines 5–6 focus on the wretched 'hand to mouth' living conditions of working-class people who are expected to be grateful for any kind of employment. Repulsive imagery ('squalid cottages') and broad vowel assonance ('mouth', 'dole', 'nullity') add to our understanding of the pathos Lawrence associates with such widespread hardship. The extended line lengths and turgid rhythms also suggest their relentless struggle for survival.

A significant change of emphasis occurs in **line 7**, however, when **the poet broadens his scathing criticism**. Up until this point, the 'they' targeted by Lawrence referred to the powerful factory owners and captains of industry. Now he turns his attention to the **wider establishment forces** in politics and education: 'board-school education, newspapers, and the cinema'. From his point of view, ordinary people are not just oppressed by poverty, but are also controlled through the conservative school system. In addition, their lives are further diminished by cheap journalism and popular entertainment.

The tone becomes increasingly melodramatic as Lawrence rages against the ruling class – those who misuse power to stifle creativity and reduce the common worker to a passive 'animated carcass' (**line 9**). In a series of exasperated outbursts, he again attacks the country's press and media, and castigates the film industry – presumably for producing undemanding escapism designed for 'goggling eyes'. The 'ha'penny press' is further accused of keeping readers' minds 'stuffed up' with useless information.

The poet's central argument that most ordinary citizens are systematically diverted from improving their lives builds to a climax in the **final lines**. Questions now begin with the exclamatory 'Oh', highlighting the anguish he feels. The plaintive repetition of 'what have they done to you?' is all but an **admission of utter despair**. In contrast to the protracted oratorical style throughout the poem, the ending is terse and to the point. Lawrence's reference to his 'fellow-men' (**line 16**) has particular significance both with and without irony. While he is aiming a final cynical blow at those who have no respect for humanity, there is no denying the poet's own tender feeling for other people.

Indeed, the entire poem is primarily a persuasive expression of Lawrence's aversion to modernity – articulated through repetitive language describing the monotonous, menial tasks of factories and the enslavement of his fellow Britons. In strongly denouncing the dehumanising effects of industrialisation, the poet raises interesting questions about modern society and community, about freedom and constraint. It is left to readers to decide whether Lawrence's use of hyperbole and excessive rhetoric enriches or devalues his sentiments.

ANALYSIS

'D. H. Lawrence writes dramatic poems that often combine polemical commentary with heartfelt compassion.' Discuss this view, with particular reference to 'What Have They Done To You?'.

Sample Paragraph

When we first studied 'What Have They Done To You?', it actually seemed much more like a political speech rather than a poem. Lawrence held very strong views and believed that the traditional English way of life had changed for the worst. In his opinion, factory towns and sweatshops had turned workers into slaves. The poem has a dramatic opening, with an oratorical tone: 'What have they done to you, men of the masses?' The poem is filled with persuasive techniques, especially repetition. Lawrence uses negative images of 'squalid' houses and assembly-line workers being 'devoured' by the 'vast maw of iron'. He views modern-day life as totally unnatural. Although the language suggests savagery, there is always a sense that the poet's main concern is with the vulnerable workers and their poverty-stricken families. Expressive verbs such as 'took away' and 'stole' express his compassionate concern for these unfortunate people. The 'animated carcass' comparison combines Lawrence's anger at their mistreatment with his sympathy for such people. This dual tone goes through the poem. He ends with the expression, 'Oh look at my fellow-men' – which, for me, perfectly sums up his heartfelt attitude.

Examiner's Comment

A high-grade response. The introductory comments showed engagement with Lawrence's strongly held views. Points were developed and aptly illustrated with accurate quotation. Some impressive discussion regarding the poet's persuasive style and use of negative language was balanced by illustrations of his sympathetic tone.

N.B. Access your ebook for additional sample paragraphs and a list of useful quotes with commentary.

CLASS/HOMEWORK EXERCISES

1. 'Lawrence is severely critical of what he views as "a state of suppression" in which individuals are tormented and made inhuman by the processes of industrialisation.' Discuss this statement with reference to 'What Have They Done To You?'.

2. In your opinion, how relevant is 'What Have They Done To You?' to modern times? Support your answer with reference to the poem.

SUMMARY POINTS

- Key themes: the suppression of natural human individuality by industrialisation.
- Contrasting tones: anger, frustration, sympathy, irony, anguish, dejection.
- Effective use of metaphorical language, onomatopoeia and vivid imagery.
- Rhetorical style – repetition, questions, speech rhythms, emotive language, etc.

10 BABY MOVEMENTS II: 'TRAILING CLOUDS'

As a drenched, drowned bee
Hangs numb and heavy from the bending flower, *dips, droops.*
 So clings to me,
My baby, her brown hair brushed with wet tears
 And laid laughterless on her cheek,   5
Her soft white legs hanging heavily over my arm
 Swinging to my lullaby.
My sleeping baby hangs upon my life
 As a silent bee at the end of a shower
 Draws down the burdened flower.   10
She who has always seemed so light
 Sways on my arm like sorrowful, storm-heavy boughs,
Even her floating hair sinks like storm-bruised young leaves
Reaching downwards:
 As the wings of a drenched, drowned bee   15
 Are a heaviness, and a weariness.

'the burdened flower'

Glossary

2	*numb*: dazed, deadened.	10	*burdened*: laden, weighed down.
3	*clings*: attaches.	12	*boughs*: small branches.

INITIAL RESPONSE

1. Why, in your opinion, does Lawrence compare the sleeping child to 'a drenched, drowned bee'? Support your answer with reference to the text

2. Lawrence makes use of sound throughout the poem. Choose one aural image from the poem and briefly comment on its effectiveness.

3. Write your own personal response to the poem, highlighting the impact it made on you.

A Note on Imagism

Imagism is the name given to a type of poetry that aimed at clarity of expression through the use of precise visual images. It originated in early 20th-century Anglo-American literature and was part of the wider Modernist movement. Imagist poets do not directly describe the themes behind the images they use; instead, the images themselves become the primary subject of the poems. Some of D. H. Lawrence's early poetry reflects the influence of the leading Imagist poet of this time, Ezra Pound.

STUDY NOTES

'Trailing Clouds' is part of a two-poem sequence called Baby-Movements, *one of D. H. Lawrence's earliest works. It was first published in 1909, apparently based on a description of his landlady's baby daughter. The poem was later re-named 'A Baby Asleep After Pain'. Lawrence's original title had been taken from a poem by William Wordsworth ('trailing clouds of glory do we come/From God, who is our home'). Wordsworth believed in the eternal spiritual nature of life.*

Lawrence's **opening lines** are dominated by the striking image of a 'drenched, drowned bee'. The speaker – most likely the voice of the baby's mother – compares the clinging infant to the dying insect on the 'bending flower'. Lawrence is fond of images drawn from the natural world, such as the **bee and flower motif**. His rhythms are apparently casual, yet carefully controlled. The alliterative 'd' sound suggests a laden inertia. Broad vowel assonance ('Hangs numb and heavy') adds to the pain the bee feels.

Lines 4-7 focus closely on the mother's natural sense of connection with her child ('My baby') and their close physical interaction. There is a hypnotic, dreamlike quality to the description. The combined force of **multiple sound effects** – alliteration, assonance and sibilance – is remarkable for the lucidity, lightness and vivid precision that Lawrence achieves. The infant's hair is 'brushed with wet tears/And laid laughterless on her cheek'. The poet does not treat his images as abstract or merely visual. They are dynamic and changeable – 'legs hanging heavily', 'Swinging'. Tactile imagery emphasises the contact between bodies. The baby appears to be almost an extension of her mother's body ('over my arm'). Such clarity of diction and use of luminous details are characteristic of Lawrence. The mother's attentive rocking movement is matched by instinctive tenderness echoed in the gentle sound of the 'lullaby'.

The poem's central simile is repeated in **lines 8-10**. This fragile helpless child is utterly reliant on her mother: 'My sleeping baby hangs upon my life'. Is there a hint that the strain is nearly too much to bear? The **lethargic mood** continues, expressed mostly through onomatopoeic effects: 'Draws down the burdened flower'. While Lawrence cannot resist the impulse to rhyme ('shower', 'flower'), the restraint in the ebb and flow of the language is mesmerising.

Imagistic in its loosened rhythms, the poem repeatedly focuses on the similarity between the dazed, heavy bee and the infant in her mother's arms. But the **tone changes** towards the end as the reality of the baby's dependency becomes evident. The child is no longer 'so light'; indeed, her mother's arms now seem 'like sorrowful, storm-heavy boughs' (**line 12**). Once again, the powerful assonance adds to the poignancy. There is a disquieting awareness of being weighed down – both physically and emotionally. Is this a natural reaction to parental responsibility? Or a deeper realisation about the cycle of life and death?

Over the course of this short poem, Lawrence has interwoven a lyrical scene with a disturbing dramatic situation. The **final lines** are infused with a deep sense of despondency. In a nightmarish sequence, the child's 'floating hair' is now sinking 'like storm-bruised young leaves'. We are left with a distressing image of a person struggling helplessly, being **overwhelmed by a greater natural power** just like the 'drenched, drowned bee'. D. H. Lawrence's poetry often shows a concern with the pressures of life and culture. His oblique approach is open to various interpretations about the experience of motherhood, but there is no denying the concluding mood of complete surrender to an inevitable 'weariness'.

ANALYSIS

'D. H. Lawrence's poems can offer revealing insights into disturbing themes.' Discuss this view, with particular reference to 'Trailing Clouds'.

Sample Paragraph

The title seemed ambiguous. Nature is beautiful, but can quickly become stormy. In comparing the tiny baby to a drowned bee, the poet appeared to be already mourning the child's life. The baby 'clings' to its parent for dear life. To me, the verb suggested desperation – as though life is a struggle that ends in death for everyone. The child has been crying and its wet hair lies 'laughterless'. The mood is negative throughout. There are so many downbeat references to the baby, 'legs hanging heavily'. Nature grows even more ominous with the mention of 'storm-heavy boughs' and a truly stark image of the baby drowning like the bee. The ending is surreal, a feeling of being out of control, 'Reaching downwards'. Lawrence seems to be exploring the idea of human life being determined by time and fate. As in the natural world, humans are subject to unknown forces outside their power. The final lines comparing the bee's wings to 'a weariness' are the most disturbing of all and emphasises Lawrence's pessimistic outlook on life.

Examiner's Comment

A solid high-grade response that explored interesting aspects of the poem and included some well-focused discussion about Lawrence's 'negative outlook'. Effective points on imagery and mood were effectively illustrated. Expression was impressive throughout, with some good use of vocabulary ('ambiguous', 'ominous', 'surreal'). Overall, a good personal answer.

N.B. Access your ebook for additional sample paragraphs and a list of useful quotes with commentary.

CLASS/HOMEWORK EXERCISES

1. Identify and comment on Lawrence's portrait of the sleeping child in the poem, '"Trailing Clouds"'. In your opinion, is it realistic or sentimental? Support your answer with reference to the text.

2. 'Lawrence often makes use of carefully organised imagery to create thought-provoking moments of drama and tension.' To what extent is this true of '"Trailing Clouds"'? Support your answer with reference to the poem.

SUMMARY POINTS

- Imagistic style – effective use of repetition, rhyme, visual and aural imagery.
- Poem is structured around the extended bee and flower simile.
- Lawrence explores aspects of life's transience and touches on spiritual themes.
- Contrasting moods and atmospheres – tender, reflective, oppressive, fearful, etc.

11 BAVARIAN GENTIANS

Not every man has gentians in his house
In soft September, at slow, sad Michaelmas.
Bavarian gentians, tall and dark, but dark
darkening the daytime torch-like with the smoking blueness of Pluto's gloom,
ribbed hellish flowers erect, with their blaze of darkness spread blue,   5
blown flat into points, by the heavy white draught of the day.

Torch-flower of the blue-smoking darkness, Pluto's dark-blue blaze
black lamps from the halls of Dis, smoking dark blue
giving off darkness, blue darkness, upon Demeter's yellow-pale day
whom have you come for, here in the white-cast day?   10

Reach me a gentian, give me a torch!
let me guide myself with the blue, forked torch of a flower
down the darker and darker stairs, where blue is darkened on blueness
down the way Persephone goes, just now, in first-frosted September,
to the sightless realm where darkness is married to dark   15
and Persephone herself is but a voice, as a bride,
a gloom invisible enfolded in the deeper dark
of the arms of Pluto as he ravishes her once again
and pierces her once more with his passion of the utter dark
among the splendour of black-blue torches, shedding fathomless darkness   20
        on the nuptials.

Give me a flower on a tall stem, and three dark flames,
for I will go to the wedding, and be wedding-guest
at the marriage of the living dark.

'blaze of darkness spread blue'

Glossary

Bavarian Gentians: small trumpet-shaped blue flower.

2 *Michaelmas*: feast of St Michael the Archangel, September 29, protector against the dark of night.

4 *Pluto*: ruler of the underworld (Hades), god of death and earth's fertility.

8 *Dis*: Roman god of the underworld where souls go after death.

9 *Demeter*: goddess of the harvest and agriculture; mother of Persephone.

14 *Persephone*: abducted bride of Pluto.

20 *nuptials*: wedding ceremony.

INITIAL RESPONSE

1. Based on your reading of the poem, outline Lawrence's attitude to death. Support your answer with reference to the text.

2. Choose one aural image from the poem that appeals to you and comment briefly on its effectiveness.

3. Write your own personal response to the poem, highlighting the impact it made on you.

STUDY NOTES

'Bavarian Gentians' is one of D. H. Lawrence's final poems, published posthumously in 1932. He wrote the poem in September 1929 when he was suffering from tuberculosis, a disease of the lungs, from which he would soon die. Lawrence's early life had been spent in the English coal mining town of Eastwood. Later on, he wrote of remembering 'a sort of inner darkness, like the gloss of coal in which we moved and had our being'.

The **first stanza** opens with a modest, off-hand observation: 'Not every man has gentians in his house/In soft September, at slow, sad Michaelmas'. The sensual evocation of autumn is conveyed in the slow, reflective pace of the two run-on lines where sibilant 's' sounds establish a soporific (sleep-inducing) mood. The September setting is significant – the month facing into winter, the season of decay. Michaelmas (**line 2**) is the Christian feast of St Michael, known as the 'protector against the devil, especially at the time of death'. For Lawrence, the gentians signify the shadow of death. The depressive person often obsesses over a particular object or event and Lawrence is fascinated by the intense blue of the flowers. The colour blue has long been associated with sadness; people in a downbeat mood are said to be suffering from 'the blues'. The tone is **dejected and dreamy**, seducing the reader with its slow rhythm. However, the momentum builds through slightly modified repetition, 'tall and dark', 'dark/darkening'.

The flowers seem to throw no light at all on the day. Then suddenly, they change into magical tokens, becoming 'torch-like' (**line 4**). In the poet's imagination, their deep colour reminds him of the blue-black of the fires of Hell, 'smoking blueness of Pluto's gloom'. The reader is persuaded by Lawrence's **obsessive preoccupation** to closely observe every detail of the 'ribbed hellish flowers erect'. Their majestic 'blaze of darkness' (**line 5**) is again linked to the flash of fire. Their posture ('blown flat into points' by 'the heavy white draught' of wind) is carefully noted. The bright white of the day is a stark contrast to the darkness of both the flowers and Pluto's wretched Underworld. All through this section, the languor is similar to falling into a trance brought on by the contemplation of these beautiful blue flowers.

In the **second stanza**, the tone is one of **incantation**. The poet now chants the compound name of 'torch-flowers'. He himself seems almost hypnotised and in turn mesmerises readers through the penetrating focus on the colour of the gentians, 'blue-smoking darkness', 'black lamps', 'smoking dark blue', 'blue darkness'. The phrase 'giving off darkness' references John Milton's poetic description of Hell in his 'Divine Comedy' where 'flames' emit 'no light'. Of course, the paradox in this case is that these 'torch-flowers' create no light.

The infernal darkness of the gentians not only alludes to Lawrence's gloomy mood, but also to the darkness of the Underworld where Pluto reigns supreme 'in the halls of Dis'. Image after image of darkness permeate these lines just as Lawrence's infected lungs became flooded with tuberculosis and he faced up to imminent death. The poet is all too aware of the answer to his question (**line 10**), 'whom have you come for here in the white-cast day?' The combined force of irregular metre and sonorous sound effects add to the **unsettling atmosphere**.

Throughout the poem, Lawrence alludes to **Greek myth**. Pluto, the ruler of the underworld, abducts Persephone, the daughter of the goddess of fertility, Demeter. Although Pluto makes Persephone his queen, Demeter secures a compromise: Persephone can return each April to her mother for six months, after which (in 'first-frosted September') she must go back to her husband and the Underworld. During the time Persephone is away from her mother, Demeter mourns her absence and the countryside becomes barren. When Persephone returns in springtime, the earth becomes fertile once again.

In the **third stanza**, the mood changes dramatically. The tone turns imperative, electrified into action through energetic verbs, 'Reach me', give me'. Lawrence now intends to use the gentians as a torch to lead him into death. **No longer a helpless victim** (in stark contrast to the abducted Persephone), he is determined to act independently: 'let me guide myself'. Long run-on lines spiral into a vortex while the poet descends 'down the darker and darker stairs'. Emphatic use of the heavy alliterative 'd' sound suggests the wretched atmosphere of the underworld where 'blue is darkened on blueness'. The colour of the flowers is becoming extinguished by the enveloping darkness.

It is a vision of unrelenting gloom: 'the sightless realm where darkness is married to dark'. The cadence of the line falls on the last monosyllabic word imitating Persephone's (and the poet's) descent into Hades. She now loses her body – becoming 'but a voice' – and is cloaked in 'the arms of Pluto' who claims his bride in a macabre fantasy 'among the splendour of black-blue torches'. Pluto's desire for Persephone ('his passion of the utter dark;') is reflected in the strong sexual imagery. Throughout this **surreal Gothic scene**, the gentians shine in the incomprehensible atmosphere of an extraordinary wedding, not with light but 'shedding fathomless darkness on the nuptials'.

In the **concluding three lines**, the tone changes once more. There is a sense of **dignified acceptance** in the poet's formal request, 'Give me a flower', contrasting with the earlier desperate grasp ('Reach'). Calmly and courageously, Lawrence accepts the inevitable invitation of death: 'I will go to the wedding'. Paradoxically, he describes the place where Pluto and Persephone have their marriage ceremony as 'the living dark'. This refers to the ability of the dark earth to receive the dead flower's seed in autumn and to bring it back to life the following spring. Nature buries and regenerates. The compelling drama concludes with the poet preparing to enter this dark realm forever. Does he hope for an afterlife in death?

'Bavarian Gentians' is sustained by a combination of repetitive rhythm, monotonous melody and the obsessive litanies expressing the poet's deepest thoughts and fears. In the end, Lawrence succeeds in uniting the natural beauty of the blue flowers with an overflowing description of their colour, leading to an erotically and morbidly charged descent into the mythical Underworld. He is a poet without a mask.

ANALYSIS

'D. H. Lawrence's last poems study death with precise, reverential fascination.' Discuss this view, with particular reference to 'Bavarian Gentians'.

Sample Paragraph

'Bavarian Gentians' explores the fall towards oblivion through a keen description of its seductive powers. Hypnotically, the poet weaves the 'blue-smoking darkness' of the flowers through the poem so that they become both the guide to death as well as an emblem of it. Strict observation not only of the flower's colour but also its texture ('ribbed') and shape ('blown flat into points') causes this beautiful flower to become a focal point, enabling both the poet and reader to pass from acute awareness to a trance-like state of meditation. The terror of the descent into nothingness is conveyed in the spine-chilling alliterative phrase 'down the darker and darker stairs'. Soft sweeping syllables swirl as Lawrence relates the classic myth of Pluto and Persephone's nuptials ('splendour', 'shedding fathomless darkness'). He presents us with the threshold of life and death as the earth buries and nurtures. Pluto embraces his bride just as death claims the poet. The poem ends on a dignified note. Respectfully, Lawrence accepts the invitation in the carefully paused line, 'for I will go to the wedding, and be wedding guest'. The struggle with death now loses importance as the poet quietly approaches 'the living dark'. This entrancing poem reveals death through awed, detailed absorption.

Examiner's Comment

A mature and thoughtful response to the question. Informed discussion points focus throughout on the poet's precise style and reverential tone. Excellent use of accurate quotations and support reference. Expression is also impressive: varied sentence length, wide-ranging vocabulary and good control of syntax. Top-grade standard.

N.B. Access your ebook for additional sample paragraphs and a list of useful quotes with commentary.

CLASS/HOMEWORK EXERCISES

1. 'Lawrence's sensual language and vivid imagination convey his intense vision of life.' In your opinion, how true is this of 'Bavarian Gentians'? Support your answer with reference to the poem.

2. 'D. H. Lawrence's dark themes are explored through honest free verse.' To what extent is this evident in 'Bavarian Gentians'? Support your answer with reference to the poem.

SUMMARY POINTS

- Direct, immediate exploration of death, oblivion, self-awareness.
- Rolling, dreamlike style, irregular line length and metre.
- Repetition and other aural effects create spell-binding fantasy.
- Use of Greek mythology enriches the poem's universal appeal.
- Dramatic impact of colour imagery patterns.
- Poet's own journey towards death portrayed through moods of awareness, anger, terror and acceptance.

LEAVING CERT SAMPLE ESSAY

'D. H. Lawrence's poetry is notable for both its provocative subject matter and distinctive language use.' Discuss this view, supporting your answer with suitable reference to the poems by Lawrence on your course.

Marking Scheme Guidelines

Responses to the question should contain clear evidence of engagement with the poetry by Lawrence on the course. Expect a wide variety of approaches in the candidates' answering, but they should focus on the poet's distinctive language use in exploring provocative themes and issues.

Indicative material:

- Unusual viewpoint and perspective, often challenging and confrontational.
- Personal approach to love, memory, death, nature, modernity, cosmic harmony.
- Experimental style, free verse, range of tones, striking description.
- Startling imagery, contrasting moods, irregular rhyme, rhythm and line length.

Sample Essay
(Lawrence's provocative subject matter and distinctive language use)

1. *D. H. Lawrence, rebel and mystic, believed 'when genuine passion moves you, say what you've got to say'. Exploring disturbing, challenging, sensual and vexing themes, Lawrence employed free verse and precise diction to create deep, resonant, unforgettable poetry. As readers, we are challenged and consoled in diverse poems such as 'Piano', 'The Mosquito', 'Snake' and 'Blue Gentians', which investigate relationships, memory, loss, nature and death.*

2. *A gentle, conversational remark opens Lawrence's paradoxical memory poem, 'Piano'. 'Softly in the dusk, a woman is singing to me'. This catapults reader and poet down the 'vista' of the past where exact details and the use of the present tense brings to life the tender scene of a little child 'sitting under the piano,' 'pressing the small, poised feet of a mother'. Both reader and poet vividly experience the recollection through Lawrence's skilful use of onomatopoeia ('boom', 'tinkling') and assonance ('tingling strings'). The past is being brought into the present. However, Lawrence avoids sentimental clichés. Instead, he honestly confronts the uncomfortable reality that none of us can ever go back to the security of a simpler past, 'with winter outside'. The adult poet who cannot become a child again weeps inconsolably 'Down the flood of remembrance'. Long, irregular run-on lines capture the non-stop flow of memories, 'the insidious mastery of song/Betrays me back'. The effect is bound to provoke readers who can usually relate to nostalgic feelings.*

3. In the poems 'The Mosquito' and 'Snake', Lawrence creates brilliant evocations of the natural world, catching its physical presence with vigour. The poet showcases nature's creatures, which are all instinct and immediacy without the human's restrictions. A confrontation between the refined, civilised human mind and the subterranean forces of the earth is dramatised in 'Snake'. Through an inventive use of syntax, the poet describes a creature that does not rationalise but acts on natural intuition – he 'flickered his two-forked tongue from his lips'. When describing the logical human narrator, the poet uses much more complex expression – 'The voice of my education said to me/He must be killed,/For in Sicily ... the gold are venomous'. As in the poem 'Piano', the narrator wants to relive the past, 'I wished he could come back', but no amount of wishing will change what has been done. Lawrence confronts the reader with yet another uncomfortable truth.

4. However, in 'The Mosquito', this conflict between man and creature has a different outcome. Lawrence is furious that this little insect has dared to cross the boundaries of 'otherness' and attacked him. Unlike the narrator in 'Snake', who is filled with guilt for attacking the snake, the insect glories in his attack on the man, entering into a state of ecstasy, 'enspasmed in oblivion'. This time, the poet uses repetition to effectively describe the aftermath of the encounter, 'Such silence', 'Such gorging', 'Such obscenity'. There is no guilt, the insect is at one with the natural world, a mosquito has followed its natural instinct. In these poems, Lawrence clearly shows the beautiful diversity of nature, the snake's 'yellow-brown slackness soft-bellied', an insect's 'shredded shank' and 'streaming legs'. He is demonstrating how humans have lost a sense of oneness with the universe.

5. Lawrence also makes inventive use of animals as images in 'Call into Death' and '"Trailing Clouds"'. The bird images, 'white bird among snow-berries'; 'gently rustling in heaven like a/bird' in 'Call into Death' shows how life continues, even if unseen, and this can be an image for what happens in death. The life force continues in a different form to that of the mortal human. The disturbing image of a 'drenched drowned bee' in '"Trailing Clouds"' suggests Lawrence's desire for oblivion.

6. In 'Bavarian Gentians', the subject of death is again addressed. Similar to 'Piano', the poem opens with a simple observation, 'Not every man has gentians in his house'. Through the hypnotic repetition of 'blue-smoking darkness', the poet then confronts the terrifying reality of death – 'darkness is married to dark'. He uses the beautiful Greek myth of Persephone and Pluto to show how life continues even after death, although in a different form. Lawrence is going towards death voluntarily, 'let me guide myself', lit by the dark blue gentians, 'Torch-flowers of the blue-smoking darkness'. The poet accepts death in the image of a 'wedding guest' about to take his place in the 'living dark'. Lawrence rebels against the 'normal approach' to dying. Through his absorbing rhythms and interweaving lines, he invites the reader to take part in this magnificent final journey.

7. *I found Lawrence to be an extraordinary poetic voice through poems that grow naturally from intense emotion, with their irregular line-length, rhyme and rhythm. Clear-cut, accurate descriptions, repetition, sound-effects and clever contrasts all add to these disturbing, challenging poems which cause the modern reader to stop and consider some of life's great questions.*

(approx. 825 words)

Examiner's Comment

An accomplished high-grade response showing very good engagement with Lawrence's poetry. The opening gives a useful overview, mentioning the poems that will be discussed. Focus is maintained on the poet's unusual approach in challenging conventional views. Cross-referencing works very well, reflecting a broad appreciation of themes and style – and excellent use is made of supportive reference and quotation. Paragraph 5 is slight, however, and points lack development. Otherwise, expression is impressive throughout and the essay is rounded off confidently.

MARKING
SCHEME
GRADE: H1
P = 15/15
C = 13/15
L = 13/15
M = 5/5
Total = 46/50

N.B. Access your ebook for additional sample paragraphs and a list of useful quotes with commentary.

SAMPLE LEAVING CERT QUESTIONS ON LAWRENCE'S POETRY

(45–50 MINUTES)

1. 'D. H. Lawrence's stark, innovative poetry celebrates sensuality in an over-intellectualised world.' Discuss this view, supporting your answer with reference to the poems by Lawrence on your course.

2. 'Lawrence's intensely confessional poetry contains a richness of wide-ranging imagery.' Discuss this statement, supporting your answer with reference to the poetry of Lawrence on your course.

3. 'D. H. Lawrence, the rebel poet, is passionately in love with language.' To what extent do you agree with this view? Support the points you make with reference to the poems by Lawrence on your course.

Sample Essay Plan (Q1)
'D. H. Lawrence's stark, innovative poetry celebrates sensuality in an over-intellectualised world.' Discuss this view, supporting your answer with reference to the poems by Lawrence on your course.

- Intro: Lawrence – master craftsman, profound thinker – creator of raw, honest poetry glorying in nature's creative beauty, critical of modern society. Unique and intense poetic voice – free verse, precise description, experimental structures, startling imagery patterns.

- Point 1: 'Delight of Being Alone' and 'Absolute Reverence' champion Lawrence's belief in living through the senses – 'It makes me realise the delicious pleasure of the moon/that she has in travelling by herself' (emphatic sibilance and line length). Worships divine in nature – 'But to something unseen, unknown … I feel absolute reverence'. Curt dismissal of modern analytical approach, 'Say no more!'

- Point 2: 'What Have They Done to You?' – extended reflection on dehumanising effects of modern industrialisation. Use of contrasting verbs to showcase the difference between oppressed work force, confined and passive ('creeping') and capitalist employers. Repetition of refrain 'What have they done to you?' mimics monotonous factory work.

- Point 3: 'Humming-Bird' – visualising creature's physicality. Assonance highlights natural beauty of bird, 'This little bit chipped off in brilliance'. Dynamic verbs used to describe bird ('flashed', 'whizzing', 'pierced'). Similarly, in 'Snake', the conflict focuses on the relationship between nature and human nature.

- Point 4: 'Intimates' – honest exploration of deadening effect of modern relationships. In this domestic drama, the couple communicate through words rather than senses. Contrasting language and varying tones throughout.

- Conclusion: Poetry defined by two elements: Lawrence's glorification of the natural world and his condemnation of modern civilisation. Recurring tensions between heart and head. Unique style dominated by careful observation, searing honesty, varied structure and innovative language use.

Sample Essay Plan (Q1)

Develop one of the above points into a paragraph.

Sample Paragraph: Point 4

The difficulty the modern world has in forming successful relationships is explored in the ironically titled 'Intimates'. Lawrence focuses on a bitter marital row. The couple's knowledge of each other does not add warmth and intimacy, but is used to bombard each other with hurtful weapons. The opening question, 'Don't you care for my love?' suggests an unhappy woman who craves attention and affection. The man's startling reaction, 'I handed her the mirror', prefaces his spiteful attack. The poet juxtaposes the polite, formal request 'please', which is transformed into sharp sarcasm as part of a withering list of directions aimed at his partner. Their relationship is defined by the words they say. His fury at the woman's assumed superiority is conveyed in the references to the 'proper person', 'head-quarters', 'supreme authority'. Now the woman is invited to see herself as she really is, the source of power, not a helpless victim. The contrasting line lengths at the conclusion highlight the woman's 'spellbound' inspection of herself. The relationship is cold, lacking sensuality or feeling. The man's final comment, 'while I fled', imitates his frantic dash for freedom from the stifling verbal arguments. This relationship is doomed because it is based on harsh intellectualising.

Examiner's Comment

As part of a full essay, this is an informed response that illustrates Lawrence's interest in the tension between emotion and rationality. Key sentences address the essay wording, e.g. 'Their relationship is defined by the words they say'. The paragraph traces the progress of thought within the poem, using apt references along the way to illustrate discussion points. Syntax is well controlled and there is no awkwardness in the expression. Expressive adjectives such as 'startling' and 'stifling' maintain the focus on an important element of the question ('innovative'). A confident, top-grade answer.

N.B. Access your ebook for additional sample paragraphs and a list of useful quotes with commentary.

LAST WORDS ”

'Lawrence was in a direct line of descent from such earlier poets as Blake, Coleridge and Whitman, for whom imagination was everything.'

Keith Sagar

'The accuracy of Lawrence's observations haunts the mind permanently.'

Kenneth Roxroth

'These are my tender administrations to the mental and emotional wounds we suffer from.'

D. H. Lawrence

EILÉAN NÍ CHUILLEANÁIN

1942-

'I chose poetry because it was different.'

E iléan Ní Chuilleanáin is regarded by many as one of the most important contemporary Irish women poets. Her subject matter ranges from social commentary and considerations of religious issues to quiet, introspective poems about human nature. She has also translated poetry from a number of languages. Ní Chuilleanáin is noted for being mysterious and complex; her poems usually have subtle messages that unfold only through multiple readings. She is well read in history and a strong sense of connection between past and present characterises her work, in which she often draws interesting parallels between historical events and modern situations. Many of her poems highlight the contrast between fluidity and stillness, life and death, and of the undeniable passing of time and humanity's attempts to stop change. They are usually intricately layered, often subtle half-revelations, but always both carefully controlled and even startling. She herself has frequently referred to the importance of secrecy in her poetry. Most critics agree that Ní Chuilleanáin's poems resist easy explanations and variously show her interest in explorations of transition, the sacred, women's experience and history.

INVESTIGATE FURTHER

To find out more about Eiléan Ní Chuilleanáin or to hear readings of her poems not available in your ebook, you could search some useful websites such as YouTube, poetryarchive.org and bbc. co.uk. Also view the additional material available in your ebook.

Prescribed Poems

6 **'All for You'**

This multi-layered narrative offers glimpses of salvation and hope. Resonating with detailed references to the Bible story of the birth of Jesus, the poem focuses on the experience of Christian faith as imagined through the imposing challenge and triumph of religious vocations.   **341**

7 **'Following'**

A vividly realised journey by a young girl through a busy Irish fair day invites readers into this mysterious story. The power of memory is central to the poem, which suggests that the past is not dead. Ní Chuilleanáin's final lines offer readers a sense of comfort and hope.   **346**

8 **'Kilcash'**

This version of the old Irish elegy, *Caoine Cill Chais*, mourns the death of Margaret Butler, Viscountess Iveagh. However, the traditional lament for the lost Catholic aristocracy suggests unanswered questions about Ireland's troubled and complex history.   **351**

9 **'Translation'**

Ní Chuilleanáin's poem was read at the reburial ceremony to commemorate Magdalene laundry women from all over Ireland. 'Translation' links the poet's work with the belated acknowledgement of the stolen lives of generations of Irishwomen in some Magdalene convents.   **357**

10 **'The Bend in the Road'**

The poet recalls a journey when a child was suffering from car sickness. For her, the roadside location marks the realisation of time passing. This recollection is not static, but becomes interwoven with other memories of absence and loss that have deep personal significance.   **362**

* **The poems marked with an asterisk are also prescribed for the Ordinary Level course.**

① LUCINA SCHYNNING IN SILENCE OF THE NICHT 🔊

Moon shining in silence of the night
The heaven being all full of stars
I was reading my book in a ruin
By a sour candle, without roast meat or music
Strong drink or a shield from the air   5
Blowing in the crazed window, and I felt
Moonlight on my head, clear after three days' rain.

I washed in cold water; it was orange, channelled down bogs
Dipped between cresses.
The bats flew through my room where I slept safely.   10
Sheep stared at me when I woke.

Behind me the waves of darkness lay, the plague
Of mice, plague of beetles
Crawling out of the spines of books,
Plague shadowing pale faces with clay   15
The disease of the moon gone astray.

In the desert I relaxed, amazed
As the mosaic beasts on the chapel floor
When Cromwell had departed and they saw
The sky growing through the hole in the roof.   20

Sheepdogs embraced me; the grasshopper
Returned with a lark and bee.
I looked down between hedges of high thorn and saw
The hare, absorbed, sitting still
In the middle of the track; I heard   25
Again the chirp of the stream running.

'shining in silence of the night'

Glossary

Title: Lucina is another name for Diana, the moon goddess. In Roman mythology, Lucina was the goddess of childbirth. Ní Chuilleanáin's title comes from the opening line of 'The Antichrist', a satirical poem by the Scottish poet William Dunbar (*c.* 1460–1517).

9   *cresses*: small strongly flavoured leaves.

12   *plague*: curse, diseased group.

14   *spines*: inner parts, backs.

16   *astray*: off course.

18   *mosaic*: mixed, assorted.

19   *Cromwell*: Oliver Cromwell (1599–1658), controversial English military and political leader who led an army of invasion in 1649–50, which conquered most of Ireland. Cromwell is still regarded largely as a figure of hatred in the Irish Republic, his name being associated with massacre, religious persecution and mass dispossession of the Catholic community.

26   *chirp*: lively sound, twitter.

INITIAL RESPONSE

1. How would you describe the atmosphere in the poem's opening stanza? Refer to the text in your answer.

2. Choose one image taken from the natural world that you found particularly interesting. Comment briefly on its effectiveness.

3. Based on your reading of this poem, do you think Ní Chuilleanáin presents a realistic view of Irish history? Give reasons for your response.

STUDY NOTES

Eiléan Ní Chuilleanáin takes her title from a Middle Scots poem by William Dunbar. 'Lucina Schynning in Silence of the Nicht' is set in a ruin somewhere in Ireland, after Oliver Cromwell had devastated the country in 1649. However, Ní Chuilleanáin's beautiful and haunting poem is much more than a meditation on an historical event. The poet achieves immediacy by means of a dramatic monologue that recreates the whisperings of desolation in the aftermath of Cromwell's march through Ireland.

As in so many of her poems, Ní Chuilleanáin invites readers into a **strangely compelling setting**. The poet personifies the moon, creating an uneasy atmosphere. Silence enhances the dramatic effect: 'The heaven being all full of stars'. This eerie scene is described in a series of random details. The language – with its archaic Scottish dialect – is note-like and seemingly timeless. There is a notable absence of punctuation and a stilted rhythm as the unknown speaker's voice is introduced: 'I was reading my book in a ruin' (**line 3**). The series of fragmentary images – 'a sour candle', 'the crazed window' – are immediately unsettling, drawing us back to a darker age in Ireland's troubled history.

Characteristically, Ní Chuilleanáin leaves readers to unravel the poem's veiled meanings and the identity of the dispossessed narrator is never made known. Instead, this forlorn figure 'without roast meat or music' is associated with material and cultural deprivation – **a likely symbol of an oppressed Ireland**? Does the absence of 'Strong drink or a shield' add to the notion of a defeated people? Despite the obvious indications of almost incomprehensible suffering, some respite can still be found: 'I felt/ Moonlight on my head, clear after three days' rain' (**line 7**). This simple image of nature – illuminating and refreshing – suggests comforting signs of recovery.

Ní Chuilleanáin's startling drama moves into the wild Irish landscape: 'I washed in cold water; it was orange'. The sense of native Irish resistance against foreign invasion is clearly evident in the reference to Dutch-born Protestant William of Orange, who defeated the army of Catholic James II at the Battle of the Boyne in 1690. But the poet focuses on the speaker's experience of displacement, illustrating the **alienation which existed within nationalist Ireland**. The narrator, surrounded by animal life and the open sky, becomes an extension of animate and inanimate nature: 'The bats flew through my room ... Sheep stared at me' (**line 10**).

In an increasingly surreal atmosphere, the mood becomes much more disturbed. The poet's apocalyptic dream-vision highlights the 'waves of darkness' in an uninterrupted nightmarish sequence of repulsive images: 'plague/Of mice, plague of beetles/Crawling'. The **emphatic repetition of 'plague' resonates with images of widespread misery, disease and famine**. Nor does the poet ignore the distorted history of Ireland that has resulted from prejudice, propaganda and vested interest 'Crawling out of the spines of books' (**line 14**). What stands out, however, is Ní Chuilleanáin's ability to suggest distressing glimpses of our island's dark past, poignantly depicted in her heart-rending language describing innocent death: 'Plague shadowing pale faces with clay/The disease of the moon gone astray'.

There is a distinctive change of mood in **lines 17–20** as the speaker reflects on the aching aftermath in the period after 'Cromwell had departed'. References to Christian retreat and renewal indicate the **consolation provided by religious faith**: 'In the desert I relaxed, amazed/As the mosaic beasts on the chapel floor'. This sense of wonder through the possibility of spiritual fulfilment is developed in the metaphorical image of 'The sky growing through the hole in the roof'. As always, landscape and nature are features of Ní Chuilleanáin's poem, allowing readers access to her subtle thinking.

In sharp contrast to the earlier trauma, the final tone is remarkably composed and harmonious. The language – which has been somewhat archaic throughout much of the poem – is noticeably biblical: 'Sheepdogs embraced me; the grasshopper/Returned with a lark and bee'. **There is an unmistakable sense of survival and newfound confidence** in **line 23**: 'I looked down between hedges of high thorn'. Ní Chuilleanáin's recognition of 'The hare, absorbed, sitting still' (a cross-reference to her poem 'On Lacking the Killer Instinct') reinforces the feeling of quiet resignation. Is she alluding to the maturity and relative peace of the present Irish state? At any rate, the poem ends on a hopeful note of vigorous resilience, with one of nature's liveliest sounds, 'the chirp of the stream running'.

Throughout this elusive poem, Ní Chuilleanáin has explored fascinating aspects of Irish history – a story that has been often lost in the 'silence of the night'. So much of Ireland's past is marked by exploitation and resistance. The poem has deep undercurrents of countless conflicts springing from both without and within. The moon has long been associated with love, beauty, loneliness, lunacy and death. Some critics have suggested that Ní Chuilleanáin's poem uses the moon to symbolise the struggle of women through the centuries. As usual, readers are free to judge for themselves. However, there is little doubt that 'Lucina Schynning in Silence of the Nicht' presents us with **an intense, self-enclosed world** – but one where the tensions and aspirations of Ireland's complex story are imaginatively encapsulated.

ANALYSIS

'Eiléan Ní Chuilleanáin's poems offer rich rewards to the perceptive reader.' Discuss this view, with particular reference to 'Lucina Schynning in Silence of the Nicht'.

Sample Paragraph

While I first found Ní Chuilleanáin's poetry obscure and quite difficult, I really enjoyed reading 'Lucina Schynning'. The strange title and eerie atmosphere under the moonlight is typical of a poet who makes us, the reader, imagine the 'world' of the poem. I found it all very dramatic. The narrative voice seemed very traumatised and was convincing as it represented Ireland's troubled history – 'I washed myself in cold water', 'Behind me, waves of darkness'. What I really liked about the poet was that she suggested, rather than explained. The description of Irish people starving and dying was very moving – especially because of the word 'plague'. Ní Chuilleanáin's images of suffering were balanced by the positive ending. The character in the poem was at one with nature – 'sheep embraced me'. The poem asked many questions about how people today look at the past. I thought the final lines were really encouraging. The poet used many simple nature images of the hare 'sitting still' and the 'chirp of the stream' to show a present-day Ireland where there is peace and contentment – unlike the war-torn past of the history books. Overall, I did enjoy 'Lucina Schynning' as it reminded me that there is still meaning in the beauty of nature.

Examiner's Comment

This sensitive reaction to Ní Chuilleanáin's poem reflected on both the subject matter and style of the text using accurate quotations to support the discussion points. The poem's narrative was disclosed by drawing together its significant details. Very impressive vocabulary throughout: 'the pattern on the floor of the church curled into serenity while Ireland regained some of its equilibrium'. A solid high-grade response.

N.B. Access your ebook for additional sample paragraphs and a list of useful quotes with commentary.

CLASS/HOMEWORK EXERCISES

1. 'Ní Chuilleanáin's distinctive poetry is filled with subtle messages.' Discuss this statement, with particular reference to 'Lucina Schynning in Silence of the Nicht'.

2. 'Eiléan Ní Chuilleanáin's "Lucina Schynning in Silence of the Nicht" is a highly atmospheric poem that has an elusive dreamlike quality.' To what extent do you agree or disagree with this statement? Support your answer with reference to the poem.

SUMMARY POINTS

- Evocative mid-seventeenth century Irish setting.
- Dramatic monologue form recreates Irish alienation after Cromwell's invasion.
- Themes include suffering, loss, human resilience and the celebration of nature.
- Effective use of startling imagery, repetition, sibilance and alliteration.

❷ THE SECOND VOYAGE

Odysseus rested on his oar and saw
The ruffled foreheads of the waves
Crocodiling and mincing past: he rammed
The oar between their jaws and looked down
 In the simmering sea where scribbles of weed defined   5
 Uncertain depth, and the slim fishes progressed
 In fatal formation, and thought
                  If there was a single
Streak of decency in these waves now, they'd be ridged
Pocked and dented with the battering they've had,   10
And we could name them as Adam named the beasts,
Saluting a new one with dismay, or a notorious one
With admiration; they'd notice us passing
And rejoice at our shipwreck, but these
Have less character than sheep and need more patience.   15

I know what I'll do he said;
I'll park my ship in the crook of a long pier
(And I'll take you with me he said to the oar)
I'll face the rising ground and walk away
From tidal waters, up riverbeds   20
Where herons parcel out the miles of stream,
Over gaps in the hills, through warm
Silent valleys, and when I meet a farmer
Bold enough to look me in the eye
With 'where are you off to with that long   25
Winnowing fan over your shoulder?'
There I will stand still
And I'll plant you for a gatepost or a hitching-post
And leave you as a tidemark. I can go back
And organise my house then.   30
                But the profound
Unfenced valleys of the ocean still held him;
He had only the oar to make them keep their distance;
The sea was still frying under the ship's side.
He considered the water-lilies, and thought about fountains   35
Spraying as wide as willows in empty squares,

The sugarstick of water clattering into the kettle,
The flat lakes bisecting the rushes. He remembered spiders and frogs
Housekeeping at the roadside in brown trickles floored with mud,
Horsetroughs, the black canal, pale swans at dark;   40
His face grew damp with tears that tasted
Like his own sweat or the insults of the sea.

'the simmering sea'

Glossary

1   *Odysseus*: Greek mythic king and warrior. He is also the literary hero of Homer's epic tale, *The Odyssey*, which tells of Odysseus's 10-year struggle to return home from the Trojan War.
2   *ruffled:* wrinkled, tangled.
3   *Crocodiling*: gliding.
3   *mincing*: moving daintily.

10   *Pocked*: disfigured.
12   *notorious*: infamous.
21   *herons*: long-necked wading birds.
21   *parcel*: mark, measure.
26   *Winnowing*: probing.
38   *bisecting*: cutting through.

INITIAL RESPONSE

1. From your reading of the first stanza (lines 1–15), describe Odysseus's relationship with the sea. Refer to the text in your response.

2. Select two interesting images from the poem and comment on the effectiveness of each.

3. Write your own personal response to 'The Second Voyage', supporting the points you make with reference to the text.

STUDY NOTES

The relationship between past and present is one of Eiléan Ní Chuilleanáin's recurring themes. In addressing the present within the context of history, she often explores contrasts, such as life and death, motion and stillness, and the inevitable tension between time passing and people's desire to resist change. 'The Second Voyage' refers to the Greek hero Odysseus, whose first epic journey was a relentless battle with the treacherous ocean. But growing frustrated by the endless struggle against nature, he decides that his next voyage will be on land and therefore less demanding.

From the outset, Odysseus is presented as a slightly bemused and ridiculous figure. There is a cartoon-like quality to the exaggerated ocean setting as Ní Chuilleanáin immediately portrays this legendary hero resting on his oar and watching the 'ruffled foreheads of the waves/Crocodiling and mincing past' (**line 3**). The poet expands this metaphor, describing the waves as great beasts to be challenged: 'he rammed/The oar between their jaws'. **Ní Chuilleanáin's derisive humour mocks the great wanderer's inflated sense of his own masculinity.** But there is no denying that Odysseus is still excited by the 'Uncertain depth' beneath him. For him, anything is possible at sea, where he is truly in his element. The personification is childlike, suggesting his peevish annoyance at being unable to conquer the ocean waves, which don't possess 'a single/Streak of decency' (**line 9**).

Ní Chuilleanáin's tone is playfully critical. As always, the poet's skill lies in her vigorous images, such as the 'slim fishes' beneath 'scribbles of weeds'. Odysseus's powerful physicality is contrasted with the seemingly pretty waves, which somehow resist the 'battering they've had'. Lording over this surreal scene and filled with disappointment, the egotistical Greek warrior thinks about the Garden of Eden. He is soon envying Adam, who was given God-given control over all living things and had 'named the beasts' of the earth. Completely unaware of the irony of his excessive pride, Odysseus is overwhelmed by self-pity and resorts to ridiculing these foolish waves, which fail to 'rejoice at our shipwreck' (**line 14**).

Ní Chuilleanáin develops the whimsical drama by letting us hear Odysseus's petulant voice as he prepares to seek recognition onshore. Armed with renewed confidence and his trusty oar – ('I'll take you with me he said to the oar') – he sets out to 'face the rising ground' and seek affirmation far away 'From tidal waters'. But despite the purposeful rhythm and self-assured tone, there is a strong underlying sense that he is deluding himself. The landscape might be serenely beautiful, but it is confined. Unlike the boundless sea, birds define it: 'herons parcel out the miles of stream' (**line 21**). Yet the brave warrior is eager to boast of his exploits in the outside world and hopes to tell his story to the first farmer he meets who is 'Bold enough to look me in the eye'. **Odysseus even tries to convince himself that it is time to put down roots**, to plant his oar as 'a gatepost or a hitching-post'. Then he will be ready to return home and 'organise my house'. However, the laboured rhythm and imposing multi-syllabic language convey his half-heartedness about settling down.

Indeed, there are already signs that Odysseus will never surrender the freedom and adventure of dangerous ocean voyages. The powerful oar, which once signified dynamism and exhilaration, is now seen as a decorative symbol of stillness, a 'Winnowing fan'. Unable to deny his true destiny any longer, **he accepts that he cannot ignore his urge to control the sea**: the 'Unfenced valleys of the ocean still held him' (**line 32**). But his ironic situation remains; while the freedom he yearns for is unattainable on land, he is still unable to conquer the seemingly infinite sea.

The poem's final section is sympathetic to Odysseus's dilemma. Ní Chuilleanáin replaces the pompous first-person pronouns with her own measured narrative account: 'He considered the water-lilies, and thought about fountains' (**line 35**). The poet makes extensive use of **contrasting water images to highlight land and sea**. Unlike the water 'frying under the ship's side', settled life appears controlled, but unattractive ('Horsetroughs, the black canal'). His uneasy memories of home ('water clattering', 'pale swans at dark') are ominous. For Odysseus, his second excursion into landlocked civilisation offers so little fulfilment that 'His face grew damp with tears'. The hero is forever drawn to that first epic voyage and the wonderful experience of ocean living, with which he is inextricably bound: 'Like his own sweat or the insults of the sea'.

The fluctuating water images – another familiar feature of Eiléan Ní Chuilleanáin's writing – reflect the complex narrative threads throughout the poem. Transitions of various kinds are central to her work. The poet has also been very involved in translating texts, and believes that because of the limits imposed by the translator, the process can never be completely true to the original language. Some literary critics see 'The Second Voyage' as an **extended metaphor exploring how language and culture resist translation**, but like so many of Ní Chuilleanáin's enigmatic poems, the ultimate interpretation is left to individual readers themselves.

'Ní Chuilleanáin's poetry makes effective use of contrasts to illuminate her themes.' Discuss this view, with particular reference to 'The Second Voyage'.

Sample Paragraph

Contrasting themes, such as life and death, permanence and transience, and motion and stillness are all prominent within Eiléan Ní Chuilleanáin's 'The Second Voyage'. Such contrasts make it easier to understand her poetic world. The opening description of arrogant Odysseus who 'rammed' his oar against the waves shows a macho larger-than-life character whose extrovert behaviour could not be more unlike the silent sea with its 'Uncertain depth' which he will never tame. Momentarily, the irritated hero makes up his mind to undertake a new 'voyage' by seeking glory on land. But the reality of settled life disappoints him. Revealing images of fixed landmarks – 'a gatepost', 'hitching-post', 'tidemark' – all convey the sense of motionless disinterest. Odysseus is immediately aware of the contrasting dynamic qualities of the sea's 'Unfenced valleys'. Throughout the last stanza, Odysseus debates the relative attractions of land and sea. I found it interesting that the man-made images were all water-based – 'fountains', 'brown trickles', 'the black canal' – and all lacking the mystery and danger of the open sea which Odysseus longs for. The ending of the poem rounds off the choices facing Odysseus. Once again, Ní Chuilleanáin succeeds in juxtaposing his love-hate obsession with the mysterious ocean as his tears taste 'Like his own sweat or the insults of the sea'.

Examiner's Comment

The introductory overview established a very good basis for exploring interesting contrasts within the poem. There is some well-focused personal engagement with the text: 'I found it interesting that the man-made images were all water-based'. Suitable quotations provide valuable support. Diction and expression – in the final sentence, for example – are also excellent. This confident response fully merits the top grade.

N.B. Access your ebook for additional sample paragraphs and a list of useful quotes with commentary.

1. 'Eiléan Ní Chuilleanáin presents readers with unsettling scenes, both real and otherworldly.' Discuss this statement, with particular reference to 'The Second Voyage'. Refer to the text in your answer.

2. 'In "The Second Voyage", Ní Chuilleanáin addresses the idea of transition and the difficulties associated with change.' Discuss this view, supporting your answer with reference to the poem.

SUMMARY POINTS

- Imaginative use of mythic tale of Greek hero.
- Sardonic humour evident in vivid personification of the sea.
- Unsettling scenes, both real and otherworldly.
- Contrasting themes (transience, masculinity, freedom, etc.).
- Vibrant water imagery is a powerful motif.
- Alliteration and sibilance create dynamic sound effects.
- Direct dialogue adds immediacy.

❸ DEATHS AND ENGINES 🔊

We came down above the houses
In a stiff curve, and
At the edge of Paris airport
Saw an empty tunnel
– The back half of a plane, black   5
On the snow, nobody near it,
Tubular, burnt-out and frozen.

When we faced again
The snow-white runways in the dark
No sound came over   10
The loudspeakers, except the sighs
Of the lonely pilot.

The cold of metal wings is contagious:
Soon you will need wings of your own,
Cornered in the angle where   15
Time and life like a knife and fork
Cross, and the lifeline in your palm
Breaks, and the curve of an aeroplane's track
Meets the straight skyline.

The images of relief: 20
Hospital pyjamas, screens round a bed
A man with a bloody face
Sitting up in bed, conversing cheerfully
Through cut lips:
These will fail you some time.   25

You will find yourself alone
Accelerating down a blind
Alley, too late to stop
And know how light your death is;

You will be scattered like wreckage,   30
The pieces every one a different shape
Will spin and lodge in the hearts
Of all who love you.

'snow-white runways'

Glossary

7	*Tubular*: cylindrical, tube shaped.	27	*Accelerating*: speeding.
13	*contagious*: catching.	32	*lodge*: settle.
23	*conversing*: chatting.		

INITIAL RESPONSE

1. Describe the atmosphere at the airport in the first two stanzas. Refer to the text in your response.

2. Based on your reading of lines 13–25, choose one image that you found particularly memorable and comment on its effectiveness.

3. Write your personal response to 'Deaths and Engines', referring closely to the poem in your answer.

STUDY NOTES

'Deaths and Engines' contextualises Eiléan Ní Chuilleanáin's experience of death – and particularly her father's death – within the setting of another 'burnt-out' ruin: the abandoned wreckage of an aircraft engine. Characteristically, the poet's metaphorical sense is so complete that at times it dominates the poem, constantly inviting readers to tease out meaningful connections within the language.

As with so many of her poems, Ní Chuilleanáin begins mid-narrative – as dreams often do – with an aeroplane coming in to land in Paris. The sense of danger as the plane descends in 'a stiff curve' is typical of the edgy imagery found in **stanza one**. **The memory immediately suggests a moment of insight – of coming down to earth**: 'We came down above the houses/In a stiff curve'. Details are stark – particularly the absorbing description of the 'empty tunnel' and the peculiar sight of the 'back half of a plane' that has been 'burnt-out and frozen' against the wintry landscape. The contrast of the deserted 'black' wreckage 'On the snow' accentuates the visual effect, adding drama to the memory.

Stanza two emphasises the surreal nature of the hushed 'snow-white runways in the dark'. The poet continues to construct a dreamlike sense of uneasy silence and chilling alienation. The only sounds coming over the loudspeakers are the unsettling 'sighs/Of the lonely pilot'. There is an underlying suggestion of a weary individual – perhaps facing death. This is given a wider relevance by the unnerving opening of **stanza three**: 'The cold of metal wings is contagious'. For the poet, this insightful moment marks a changing perspective: 'Soon you will need wings of your own'. The 'you' might refer to Ní Chuilleanáin's dying father or the poet herself or possibly the reader. From this point onwards, the metaphor of the wrecked aircraft is central to the fragmentary memories of her father's illness and death. **The poet interweaves two narratives**: the trajectory of the plane as it 'Meets the straight skyline' and the mark of her father's natural life span ('the lifeline in your palm'). Ní Chuilleanáin uses the memorable image of the crossed knife and fork to suggest the inescapable destiny that confronts the dying.

The poet's familiar preoccupations of tension and mystery are even more obvious in **stanza four**. Disjointed scenes of 'Hospital pyjamas, screens round a bed' are introduced as 'images of relief'– at least temporarily. **But the prevailing mood is of inevitable death** – 'These will fail you some time'. The poet expresses the final reality of every human being in **stanza five**: 'You will find yourself alone'. Ní Chuilleanáin conveys the nightmarish realisation of irreversible death through recognisable images of losing control: 'Accelerating down a blind/Alley, too late to stop'. Run-on lines and a persistent rhythm add to the sense of powerlessness. Once again, there are echoes of the 'empty tunnel' and the 'burnt-out' plane. Nevertheless, in imagining her father's final moments, the poet can relate to his experience of dying as a release, so that they both understood 'how light your death is'.

The resigned tone of **stanza six** reflects Ní Chuilleanáin's deeper understanding of mortality. In celebrating her father's life within a context of enduring love, the poet is able to simultaneously dismantle and preserve the relationship she has had with her father. She returns to the image of the wrecked aeroplane, accepting that in death, 'You will be scattered like wreckage'. However, far from feeling sadness for her father's loss, **Ní Chuilleanáin takes comfort in knowing that he will live 'in the hearts/Of all who love you'**. The sentiment is subdued and poignant, and all the more powerful since it comes from a poet who rarely expresses her feelings directly.

To a great extent, the poem is about families and how they process their personal tragedies. As always, Ní Chuilleanáin's oblique approach is open to many interpretations. But she seems to be suggesting that it takes the sudden shock of death to acknowledge the closeness of relationships in our lives. Typically, in dealing with such emotional subjects as separation, grief and the death of a loved one, **the poet never lapses into sentimentality**. 'Deaths and Engines' was written during the escalation of violence in Northern Ireland, and some critics have understood the poem as a commentary on the human cost of conflict. In the end, readers are left to make up their own minds.

ANALYSIS

'Ní Chuilleanáin's poems of separation and estrangement transcend the limits of personal experience.' Discuss this view, with particular reference to 'Deaths and Engines'.

Sample Paragraph

One of the most interesting aspects of Eiléan Ní Chuilleanáin's poetry is her focus on the natural life cycle. Even though she deals with the distressing subject of her father's death in 'Deaths and Engines', I found the poem to be more uplifting than depressing. In closely comparing his death to the wrecked plane she saw in Paris, 'Tubular, burnt-out and frozen', she eventually realises that all the 'pieces' of the wreckage 'Will spin and lodge in the hearts/Of all who love you'. Just because death has separated her from her father physically does not mean the end of their love. The poem also shows Ní Chuilleanáin empathising with her father and stressing the individual experience of death for every human being: 'You will find yourself alone/Accelerating down a blind/Alley, too late to stop'. Her message is simple – every individual must face death unaccompanied. In her poems, Ní Chuilleanáin can really accept the natural cycle – and this has meaning for every reader. In 'Fireman's Lift', for example, she also came to terms with a close family death – that of her mother – by comparing her passing to the glorious Assumption of the Virgin Mary. I believe that such poems transcend the individual and emphasise the naturalness of separation and loss.

Examiner's Comment

This is a well-focused response to the question and shows a close understanding of the poem, particularly in the cross-reference to 'Fireman's Lift'. Accurate quotations are used effectively to support key points. Expression is fluent, varied and clear, with some good personal engagement, such as in the final sentence. A very assured performance securing the highest grade.

N.B. Access your ebook for additional sample paragraphs and a list of useful quotes with commentary.

CLASS/HOMEWORK EXERCISES

1. 'What defines Eiléan Ní Chuilleanáin's poetry is its imaginative power and precision of language.' Discuss this statement, with particular reference to 'Deaths and Engines'.

2. 'In "Deaths and Engines", Ní Chuilleanáin explores aspects of suffering and death by effectively using the metaphor of an aeroplane coming in to land.' Discuss this view, with reference to the poem.

SUMMARY POINTS

- Key themes – memory, family bonds and coming to terms with death.
- An underlying sense of tension pervades the poem.
- Effective use of metaphor, contrast and repetition throughout.
- Positive conclusion: love can transcend death.

4 STREET 🔊

He fell in love with the butcher's daughter
When he saw her passing by in her white trousers
Dangling a knife on a ring at her belt.
He stared at the dark shining drops on the paving-stones.

One day he followed her   5
Down the slanting lane at the back of the shambles.
A door stood half-open
And the stairs were brushed and clean,
Her shoes paired on the bottom step,
Each tread marked with the red crescent   10
Her bare heels left, fading to faintest at the top.

'And the stairs were brushed and clean'

Glossary

3   *Dangling*: hanging freely, displaying.
6   *shambles*: untidy market scene; place of slaughter.
10 *tread*: undersole of a shoe; top surface of a step in a
    staircase.

10 *crescent*: half-moon; sickle shape.
11 *fading*: dwindling, perishing.
11 *faintest*: weakest, exhausted.

INITIAL RESPONSE

1. Why do you think Ní Chuilleanáin chose to name her poem 'Street' and yet gives the street no name? Give reasons for your response.

2. Which image did you find most intriguing in the poem? Refer closely to the text in your answer.

3. Were you satisfied by the poem's conclusion? Briefly explain your response.

STUDY NOTES

'Street' is a short lyric poem from Ní Chuilleanáin's collection The Magdalene Sermon *(1989). Mary Magdalene was the first person to witness the Resurrection of Christ and these poems reflect on women's religious experiences. The poems also depict edges, borders and crossings between different kinds of worlds as though passing through thresholds and intersections from one realm of experience to another, just as Christ rose from the dead. Characteristically, the poet reveals and conceals women and their strange responsibilities in a graceful, luminous voice.*

Ní Chuilleanáin believed in the importance of the ordinary and the domestic as new metaphors for human experience. In the **first section** of the poem, she quietly tells a somewhat unusual tale, giving readers a memorable glimpse into another reality. It is the story of a man falling in love with a woman, 'the butcher's daughter'. Flowing run-on lines depict the rising emotions of the man as he catches sight of her 'in her white trousers'. This colour is often associated with purity and innocence, but it is also the traditional colour butchers wear in their work. **A close-up shot captures a disturbing detail.** 'Dangling' describes the careless movement of the knife as it sways from the 'ring at her belt'. The verb is carefully positioned at the beginning of the line, as it tantalises and entices like a piece of shining jewellery; yet this knife has a deadly purpose. The man is captivated: 'He stared at the dark shining drops on the paving-stones'. Has this knife recently been used? Has blood just been spilled? Is he, as if in a fairytale, suddenly enthralled by the glittering yet lethal trade of the slaughterer?

In the **second section**, the narrative continues, becoming increasingly menacing: 'One day he followed her'. The assonant 'ow' sound disquietly enhances his journey. Ní Chuilleanáin specialises in the 'poetic of descriptive places'. The man's journey takes him 'Down the slanting lane at the back of the shambles'. **Varying line lengths add to the growing tension.** The adjective 'slanting' suggests a sinister backstreet where everything is oblique, tilted, half-concealed. The 'shambles' is a rough market where meat is carved and animals are slaughtered. To the outside world, it is a place of violence and mayhem. Is Ní Chuilleanáin making a hidden reference to the slaughter of Christ on the cross? 'A door stood half-open'. Does the door admit or shut out? Is this a symbol of the threshold between life and death which Christ breached? As always, the poet invites the reader to make sense of the clues. A secret is being half-revealed, a mystery is being highlighted. Where does the door lead?

Eiléan Ní Chuilleanáin often peoples her poems with women who studiously attend to their chores. (Mary Magdalene attended to Jesus, washing his feet with her tears and drying them with her hair.) Here 'the stairs were brushed and clean'. Are they awaiting a visit or is this the attention to hygiene which is normal in the butchering trade? This poet's population of silent figures disclose little information. The 'butcher's daughter' had left 'shoes paired on the bottom step'. Yet even this tangible detail reveals only mystery. The full narrative is missing. Is there a suggestion that the man and woman will soon be a pair as well? An inviting flight of stairs leads to all sorts of possibilities. **Ní Chuilleanáin has created a typically ambivalent scenario** filled with underlying danger and excitement. This dreamlike encounter is imbued with an unforgettable atmosphere of edgy anticipation as profound silence echoes.

The poem concludes with a defined image. The girl's 'bare heels' have left traces which become more indistinct as they ascend the stairs. This is emphasised by the alliterative phrase 'fading to faintest'. These are 'marked with the red crescent', like a secret sign beckoning through the enjambed lines. **The mystery resonates.** What really is marked with the bow shapes? The stairs? Her shoes? The heels? Readers are kept wondering. What does the future hold for this couple? Detailed close-ups have been presented, yet there are tantalising gaps in the narrative as we are left like the man who was enticed by the 'Dangling' knife, lured into this ominous atmosphere. As in so many of her elusive dramas, disrupting patterns of communication allows the poet to draw attention to the problem of communication itself. Is this the rounded insight to be glimpsed in the poem?

ANALYSIS

'Poems of waiting, dramatic and incident rich, are told quietly by Ní Chuilleanáin.' Discuss this statement in relation to the poem 'Street'.

Sample Paragraph

I felt that the poem 'Street' inveigled me into its dreamlike, surreal yet tangible world rather like the man is lured by the 'butcher's daughter'. I was caught as if in a dream, that state of consciousness which shimmers between sleep and wakefulness, where details are clearly recognisable, 'the dark shining drops', 'the red crescent/her bare heels left', yet their meaning is shrouded in mystery. Just as the 'half-open' door both invites and repels, this poem reveals and conceals as the reader wonders what is about to happen. Will the encounter take place between the man and the woman?

Will he disappear at the top of the steps? Is she waiting for him there or has she disappeared? What has she been doing? What will she do? The reader has been brought like the man on a 'slanting' journey. The full view of the lane was obscured from him, the full story is hidden from the reader by the obliqueness of the poem. Yet just like a dream the atmosphere is unforgettable, the waiting is palpably ominous. The poem disappears at its conclusion as the 'red crescent' marks flow 'fading to faintest at the top'. Suspense and tension reverberate. As in life nobody knows what will happen next. This tale is told calmly as the poet carefully positions the instrument of allure at the edge of the line 'Dangling' to highlight its swaying inviting movement. The reader is led like the man, by well-realised signs, 'drops', a 'lane', a 'door', 'stairs' and footprints as if following a trail in a fairytale. Yet the poet does not release the dramatic tensions at the poem's conclusion leaving it to resonate in the reader's consciousness.

Examiner's Comment

This response shows a remarkably close reading of the poem, using suitable reference and quotation to address the task in the question throughout. Discussion is coherent and the analysis incisive, especially the point about the dreamlike atmosphere. Expression is also impressive – fluent, varied and well controlled: 'the full story is hidden from the reader by the obliqueness of the poem'. Fully deserves the top grade.

N.B. Access your ebook for additional sample paragraphs and a list of useful quotes with commentary.

CLASS/HOMEWORK EXERCISES

1. 'Ní Chuilleanáin's poetry is oblique, yet concrete.' Discuss this statement in relation to 'Street'.

2. 'Ní Chuilleanáin creates an unnerving nightmarish atmosphere in her poem, "Street".' To what extent do you agree with this view? Support your answer with reference to the text.

SUMMARY POINTS

- Highly dramatic poem filled with suspense and intrigue.
- Close-up details create interest.
- Run-through lines add a sense of urgency.
- Sense of mystery resonates at the end.

⑤ FIREMAN'S LIFT

I was standing beside you looking up
Through the big tree of the cupola
Where the church splits wide open to admit
Celestial choirs, the fall-out of brightness.

The Virgin was spiralling to heaven,   5
Hauled up in stages. Past mist and shining,
Teams of angelic arms were heaving,
Supporting, crowding her, and we stepped

Back, as the painter longed to
While his arm swept in the large strokes.   10
We saw the work entire, and how light

Melted and faded bodies so that
Loose feet and elbows and staring eyes
Floated in the wide stone petticoat
Clear and free as weeds.   15

This is what love sees, that angle:
The crick in the branch loaded with fruit,
A jaw defining itself, a shoulder yoked,

The back making itself a roof
The legs a bridge, the hands   20
A crane and a cradle.

Their heads bowed over to reflect on her
Fair face and hair so like their own
As she passed through their hands. We saw them
Lifting her, the pillars of their arms   25

(Her face a capital leaning into an arch)
As the muscles clung and shifted
For a final purchase together
Under her weight as she came to the edge of the cloud.

Parma 1963 – Dublin 1994

'spiralling to heaven'

Glossary

Fireman's Lift: The term refers to a technique commonly used by emergency service workers to carry someone to safety by placing the carried person across the shoulders of the carrier.

The Assumption of the Virgin: Roman Catholic Church teaching states that the Virgin Mary, having completed the course of her earthly life, was assumed (or elevated) body and soul into heavenly glory.

Antonio Allegri da Correggio (1489–1534), usually known as Correggio, was the foremost painter of the Parma school of the Italian Renaissance. One of his best-known works, *The Assumption of the Virgin*, is a fresco which decorates the dome of the Duomo (Cathedral) of Parma, in northern Italy.

2 *cupola*: dome-shaped roof.
4 *Celestial*: heavenly, divine.
5 *spiralling*: whirling, twisting.
17 *crick*: arch, strain.
18 *yoked*: forced, strained.
26 *capital*: upper section of a column supporting a ceiling or arch.

INITIAL RESPONSE

1. Based on your reading of the poem, comment on the appropriateness of the title, 'Fireman's Lift'.

2. Choose one visual image from the poem which you consider particularly effective. Briefly explain your choice.

3. Write your own short personal response to the poem.

STUDY NOTES

This extraordinary poem describes the scene depicted in the painter Correggio's masterpiece, Assumption of the Virgin. *In 1963 Eiléan Ní Chuilleanáin and her mother had visited Parma Cathedral. Following her mother's death in 1994, the poet used the visit as the setting for 'Fireman's Lift', describing it as a 'cheering-up poem, when my mother was dying because I absolutely knew that she would want me to write a poem about her dying …'*

The poem begins with Ní Chuilleanáin's vivid memory of the moment when she and her mother were looking up at Correggio's celebrated ceiling mural. In the **opening stanza**, she invites readers into the Italian setting: 'I was standing beside you looking up/Through the big tree of the cupola'. There is an **immediate dreamlike sense of intimacy and closeness between mother and daughter**, as though they were both aware that something significant was happening. From the outset, the focus is on the majestic painting's mystery and symbolism, reaching heavenwards to imagined 'Celestial choirs'.

Stanza two emphasises the struggle of the angels to lift Mary into the heavens, and the awkwardness and wonder of being pushed in such a similar manner to birth. We are encouraged to become part of the dynamic scene within the reality of this great spectacle. The dynamic verbs 'spiralling' and 'heaving' suggest **the physical effort involved in raising the Virgin from her earthly life**. Line breaks and frequent commas are used to create a sluggish pace. Ní Chuilleanáin is drawn to the collective energy which becomes a fireman's lift of 'Teams of angelic arms', and the effort to raise Mary 'Past mist and shining' is relentless.

Ní Chuilleanáin then considers the overwhelming effect of Correggio's 'work entire', designed to give the illusion of real and simulated architecture within the painted fresco. This awe-inspiring achievement is reflected in the pulsating run-through rhythms and hushed tones of **stanzas three** and **four**. **Dramatic images of the angelic figures and saints assisting Mary's Assumption give expression to the artist's powerful vision**: 'Melted and faded bodies' are intermingled with 'elbows and staring eyes'. Within the dome/petticoat image, Ní Chuilleanáin describes Correggio's Virgin passing into another glorious life. All the time, this vortex of bodies and faces around her are fully engaged in assisting Mary to reach the waiting Christ.

Stanza five defines an important turning point for the poet, who can now make sense of her mother's death through a fresh understanding of Correggio's perspective: 'This is what love sees, that angle'. **The assured tone marks a coming-to-terms with deep personal loss.** Ní Chuilleanáin's renewed appreciation of the painting enables her to accept the burden of letting the dead go. Her resignation is evident in the poignant image of a 'branch loaded with fruit', an obvious symbol of the natural cycle.

Stanzas six and **seven** return to **Correggio's mesmerising skill in his interaction of art and architecture** within the cathedral dome. This intricate collusion is seen in sharper focus, providing a context for Ní Chuilleanáin to reassert her changing relationship with her mother. The restless limbs of the painted angels are in perfect harmony with the great Duomo ceiling: 'The back making itself a roof/ The legs a bridge'. This intriguingly harmonious composition merging paint and plaster adds to the urgency of ensuring that the dying soul achieves its ultimate ascension to heaven.

The **final stanzas** observe the figures attending on Mary, 'heads bowed over to reflect on her/Fair face'. Their tenderness is evident in both sound and tone. The poet has said that, on one level, 'Fireman's Lift' is about the nurses who looked after her mother when she was dying. Typically, the poet broadens our understanding of suffering, showing people caring and concerned. The concluding lines, however, acknowledge **the strength of spirit which Ní Chuilleanáin singles out as the hallmark of her mother's life and death**. This is reflected in the purposeful expression on the Virgin's face: 'As the muscles clung and shifted/For a final purchase'. Tactile 'u' sounds ('usc', 'ung', 'urch', etc.) and the drawn-out rhythms emphasise that body goes with soul in the movement across this threshold: 'to the edge of the cloud'.

Death and rebirth are recurring themes in Ní Chuilleanáin's work. But in honouring her mother's life and associating her passing with the Assumption of the Virgin, the poet has brought together Italian art, religion and a deep sense of sorrow. Essentially, however, **'Fireman's Lift' is a moving expression of the poet's enduring love** for her mother. It is not unusual for readers of Ní Chuilleanáin's poetry to encounter beautiful images which leave them searching. Nevertheless, this poem has a universal significance. It is infused with an astounding sense of love, loss and triumph as the ascending figure disappears into the clouds. Poised on the edge of this unknowable boundary, the rest is mystery.

ANALYSIS

'For Eiléan Ní Chuilleanáin, boundaries and transitions are central concerns.' Discuss this view with particular reference to 'Fireman's Lift'.

Sample Paragraph

I found 'Fireman's Lift' both puzzling and interesting. Ní Chuilleanáin managed to link her mother's death with the famous painting by Antonio Correggio, *The Assumption of the Virgin*. In describing her memory of a holiday visit to Parma Cathedral, the poet seemed to enter the reality of the mural and see her own relationship with her mother in a new way – almost like one of the angels who desperately tries to raise Mary to heaven, 'Teams of angelic arms were heaving'. The transition is shown in terms of brute strength – the Virgin is 'Hauled up in stages'. But the poet also reflects the transition between this life and the next in the optical illusions painted on the dome's structure. Everything appears to be integrated – for example, the hands of angels act as a 'crane and a cradle' supporting Mary. She leans on the 'pillars of their arms'. This metaphor blurs the distinction between stonework and painted figures. The poet sees no difference between her own prayers for her mother's soul and the work of the saints who raise the Virgin. To me, Ní Chuilleanáin is absorbed in the art work. I found this typical of her poetry in that she wanders beyond borders and margins, just as Correggio did within his celebrated painting.

Examiner's Comment

An incisive response which addresses this challenging question directly. There is good personal interaction: 'To me, Ní Chuilleanáin is absorbed in the artwork', and effective use of supportive references. Clearly made points explore the poet's emphasis on the blurred lines within the Correggio painting, and between it and Ní Chuilleanáin's own involvement. Such in-depth analysis merits the top grade.

N.B. Access your ebook for additional sample paragraphs and a list of useful quotes with commentary.

CLASS/HOMEWORK EXERCISES

1. 'Eiléan Ní Chuilleanáin's poems explore the persistence of memory in a highly distinctive style.' Discuss this statement with particular reference to 'Fireman's Lift'.

2 '"Fireman's Lift" is typical of Ní Chuilleanáin's poems in that it is layered with hidden meaning.' To what extent do you agree with this view? Support your answer with reference to the text.

SUMMARY POINTS

- Characteristic narrative opening recalling a significant memory.
- Effective use of run-on lines, symbolism, dramatic images of art and architecture.
- Vivid details and powerful verbs suggest physical effort.
- Key themes – death, rebirth, family relationships and enduring love.

6   ALL FOR YOU 🔊

Once beyond the gate of the strange stableyard, we dismount.
The donkey walks on, straight in at a wide door
And sticks his head in a manger.

The great staircase of the hall slouches back,
Sprawling between warm wings. It is for you.   5
As the steps wind and warp
Among the vaults, their thick ribs part; the doors
Of guardroom, chapel, storeroom
Swing wide and the breath of ovens
Flows out, the rage of brushwood,   10
The roots torn and butchered.

It is for you, the dry fragrance of tea-chests
The tins shining in ranks, the ten-pound jars
Rich with shrivelled fruit. Where better to lie down
And sleep, along the labelled shelves,   15
With the key still in your pocket?

'steps wind and warp/Among the vaults'

Glossary

6	*wind*: curve, meander.		7	*ribs*: curved structures that support a vault.
6	*warp*: bend, buckle.		10	*brushwood*: undergrowth, small twigs and branches.
7	*vaults*: large rooms often used for storage; chambers beneath a church.			

INITIAL RESPONSE

1. Based on your reading of the poem, comment on the appropriateness of the title, 'All for You'.

2. Choose one memorable image from the poem and briefly explain its effectiveness.

3. Write your own individual response to the poem, referring closely to the text in your answer.

STUDY NOTES

'All for You' comes from Eiléan Ní Chuilleanáin's The Brazen Serpent *(1994). The book's title refers to the biblical story of Moses and the Israelites in the desert. God had become angry with his people, as they had spoken against their leader, Moses, and He let fierce snakes crawl among them and bite them. Moses prayed for the people and God instructed Moses to make a bronze serpent and place it upon a pole in public view. Anyone who was bitten could then look on the brazen snake and they would be cured. This foreshadows the raising onto the cross of Jesus Christ, who died to save sinners. Therefore, God made this sacrifice 'All for You'. Ní Chuilleanáin's collection of poems brings the possibility of hope, of getting through bad times, of being redeemed.*

Ní Chuilleanáin **collapses time and distinctions betweeen places** in 'All for You'. Line by line, the reader is drawn into deeper water until the bottom can no longer be touched, a recurring feature of this poet's complex work. The **first three lines** describe a scene that resonates with detail from the Bible story of the birth of Jesus: 'the strange stableyard', 'The donkey', the 'manger'. Why is the stableyard 'strange'? In the biblical account, Joseph and Mary had to leave their home town and travel to Bethlehem to be listed for a tax census. As is often the case with Ní Chuilleanáin's dramatic presentations, the reader must piece together a bare minimum of narrative sense. However, there is a sense of inevitability about the journey being described.

In **lines 4–11**, a noticeably different time and space is realised. What follows is **a series of evocative images and metaphors relating to a transitional experience.** Personification brings a staircase vividly to life as it 'slouches back', lolling and slumping – 'Sprawling' almost like a reclining animal as it sits between the 'warm wings' of the hall. Is it ominous or welcoming? It is waiting, as the bronze serpent awaited the Israelites, like a gift 'for you'. Ní Chuilleanáin does not determine the identity of 'you', instead leaving it open to speculation so that 'you' could have a universal application and refer to anyone. Is this gift for all? The poet's descriptive talent engages the reader as the grand staircase is depicted with great clarity, yet its full significance is never defined. Alliteration ('wind and warp') conveys the stairs' sinuous movement, curling like an uncoiling animal through the 'thick ribs' of the intimidating vaults.

The architectural metaphor is a strong element in Ní Chuilleanáin's poetry, which is full of mysterious crannies and alcoves. Could this imposing building be a convent waiting to welcome a young woman as its doors open, revealing the imposing interior of 'guardroom, chapel' and 'storeroom'? The poet's three aunts were nuns and she has commented, 'One is constantly made aware of the fact that the past does not go away, that it is walking around the place causing trouble at every moment.' Is this reference therefore autobiographical or does it encompass a wider significance? Could the staircase lead to salvation and heaven?

A rush of heat from the nearby ovens is suddenly palpable – again conveyed through the poet's effective working of personification: 'the breath of ovens/Flows out'. Ní Chuilleanáin uses a violent image to describe the fierce temperature: 'the rage of brushwood'. This is continued in the savagery with which the kindling has been collected: 'roots torn out and butchered'. Is there an echo of the biblical tale of the burning bush from the **Book of Exodus**, where God directed Moses to the Promised Land? This story teaches that we should be able to obey God whenever he calls us. Is the poet also referencing the story of Christ, 'butchered' on the cross for the sins of the world? The forceful rhythm of these dramatic lines creates an intensity, a climax of dread, almost like an ecstatic spiritual experience.

There is a marked **change of tone** in the **last five lines**. All the tension eases within the ordered space of the building's provisions store. Readers are now immersed in the moment, smelling the 'dry fragrance of tea-chests', observing 'tins shining in ranks, the ten-pound jars'. Repetition of the rich 'r' sound suggests the store's abundance of goods. Yet there is also an unease secreted in this image of confined order. The fruit is 'shrivelled', the fragrance is 'dry'. Is there a life withering, unable to reproduce? Is this another central dimension of religious life? The poem concludes with a rhetorical question intimating that there is nowhere better to take rest, just as Joseph and Mary did long ago in that 'strange stable yard', than here 'along the labelled shelves'. The body's surrender and submission to God's will enables it to act.

Another biblical reference is suggested in the final detail of the 'key still in your pocket'. In Isaiah 33:6, faith is the key to salvation: 'He will be the sure foundation of your times, a rich store of salvation and wisdom and knowledge; the fear of the Lord is the key to this treasure.' Ní Chuilleanáin's poem focuses on the experience of Christian faith as imagined through the imposing challenge and triumph of religious vocations. The 'key' image is typically contradictory – symbolising both confinement and freedom. Is the poet presenting the central paradox of Christian belief? Can the soul's redemption only be achieved through submission to God's will? Characteristically, Ní Chuilleanáin's multi-layered narrative has been subtly woven, offering a glimpse, perhaps, of salvation and hope.

ANALYSIS

'Eiléan Ní Chuilleanáin's poetry is an unshaped fire demanding to be organised into a sequence of words and images.' Discuss this statement in relation to 'All for You'.

Sample Paragraph

'All for You' is an unsettling poem which seems to emerge from the subconscious like an unformed fire. This poet's work resists containment as she wanders beyond borders. The poem springs from the idea of a gift which is 'All for You'. This can be the reward of spiritual salvation as the continuous references to the Bible – the story of Christ's birth is interwoven with references to Old Testament scenes, such as 'the rage of brushwood'. Like an 'unshaped fire', the poem's religious theme 'Flows out' like the heat from the ovens. Yet it is carefully layered. Fragmentary narratives are overlaid and remain long after the poem is read. I thought the image of the writhing staircase which 'slouches back' was very effective as it suggested the brazen serpent which Moses erected to gain salvation for his own people. The image also symbolised the harsh ladder of life which Christians must climb to reach salvation. Ní Chuilleanáin's use of alliteration, 'wind and warp', emphasised the twisting turns life takes and also called to mind the uncoiling serpent – the devil, perhaps. The poet has often written about nuns and she includes several interesting images relating to the enclosed life of a convent. I got the sense of being in a strange building with old-fashioned rooms and vaults. The storeroom imagery reflected the enclosed religious world, with 'the dry fragrance of tea-chests' and 'shrivelled fruit'. The sense of routine and order was also present: 'The tins shining in ranks'. Ironically, this strict religious life of submission represented the 'key' to salvation. The repetition of 'It is for you' suggests a generous God wishing to give a precious gift and what gift could be more important than the gift of hope? All the poet's ideas are expressed in patterns of visionary and spiritual language which can be seen as a powerful 'unshaped fire'.

Examiner's Comment

A clear personal response to a challenging question. Key discussion points are very well developed and effectively illustrated. This shows a good understanding of this complex poem – and particularly the poet's use of dense symbols and overlapping images. Expression throughout is confident, fluent and well controlled. An excellent response that merits the highest grade.

N.B. Access your ebook for additional sample paragraphs and a list of useful quotes with commentary.

CLASS/HOMEWORK EXERCISES

1. 'Ní Chuilleanáin's language is supple and acute enough to undertake its most difficult subject: how we perceive and understand the world.' Discuss this statement in relation to the prescribed work of the poet on your course.

2. '"All for You" illustrates Ní Chuilleanáin's deep interest in the mysteries of Christianity.' To what extent do you agree with this view? Support your answer with reference to the poem.

SUMMARY POINTS

- The poem explores various aspects of choosing the Christian life.
- Personification and architectural imagery create a sense of mystery.
- Effective use of Biblical and religious references.
- Descriptive details and provocative images add drama.

⑦ FOLLOWING 🔊

So she follows the trail of her father's coat through the fair
Shouldering past beasts packed solid as books,
And the dealing men nearly as slow to give way –
A block of a belly, a back like a mountain,
A shifting elbow like a plumber's bend –   5
When she catches a glimpse of a shirt-cuff, a handkerchief,
Then the hard brim of his hat, skimming along,

Until she is tracing light footsteps
Across the shivering bog by starlight,
The dead corpse risen from the wakehouse   10
Gliding before her in a white habit.
The ground is forested with gesturing trunks,
Hands of women dragging needles,
Half-choked heads in the water of cuttings,
Mouths that roar like the noise of the fair day.   15

She comes to where he is seated
With whiskey poured in two glasses
In a library where the light is clean,
His clothes all finely laundered,
Ironed facings and linings.   20
The smooth foxed leaf has been hidden
In a forest of fine shufflings,
The square of white linen
That held three drops
Of her heart's blood is shelved   25
Between the gatherings
That go to make a book –
The crushed flowers among the pages crack
The spine open, push the bindings apart.

'And the dealing men nearly as slow to give way'

Glossary

Following: coming after in time or sequence, people about to be mentioned or listed; those who admire or support somebody.
2 *beasts*: animals at an Irish mart.
3 *dealing men*: dealers, men who bargain as they buy and sell animals at an Irish fair.
5 *plumber's bend*: length of 18 inches from the bend of the elbow to the tip of the middle finger.
7 *brim*: edge.
10 *wakehouse*: house, particularly in Ireland, where a dead person is laid out; people come to console the grieving relatives and to pay their respects to the deceased.

14 *cuttings*: small pieces of plants.
20 *facings*: strengthening linings; collar, cuffs and trimmings on a uniform coat.
20 *linings*: layers of material used to cover and protect.
21 *foxed*: soiled; marked with fox-like reddish spots and stains, often found on old books and documents.
21 *leaf*: single sheet of paper.
22 *shufflings*: walking slowly and awkwardly.
29 *spine*: vertical back of book to which pages are attached.
29 *bindings*: material which holds pages together.

INITIAL RESPONSE

1. Based on your reading of the poem, show how Eiléan Ní Chuilleanáin conjures up the atmosphere of an Irish fair day. Refer closely to the text in your response.

2. In your opinion, how many settings are there in this poem? Which one did you prefer? Give reasons for your choice, quoting to support your answer.

3. Choose one vivid image from the third stanza of the poem and briefly explain its effectiveness.

STUDY NOTES

Eiléan Ní Chuilleanáin often assumes a storytelling role in her poems as she relates memories from the past. She readjusts the perspective of readers by taking us into the lives of ordinary people who literally and physically made history. In her collection The Brazen Serpent, *Ní Chuilleanáin highlights family and women as makers of history. She hints at the untold through her use of characters, silences and secrets. These confidential witnesses, like the poet herself, reconstruct subtle revelations of family unease and discontentment. Female imagery expresses what is silenced. The poet frequently explores religious themes as well as death and rebirth. Quietly and precisely, she offers us the comfort that the past does not go away.*

In the **opening section**, the poet begins her story in her usual oblique, non-confessional style, yet deeply engages the reader despite her seeming detachment. A vividly realised journey by a girl through the hurly-burly of an Irish fair day catapults the reader into the story. She is trying to follow her father through the dense crowds: 'the trail of her father's coat through the fair'. Long run-on lines and broad vowels convey the difficulty of negotiating the route as she attempts to push past 'beasts packed as solid as books'. This unusual simile illustrates the tightly packed rows of animals. Nor could she easily make her way through the dealers, men caught up in the very serious business of buying and selling, making a deal. Their thick-set bodies, bulky like their animals, are described through a tumbling list of similes and metaphors to highlight their immobile weight: 'A block of a belly, a back like a mountain'. A 'shifting elbow' is like the measure used in plumbing. All these images reinforce the **tough, masculine world of the fair**. Ní Chuilleanáin has pushed the reader, through her unwavering gaze, into the poem's self-enclosed world.

Suddenly, in **line 6**, the girl catches a glimpse of her father. This is shown by a list of his clothing: 'a shirt-cuff, a handkerchief,/Then the hard brim of his hat'. His progress is swift and effortless. He moves as swiftly as the punctuation (a series of fast-moving commas) accelerates the motion of the line. Sharp contrast in the verbs used to describe the progress of the girl and her father **highlight their different rates of success in moving through the fair**. The girl is struggling, 'Shouldering past', while the father moves with ease, 'skimming along'. Is Ní Chuilleanáin suggesting that a woman finds it difficult to negotiate a man's world? The poet has hypnotically caught the excitement as well as the danger of the fair day.

Distance and time blur in the **second section**. Ní Chuilleanáin shifts the scene and time frame from the noise and physical bulk of the fair to the **'shivering bog'**. Personification and slender vowels effectively convey the cold 'starlight' scene as she is revisiting, 'tracing light footsteps', mapping faint prints. **A surreal, nightmarish world is presented**, as 'The dead corpse risen from the wakehouse' appears 'before her in a white habit'. Whose corpse is this? The effortless sense of 'Gliding' suggests the agile movement of the father. Momentarily, the packed animals of the fair have given way to the ground 'forested with gesturing trunks'. Now the heavy trees are highlighting her way, as she will ultimately follow her father into death. Thin waving rushes are evocatively described as 'Hands of women dragging needles'. Their slow cumbersome movement is presented in visionary terms. Is this a reference to the story from the Bible when the Pharaoh of Egypt decreed that because of the increasing numbers of Israelites, all first-born boys were to be drowned in the River Nile? Are these the half-choked heads? Is this the wail of Israelite women and children as they cry and 'roar' like the beasts in the fair, aware of their fate? Or is it a reference to the subordination of women as they work?

In the poem's **concluding section**, the girl meets her father in a much more hospitable setting with 'whiskey poured in two glasses', 'His clothes all finely laundered'. Within these domestic interiors of the poet's imagination lies the remote **possibility of utopia**. The 'square of white linen', redolent of the survivor's suffering, shrunk and stained by the body's signifiers of hurt, becomes a relic of love and loss. Ní Chuilleanáin has commented, 'A relic is something you enclose, and then you enclose the reliquary in something else. In the *The Book of Kells* exhibition, the book satchel is in leather, which is meant to protect, and there is a shrine which in turn is meant to protect the book'. A relic is associated with people seeking comfort in difficult times. The past is beautifully evoked in the phrase 'The smooth foxed leaf has been hidden', with its haunting image of time-stained pages. Inside the book are 'crushed flowers', reminders that love was violated, yet something of it remains. These memories have tremendous power; they 'crack' and push apart as if being reborn. Living and dead touch each other through such memories. The dust and noise of the cattle market, the cold starry bog have all evaporated to be replaced by this interior where the 'light is clean', making it easy to see. Comfort and hope are being offered as the poem suggests that the past is not dead.

ANALYSIS

'Ní Chuilleanáin's poems explore how the most basic legends – family stories – fragment and alter in each individual's memory.' Discuss this statement with particular reference to the poem 'Following'.

Sample Paragraph

I think we tell ourselves stories about the past and I wonder do we need to revisit them in order to see the past differently, to assimilate it and move on in hope? Ní Chuilleanáin's poem, 'Following', dredges up fragments of uniquely Irish family stories (the fair day, a wake, women sewing) and rearranges them, as cards are moved in 'shufflings'. This reconstructs and transforms the past so that we can see and understand from a new perspective. We are brought as followers, just like the girl in the fair, on a journey to discover that the past is not dead, but resonates through the present by means of relics, 'The square of white linen', and so gives hope and comfort to those left behind. The title suggests to me that we are all following one another on the same journey through life, but at different paces, as the girl and the father in the fair. In the masculine world of the fair, 'beasts packed solid as books' the girl found it hard to negotiate her way. The poet has identified the difficult role women have in life, 'dragging needles', employed in repetitive domestic drudgery. These women are unable to express their opinions and concerns, 'Half-choked'. The legends become 'crushed flowers' yet the poet suggests that they are so potent that they can 'crack' open and push apart the book in which they are enclosed. I felt that she was communicating the message of hope that the past does not stay in the past but reverberates and pulses through the present. Our memories do not remain 'shelved' but live again in the present through the power of relics.

Examiner's Comment

This is a very impressive response which fully deserves the highest grade. The focus throughout is firmly placed on addressing the various parts of the question. Quotations are integrated effectively and the answer ranges widely from the title to the individual stories and the imagery used in conveying the narratives. Language is carefully controlled to express points clearly, e.g. 'This reconstructs and transforms the past so that we can see and understand from a new perspective'.

N.B. Access your ebook for additional sample paragraphs and a list of useful quotes with commentary.

CLASS/HOMEWORK EXERCISES

1. 'The mysterious writing style of Ní Chuilleanáin allows the reader to explore the poems on many levels, each tracking a different aspect of the cycle of life.' Discuss this statement in relation to the prescribed poems of this poet on your course.

2. 'Ní Chuilleanáin's unsettling poetic voice can often seem deceptively simple.' Discuss this statement with particular reference to the poem 'Following'. Support your answer with reference to the text.

SUMMARY POINTS

- The poet assumes a familiar story-telling role in this mystery tale.
- Themes include Irish identity and the power of memory.
- Effective use of commas, dashes and run-on lines.
- Prominent sound effects (alliteration and assonance) add emphasis.

8 KILCASH

From the Irish, c.1800

What will we do now for timber
With the last of the woods laid low –
No word of Kilcash nor its household,
Their bell is silenced now,
Where the lady lived with such honour,   5
No woman so heaped with praise,
Earls came across oceans to see her
And heard the sweet words of Mass.

It's the cause of my long affliction
To see your neat gates knocked down,   10
The long walks affording no shade now
And the avenue overgrown,
The fine house that kept out the weather,
Its people depressed and tamed;
And their names with the faithful departed,   15
The Bishop and Lady Iveagh!

The geese and the ducks' commotion,
The eagle's shout, are no more,
The roar of the bees gone silent,
Their wax and their honey store   20
Deserted. Now at evening
The musical birds are stilled
And the cuckoo is dumb in the treetops
That sang lullaby to the world.

Even the deer and the hunters   25
That follow the mountain way
Look down upon us with pity,
The house that was famed in its day;
The smooth wide lawn is all broken,
No shelter from wind and rain;   30
The paddock has turned to a dairy
Where the fine creatures grazed.

Mist hangs low on the branches
No sunlight can sweep aside,
Darkness falls among daylight   35
And the streams are all run dry;
No hazel, no holly, no berry,
Bare naked rocks and cold;
The forest park is leafless
And all the game gone wild.   40

And now the worst of our troubles:
She has followed the prince of the Gaels –
He has borne off the gentle maiden,
Summoned to France and to Spain.
Her company laments her   45
That she fed with silver and gold:
One who never preyed on the people
But was the poor souls' friend.

My prayer to Mary and Jesus
She may come safe home to us here   50
To dancing and rejoicing
To fiddling and bonfire
That our ancestors' house will rise up,
Kilcash built up anew
And from now to the end of the story   55
May it never again be laid low.

'long walks affording no shade now'

Glossary

Title: Eiléan Ní Chuilleanáin's translation of the early 19th-century ballad *Caoine Cill Chais* (The Lament for Kilcash), an anonymous lament that the castle of Cill Chais stood empty, its woods cut down and all its old grandeur disappeared. Kilcash was one of the great houses of a branch of the Butler family near Clonmel, Co. Tipperary, until well into the 18th century. Ní Chuilleanáin's poem encompasses several generations of the Butler family, but the presiding spirit is that of Margaret Butler, Viscountess Iveagh (who died in 1744).

2   *the last of the woods*: a reference to the mass clearance of native Irish forests by plantation settlers to create agricultural land and to fuel the colonial economy. The woodland belonging to the Butlers of Kilcash were sold in 1797 and 1801.

5   *the lady*: Margaret Butler, Viscountess Iveagh, a staunch Catholic (d.1744).

16   *The Bishop*: Catholic clergy – including Lady Iveagh's brother-in-law – were often given shelter in Kilcash.

17   *commotion*: noise, clamour.

24   *lullaby*: soothing song.

31   *paddock*: enclosure.

42   *prince of the Gaels*: probably a reference to the 18th Earl of Ormonde.

43   *the gentle maiden*: Countess, wife of the 18th Earl.

47   *preyed*: harmed, took advantage of.

INITIAL RESPONSE

1. From your reading of the poem, what is your impression of Lady Iveagh? Refer to the text in your answer.

2. Choose one interesting image from 'Kilcash' that you consider particularly effective. Give reasons to explain why this image appealed to you.

3. Write your own individual response to the poem, referring closely to the text in your answer.

STUDY NOTES

'Kilcash' comes from Eiléan Ní Chuilleanáin's The Girl Who Married the Reindeer (2001). Many of the poems in this collection deal with outsiders and the dispossessed. Kilcash was the great house of one of the branches of the Butler family near Clonmel, Co. Tipperary, until the 18th century. The Butlers were Catholic landed gentry who had come to Ireland as part of an Anglo-Norman invasion during the 12th century and had taken over vast amounts of land. Over time, the family became absorbed into Irish ways. Ní Chuilleanáin's version of the traditional Irish elegy, Caoine Cill Chais, mourns the death of Margaret Butler, Viscountess Iveagh.

Stanza one opens with a plaintive voice lamenting 'What will we do now for timber'. The ballad was originally composed in the early 1800s following the demise of the Butlers of Kilcash and the eventual clearing of the family's extensive woodlands, which had supplied timber for local people. **The early tone typifies the entire poem's sense of hopelessness now that the woods are 'laid low'.** The systematic felling of trees is symbolic of the decline of this aristocratic Catholic family. Following colonisation, the Irish were consigned to Nature as a symbol of their barbarity. In some British circles, they were referred to as the 'natural wild Irish' because the country's remote boglands and forests offered shelter to Irish rebels. The poem emphasises the uneasy silence around Kilcash and the speaker pays extravagant tribute to 'the lady' of the house, who is immediately associated with Ireland's Catholic resistance: 'Earls came across oceans to see her'.

As always, Ní Chuilleanáin's approach is layered, recognising the genuine feelings of loss while suggesting a misplaced dependence on all those who exploited the native population. For the most part, however, the poem's anonymous narrator appears to express the desolation ('long affliction') felt by the impoverished and leaderless Irish of the time. There is no shortage of evidence to illustrate what has happened to the 'fine house'. Throughout **stanzas two** and **three**, broad assonant sounds add to the maudlin sentiments. **The 'neat gates knocked down' and the 'avenue overgrown' reflect the dramatic turnaround in fortunes.** But is Ní Chuilleanáin's translation of the old song also unearthing an underlying sense of delight in the sudden fall of the mighty? There is 'no shade now' for the once powerful gentry as well as the impoverished community. Many of the references to the 'stilled' birds and animals can also be seen as both a loss and a possible release from an unhappy phase of oppression and dependence.

Images of hardship taken from nature dominate **stanzas four** and **five**. The abandoned peasants are depicted as pitiable. The atmosphere becomes increasingly disturbing as the natural world order is transformed: 'Darkness falls among daylight/And the streams are all run dry'. **As in so many other Irish legends, the landscape reflects the terms of the Butlers' exile: 'The forest park is leafless'.** Negative language patterns – 'No sunlight', 'No hazel, no holly' – highlight the sense of mordant despondency resulting from abandonment. Relentlessly, the regular lines and ponderous rhythm work together to create a monotonous trance-like effect. The extravagant praise for 'the gentle maiden' (a likely reference to the wife of the 18th Earl) dominates **stanza six**. As a representative of the Butler dynasty, her absence is seen as 'the worst of our troubles' and she is glorified as someone 'who never preyed on the people' despite her privileged lifestyle.

The prayer-like tone of the **final stanza** is in keeping with the deep yearning for a return to the old ways in Kilcash. The Catholic allusion also reinforces the central importance of religion in expressing political and cultural identity. In wishing to restore the former Gaelic order, the speaker imagines lively scenes of communal celebration: 'fiddling and bonfire'. **The aspiration that the castle will be 'built up anew' offers a clear symbol of recovery.** This rallying call is in keeping with traditional laments and is characteristic of the poet's sympathies for the oppressed. Ní Chuilleanáin has retained the rhetorical style of Gaelic poetry throughout, revealing the experience of isolated communities through numerous images of restless desolation and uncomfortable silences.

'Kilcash' marks a significant transition in Irish history. As the old native aristocracy suffered military and political defeat and, in many cases, exile, the world order that had supported the bardic poets disappeared. In these circumstances, it is hardly surprising that much Irish poetry of this period laments these changes and the poet's plight. However, **Ní Chuilleanáin's translation of the old ballad differs from other versions in being more ambivalent towards Viscountess Iveagh and what she represented**. Is the poem a poignant expression of loss and a genuine tribute to those landlords who were seen as humane? Does the poet satirise the subservient native Irish who had been conditioned to accept some convenient generosity from the Catholic gentry? To what extent did the original lament present a romantic distortion of Ireland's history? Readers are left to decide for themselves.

ANALYSIS

'Eiléan Ní Chuilleanáin's poems retain the power to connect past and present in ways that never cease to fascinate.' Discuss this statement, with particular reference to 'Kilcash'.

Sample Paragraph

On a first reading, I thought that 'Kilcash' was a simple adaptation of the old Gaelic ballad, 'Caoine Cill Chais'. After studying the poem, however, I feel that Eiléan Ní Chuilleanáin has raised many interesting questions about Irish history. For a start, the poem is a translation and the original bard's view of the 18th century Butler line is buried beneath Ní Chuilleanáin's. The opening lament of the deprived peasants seems self-pitying – 'What will we do now for timber'. The compliments paid to Lady Iveagh (Margaret Butler) are lavish and focus on her Catholic faith and support for the old Gaelic culture – 'Earls came across oceans to see her'. As a young person looking back on this period of upheaval, I could appreciate the way dispossessed Irish people had become dependent on the Catholic gentry as symbols of freedom. The poem repeatedly places 'the lady' as the epitome of hope – 'the poor souls' friend'. It was interesting to see how the flight of the Butlers reduced people to complete dependence, so that all they could do was pray for a miraculous reversal of history 'that our ancestors' house will rise up'. The main insight I gained from the poem was that colonisation – whether by Catholic or Protestant landlords – had broken the Irish spirit. Ní Chuilleanáin manages to link past and present very subtly, broadening our view of the complex relationships between powerful interests and a conquered population.

Examiner's Comment

An assured personal response, focused throughout and very well illustrated with suitable quotations. The paragraph carefully highlights Ní Chuilleanáin's exploration of the plight of the native Irish community in various ways: 'the original bard's view of the eighteenth century Butler line is buried beneath Ní Chuilleanáin's'. Points are clearly expressed throughout in this excellent, top-grade answer.

N.B. Access your ebook for additional sample paragraphs and a list of useful quotes with commentary.

CLASS/HOMEWORK EXERCISES

1. 'Ní Chuilleanáin's distinctive poetic world provides an accessible platform for voices from the margin.' Discuss this view, with particular reference to 'Kilcash'.

2. 'In her poem, "Kilcash", Ní Chuilleanáin explores themes of loss and dispossession.' To what extent do you agree with this statement? Support your answer with reference to the text.

SUMMARY POINTS

- Traditional lament for Catholic aristocracy raises questions about Ireland's past.
- Desolate landscape and negative language reflect the mood of hopelessness.
- Regular rhythm, the prayer-like tone and stark images emphasise the atmosphere.
- Ambivalent ending intrigues readers about the poet's own viewpoint.

9 TRANSLATION 🔊

for the reburial of the Magdalenes

The soil frayed and sifted evens the score –
There are women here from every county,
Just as there were in the laundry.

White light blinded and bleached out
The high relief of a glance, where steam danced   5
Around stone drains and giggled and slipped across water.

Assist them now, ridges under the veil, shifting,
Searching for their parents, their names,
The edges of words grinding against nature,

As if, when water sank between the rotten teeth   10
Of soap, and every grasp seemed melted, one voice
Had begun, rising above the shuffle and hum

Until every pocket in her skull blared with the note –
Allow us now to hear it, sharp as an infant's cry
While the grass takes root, while the steam rises: 15

　　　Washed clean of idiom · the baked crust
　　　Of words that made my temporary name ·
　　　A parasite that grew in me · that spell
　　　Lifted · I lie in earth sifted to dust ·
　　　Let the bunched keys I bore slacken and fall ·   20
　　　I rise and forget · a cloud over my time.

'Washed clean of idiom'

Glossary

Subtitle: The Magdalenes refers to Irish women, particularly unmarried mothers, who were separated from their children and forced to work in convent laundries. Inmates were required to undertake hard physical labour, including washing and needlework. They also endured a daily regime that included long periods of prayer and enforced silence. In Ireland, such institutions were known as Magdalene laundries. It has been estimated that up to 30,000 women passed through such laundries in Ireland, the last one of which (in Waterford) closed on 25 September 1996.

1	*frayed*: ragged.
1	*sifted*: sorted, examined.
3	*the laundry*: clothes washing area.
13	*blared*: rang out, resounded.
16	*idiom*: language, misinterpretation.
18	*parasite*: bloodsucker.

INITIAL RESPONSE

1. Comment on the effectiveness of the poem's title, 'Translation', in relation to the themes that Ní Chuilleanáin addresses in the poem.

2. Choose one image from the poem that you found particularly interesting. Briefly explain your choice.

3. How does the poem make you feel? Give reasons for your response, supporting the points you make with reference to the text.

STUDY NOTES

During the early 1990s, the remains of more than 150 women were discovered at several Dublin religious institutions as the properties were being excavated. The bones, from women buried over a very long period, were cremated and reburied in Glasnevin Cemetery. Eiléan Ní Chuilleanáin's poem was read at the reburial ceremony to commemorate Magdalene laundry women from all over Ireland. 'Translation' links the writer's work with the belated acknowledgement, in the late 20th century, of the stolen lives and hidden deaths of generations of Irishwomen incarcerated in Magdalene convents.

The poem begins with a macabre description of the Glasnevin grave where the reburial is taking place: 'The soil frayed and sifted evens the score'. Ní Chuilleanáin expresses the feelings of the mourners ('here from every county') who are **united by a shared sense of injustice**. This dramatic ceremony represents a formal acknowledgement of a dark period in Ireland's social history. **Line 4** takes readers back in time behind convent walls and imagines the grim laundry rooms in which the Magdelene women worked: 'White light blinded and bleached out/The high relief of a glance'.

The poet's delicate and precise language contrasts the grinding oppression of routine manual labour with the young women's natural playfulness. **Their stolen youth and lost gaiety are poignantly conveyed through familiar images of the laundry**, 'where steam danced/Around stone drains and giggled and slipped across water' (**line 6**). Vigorous verbs and a jaunty rhythm add emphasis to the sad irony of their broken lives. The relentless scrubbing was intended to wash away the women's sins. However, no matter how much the women washed, they were considered dirty and sinful throughout their lives.

All through the poem, Ní Chuilleanáin focuses on the importance of words and naming as though she herself is aiming to make sense of the shocking Magdalene story. But how is she to respond to the women who have come to the graveyard, 'Searching for their parents, their names'? Typically, the language is dense and multi-layered. In death, these former laundry workers are mere 'ridges under the veil' of the anonymous earth. The metaphor in **line 7** also evokes images of the stern Magdalene nuns. **Ní Chuilleanáin sees all these women as victims of less enlightened times**, ironically recalled in the prayer-like note of invocation: 'Assist them now'.

The poem's title becomes clear as we recognise **Ní Chuilleanáin's intention to communicate ('translate') decades of silence into meaningful expression on behalf of the Magdalene laundry inmates**. Their relentless efforts to eventually become a 'voice' is compared to the almost impossible challenge of 'rising above the shuffle and hum' within the noisy laundry itself. In **line 9**, Ní Chuilleanáin visualises the women setting 'The edges of words grinding against nature' until their misrepresentation is overcome as it is turned to dust along with their bodies.

From **line 13**, much of the **focus is placed on exploring the experience of one of the nuns who managed the laundries**. As the true history emerges, she is also being cleansed of 'the baked crust/ Of words that made my temporary name'. The 'temporary name' is her name in religion, that is, the saint's name she chose upon entering strict convent life, which, as Ní Chuilleanáin notes, involved relinquishing her previous identity as an individual. She too has been exploited and the poet's generous tone reflects an understanding of this woman, who is caught between conflicting influences of duty, care, indoctrination and doubt, 'Until every pocket in her skull blared'. The evocative reference to the 'infant's cry' echoes the enduring sense of loss felt by young mothers who were forced to give up their babies shortly after birth.

In the poem's **final lines**, we hear the voice of a convent reverend mother, whose role is defined by 'the bunched keys I bore'. The reburial ceremony has also cleansed her from 'that spell' which maintained the cruel system she once served. Almost overwhelmed, she now recognises the 'parasite' power 'that grew in me' and only now can the keys she carries, an obvious symbol of her role as gaoler, 'slacken and fall'. **Bleak, disturbing images and broken rhythms have an unnerving, timeless effect.** This woman's punitive authority over others has haunted her beyond the grave.

In the end, Ní Chuilleanáin's measured and balanced approach shows genuine compassion for all institutionalised victims, drawing together the countless young women and those in charge in their common confinement. In addition to their time spent in convents, they are now reunited, sifting the earth that they have all become. **The tragic legacy of these institutions involves women at many levels.** Nevertheless, the poem itself is a faithful translation, as these victims have been raised from their graves by the poet's response to their collective dead voice. Ní Chuilleanáin relates their compelling story to 'Allow us now to hear it'. She also tenderly acknowledges the complete silencing of the Irish Magdalenes as they did their enforced and, in some cases, lifelong penance.

Although Eiléan Ní Chuilleanáin's mournful 'translation' reveals glimpses of their true history, **none of these Magdalene women can ever be given back the lives they had before they entered the laundries**. The poem stops short of pretending to even the score in terms of power between those in authority and the totally subservient and permanently disgraced women under their control. At best, their small voices rise up together like 'steam' and form a 'cloud over my time' (**line 21**). This metaphor of the cloud can be construed as a shadow of shame over Irish society, but it can also be seen as a warning that the cycle of abuse is likely to be repeated.

ANALYSIS

'Ní Chuilleanáin's poems often address important aspects of women's experiences in an insightful fashion.' Discuss this view, with particular reference to 'Translations'.

Sample Paragraph

I would completely agree that 'Translations' deals with an issue which is important to Irish women. The scandal of what happened to the unfortunate girls who were locked up in Magdalene convents deserves to be publicised. Eiléan Ní Chuilleanáin's poem certainly gave me a deeper understanding of their disturbing story. The dramatic opening description of the reburial service was attended by relatives 'from every county', suggesting the scale of the mistreatment. The details of the cold laundries – where 'White light blinded' seemed a subtle way of symbolising the misguided actions of those religious orders who punished young girls. I admired the poet's fair treatment of those nuns who are also presented as being imprisoned, even replacing their own natural identities with 'temporary' saints' names. The poem's last stanza was revealing as it envisaged one of the severe nuns who was still confused by her part in the cruelty. She only recognises the 'parasite' of heartless authority within her when it is too late. The poet makes it clear that she was a product of an oppressive Catholic Ireland and under the 'spell' of misguided power. In my opinion, 'Translation' succeeds in explaining the true story of the Magdalene women. It is all the more powerful because

Ní Chuilleanáin avoids being over-emotional. Her quiet tone conveys sensitivity and sadness for this dreadful period in Irish history which still lingers like 'a cloud over my time'.

Examiner's Comment

This top-grade response shows a clear understanding of Ní Chuilleanáin's considered approach to her theme, empathising with both those imprisoned and those in charge. Short quotations are well integrated while discussion points are clear and coherent, ranging over much of the poem. There is also some very good personal interaction, including the final sentence. An excellent standard.

N.B. Access your ebook for additional sample paragraphs and a list of useful quotes with commentary.

CLASS/HOMEWORK EXERCISES

1. 'Eiléan Ní Chuilleanáin's poetry offers a variety of interesting perspectives that vividly convey themes of universal relevance.' Discuss this statement with particular reference to 'Translation'.

2. 'In her poem, "Translation", Ní Chuilleanáin's poetic voice is both critical and compassionate.' Discuss this statement with particular reference to the text.

SUMMARY POINTS

- The poet addresses aspects of the Magdalene laundries scandal.
- Several changes and translations are explored in the poem.
- Sensuous imagery evokes the harsh atmosphere in the laundry.
- Effective use of sound, contrast, mood, and viewpoint throughout.

10 THE BEND IN THE ROAD 🔊

This is the place where the child
Felt sick in the car and they pulled over
And waited in the shadow of a house.
A tall tree like a cat's tail waited too.
They opened the windows and breathed   5
Easily, while nothing moved. Then he was better.

Over twelve years it has become the place
Where you were sick one day on the way to the lake.
You are taller now than us.
The tree is taller, the house is quite covered in   10
With green creeper, and the bend
In the road is as silent as ever it was on that day.

Piled high, wrapped lightly, like the one cumulus cloud
In a perfect sky, softly packed like the air,
Is all that went on in those years, the absences,   15
The faces never long absent from thought,
The bodies alive then and the airy space they took up
When we saw them wrapped and sealed by sickness
Guessing the piled weight of sleep
We knew they could not carry for long;   20
This is the place of their presence: in the tree, in the air.

'This is the place'

Glossary

11 *creeper*: climbing plant.	13 *cumulus*: rounded, fluffy.

INITIAL RESPONSE

1. Based on your reading of the poem, comment on the appropriateness of the title, 'The Bend in the Road'.

2. Choose one image from 'The Bend in the Road' that you consider effective. Give reasons why this image appealed to you.

3. How would you describe the poem's conclusion? Is it mysterious? Hopeful? Comforting? Bitter? Briefly explain your response.

STUDY NOTES

'The Bend in the Road' is part of Eiléan Ní Chuilleanáin's poetry collection The Girl Who Married the Reindeer. *In many of these poems, the autobiographical becomes transformed as Ní Chuilleanáin takes a moment in time and fills it with arresting images, exact description, stillness and secrecy, linking together selected memories from various times and places. This poem's title suggests that the road will go on even though it is not visible at the moment.*

   Stanza one opens with Ní Chuilleanáin pointing to the exact place where 'the child/Felt sick in the car and they pulled over'. The memory of such a familiar occurrence is given significance by the use of the demonstrative pronoun, 'This'. Run-on lines catch the flurry of activity as concerned adults attend to the sick child. Everything is still as they 'waited' for the sickness to pass. This suspended moment resonates as they linger 'in the shadow of a house'. **For a split second, an ominous – almost surreal – atmosphere begins to develop.** The poet introduces a slightly sinister simile, 'A tall tree like a cat's tail', peeking in from the world of fairytale. Then the tree is personified: it 'waited too' as people and landscape merge in the moment of hush. Suddenly, a simple action ('They opened the windows') relieves the tension and everyone 'breathed/Easily'. The position of the adverb at the beginning of the line captures the relief at the recovery of the child. Yet the stationary atmosphere remained: 'while nothing moved'. However, the routine narrative of everyday life quickly resumes: 'Then he was better'.

   In the **second stanza**, this roadside location takes on the shared resonance of memory: 'Over twelve years'. Readers are left imagining how the adults and child, when passing 'the place', would point it out as 'Where you were sick one day on the way to the lake'. The length of the line mirrors the long car journey. There is a sense of time being concentrated. Ní Chuilleanáin marvels at how the child has grown to adulthood: 'You are taller now than us'. The place has also changed – and even the tree is 'taller'. Assonance pinpoints how the nearby house is becoming yet more mysterious, 'quite covered in/With green creeper'. The insidious 'ee' sound mimics the silent takeover of the house by nature, as it recedes more and more into the shadows. Nature is alive. Creepings and rustlings stir, dispersing solidity and sureness. The poet cleverly places the line as if on a bend at the turn of a line: 'the bend/In the road is as silent as ever it was on that day'. Everything seems focused on the serenity of the place. **A bend in a road prevents seeing what is coming next. Is this an obvious symbol of the human experience?** No one knows what lies ahead. The tone of this reflective stanza is introspective as Ní Chuilleanáin considers the undeniable passing of time and the human condition.

In the **final stanza**, memory and place interplay with other recollections. The poet's attention turns towards the sky, which she imagines 'Piled high' with past experiences. A lifetime's memories now tower 'like the one cumulus cloud/In a perfect sky'. The alliteration of the hard 'c' successfully captures the billowing cloud as it sails through the sky. **Similarly, the recollections of 'all that went on in those years' heave and surge as they drift through the poet's consciousness.** Naturally, they flow from the exact description of 'the bend/In the road'. They are now visible as feelings of loss expand into the present: 'The faces never long absent from thought'. Ní Chuilleanáin had lost not only her father and mother, but also her sister. But she remembers them **similarly** as they were, 'bodies alive then and the airy space they took up', just as the cloud in the sky. Poignantly, the poet also recalls them in their final sickness, 'wrapped and sealed by sickness', as if they had been parcelled for dispatch away from the ordinary routine of life by the ordeal of suffering.

However, the harsh reality of sickness and old age is also recognised: 'We knew they could not carry for long'. Just as the cloud grows bigger as it absorbs moisture, finally dissolving into rain, so did the poet's loved ones buckle beneath the weight of their illness, under the 'piled weight of sleep'. **Ní Chuilleanáin finds constant reminders of her family's past in the natural world.** She uses a simple image of cloud-like shapes of pillows and bed-covers as they surrender to sickness. Characteristically, the thinking within the poem has progressed considerably. The poet has widened its scope, its spatial dimension, to include those external experiences to which she so eloquently pays witness. Indeed, the poem now stands as a monument to silence and time, absence and presence, past and present. The moment of stillness is evoked. This roadside location takes on a special importance. It marks the place where lost family members now reside. Ní Chuilleanáin's alliterative language is emphatic: 'This is the place of their presence'. They belong 'in the tree, in the air'. As in so many of her poems, Ní Chuilleanáin honours the invisible, unseen presence of other thoughts and feelings that – just like the bend in the road – lie waiting in silence to be discovered and brought to life again.

ANALYSIS

'Eiléan Ní Chuilleanáin's poetry illuminates moments of perception in exact description.' Discuss this view in relation to 'The Bend in the Road'. Use suitable reference and quotation to support the points you make.

Sample Paragraph

I agree that Ní Chuilleanáin's poem 'The Bend in the Road' is filled with meticulously accurate description. The opening lines pinpoint the exact place where 'the child/Felt sick in the car' and they 'pulled over'. The ordinary conversational language, 'They opened the windows', 'Then he was better', brings me into this precise moment in time and place. I can see the dark, cool shadow of the house. I experience the tree, as if a child, through the almost cartoon-like simile, 'A tall tree like a cat's tail'. Yet, an otherworldly experience hovers as personification transforms the tree into a living being; it 'waited too'. The poet reveals that 'nothing moved' as if all was in suspense awaiting some dramatic revelation. And then it is displayed. The place has become a metaphor for the reality of being human. Everything in life changes. The poet suddenly realises that the child has now grown into a man, 'You are taller than us now'. Nothing has remained the same, 'The tree is taller'. Assonance subtly illustrates the changed house now overgrown with 'green creeper'. Another layer is added with the perception that the place has become suffused with the 'presence' of those 'faces never long absent from thought'. This still, silent moment has allowed boundaries to be crossed as memories float 'Piled high, wrapped lightly, like the one cumulus cloud/In a perfect sky'. I now began to understand that in a static moment, the conventional distinctions between life and death, being and memory, all recede and become blurred. The past now lives again, 'in the tree, in the air'. Through carefully observed, precise description of material things, this poet transports readers into a different place to an understanding that many experiences, 'all that went on in those years', can be savoured in various forms, 'softly packed like the air'.

Examiner's Comment

This is a top-grade personal response that addresses the poet's interest in transience and memory. Apt, accurate quotes provide good support for developed discussion points which range effectively through the poem. There is some highly impressive focus on aspects of the poet's distinctive style. Expression is also excellent throughout, e.g. 'The place has become a metaphor for the reality of being human'.

N.B. Access your ebook for additional sample paragraphs and a list of useful quotes with commentary.

CLASS/HOMEWORK EXERCISES

1. 'Space in Ní Chuilleanáin's poetry is used as an expression of one's experience of the world and is a metaphor for the linking together of self and the world, within and without.' Discuss this statement, with particular reference to 'The Bend in the Road'.

2. 'The evocative power of a specific location is central to Ní Chuilleanáin's "The Bend in the Road".' Discuss this view, supporting your answer with reference to the poem.

SUMMARY POINTS

- Key themes include memory, family, transience, loss and grief.
- Symbolism used throughout the poem to suggest meaning.
- Effective use of assonance and alliteration to create atmosphere.
- Recurring references to sickness add unity to the poem.

11 ON LACKING THE KILLER INSTINCT 🔊

One hare, absorbed, sitting still,
Right in the grassy middle of the track,
I met when I fled up into the hills, that time
My father was dying in a hospital –
I see her suddenly again, borne back   5
By the morning paper's prize photograph:
Two greyhounds tumbling over, absurdly gross,
While the hare shoots off to the left, her bright eye
Full not only of speed and fear
But surely in the moment a glad power,   10

Like my father's, running from a lorry-load of soldiers
In nineteen twenty-one, nineteen years old, never
Such gladness, he said, cornering in the narrow road
Between high hedges, in summer dusk.
                         The hare   15
Like him should never have been coursed,
But, clever, she gets off; another day
She'll fool the stupid dogs, double back
On her own scent, downhill, and choose her time
To spring away out of the frame, all while   20
The pack is labouring up.
                   The lorry was growling
And he was clever, he saw a house
And risked an open kitchen door. The soldiers
Found six people in a country kitchen, one   25
Drying his face, dazed-looking, the towel
Half covering his face. The lorry left,
The people let him sleep there, he came out
Into a blissful dawn. Should he have chanced that door?
If the sheltering house had been burned down, what good   30
Could all his bright running have done
For those that harboured him?
               And I should not
Have run away, but I went back to the city
Next morning, washed in brown bog water,   35
And I thought about the hare, in her hour of ease.

'While the hare shoots off to the left'

Glossary

1	*hare*: mammal resembling a large rabbit.		16	*coursed*: hunted with greyhounds.
1	*absorbed*: engrossed, immersed, preoccupied.		20	*frame*: picture, enclosure.
7	*absurdly*: ridiculously, nonsensically.		21	*labouring*: moving with difficulty.
7	*gross*: disgusting, outrageous.			

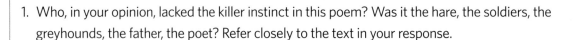

INITIAL RESPONSE

1. Who, in your opinion, lacked the killer instinct in this poem? Was it the hare, the soldiers, the greyhounds, the father, the poet? Refer closely to the text in your response.

2. The poet alters time and place frequently in this poem. With the aid of quotations, trace these changes as the poem develops.

3. Did you find the poem's conclusion satisfying or mystifying? Give reasons for your response, referring closely to the text.

STUDY NOTES

'On Lacking the Killer Instinct' is part of Eiléan Ní Chuilleanáin's The Sun-fish collection. A sunfish is so-called due to its habit of basking on the water's surface. Ní Chuilleanáin often presents daily life with a sense of mystery and otherworldliness as the poems move between various realms of experience. Each scene lies open to another version of the narrative. She blurs the distance between past and present in this three-part poem. History, which is something of an Irish obsession, always informs the present. This poet discovers and remembers. As she herself has said, 'In order for the poem to get written, something has to happen.'

The title of the poem immediately intrigues and unsettles. The **opening lines** focus on a stationary hare, silent, engrossed, 'absorbed', at rest. It is a vivid picture. Why is this hare preoccupied? The sibilant alliterative phrase, 'sitting still', captures the motionless animal in 'the middle of the track'. This **naturalistic setting** and image is brought into high resolution as the poet recounts that her own journey 'up into the hills' caused her to meet this creature. Ní Chuilleanáin juxtaposes the stillness of the wild hare with her own headlong flight from the awful reality, 'that time/My father was dying in a hospital'. In describing this terrible experience, her tone is remarkably controlled – detached, yet compassionate.

Another narrative thread is introduced in **line 6** when the poet recalls the 'morning paper's prize photograph'. Here the predators are presented as ungainly, almost comical characters incapable of purposeful action: 'Two greyhounds tumbling over, absurdly gross'. The broad vowels and repetition of 'r' highlight the hounds' unattractively large appearance. Irish coursing is a competitive sport where dogs are tested on their ability to run and overtake the hare, turning it without capturing it. It is often regarded as a cruel activity that causes pain and suffering to the pursued creature. From the start of the poem, **readers are left wondering who exactly lacks the killer instinct**. Do the dogs not have the urge to pounce and kill? Has the hare got the killer instinct, running for its life, showing the strong will to survive against all odds? The rapid run-on lines mimic the speed and agility of the hare exulting in 'glad power'.

In **line 11**, the **reader is taken into another realm** – a common feature of Ní Chuilleanáin's interconnected narratives. In this case, she recalls another pursuit. Her father was a combatant in the Irish Civil War in 1922 and was on the run. Like the hare, he fled, 'cornering in the narrow road/ Between high hedges, in summer dusk'. Both are linked through 'gladness' as they exult in their capacity to outrun their pursuers. For her father, this was a 'lorry-load of soldiers' – the compound word emphasising the unequal odds against which the poet's father struggled. This is similar to the hare's predicament against the 'Two greyhounds'. The precise placing of 'The hare' tucked away at the end of **line 15** suggests the animal's escape. Ní Chuilleanáin comments that neither the hare nor her father should ever have 'been coursed'. She is happy to think that on some other occasion, the hare is likely to outwit the 'stupid dogs' and will 'spring away out of the frame', nimbly escaping her pursuers. In Irish coursing, the hare is not run on open land but in a secure enclosure over a set distance. The heavy, panting exertions of the pursuing dogs is illustrated in the run-through line, 'all while/ The pack is labouring up'.

Ní Chuilleanáin returns to her father's story in **line 22**, imagining a moment of danger from his time as a fugitive. The scene is dominated by the threatening sound of a lorry, 'growling' like a pursuing hound. The repetition of the adjective 'clever' links her father and the hare as he too made his escape. Intent on surviving, 'he saw a house/ And risked an open kitchen door'. The **enemy soldiers go through the motions of pursuit cursorily, seemingly lacking the killer instinct** when they 'Found six people in a country kitchen'. Ní Chuilleanáin is characteristically ambivalent about why the rebels were not challenged, reminding us of the contradictory attitudes among the various combatants of the Civil War. For whatever reason, the fugitives ('one/ Drying his face, dazed-looking') were not arrested and their deception worked. The poet's father is allowed refuge: 'The people let him sleep there'. Throughout Ireland's troubled history, 'safe houses' existed that sheltered those on the run. In her mind's eye, the poet pictures her father emerging in triumph the next day 'Into a blissful dawn' (**line 29**). In a series of questions, she considers his crucial decision to stand his ground and feign innocence. In retrospect, anything might have happened to affect the outcome at 'the sheltering house'. Ní Chuilleanáin emphasises how chance has played such a significant role – not just in her father's life, but in Ireland's history.

The poet concludes by returning to the opening scene. Having observed the hare and remembered her father's encounter during the Civil War, she now realises that she should never have run away from her dying father. Her decision to return is seen as a mature one – almost like a religious ritual in which the poet cleanses herself, 'washed in brown bog water'. Is this a form of absolution to remove her guilt for running away? Typically, she uses this unifying symbol to gently draw the poem's three narratives together. After the common experience of the turbulence of the run, all three (the hare, the father and the poet herself) have entered a new state of being – calm composure. Ní Chuilleanáin reflects on 'the hare, in her hour of ease', the soft monosyllabic final word gently conveying a sense of peace and reconciliation. The poem closes as it began, with the **beautiful silent image of the hare**, self-possessed and serene after all the turmoil of the chase.

ANALYSIS

'Eiléan Ní Chuilleanáin is a quiet, introspective, enigmatic poet.' Discuss this statement with particular reference to 'On Lacking the Killer Instinct'.

Sample Paragraph

I thought the poem, 'On Lacking the Killer Instinct', moved effortlessly, mysteriously weaving three different narratives: the intently observed story of the hare and greyhounds, the quietly detached family history of her father's escape in 1921 and her own headlong flight from the city. Ní Chuilleanáin creates small clear windows into the narratives and the reader can then glimpse multi-views of human experience and discord, 'One hare … I met … that time/My father was dying in a hospital'. She celebrates resilience, the hare's 'bright eye' is full of 'a glad power'. Similarly, her father exulted in his cleverness, 'never/Such gladness' as he out-manoeuvred the 'lorry-load of soldiers'. The poet also faced up to the unpalatable fact of death and 'went back to the city/Next morning'. Her impressionistic style is similar to watching a photograph as it slowly develops before our eyes. At first there are vague unconnected shapes, but as the order establishes itself, the meaning becomes clear. Ní Chuilleanáin gazes intently on a familiar sight, the still hare, which becomes more strange under her spellbound observation and she links it to the flight and survival contest which underpins all of life. The reader is effortlessly guided through different times and places as the focus of the poet's gaze shifts from the hunt of the hare in coursing to the hunt of her father in his role in the Civil War, 'In nineteen twenty-one, nineteen years old'. She then quietly reflects on her own flight and concludes that running does not solve problems, 'what good/Could all his bright running have done/For those that harboured him?' In the end, this poet poses questions that resonate. Does she too lack the killer instinct, the capacity to seize and capture rather than suggest? The long monosyllabic word 'ease' suggests that staying calm and still is more effective than running. Yet who lacked the killer instinct, the hare, the greyhounds, the father, the soldiers, the poet? Is the killer instinct worth having? This enigmatic, introspective poet leaves us with an image of quiet stillness to ponder.

Examiner's Comment

This lengthy paragraph offers a very clear and focused response to a testing question. Interesting critical discussion – aptly illustrated by accurate quotations – ranges widely, tracing the subtle development of the poem's various narrative threads. Impressive use of language throughout adds clarity to the key points. The questions posed towards the end round off the discussion effectively in this excellent top-grade answer.

N.B. Access your ebook for additional sample paragraphs and a list of useful quotes with commentary.

CLASS/HOMEWORK EXERCISES

1. 'Eiléan Ní Chuilleanáin's poems elude categories and invite and challenge the reader in equal measure.' Discuss this statement with particular reference to 'On Lacking the Killer Instinct'.

2. 'Ní Chuilleanáin is capable of blending multiple narratives with great skill in her poetry.' To what extent is this the case in 'On Lacking the Killer Instinct'? Support your answer with reference to the poem.

SUMMARY POINTS

- Interwoven stories: hunting the hare, her father's death and Ireland's Civil War.
- Effective use of rhythm and contrast – movement and stillness.
- Subtle blending of past and present, time and place.
- Alliterative and sibilant sound effects echo related ideas throughout.

(12) TO NIALL WOODS AND XENYA OSTROVSKAIA, 🔊 MARRIED IN DUBLIN ON 9 SEPTEMBER 2009

When you look out across the fields
And you both see the same star
Pitching its tent on the point of the steeple –
That is the time to set out on your journey,
With half a loaf and your mother's blessing.   5

Leave behind the places that you knew:
All that you leave behind you will find once more,
You will find it in the stories;
The sleeping beauty in her high tower
With her talking cat asleep   10
Solid beside her feet – you will see her again.

When the cat wakes up he will speak in Irish and Russian
And every night he will tell you a different tale
About the firebird that stole the golden apples,
Gone every morning out of the emperor's garden,   15
And about the King of Ireland's Son and the Enchanter's Daughter.

The story the cat does not know is the Book of Ruth
And I have no time to tell you how she fared
When she went out at night and she was afraid,
In the beginning of the barley harvest,   20
Or how she trusted to strangers, and stood by her word:

You will have to trust me, she lived happily ever after.

'the firebird that stole the golden apples'

Glossary

Title: An epithalamium is a poem (or song) in celebration of a wedding. Eiléan Ní Chuilleanáin has included this poem (to her son Niall and his bride, Xenya) as the introductory dedication in her poetry collection *The Sun-fish*.

9   *sleeping beauty*: European fairytale from 'La Belle au bois dormant' (Beauty of the sleeping wood) by Charles Perrault and 'Dornroschen' (Little Briar Rose) by the Brothers Grimm.

14   *the firebird*: Russian fairytale; 'Tsarevitch Ivan, the Fire Bird and the Gray Wolf' by Alexander Afanasyev.

16   *the King of Ireland's Son*: Irish fairytale; 'The King of Ireland's Son' by Padraic Colum.

17   *Book of Ruth*: religious story from the Old Testament.

21   *Or how she trusted to strangers*: In the Bible story, Boaz owned the field Ruth harvested. He was a relative of the family and by law could 'redeem' her if he married her now that she was a widow. He wished to do so because he admired how she had stood by her mother-in-law, 'For wherever you go, I will go'.

INITIAL RESPONSE

1. Do you think the references to fairytales are appropriate on the occasion of Eiléan Ní Chuilleanáin's son's marriage? Give one reason for your answer.

2. In your opinion, what is the dominant tone of voice in the poem? Is it one of warning, reassurance, hope, consolation? Briefly explain your response with reference to the poem.

3. Why do you think the poet placed the last line apart from the rest of the poem? Give one reason for your opinion.

STUDY NOTES

'I write poems that mean a lot to me.' (Eiléan Ní Chuilleanáin) This particular poem is dedicated to her son, Niall, and his new bride, Xenya, on the happy occasion of their marriage. Folklore is central to this poet's work. Her mother, Eilís Dillon, was a famous writer of children's stories. Fairytales allow Ní Chuilleanáin the opportunity to approach a subject from an oblique, non-confessional perspective. It gives distance. Story-tellers rarely comment on or explain what happens. They simply tell the tale. In this poem, Ní Chuilleanáin refers to folklore and a well-known Bible story as she addresses the young couple.

The **first stanza** opens with **warm advice** from a loving mother as she gives the young man leave to set out on his own journey through life with his new partner. Run-on lines contain a beautiful, romantic image of a harmonious vision: 'you both see the same star'. Personification and alliteration bring this natural image to radiant life, 'Pitching its tent on the point of the steeple', suggesting the new home which the young couple are about to set up for themselves. **Ní Chuilleanáin's gaze is one of relentless clarity and attentiveness. She illuminates details.** She also counsels that it is the right time to go, 'to set out on your journey' when you are prepared ('With half a loaf') and with good wishes ('and your mother's blessing'). She combines colloquial and fairytale language. The tone is warm, but also pragmatic – offering practical advice to the newlyweds to make the most of whatever they have to start with: 'half a loaf is better than none'.

Stanza two begins with the imperative warning: 'Leave behind'. The mother is advising the couple to forget 'the places that you knew'. Is 'places' a metaphor for their actual homes or their cultural environments? Or does it refer to values the young people hold sacred? She consoles them that past experiences can still be found 'in the stories'. Ní Chuilleanáin now weaves an intricate web of such stories from many different sources. The first tale is that of 'sleeping beauty in her high tower'. This classic folk story involves a beautiful princess, enchantment, and a handsome prince who has to brave the obstacles of tall trees that surround the castle and its sleeping princess. **Is Ní Chuilleanáin illustrating that the path to true love is filled with difficulties and that only the brave will be successful?** The extended run-on lines suggest the hundred years' sleep of the spellbound princess, who can only be awakened by a kiss. The poet also makes use of another familiar element of fairytales – talking animals. In this case, the 'talking cat' probably refers to Irish folklore, and the King of Cats, a renowned teller of tales. Ní Chuilleanáin is able to link the basic characteristics of the animal with human behaviour. The cat slumbers with the princess, 'Solid', stable and dependable, beside her feet. Despite the poet's realism, however, this fairytale allusion is primarily optimistic.

In **stanza three**, Ní Chuilleanáin imagines the cat awakening and telling stories in both 'Irish and Russian', a likely reference to the young couple's **two cultural backgrounds**. The poet has said that in her work she is trying 'to suggest, to phrase, to find a way to make it possible for somebody to pick up certain suggestions ... They might not be seeing what I am seeing'. The poet continues to set her personal wishes for Niall and Xenya within the context of folktales, turning to the Russian tradition: 'Tsarevitch, the Fire Bird and the Gray Wolf'. Again, the hero of this story is on a challenging mission, as he attempts to catch the 'firebird that stole the golden apples ... out of the emperor's garden'. The assonance of the broad vowel 'o' emphasises the exasperation of the repeated theft. As always in folklore, courage and determination are required before the hero can overcome many ordeals and find true happiness.

Ní Chuilleanáin introduces the Irish tradition with the story of the King of Ireland's son, who must pluck three hairs from the Enchanter's beard in order to save his own life. On his quest, he gains the hand of Fedelma, the Enchanter's youngest daughter. But he falls asleep and loses her to the King of the Land of Mist. **Is the poet simply advising her son and daughter-in-law that love must be cherished and never taken for granted?** Throughout the poem, she draws heavily on stories where heroes have to fight for what they believe in. All of these tales convey the same central meaning – that lasting love has to be won through daring, determination and sacrifice.

In the playful link into **stanza four**, Ní Chuilleanáin remarks that 'the story the cat does not know is the Book of Ruth'. This final story is not from the world of folklore, but from the Bible, (although the poet has commented that 'a lot of religious narrative is very folkloric'). The Book of Ruth teaches that **genuine love can require uncompromising sacrifice**, and that such unselfish love will be well rewarded. This particular tale of inclusivity shows two different cultures coming together. The Israelites (sons of Naomi) marry women from the Moab tribe, one of whom is Ruth. She embraces Naomi's people, land, culture and God. This is very pertinent to the newly married couple, as they are also from different lands and cultures. Not surprisingly, the biblical tale is one of loving kindness – but it also includes a realistic message. After her husband's death, Ruth chooses to stay with her mother-in-law and undertakes the backbreaking farm work of gleaning to support the family. This involves lifting the grain and stalks left behind after the harvesting of barley. The metaphor of the harvest is another reminder that married couples will reap what they sow, depending on the effort and commitment made to their relationship.

The poem's last line is placed apart to emphasise its significance. Ní Chuilleanáin tells the newlyweds that they 'will have to trust me' – presumably just as Ruth trusted her mother-in-law, Naomi. For doing this, she was rewarded with living 'happily ever after', as in the best tales. The poet's quietly light-hearted approach, however, does not lessen her own deeply felt hopes for Niall and Xenya. **All the stories she has used are concerned with the essential qualities of a loving relationship** – and share a common thread of courage, faithfulness and honesty as the couple journey to a happy future. Tales and dreams are the shadow-truths that will endure. Ní Chuilleanáin's final tone is clearly sincere, upbeat and forward looking.

ANALYSIS

'The imagination is not the refuge but the true site of authority.' Comment on this statement in relation to the poem 'To Niall Woods and Xenya Ostrovskaia, Married in Dublin on 9 September 2009'.

Sample Paragraph

I feel that Ní Chuilleanáin's poem has subtle messages which only become clear after several readings. I think the poet is counselling her son and his new bride, Xenya, that stories, 'the imagination' are where truth, 'the true site of authority' lies. Stories are not escapism, although we may scoff in this modern age at 'Once upon a time'. The stories she chooses, 'sleeping beauty in her high tower', 'the firebird that stole the golden apples' and the 'King of Ireland's Son and the Enchanter's Daughter' all suggest that perseverance and sincerity win the day. I believe that this is a good message to give to the couple as they 'set out' on their journey. Nothing worthwhile is won easily. This is not escapism, but reality. While the language, 'half a loaf and your mother's blessing', and imagery (even the beautiful lines which describe the 'star/Pitching its tent on the point of the steeple') seem to be from the land of children's fiction, they resound with good sense. I thought the inclusion of the story of Ruth was very apt as it involved two cultures which is relevant to the couple's Irish and Russian origins, but also to many other situations in this time of immigration. People in this new era will have to 'trust to strangers'. But if integrity and loving kindness is shown, as Ruth's story demonstrated long ago, the prize of a happy future can be won. 'You will have to trust me, she lived happily ever after.' I understood that Ní Chuilleanáin is showing that no matter where these imaginative tales come from, Europe, Russia, Ireland or the Bible, obstacles have to be overcome in life through resolution and perseverance. This is a tough message, there is no hiding here. I thought the poet was clever because by putting this insight into the realm of a fairy story, it does not sound like preaching which the young couple might resent, yet the message rings true throughout time from this 'site of authority' the kingdom of story-telling.

Examiner's Comment

A sustained personal response showing genuine engagement with the poem. The focused opening tackles the discussion question directly. This is followed by several clear points, e.g. 'perseverance and sincerity win the day', 'Nothing worthwhile is won easily', 'obstacles have to be overcome', tracing the development of thought throughout the poem. Accurate quotations and clear expression ensure the highest grade.

N.B. Access your ebook for additional sample paragraphs and a list of useful quotes with commentary.

CLASS/HOMEWORK EXERCISES

1. What impression of Ní Chuilleanáin do you get from reading 'To Niall Woods and Xenya Ostrovskaia, Married in Dublin on 9 September 2009'? Write at least one paragraph in response, illustrating your views with reference to the text of the poem.

2. 'Ní Chuilleanáin's poems are often seen as challenging, but ultimately rewarding.' To what extent is this true of 'To Niall Woods and Xenia Ostrovskaia, married in Dublin on 9 September 2009'? Support your answer with reference to the poem.

SUMMARY POINTS

- The advice to the young couple is couched in the language of a fairy-tale.
- Recurring references to Bible stories and legends.
- Effective use of personification, alliteration and sibilance.
- Ending is sincere, sympathetic and optimistic.

LEAVING CERT SAMPLE ESSAY

'Eiléan Ní Chuilleanáin's extraordinary poetic world reveals compelling narratives which never cease to captivate readers.' Discuss this view, supporting your answer with suitable reference to the poems on your course.

Marking Scheme Guidelines

Candidates are free to agree and/or disagree with the given statement. The poet's treatment of themes and subject matter should be addressed, as well as her individual approach, distinctive writing style, etc. Reward responses that show clear evidence of genuine engagement with the poems. Expect discussion on how Ní Chuilleanáin's poetry appeals/does not appeal to readers.

Indicative material:

- Poet's views on life/relationships.
- Recurring optimistic themes on life and rebirth; the continuous past.
- Fragmented narrative; innovative narrative blending.
- Collapse of time and place.
- Atmospheric detail; artistic and architectural references.
- Dispassionate, detached tone of storyteller.
- Focus on uniquely Irish phenomena.
- Biblical, historical and mythical references.
- Mystical/spiritual experience.
- Layered and interwoven nuances challenge the reader, etc.

Sample Essay

(Ní Chuilleanáin's extraordinary poetic world reveals compelling narratives which captivate readers)

1. *To me, Eiléan Ní Chuilleanáin's lyrical world thrives on the creeping rustlings and barely noticed stirrings of life. Enthralling stories are quietly let slip to bewitch and enchant her readers in a wide range of variety,*

from hopeful poems such as 'All for You' to the family stories of 'Fireman's Lift' and 'To Niall Woods and Xenya.'

2. *'The Bend in the Road' takes a normal event, a child becoming car-sick, and transforms it with arresting images from the surreal, ominous world of the fairytale, 'A tall tree like a cat's tail'. The poet links together selected memories from various times and places and so mesmerises the reader with the resonance from this 'bend/In the road'. The family all point, on subsequent journeys, to 'Where you were sick on the way to the lake'. Ní Chuilleanáin's intent gaze reminds us that a bend in the road, which is cleverly emphasised by its line placement, prevents seeing what is around the corner. Now the poet interjects another memory into the story, the death of loved ones 'Piled high, wrapped lightly, like the one cumulus cloud/In a perfect sky'. This place now becomes 'the place of their presence'. They live now 'in the tree, in the air' because this is where they are remembered. Ní Chuilleanáin fuses parallel narratives, the ill child, the revisited bend in the road, the sick and dying relatives to uncover the mystical truth, the past shines through the present.*

3. *The driving narrative of the young girl in 'Following' as she attempts to keep up with her father on a hectic fair day holds the readers who are pulled into this world by the unusual description of 'beasts packed solid as books'. The explosive 'b' links 'beasts' and 'books' and I can really picture the crammed animals standing in lines as they await sale. Other stories are woven into the poem, as the image of the dead father appears, not 'skimming' as before but 'Gliding' as the girl crosses the 'shivering bog'. He is now sitting in 'the library where the light is clear'. The poet is tantalising readers, challenging us to engage and 'push ... open' the poem, just as the 'crushed flowers', an evocative image for past shared memories, force the book open. Once more the reader is comforted by the message that the past is not dead. The girl's suffering is represented by 'The square of white linen'. It is not 'shelved', never to be thought of or experienced again. It will emerge, 'crack/The spine open'.*

4. *Ní Chuilleanáin has remarked that she has been 'captivated by history'. She recounts a story in the poem, 'On Lacking the Killer Instinct', which her father had told her about running away from the Black and Tans when he was a young man. The reader is submerged into the Ireland of 1922 as the soldiers hunt her father. He seeks refuge in a 'safe house'. The blessed relief of the escape is graphically conveyed in the detail, 'he came out/Into a blissful dawn'. In my opinion, the reader is delighted at the father's breath-taking escape. It is similar to the escape of the hare, recounted in the earlier part of the poem, 'her bright eye/Full not only of speed and fear/But surely in the moment a glad power'. Narratives are blended together seamlessly as the poet relates her own flight from the awful reality of her father's final illness, 'I fled up into the hills, that time/My father was dying a in hospital'.*

5. 'Fireman's Lift' also deals with the harsh truth of her mother's death. They had both visited Parma Cathedral once and their close relationship is clearly caught. 'I was standing beside you looking up/ Through the big tree of the cupola'. The strong verbs, 'spiralling' and 'heaving' capture the huge effort of the angels as they lifted Mary in to the heavens from her earthly life. The hands of the angels act as a 'crane and support' for Mary. 'Their heads bowed to reflect on her/Fair face' reminded the poet of the nurses who tended her mother in her final illness. Readers become immersed in the poem's storyline when the poet comments, 'This is what love sees, that angle'. The poet is coming to terms with the harsh reality that life has a natural cycle, 'The crick in the branch loaded with fruit'. The reader stands with mother and daughter marvelling as 'The Virgin was spiralling to heaven'. Now it is time for the poet's mother to go too.

6. Although Ní Chuilleanáin tells a story from an oblique, non-confessional perspective, this detachment does not prevent her engaging her reader. In the epithalamium, 'To Niall Woods and Xenya' she intricately weaves Russian ('the firebird') and Irish ('the Enchanter's Daughter') stories as she celebrates the two diverse cultures of the young couple. She also uses the story to gently pass on her thoughts and advice on their new life together. I thought the phrase, 'you both see the same star', showed how she understood that the young couple had a shared vision of life. But Ruth's story from the Bible was most fascinating. She had to show courage to succeed as she trusted to strangers. The young people will also need these qualities if they are to succeed in the best tradition of the fairytale to 'live happily ever after'. This, of course, is what every reader dreams of.

7. For me, Ní Chuilleanáin has opened a poetic world in which she intertwines stories from the fabric of her own family life, 'poems that mean a lot to me', with those from many other varied sources. The reader stands fascinated and delighted by a bend in the road, a hare 'sitting still', 'The sleeping beauty in her high tower', the Virgin Mary as 'she came to the edge of the cloud', a 'key still in your pocket', all thanks to the gaze and skill of a remarkable poet.

(approx. 990 words)

Examiner's Comment

This is a top-grade personal response that shows clear engagement with Ní Chuilleanáin's poems. Effective use is made of accurate quotations and detailed reference to support perceptive critical discussion. For example, in paragraph 3: 'The explosive "b" links "beasts" and "books" and I can really picture the crammed animals standing in lines as they await sale'. This clearly organised essay is very well written and highly impressive.

MARKING
SCHEME
GRADE: H1
P = 15/15
C = 13/15
L = 13/15
M = 5/5
Total = 46/50

N.B. Access your ebook for additional sample paragraphs and a list of useful quotes with commentary.

SAMPLE LEAVING CERT QUESTIONS ON NÍ CHUILLEANÁIN'S POETRY

1. 'Ní Chuilleanáin's beguiling poems emerge from an intense but insightful imagination.' Do you agree with this assessment of her poetry? Write a response, supporting your points with reference to the poems on your course.

2. 'Eiléan Ní Chuilleanáin is a truly original poet who leads us into altered landscapes and enhances our understanding of the world around us.' To what extent would you agree with this statement? In your response, refer to the poems on your course.

3 'Ní Chuilleanáin's subject matter can be challenging at times, but her writing style is always highly impressive.' Write a response to this view, supporting the points you make with suitable reference to the poetry on your course.

Sample Essay Plan (Q1)

'Ní Chuilleanáin's beguiling poems emerge from an intense but insightful imagination.' Do you agree with this assessment of her poetry? Write a response, supporting your points with reference to the poems on your course.

- Intro: Ní Chuilleanáin's innovative treatment of a broad thematic range – Irish history, myth, transience, memory, relationships, loss, religious life, the dispossessed, etc.

- Point 1: 'Fireman's Lift' – compelling treatment of her mother's death. Importance of dramatic setting as a context for personal experiences/memories. Poet's sympathetic tone, atmospheric detail, artistic references.
- Point 2: 'Translation' – perceptive account of the Magdalene laundry workers. Sensitive approach to women victims. Use of effective symbols. Collapse of time. Silence and understated meanings. Imaginative and interwoven nuances affect readers.

- Point 3: Dispassionate, detached tone of storyteller – 'Deaths and Engines', 'Kilcash'. Underlying sense of the poet's compassion. Interlinked layered narrative threads entice the reader.

- Conclusion: Poetry can challenge/excite responses – Ní Chuilleanáin's mesmeric exploration of universal themes invites readers to unravel the secrets of her work.

Sample Essay Plan (Q1)

Develop one of the above points into a paragraph.

Sample Paragraph: Point 2

'Translation' offers an intriguing account of a dark period in recent Irish history. Ní Chuilleanáin's quiet dramatisation of the Magdalene laundry victims begins in Glasnevin Cemetery, with an unnerving description: 'soil frayed and sifted evens the score'. This image is typical of the poet, suggesting both the surface of the communal grave and the horrifying injustice that has happened over the years. In death, these women have become 'ridges under the veil' of the earth. The reference also conveys a sense of the strict Magdalene nuns who are also viewed as victims of an unchristian era. Time and places blend throughout the poem. The poet's concentrated vision of the laundries is associated with their exploitation – 'where steam danced/Around stone drains and giggled and slipped across water'. She contrasts the girls' youthful spirit with the cold conditions around them. I could make sense of the poem's title as Ní Chuilleanáin's aim was to reveal (or 'translate') the true Magdalene story. Without a trace of sentimentality, 'Translation' movingly recalls a whole generation of women whose lives were ruined. Generously, the ending focuses on the authoritarian figure of an unnamed nun who is envisioned in death and who finally understands the tragedy – 'Allow us now to hear it, sharp as an infant's cry'. This line suggested the communal suffering shared by the nuns and the unmarried mothers who were separated from their babies. The poet's intense depiction of the Magdalene experience is highly compelling, allowing me to relate to this truly regrettable 'cloud over my time'.

Examiner's Comment

As part of a full essay, this is a strong, top-grade paragraph that shows clear engagement with the poem. The discussion relating to Ní Chuilleanáin's dense imagery is particularly impressive. Apt – and accurate – quotations are used effectively. Language use is also excellent throughout.

N.B. Access your ebook for additional sample paragraphs and a list of useful quotes with commentary.

LAST WORDS

'There is something second-sighted about Eiléan Ní Chuilleanáin's work. Her poems see things anew, in a rinsed and dreamstruck light.'

Seamus Heaney

'Ní Chuilleanáin's eccentric poems uncover hidden dramas in many guises, and she continually holds us captive by her luminous voice.'

Molly Bendall

'Inspiration comes from everywhere, from the places I go and the things I do. I never write unless I have an idea that seems really interesting to me.'

Eiléan Ní Chuilleanáin

SYLVIA PLATH

1932– 1963

'Out of the ash
I rise with my red hair
And I eat men like air.'

orn in Boston, Massachusetts, in 1932, Sylvia Plath is a writer whose best-known poems are noted for their intense focus and vibrant, personal imagery. Her writing talent – and ambition to succeed – was evident from an early age. She kept a journal during childhood and published her early poems in literary magazines and newspapers. After studying Art and English at college, Plath moved to Cambridge, England, in the mid-1950s. Here she met and later married the poet Ted Hughes. The couple had two children, Frieda and Nicholas, but the marriage was not to last. Plath continued to write through the late 1950s and early 1960s. During the final years of her life, she produced numerous confessional poems of stark revelation, channelling her long-standing anxiety and doubt into poetic verses of great power and pathos. At her creative peak, Sylvia Plath took her own life on 11 February 1963.

INVESTIGATE FURTHER

To find out more about Sylvia Plath, or to hear readings of her poems, you could search some useful websites such as YouTube, poetryarchive.org. and bbc.co.uk. Also view the additional material available in your ebook.

Prescribed Poems

* The poems marked with an asterisk are also prescribed for the Ordinary Level course.

About inspiration being everywhere

Bleakness

Death, Dark

1 BLACK ROOK IN RAINY WEATHER

Foreboding

On the stiff twig up there
Hunches a wet black rook
Arranging and rearranging its feathers in the rain.   _Shes rearranging words_
rooks arranging feathers
I do not expect a miracle
Or an accident   5

enjambement - run online (keeps flow)

to be inspired. To set the sight on fire
In my eye, nor seek
Any more in the desultory weather some design,
But let spotted leaves fall as they fall,
Without ceremony, or portent.   10

Although, I admit, I desire,
Occasionally, some backtalk
From the mute sky, I can't honestly complain:
A certain minor light may still
Lean incandescent   15

Out of kitchen table or chair   _inspiration from nothing._
angelic   As if a celestial burning took
force   Possession of the most obtuse objects now and then –
(holiness, Thus hallowing an interval
heavenly). Otherwise inconsequent   20

By bestowing largesse, honour,
One might say love. At any rate, I now walk   _walking wary   as inspiration_
Wary (for it could happen   _is everywhere_
Even in this dull ruinous landscape); skeptical,   _note use of brackets_
Yet politic; ignorant   25 _very conversational._

Of whatever angel may choose to flare
Suddenly at my elbow. I only know that a rook
Ordering its black feathers can so shine
As to seize my senses, haul   _actual happiness_
My eyelids up, and grant   30

forced

A brief respite from fear
Of total neutrality. With luck,
Trekking stubborn through this season
Of fatigue, I shall
Patch together a content

writers block, working hard, trek, effort.

35

Of sorts. Miracles occur,
If you care to call those spasmodic

- glimpses

Tricks of radiance miracles. The wait's begun again,
The long wait for the angel,
For that rare, random descent.

- divine angel

40

blessed, gifted by the angel

'Hunches a wet black rook'

Glossary

8   *desultory*: unexceptional, oppressive.
10 *portent*: omen.
15 *incandescent*: glowing.
19 *hallowing*: making holy.
20 *inconsequent*: of no importance.

21 *largesse*: generous, giving.
24 *skeptical*: wary, suspicious.
25 *politic*: wise and likely to prove advantageous.
37 *spasmodic*: occurring in bursts.

INITIAL RESPONSE

1. What is the mood of the poet? How does the weather described in the poem reflect this mood?

2. In your opinion, why do you think Plath sees light coming from ordinary household objects such as kitchen tables and chairs?

3. What do you think the final stanza means? Consider the phrase 'The wait's begun again'. What is the poet waiting for?

STUDY NOTES

'Black Rook in Rainy Weather' was written while Plath was studying in Cambridge in 1956. It contains many of her trademarks, including the exploration of emotions, the use of weather, colour and natural objects as symbols, and the dreamlike world. She explores a number of themes: fear of the future, lack of identity and poetic inspiration.

Stanza one begins with the straightforward description of a bird grooming itself, which the poet observes on a rainy day. But on closer inspection, the mood of the poem is set with the words 'stiff' and 'Hunches'. The bird is at the mercy of the elements ('wet') and there is no easy movement. **This atmospheric opening is dull and low key.** The black rook is a bird of ill omen. But the bird is presenting its best image to the world as it sits 'Arranging and rearranging its feathers'. Plath longed to excel in both life and art. If she were inspired by poetry, the rook would take on a new light as if on fire. Yet she doesn't see this happening. Even the weather is 'desultory' in the fading season of autumn. Poetic inspiration is miraculous; it is not ordinary. The world is experienced in a heightened way. Notice the long line, which seems out of proportion with the rest as she declares that she doesn't expect any order or 'design' in the haphazard weather. The decaying leaves will fall with no ritual, without any organisation, just as they will. **This is a chaotic world**, a random place with no design, just as poetic inspiration happens by chance. It is also accidental, like the falling leaves. We cannot seek it, we receive it. It is active, we are passive.

After this low-key opening, the poem starts to take flight in **stanzas three** and **four** when the poet states: 'I desire'. Plath employs a witty metaphor as she looks for 'some backtalk' from the 'mute sky'. She would like to connect with it. It could happen on her walk, or even at home if she were to experience a 'certain minor light' shining from an ordinary, everyday object like a chair. The association of fire and light makes an ordinary moment special. It is 'hallowing'; it is giving generously ('largesse'). She is hoping against hope. Plath may be sceptical, but she is going forward carefully in case she misses the magic moment. She must stay alert and watchful. She must also be 'politic', wise.

Stanzas six, **seven** and **eight** explore poetic inspiration. Plath doesn't know if it will happen to her or how it will happen. Two contrasting attitudes are at loggerheads: hope and despair. The rook might inspire her: 'Miracles occur'. If she were motivated, it would relieve 'total neutrality', this nothingness she feels when living uninspired. Although she is tired, she is insistent, 'stubborn'. The poet will have to 'Patch' something together. She shows human vulnerability, but she is trying. This determination is a very different tone from the negative one at the beginning.

Literature was as important to Plath as friends and family. What she can't live without, therefore, is inspiration – her life would be a dark, passionless existence. Depression is an empty state with no feeling or direction, yet her view of creativity is romantic. It is miraculous, available only to a chosen few. 'The long wait for the angel' has begun. Notice the constant use of the personal pronoun 'I'. This is a poet who is very aware of self and her own personal responses to events and feelings. The outside world becomes a metaphor for her own interior world.

Plath uses both archaic language and slang, as if reinforcing the randomness of the world. This is also mirrored in the run-on lines. All is haphazard, but carefully arranged, so even the extended **third-to-last line** stretches out as it waits for the 'random descent' of inspiration. In this carefully arranged disorder, two worlds are seen. One is negative: 'desultory', 'spotted', 'mute', 'dull', 'ruinous', 'stubborn', 'fatigue'. This is indicative of her own bleak mood. The other world is positive: 'fire', 'light', 'incandescent', 'celestial', 'hallowing', 'largesse', 'honour', 'love', 'shine'. Here is the possibility of radiance.

ANALYSIS

'Plath's poems are carefully composed and beautifully phrased.' Write a paragraph in response to this statement, illustrating your answer with close reference to the poem 'Black Rook in Rainy Weather'.

Sample Paragraph

Just like the rook, Plath 'arranges and rearranges' her words with infinite care to communicate the contrast between the dull life of 'total neutrality' which occurs when she is not inspired, when nothing sets 'the sight on fire'. I particularly admire how she artfully arranges disorder in the poem. This mirrors the chance of poetic inspiration. Long lines poke untidily out of the first three stanzas, seeking the 'minor light' to 'Lean incandescent' upon them. I also like how the lines run in a seemingly untidy way into each other, as do some stanzas. **Stanza three** goes into **four**, as it describes the chance of a light coming from an ordinary object, such as a kitchen chair, which is seen only if the poet is inspired. The alliteration of 'rare, random' in the last line mirrors the gift of poetic technique which will be given to the poet if she can receive the blessed benediction of poetic inspiration. 'Miracles occur'.

Examiner's Comment

Close reading of the poem is evident in this top-grade original response to Plath's poetic technique. Quotations are very well used here to highlight the poet's ability to create anarchic order.

N.B. Access your ebook for additional sample paragraphs and a list of useful quotes with commentary.

CLASS/HOMEWORK EXERCISES

1. Plath criticised the poem, 'Black Rook in Rainy Weather' for its 'glassy brittleness'. In your opinion, what does she mean? Refer to both the content and style of the poem, supporting your answer with reference to the text.

2. In your opinion, has the poet given up hope of being inspired? Use reference to the poem in your answer.

SUMMARY POINTS

- Waiting for poetic inspiration, the hope for something better.
- Despondency – negative adjectives, harsh verbs.
- Miracle of inspiration, contrasting imagery of fire and light.
- Careful rhyme patterns echo design of the rook's plumage.
- Language – colloquial and formal, slang and religious terminology.

❷ THE TIMES ARE TIDY

Unlucky the hero born   ① *stagnant nothing new*
In this province of the stuck record   ②
Where the most watchful cooks go jobless   *Dedicated men go/redundant*
And the mayor's rôtisserie turns   *jobless.*
Round of its own accord.   5

There's no career in the venture
Of riding against the lizard,
Himself withered these latter-days   ③ *ineffectual*
To leaf-size from lack of action:
History's beaten the hazard.   10

The last crone got burnt up
More than eight decades back
With the love-hot herb, the talking cat,   ④ *witches/mystery/dark.*
But the children are better for it,
The cow milks cream an inch thick.   ⑤   15
unnatural.

'riding against the lizard'

Glossary

2	*province*: a remote place.		4	*rôtisserie*: meat on a rotating skewer.
2	*stuck record*: the needle would sometimes get jammed on a vinyl music album.		7	*lizard*: dragon.
			11	*crone*: old witch.

INITIAL RESPONSE

1. What is suggested by the poem's title? Is Plath being cynical about modern life? Develop your response in a short paragraph.

2. Select one image from the poem which suggests that the past was much more dangerous and exciting than the present. Comment on its effectiveness.

3. Do you agree or disagree with the speaker's view of modern life? Give reasons for your answer.

STUDY NOTES

'The Times Are Tidy' was written in 1958. In this short poem, Plath casts a cold eye on contemporary life and culture, which she sees as bland and unadventurous. The poem's ironic title clearly suggests Plath's dissatisfaction with the over-regulated society of her day. Do you think you are living in an heroic age or do you believe that most people have lost their sense of wonder? Is there anyone in public life whom you really admire? Perhaps you despair of politicians, particularly when their promises sound like a 'stuck record'.

Stanza one is dominated by hard-hitting images reflecting how the world of fairytale excitement has disappeared. From the outset, **the tone is scornful and dismissive**. Plath believes that any hero would be totally out of place amid the mediocrity of our times. True talent ('the most watchful cooks') is largely unrewarded. The unexpected imagery of the 'stuck record' and the mayor's rotating spit symbolise complacent monotony and lack of progress, particularly during the late 1950s, when Plath wrote the poem. Both images convey a sense of purposeless circling, of people going nowhere. It seems as though the poet is seething with frustration at the inertia and conformity of her own life and times.

Plath's **darkly embittered sense of humour** becomes evident in **stanza two**. She laments the current lack of honour and courage – something which once existed in the world of fairytales. Unlike the past, contemporary society is compromised. There are no idealistic dragon-slayers any more. The worker who dares to stand up and criticise ('riding against the lizard') is risking demotion. The modern dragon – a metaphor for the challenges we face – has even been reduced to a mere lizard. Despite this, we are afraid of confrontation and prefer to retreat. The verb 'withered' suggests the weakness and decay of our safe, modern world. The poet openly complains that 'History's beaten the hazard'. Over time, we have somehow defeated all sense of adventure and daring. These qualities belong in the distant past.

In **stanza three**, Plath continues to contrast past and present. Witches are no longer burned at the stake. This might well suggest that superstition has disappeared, and with it, all imagination. The last two lines are ironic in tone, reflecting the poet's deep disenchantment with the excesses of our consumer society. The final image – 'the cow milks cream an inch thick' – signifies overindulgence. At one time, it was thought that supernatural forces could reduce the milk yield from cows.

The poet clearly accepts that society has changed for the worse. Children may have everything they want nowadays, but they have lost their sense of wonder and excitement. She laments the loss of legendary heroism. Medieval dragons and wicked witches (complete with magic potions and talking cats) no longer exist. Her conclusion is that life today is unquestionably less interesting than it used to be. Unlike so much of Plath's work, the personal pronoun 'I' is not used in this poem. However, the highly contemptuous views and weary, frustrated tone clearly suggest that Plath feels unfulfilled.

ANALYSIS

Write a paragraph on Plath's critical tone in 'The Times Are Tidy'.

Sample Paragraph

The tone of voice in 'The Times Are Tidy' is almost irrationally critical of modern life. Plath has nothing good to say about today's world as she sees it. The poem's title is glib and self-satisfied, just like the neatly organised society that Plath seems to despise. The opening comment – 'Unlucky the hero born/In this province' – emphasises this negative tone. The poet's mocking attitude becomes increasingly disparaging as she rails against the unproductive images of easy living – 'the stuck record' and 'the mayor's rôtisserie'. Plath goes on to contrast today's apathetic society with the more spirited medieval era, when knights in armour existed. The poet deliberately omits all the positive aspects of modern life and chooses to give a very one-sided view of the world. Plath ends on a sarcastic note, sneering at the advances of our world of plenty – 'cream an inch thick'. The voice here – and indeed, throughout the entire poem – is both sardonic and superior.

Examiner's Comment

This short top-grade paragraph demonstrates strong analytical skills and is firmly focused on Plath's judgmental tone. The supporting references range widely and effectively illustrate the poet's critical attitude. Quotations are particularly well integrated and the management of language is assured throughout.

N.B. Access your ebook for additional sample paragraphs and a list of useful quotes with commentary.

CLASS/HOMEWORK EXERCISES

1. Outline the main theme in 'The Times Are Tidy'. In your answer, trace the way the poet develops her ideas during the course of the poem.

2. Trace the changing tones in the poem, 'The Times are Tidy'. Support your answer with close reference to the text.

SUMMARY POINTS

- Poet's distaste for pursuit of materialism prevalent in 1950s American society.
- Collapse of moral standards in public life.
- Death of the spirit of adventure, no challenge to society's smugness.
- Humour and irony, derisive tone, entertaining images and sound effects.
- Contrast between modern 'tidy' times and 'untidy' times of legend.

(handwritten) Rebirth
Inspiration — motivation.

(handwritten) signing to a child.

③ MORNING SONG *(handwritten)* — birds — new beginning — possibilities — hope.

(handwritten) comparing life to a watch.

Love set you going like a fat gold watch. *(handwritten)* — simile — Treasure, precious — Fat/pudgy baby.
The midwife slapped your footsoles, and your bald cry *(handwritten)* exposed, undefined, purity, vulnerable.
Took its place among the elements.
(handwritten) 2 ideas

(handwritten) rost, helpless, uprooted, no direction, uncertain.
Our voices echo, magnifying your arrival. New statue. *(handwritten)* classical, beauty, skill, chizeled life
In a drafty museum, your nakedness *(handwritten)* life is dark, cold, unwelcoming, alien, ready to be morphed
(handwritten) Put statue + museum together.
Shadows our safety. We stand round blankly as walls.
(handwritten) Isolation, helpless, no plan,

I'm no more your mother *(handwritten)* hard on herself, expects a lot.
Than the cloud that distils a mirror to reflect its own slow
Effacement at the wind's hand.

All night your moth-breath   10
Flickers among the flat pink roses. I wake to listen:
A far sea moves in my ear.
(handwritten) lost the idea of being a beautiful woman.
(handwritten) Stumbling through Parenthood,
One cry, and I stumble from bed, cow-heavy and floral *(handwritten)* still asleep, getting used to changes.
In my Victorian nightgown. *(handwritten)* bed leg rudely accepts her role.
Your mouth opens clean as a cat's. The window square   15
(handwritten) Sterile image

Whitens and swallows its dull stars. And now you try
Your handful of notes;
The clear vowels rise like balloons.
(handwritten) Pure, innocent, no views.

'clear vowels rise'

Glossary

2	*midwife*: a person trained to assist at childbirth.	11	*pink roses*: images on the wallpaper.
3	*elements*: primitive, natural, atmospheric forces.	18	*vowels*: speech sounds made without stopping the
9	*Effacement*: gradual disappearance.		flow of the breath.

INITIAL RESPONSE

1. Comment on the suitability and effectiveness of the simile in line 1.

2. What is the attitude of the mother to the new arrival? Does her attitude change in the course of the poem? Refer to the text in your answer.

3. A metaphor links two things so that one idea explains or gives a new viewpoint about the other. Choose one metaphor from the poem and comment on its effectiveness.

STUDY NOTES

'Morning Song' was written in 1961. Plath explores the complex issues of the relationship between a mother and her child, celebrating the birth of the infant but also touching on deep feelings of loss and separation.

Do all mothers immediately welcome and fall in love with a new baby? Are some of them overwhelmed or even depressed after giving birth? Are parents often anxious about the new responsibilities a baby brings? Plath wrote this poem after two intensely personal experiences, celebrating the birth of her daughter, Frieda, who was 10 months old and shortly after a miscarriage. The poem is realistic and never strays into sentimentality or cliché. The title 'Morning' suggests a new beginning and 'Song' a celebration.

Stanza one describes the arrival of the child into the world in a strong, confident, rhythmic sentence announcing the act of creation: 'Love set you going'. The simile comparing the child to a 'fat gold watch' suggests a plump baby, a rich and precious object. Broad vowel effects emphasise the physical presence of the baby. The 'ticking' sound conveys action and dynamism, but also the passage of time. Plath's child is now part of the mortal world where change and death are inevitable. At this moment of birth, the baby is the centre of attention as the midwife and parents surround her. But this is a cruel world, as we see from the words 'slapped' and 'bald'. The infant is part of the universe as she takes her place among the 'elements'. The verbs in this stanza are in the past tense – **the mother is looking back at the event**. The rest of the poem is written in the present tense, which adds to the immediacy of the experience.

Stanza two has a feeling of disorientation, as if the mother feels separated from the child now that she has left the womb. There is a nightmarish, surreal quality to the lines 'Our voices echo, magnifying your arrival'. Plath sees the child as a new exhibit ('New statue') in a museum. Commas and full stops break up the flow of the lines and **the tone becomes more stilted and detached**. The child as a work of art is special and unique, but the museum is 'drafty', again a reference to the harshness of the world. The baby's vulnerability is stressed by its 'nakedness'. The midwife's and parents' frozen response is caught in the phrase 'blankly as walls'. They anxiously observe, unsure about their ability to protect. This baby also represents a threat to the parents' relationship as she 'Shadows' their safety. The child is perceived as having a negative impact on them, perhaps driving them apart rather than uniting them.

Stanza three catches the **complex relationship between child and mother**. Plath feels she can't be maternal ('no more your mother'). This is vividly shown in the image of the cloud that rains, creating a puddle. **But in the act of creation, it destroys itself and its destruction is reflected in the pool of water.** Throughout her life, the poet was haunted by a fear of her own personal disintegration and annihilation. Does she see a conflict between becoming a mother and remaining a writer? She also realises as the child grows and matures that she will age, moving closer to death, and this will be reflected in the child's gaze. The mood of this stanza is one of dislocation, estrangement and powerlessness. Notice how the three lines of the stanza run into each other as the cloud disappears.

In **stanza four**, the tone changes to one of intimate, maternal love as the caring mother becomes alert to her child's needs. The situation described is warm and homely – the 'flat pink roses' are very different to the chill 'museum' of a previous stanza. The fragile breathing of the little child is beautifully described as 'your moth-breath/Flickers'. **Onomatopoeia in 'Flickers' mimics the tiny breathing noises of the child.** The mother is anticipating her baby's needs as she wakes ('listen'). The breathing child evokes happy memories of Plath's seaside childhood ('A far sea moves in my ear'). The infant cries and the attentive mother springs into action. She laughs at herself as she describes the comical figure she makes, 'cow-heavy and floral'. She feels awkward as she 'stumble[s]' to tend her child, whose eager mouth is shown by a startling image ('clean as a cat's') when it opens wide to receive the night feed of milk. The stanza flows smoothly over into **stanza five**, just as nature flows to its own rhythm and does not obey clocks or any other man-made rules. Night becomes morning as the child swallows the milk and the window swallows the stars.

Children demand a parent's time and energy. **This child now defines herself** with her unique collection of sounds ('Your handful of notes'). This poem opened with the instinctive, elemental 'bald' cry of a newborn, but closes on a lovely, happy image of music and colour, as the baby's song's notes 'rise like balloons'.

N.B. Access your ebook for additional sample paragraphs and a list of useful quotes with commentary.

ANALYSIS

'Morning Song' opens with the word 'Love'. How does Plath treat the theme of love over the course of the poem? Support your answer with reference to the text.

Sample Paragraph

'Morning Song' treats the theme of love by addressing both the joy of parental love and also the shock new parents experience. It opens with a tender statement that the poet's daughter was conceived in love – 'Love set you going'. This warm tone changes, however, to the curiously disengaged voice of the second stanza where the parents 'stand round blankly as walls'. The enormity of the event of the birth of their child into a harsh world, 'drafty museum', seems to overwhelm them, particularly the mother who is unable to express natural maternal feelings. In the third stanza, the sense of separation deepens and Plath admits that she does not really feel like the child's mother at all. Instead, she explores her feelings of annihilation through the complex image of the disintegrating cloud, which creates only to be destroyed in the act of creation. The poem ends on a more affectionate note as the attentive mother feeds her child while listening to her baby's song 'rise like balloons'. For me, the gentle effect of this image suggests the fragility and innocence of the infant. Overall, I found Plath's mixed emotions interesting as she takes a realistic and honest approach to the complicated emotions that new parents can experience.

Examiner's Comment

A succinct, focused and well-supported response showing good personal engagement with the poem. The central point about Plath's conflicting emotions is clearly stated and the development of thought is traced throughout the poem. Excellent language control and impressive vocabulary (e.g. 'curiously disengaged voice', 'complex image of the disintegrating cloud') are in keeping with the top-grade standard.

CLASS/HOMEWORK EXERCISES

1. 'The sense of alienation is often agonisingly evoked in Plath's poetry.' To what extent is this true of 'Morning Song'? Support your answer with reference to the poem.

2. 'Sylvia Plath makes effective use of unusual and startling imagery to explore deeply personal themes.' Discuss this view with particular reference to the poem, 'Morning Song'.

SUMMARY POINTS

- Poet's ambivalent attitude to motherhood: loss of individual identity conflicting with deep love.
- Striking, unexpected imagery: contrasts between the child's delicacy and the mother's clumsiness.
- Development from inanimate objects (the watch, statue, mirror, cloud) to animate objects (moth, cow, cat, singer).
- Varying tones: tender, anxious, alienated, reflective, caring, fulfilled.
- Intense feelings of dislocation replaced by increasing sense of inter-connectedness.

4 FINISTERRE

This was the land's end: the last fingers, knuckled and rheumatic,
Cramped on nothing. Black
Admonitory cliffs, and the sea exploding
With no bottom, or anything on the other side of it,
Whitened by the faces of the drowned.   5
Now it is only gloomy, a dump of rocks –
Leftover soldiers from old, messy wars.
The sea cannons into their ear, but they don't budge.
Other rocks hide their grudges under the water.

The cliffs are edged with trefoils, stars and bells   10
Such as fingers might embroider, close to death,
Almost too small for the mists to bother with.
The mists are part of the ancient paraphernalia –
Souls, rolled in the doom-noise of the sea.
They bruise the rocks out of existence, then resurrect them.   15
They go up without hope, like sighs.
I walk among them, and they stuff my mouth with cotton.
When they free me, I am beaded with tears.

Our Lady of the Shipwrecked is striding toward the horizon,
Her marble skirts blown back in two pink wings.   20
A marble sailor kneels at her foot distractedly, and at his foot
A peasant woman in black
Is praying to the monument of the sailor praying.
Our Lady of the Shipwrecked is three times life size,
Her lips sweet with divinity.   25
She does not hear what the sailor or the peasant is saying –
She is in love with the beautiful formlessness of the sea.

Gull-colored laces flap in the sea drafts
Beside the postcard stalls.
The peasants anchor them with conches. One is told: 30
'These are the pretty trinkets the sea hides,
Little shells made up into necklaces and toy ladies.
They do not come from the Bay of the Dead down there,
But from another place, tropical and blue,
We have never been to.   35
These are our crêpes. Eat them before they blow cold.'

'and the sea exploding'

Glossary

1   *land's end*: literally 'Finisterre'; the western tip of Brittany.
3   *Admonitory*: warning.
10 *trefoils*: three-leaved plants.
13 *paraphernalia*: discarded items.
14 *doom-noise*: hopeless sounds.

19 *Our Lady of the Shipwrecked*: the mother of Christ prayed for sailors.
30 *conches*: shells.
31 *trinkets*: cheap jewellery.
36 *crêpes*: light pancakes.

INITIAL RESPONSE

1. Would you agree that this is a disquieting poem which is likely to disturb readers? Refer to the text in your answer.

2. There are several changes of tone in this poem. Describe two contrasting tones, using close reference to the text.

3. What does the poem reveal to you about Sylvia Plath's own state of mind? Use reference to the text in your response.

'Finisterre' was written in 1960 following Plath's visit to Brittany, France. As with many of her poems, the description of the place can be interpreted both literally and metaphorically.

The sea has always inspired poets and artists. It is at times welcoming, menacing, beautiful, peaceful and mysterious. Throughout her short life, Sylvia Plath loved the ocean. She spent her childhood years on the Atlantic coast just north of Boston. This setting provides a source for many of her poetic ideas. Terror and death loom large in her descriptive poem 'Finisterre', in which the pounding rhythm of storm waves off the Breton coast represents Plath's inner turmoil.

Stanza one opens dramatically and immediately creates a disturbing atmosphere. Plath describes the rocky headland as being 'knuckled and rheumatic'. In a series of powerful images ('the last fingers', 'Black/Admonitory cliffs', 'and the sea exploding'), the poet recreates the uproar and commotion of the scene. The grisly personification is startling, linking the shoreline with suffering and decay. There is a real sense of conflict between sea and land. Both are closely associated with death ('the faces of the drowned'). The jagged rocks are compared to 'Leftover soldiers' who 'hide their grudges under the water'. There is a noticeable tone of regret and protest against the futility of conflict, which is denounced as 'old, messy wars'.

Plath's negative imagery is relentless, with harsh consonant sounds ('knuckled', 'Cramped', 'exploding') emphasising the force of raging storm waves. The use of contrasting colours intensifies the imagery. As the 'sea cannons' against the headland, the atmosphere is 'only gloomy'. It is hard not to see the bleak seascape as a reflection of Plath's own unhappy state.

In stanza two, the poet turns away from the cruel sea and focuses momentarily on the small plants clinging to the cliff edge. However, these 'trefoils, stars and bells' are also 'close to death'. If anything, they reinforce the unsettling mood and draw the poet back to the ocean mists, which she thinks of as symbolising the souls of the dead, lost in 'the doom-noise of the sea'. Plath imagines the heavy mists transforming the rocks, destroying them 'out of existence' before managing to 'resurrect them' again. In a surreal sequence, the poet enters the water ('I walk among them') and joins the wretched souls who lie there. Her growing sense of panic is suggested by the stark admission: 'they stuff my mouth with cotton'. The experience is agonising and leaves her 'beaded with tears'.

Plath's thoughts turn to a marble statue of 'Our Lady of the Shipwrecked' in stanza three. Once again, in her imagination, she creates a dramatic narrative around the religious figure. This monument to the patron saint of the ocean should offer some consolation to the kneeling sailor and a grieving peasant woman who pray to the mother of God. Ironically, their pleas are completely ignored – 'She does not hear' their prayers because 'She is in love with the beautiful formlessness of the sea'. The feeling of hopelessness is all pervading. Is the poet expressing her own feelings of failure and despondency here? Or is she also attacking the ineffectiveness of religion? The description of the statue is certainly unflattering. The figure is flighty and self-centred: 'Her marble skirts blown back in two pink wings'. In contrast, the powerful ocean remains fascinating.

In the **fourth stanza**, Plath describes the local Bretons who sell souvenirs to tourists. Unlike the previous three stanzas, the mood appears to be much lighter as the poet describes the friendly stall-keepers going about their business. It is another irony that their livelihood (selling 'pretty trinkets') is dependent on the sea and its beauty. Like the statue, the locals seem unconcerned by the tragic history of the ocean. Indeed, they are keen to play down 'the Bay of the Dead' and explain that what they sell is imported 'from another place, tropical and blue'. In the final line, a stall-holder advises the poet to enjoy the pancakes she has bought: 'Eat them before they blow cold'. Although the immediate mood is untroubled, the final phrase brings us back to the earlier – and more disturbing – parts of the poem where Plath described the raging storms and the nameless lost souls who have perished at sea.

ANALYSIS

Write a paragraph on Sylvia Plath's use of detailed description in 'Finisterre'.

Sample Paragraph

The opening images of the rocks – 'the last fingers, knuckled and rheumatic' – are of decrepit old age. The strong visual impact is a regular feature of Sylvia Plath's writing. The first half of the poem is filled with memorable details of the windswept coastline. In her careful choice of descriptive terms, Plath uses broad vowels to evoke a pervading feeling of dejection. Words such as 'drowned', 'gloomy', 'rolled' and 'doom' help to create this dismal effect. The dramatic aural image, 'The sea cannons', echoes the roar of turbulent waves crashing onto the rocks. Plath's eye for close observation is also seen in her portrait of the holy statue – 'Her lips sweet with divinity'. The poem ends with a painstaking sketch of the Breton traders selling postcards and 'Little shells made up into necklaces and toy ladies'. The local people seem to have come to terms with 'the Bay of the Dead' and are getting on with life. Overall, the use of details throughout the poem leaves readers with a strong sense of place and community.

Examiner's Comment

Quotations are very well used here to highlight Plath's ability to create specific scenes and moods through precise description. The examples range over much of the poem and the writing is both varied and controlled throughout. A top-grade response.

N.B. Access your ebook for additional sample paragraphs and a list of useful quotes with commentary.

CLASS/HOMEWORK EXERCISES

1. It has been said that vivid, startling imagery gives a surreal quality to 'Finisterre'. Using reference to the poem, write a paragraph responding to this statement.

2. 'Plath's unique imagination addresses unhappiness and hopelessness.' To what extent do you agree with this statement? Support your answer with suitable reference to 'Finisterre', referring to the poem's content and style.

SUMMARY POINTS

- Fearful, ominous description of ordinary place.
- Disquieting tone of Our Lady of the Shipwrecked as aloof and self-absorbed.
- Ironic contrast between sweet appearance of statue and grim reality of shipwrecks in bay.
- Formal structure of poem contrasts with terror of situation.
- Stirking images and sounds, personification, rich symbolism.

5 MIRROR

I am silver and exact. I have no preconceptions.
Whatever I see I swallow immediately *has no feelings toward whats looking in*
Just as it is, unmisted by love or dislike. *at it - same for everyone*
I am not cruel, only truthful - *Shows you the real you unless alter your own*
The eye of a little god, four-cornered. *--woman worships it. 5 image.*
Most of the time I meditate on the opposite wall.
It is pink, with speckles. I have looked at it so long *the wall dosent change*
I think it is part of my heart. But it flickers. *but the woman does.*
Faces and darkness separate us over and over.

Now I am a lake. A woman bends over me,   10
Searching my reaches for what she really is.
Then she turns to those liars, the candles or the moon.
I see her back, and reflect it faithfully.
She rewards me with tears and an agitation of hands. *distress*
I am important to her. She comes and goes.   15
Each morning it is her face that replaces the darkness.
In me she has drowned a young girl, and in me an old woman *-age is terrible.*
Rises toward her day after day, like a terrible fish. *lack of control over your own image.*

'The eye of a little god, four-cornered'.

Glossary

1   *exact*: accurate, giving all details; to insist on payment.
1   *preconceptions*: thoughts already formed.

11   *reaches*: range of distance or depth.
14   *agitation*: shaking, trembling.

INITIAL RESPONSE

1. Select two images that suggest the dark, sinister side of the mirror. Would you consider that these images show an unforgiving way of viewing oneself?

2. What are the parallels and contrasts between a mirror and a lake? Develop your response in a written paragraph.

3. Write your own personal response to this poem, referring closely to the text in your answer.

STUDY NOTES

'Mirror' was written in 1961 as Sylvia Plath approached her twenty-ninth birthday. In this dark poem, Plath views the inevitability of old age and death, our preoccupation with image and our search for an identity.

Do you think everyone looks at themselves in a mirror? Would you consider that people are fascinated, disappointed or even obsessed by what they see? Does a mirror accurately reflect the truth? Do people actually see what is reflected or is it distorted by notions and ideals which they or society have? Consider the use of mirrors in fairytales: 'Mirror, mirror on the wall, who's the fairest of them all?' Mirrors are also used in myths, such as the story of Narcissus, who drowned having fallen in love with his reflection, and *Through the Looking Glass* is a famous children's book. Mirrors are also used in horror films as the dividing line between fantasy and reality.

In this poem, Plath often gives us a startling new angle on an everyday object. The function of a mirror is to reflect whatever is put in front of it. **Stanza one** opens with a ringing declaration by the mirror: 'I am silver and exact'. This personification has a sinister effect as the mirror describes an almost claustrophobic relationship with a particular woman. The voice of the mirror is clear, direct and precise. It announces that it reports exactly what there is without any alteration. We have to decide if the mirror is telling the truth, as it says it has no bias ('no preconceptions'). It does not judge; it reflects the image received. The mirror adopts the position of an impartial observer, but it is active, almost ruthless ('I swallow'). It is not cruel, but truthful.

Yet how truthful is a mirror image, as it flattens a three-dimensional object into two dimensions? The image sent out has no depth. The voice of the mirror becomes smug as it sees itself as the ruler of those reflected ('The eye of a little god'). Our obsession with ourselves causes us to worship at the mirror that reflects our image. In the modern world, people are often disappointed with their reflections, wishing they were thinner, younger, better looking. But **the mirror insists it tells the truth**; it doesn't flatter or hurt. The mirror explains how it spends its day gazing at the opposite wall, which is carefully described as 'pink, with speckles'. It feels as if the wall is part of itself. This reflection is disturbed by the faces of people and the dying light. The passage of time is evoked in the phrase 'over and over'.

In **stanza two**, the mirror now announces that it is 'a lake'. Both are flat surfaces that reflect. However, a lake is another dimension, it has depth. **There is danger.** The image is now drawn into its murky depths. The woman is looking in and down, not just at. It is as if she is struggling to find who she really is, what her true path in life is. Plath frequently questioned who she was. Expectations for young women in the 1950s were limiting. Appearance was important, as were the roles of wife, mother and homemaker. But Plath also wanted to write: 'Will I submerge my embarrassing desires and aspirations, refuse to face myself?' The mirror becomes irritated and jealous of the woman as she turns to the deceptive soft light of 'those liars, the candles or the moon'. The mirror remains faithful, reflecting her back. **The woman is dissatisfied with her image.** In her insecurity, she weeps and wrings her hands. Plath always tried to do her best, to be a model student, almost desperate to excel and be affirmed. Is there a danger in seeking perfection? Do we need to be kind to ourselves? Do we need to love ourselves? Again, the mirror pompously announces 'I am important to her'.

The march of time passing is emphasised by 'comes and goes', 'Each morning' and 'day after day'. The woman keeps coming back. The mirror's sense of its significance is shown by the frequent use of 'I' and the repetition of 'in me'. As time passes, the woman is facing the truth of her human condition as her reflection changes and ages in the mirror. Her youth is 'drowned', to be replaced by a monstrous vision of an old woman 'like a terrible fish'. **The lonely drama of living and dying is recorded with a dreamlike, nightmarish quality.** There is no comforting rhyme in the poem, only the controlled rhythm of time. The mirror does not give what a human being desires: comfort and warmth. Instead, it impersonally reminds us of our mortality.

ANALYSIS

What is your personal response to the relationship between the mirror and the woman? Support your views with reference to the poem.

Sample Paragraph

I feel the mirror is like an alter ego, which is coolly appraising the woman in an unforgiving way. The mirror is 'silver'. This cold metal object is heartless. Although the mirror repeatedly states that it does not judge, 'I have no preconceptions', the woman feels judged and wanting: 'She rewards me with tears and an agitation of hands.' I think the relationship between the woman and the mirror is dangerous and poisonous. She does indeed 'drown' in the mirror, as she never feels good enough. Is this the payment the mirror exacts? The complacent mirror rules her like a tyrannical 'little god, four-cornered'. It reminds me of how today we are never satisfied with our image, always wanting something else, more perfect. Plath also strove to be perfect. This obsessive relationship shows a troubled self, a lack of self-love. Who is saying that the older woman is 'like a terrible fish'? I think the mirror has become the voice of a society which values women only for their looks and youth, rather than what they are capable of achieving.

Examiner's Comment

In this fluent and personal response, close analysis of the text contributes to a distinctive and well-supported, top-grade account of the uneasy relationship between the mirror and the woman.

N.B. Access your ebook for additional sample paragraphs and a list of useful quotes with commentary.

CLASS/HOMEWORK EXERCISES

1. 'Plath's use of dramatic monologue is an unsettling experience for readers.' Discuss this statement with reference to 'Mirror'.

2. 'All who share the human condition have a bright and dark side.' Discuss Plath's exploration of this theme in her poem 'Mirror'. In your response, pay particular attention to her use of imagery.

SUMMARY POINTS

- Key themes include transience and mortality.
- Chilling personification of the mirror.
- Exploration of identity, duality of being.
- Startlingly shocking imagery conveys frightening tone.

6 PHEASANT

You said you would kill it this morning.
Do not kill it. It startles me still,
The jut of that odd, dark head, pacing

Through the uncut grass on the elm's hill.
It is something to own a pheasant,   5
Or just to be visited at all.

I am not mystical: it isn't
As if I thought it had a spirit.
It is simply in its element.

That gives it a kingliness, a right.   10
The print of its big foot last winter,
The tail-track, on the snow in our court –

The wonder of it, in that pallor,
Through crosshatch of sparrow and starling.
Is it its rareness, then? It is rare.   15

But a dozen would be worth having,
A hundred, on that hill – green and red,
Crossing and recrossing: a fine thing!

It is such a good shape, so vivid.
It's a little cornucopia.   20
It unclaps, brown as a leaf, and loud,

Settles in the elm, and is easy.
It was sunning in the narcissi.
I trespass stupidly. Let be, let be.

'in its element'

Glossary

1   *You*: probably addressed to Plath's husband.
3   *jut*: extending outwards.
7   *mystical*: spiritual, supernatural.
13 *pallor*: pale colour.

14 *crosshatch*: criss-cross trail.
20 *cornucopia*: unexpected treasure.
23 *narcissi*: bright spring flowers.

INITIAL RESPONSE

1. Explain Sylvia Plath's attitude to nature based on your reading of 'Pheasant'.

2. Compile a list of the poet's arguments for not killing the pheasant.

3. Write a paragraph on the effectiveness of Plath's imagery in the poem.

STUDY NOTES

'Pheasant' was written in 1962 and reflects Plath's deep appreciation of the natural world. Its enthusiastic mood contrasts with much of her more disturbing work. The poem is structured in eight tercets (three-line stanzas) with a subtle, interlocking rhyming pattern (known as terza rima).

The poem opens with an urgent plea by Plath to spare the pheasant's life: 'Do not kill it'. In the **first two stanzas**, the tone is tense as the poet offers a variety of reasons for sparing this impressive game bird. She is both shocked and excited by the pheasant: 'It startles me still'. Plath admits to feeling honoured in the presence of the bird: 'It is something to own a pheasant'. The broken rhythm of the early lines adds an abruptness that heightens the sense of urgency. **Plath seems spellbound by the bird's beauty** ('The jut of that odd, dark head') now that it is under threat.

But the poet is also keen to play down any sentimentality in her attitude to the pheasant. **Stanza three** opens with a straightforward explanation of her attitude: 'it isn't/As if I thought it had a spirit'. Instead, **she values the bird for its graceful beauty and naturalness**: 'It is simply in its element.' Plath is keen to show her recognition of the pheasant's right to exist because it possesses a certain majestic quality, 'a kingliness'.

In **stanza four**, the poet recalls an earlier winter scene when she marvelled at the pheasant's distinctive footprint in the snow. The bird has made an even greater impression on Plath, summed up in the key phrase 'The wonder of it', at the start of **stanza five**. She remembers **the colourful pheasant's distinguishing marks against the pale snow**, so unlike the 'crosshatch' pattern of smaller birds, such as the sparrow and starling. This makes the pheasant particularly 'rare' and valuable in Plath's eyes.

The poet can hardly contain her regard for the pheasant and her tone becomes increasingly enthusiastic in **stanza six** as she dreams of having first a 'dozen' and then a 'hundred' of the birds. In a few **well-chosen details**, she highlights their colour and energy ('green and red,/Crossing and recrossing') before adding an emphatic compliment: 'a fine thing!' Her delight continues into **stanza seven**, where Plath proclaims her ceaseless admiration for the pheasant: 'It's a little cornucopia', an inspirational source of joy and surprise.

Throughout the poem, the poet has emphasised that the pheasant rightly belongs in its natural surroundings, and this is also true of the final lines. **Stanza eight** is considered and assured. From the poet's point of view, **the pheasant's right to live is beyond dispute**. While the bird is 'sunning in the narcissi', she herself has become the unwelcome intruder: 'I trespass stupidly'. Plath ends by echoing the opening appeal to spare the pheasant's life: 'Let be, let be.' The quietly insistent repetition and the underlying tone of unease are a final reminder of the need to respect nature.

It has been suggested that the pheasant symbolises Plath's insecure relationship with Ted Hughes. For various reasons, their marriage was under severe strain in 1962 and Plath feared that Hughes was intent on ending it. This interpretation adds a greater poignancy to the poem.

ANALYSIS

There are several mood changes in 'Pheasant'. What do you consider to be the dominant mood in the poem? Refer to the text in your answer.

Sample Paragraph

The mood at the beginning of 'Pheasant' is nervous and really uptight. Plath seems to have given up hope about the pheasant. It is facing death. She repeats the word 'kill' and admits to being shocked at the very thought of what the bird is facing. She herself seems desperate and fearful. This is shown by the short sentence, 'Do not kill it'. But the outlook soon changes. Plath describes the pheasant 'pacing' and 'in its element'. But she seems less stressed as she describes the 'kingliness' of the pheasant. But the mood soon settles down as Plath celebrates the life of this really beautiful bird. The mood becomes calmer and ends in almost a whisper, 'Let be, let be'. The dominant mood is calm and considered in the poem.

Examiner's Comment

This is a reasonable middle-grade answer to the question, pointing out the change of mood following the first stanza. Some worthwhile references are used to show the poem's principal mood. The expression, however, is flawed in places (e.g. repeatedly using 'But' to start sentences). This response requires more development to raise the standard.

N.B. Access your ebook for additional sample paragraphs and a list of useful quotes with commentary.

CLASS/HOMEWORK EXERCISES

1. Plath sets out to convince the reader of the pheasant's right to life in this poem. Does she succeed in her aim? Give reasons for your answer.

2. Sylvia Plath's deep appreciation of the harmonious order of the natural world is expressed in vivid imagery and terse instructions.' To what extent is this true of her poem, 'Pheasant'? Support your answer with reference to the text.

SUMMARY POINTS

- Heartfelt plea on behalf of the rights of wild creatures.
- Graphic description of beauty of bird.
- Tension, poet as intruder.
- Imperatives (verbal commands) inject urgency.
- Subtle music, casual flow of the rhythm of normal speech.

Handwritten annotations (top): Tortured minds of Plath? Thought provoking. Disturbing imagery? Use of I — so very personal. written after she found out her husband cheated.

7 ELM

Handwritten left margin: instability + despair

For Ruth Fainlight

Handwritten: The depth of depression — lowest of the low.

I know the bottom, she says. I know it with my great tap root:

It is what you fear.

I do not fear it: I have been there. *[annotation: unnerving]*

Handwritten: questioning mental state

Is it the sea you hear in me,

Its dissatisfactions?   5

Or the voice of nothing, that was your madness?

Love is a shadow.

How you lie and cry after it *[annotation: relentless sounds — constant reminder of her pain.]*

Listen: these are its hooves: it has gone off, like a horse.

All night I shall gallop thus, impetuously,   10

Till your head is a stone, your pillow a little turf, *[annotation: assonance heightens sense of hurt + pain.]*

Echoing, echoing.

Handwritten left margin: everyday things killing her. nothing doesn't hurt anymore

Or shall I bring you the sound of poisons? *[annotation: poisonous thoughts]*

This is rain now, this big hush.

And this is the fruit of it: tin-white, like arsenic. *[annotation: going toward]* 15 *[insanity]*

I have suffered the atrocity of sunsets.

Scorched to the root

My red filaments burn and stand, a hand of wires. *[annotation: harsh language sense of destruction]*

Now I break up in pieces that fly about like clubs.

A wind of such violence   20

Will tolerate no bystanding: I must shriek.

The moon, also, is merciless: she would drag me

Cruelly, being barren. *[annotation: empty nothingness]*

Her radiance scathes me. Or perhaps I have caught her.

I let her go. I let her go   25

Diminished and flat, as after radical surgery.

How your bad dreams possess and endow me.

I am inhabited by a cry.
Nightly it flaps out
Looking, with its hooks, for something to love. 30

I am terrified by this dark thing *Brutal honesty.*
That sleeps in me; *Vulnerability*
All day I feel its soft, feathery turnings, its malignity.

Clouds pass and disperse.
Are those the faces of love, those pale irretrievables? 35
Is it for such I agitate my heart?

I am incapable of more knowledge.
What is this, this face
So murderous in its strangle of branches? –

fearful.
Its snaky acids hiss. *depression building up to a hideous climax*
It petrifies the will. These are the isolate, slow faults 40 *own emotional state destroys her*
That kill, that kill, that kill.

'I am terrified by this dark thing'

Glossary

Title: The wych elm is a large deciduous tree, with a massive straight trunk and tangled branches. It was once a favourite timber of coffin makers. Plath dedicated the poem to a close friend, Ruth Fainlight, another American poet.

1   *the bottom*: lowest depths.
1   *tap root*: the main root.
15   *arsenic*: poison.

16   *atrocity*: massacre, carnage
18   *filaments*: fibres, nerves.
24   *scathes*: injures, scalds.
33   *malignity*: evil.
34   *disperse*: scatter widely.
35   *irretrievables*: things lost forever.
40   *snaky acids*: deceptive poisons.
41   *petrifies*: terrifies.

INITIAL RESPONSE

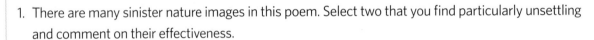

1. There are many sinister nature images in this poem. Select two that you find particularly unsettling and comment on their effectiveness.

2. Trace and examine how love is presented and viewed by the poet. Support the points you make with reference to the text.

3. Write your own individual response to this poem, referring closely to the text in your answer.

STUDY NOTES

Written in April 1962, 'Elm' is one of Sylvia Plath's most challenging and intensely dramatic poems. Plath personifies the elm tree to create a surreal scene. It 'speaks' in a traumatic voice to someone else, the 'you' of line 2, the poet herself – or the reader, perhaps. Both voices interact throughout the poem, almost always expressing pain and anguish. Critics often associate these powerful emotions with the poet's own personal problems – Plath had experienced electric shock treatment for depression. However, this may well limit our understanding of what is a complex exploration of many emotions.

The **opening stanza** is unnerving. The poet appears to be dramatising an exchange between herself and the elm by imagining what the tree might say to her. The immediate effect is eerily surreal. From the start, **the narrative voice is obsessed with instability and despair**: 'I know the bottom'. The tree is described in both physical terms ('my great tap root' penetrating far into the ground) and also as a state of mind ('I do not fear it'). The depth of depression imagined is reinforced by the repetition of 'I know' and the stark simplicity of the chilling comment 'It is what you fear'.

The bizarre exchange between the two 'speakers' continues in **stanza two**. The elm questions the poet about the nature of her **mental state**. Does the wind blowing through its branches remind her of the haunting sound of the sea? Or even 'the voice of nothing' – the numbing experience of madness?

Stanzas three and **four** focus on the dangers and disappointments of love – 'a shadow'. The tone is wary, emphasised by the comparison of a wild horse that has 'gone off'. The relentless sounds of the wind in the elm will be a bitter reminder, 'echoing' this loss of love 'Till your head is a stone'. Assonance is effectively used here to heighten the sense of hurt and abandonment. For much of the middle section of the poem (**stanzas five** to **nine**), the elm's intimidating voice continues to dramatise a series of horrifying experiences associated with insantiy. The tree has endured extreme elements – rain ('the sound of poisons'), sunshine ('Scorched to the root'), wind ('of such violence') and also the moon ('Her radiance scathes me'). The harsh imagery and frenzied language ('burn', 'shriek', 'merciless') combine to create a sense of shocking destructiveness.

Stanzas ten and **eleven** mark a turning point where the voices of the tree and the poet become indistinguishable. This is achieved by the seemingly harmless image of an owl inhabiting the branches, searching for 'something to love'. The speaker is haunted by 'this dark thing'. The poet's vulnerability is particularly evident in her stark admission: 'I feel its soft, feathery turnings, its malignity'. Plath has come to relate her unknown demons to a deadly tumour.

In the **last three stanzas**, the poet's voice seems more distant and calm before the final storm. The image of the passing clouds ('the faces of love') highlight the notion of rejection as the root cause of Plath's depression. The poem ends on a visionary note when she imagines being confronted by a 'murderous' snake that appears in the branches: 'It petrifies the will'. The scene of growing terror builds to a hideous climax until her own mental and emotional states (her 'slow faults') end up destroying her. The intensity of the final line, 'That kill, that kill, that kill', leaves readers with a harrowing understanding of Plath's paralysis of despair.

ANALYSIS

Do you think that 'Elm' has a surreal, nightmarish quality? In your response, refer to the text to support your views.

Sample Paragraph

I would agree that Sylvia Plath has created a very disturbing mood in the poem, 'Elm'. Giving the tree a speaking voice of its own is like something from a child's fairy story. Plath compares love to a galloping horse. The poem is mainly about depression and madness. So it's bound to be out of the ordinary. The speaker in the poem is confused and asks weird questions, such as 'Is it the sea you hear in me?' She is obsessive and totally paranoid. Everything is against her, as far as she imagines it. The weather is seen as an enemy even, the rain is 'tin-white like arsenic'. The end is as if she is having a bad dream and imagines a fierce hissing snake in the tree coming after her. The dramatic scenario unnerves the reader. This represents Plath's deepest nightmare, the fear of loneliness. Violent verbs such as 'suffered' and 'break up' disturb the reader while graphic images – 'a hand of wires', 'snaky acids hiss' – create a surreal atmosphere. The whole poem is hectic and confusing – especially the images.

Examiner's Comment

This short mid-grade paragraph includes some worthwhile references to the poem's disturbing aspects. The points are note-like, however, and the writing style lacks control in places. Effective use of apt quotations. Less than top-grade answer.

N.B. Access your ebook for additional sample paragraphs and a list of useful quotes with commentary.

CLASS/HOMEWORK EXERCISES

1. What evidence of Plath's deep depression and hypersensitivity is revealed in the poem 'Elm'? Refer closely to the text in your answer.

2. Plath said of her later poetry, 'I speak them to myself … aloud'. In your opinion, how effective are the sound effects and use of direct speech in the poem 'Elm'? Support your views with accurate quotation.

SUMMARY POINTS

- Inner torment, awful fear of being oneself.
- Terrifying personification of elm.
- Rich symbolism and imagery, effective sounds.
- Nightmare world, surreal mood, paralysis of fear, threat of madness.
- Simple unvarnished style, poem overflows with poet's feelings of lost love.

Symbolic

black centre - little hell flames
Colour-bright, memory, war, drug, heroin - opium

Sylvia Plath 417

POPPIES IN JULY

can become an inferno - destructive.

Little poppies, little hell flames, Toxic, threatening, dangerous - reflection of inner self.
Do you do no harm? Conversational - can she contain the threat.

frustrating
You flicker. I cannot touch you. movement - change | cant fix the problem, elusive.
I put my hands among the flames. Nothing burns. cant feel anything anymore
sense of nothingness in her head.

And it exhausts me to watch you tired of whats happening in her head.
Flickering like that, wrinkly and clear red, like the skin of a mouth.

A mouth just bloodied. stained,
Little bloody skirts!

There are fumes that I cannot touch. fears she cant conquer, never be pure
Where are your opiates, your nauseous capsules? 10 inside

release.
If I could bleed, or sleep! – Pain inside, trying to manage, cant
If my mouth could marry a hurt like that!

Or your liquors seep to me, in this glass capsule,
Dulling and stilling.

But colorless. Colorless. nothingness 15

'You flicker. I cannot touch you'.

Glossary

1	*hell flames*: most poppies are red, flame-like.		13	*liquors*: drug vapours.
9	*fumes*: the effects of drugs.		13	*capsule*: small container.
10	*opiates*: sleep-inducing narcotics.		15	*colorless*: drained, lifeless.
10	*nauseous*: causing sickness.			

INITIAL RESPONSE

1. Examine the title, 'Poppies in July', in light of the main subject matter in the poem. Is the title misleading? Explain your answer.

2. What evidence can you find in 'Poppies in July' that the speaker is yearning to escape?

3. Colour imagery plays a significant role in the poem. Comment on how effectively colour is used.

STUDY NOTES

Like most confessional writers, Sylvia Plath's work reflects her own personal experiences, without filtering any of the painful emotions. She wrote 'Poppies in July' in the summer of 1962, during the break-up of her marriage.

The **first stanza** is marked by an uneasy sense of foreboding. The speaker (almost certainly Plath herself) compares the blazing red poppies to 'little hell flames' before directly confronting them: 'Do you do no harm?' **Her distress is obvious** from the start. The poem's title may well have led readers to expect a more conventional nature poem. Instead, the flowers are presented as being highly treacherous, and all the more deceptive because they are 'little'.

Plath develops the fire image in **lines 3–6**. However, even though she places her hands 'among the flames', she finds that 'Nothing burns' and she is forced to watch them 'Flickering'. It almost seems as though she is so tired and numb that **she has transcended pain** and can experience nothing: 'it exhausts me to watch you'. Ironically, the more vivid the poppies are, the more lethargic she feels.

The uncomfortable and disturbed mood increases in the **fourth stanza** with two **startling images**, both personifying the flowers. Comparing the poppy to 'A mouth just bloodied' suggests recent violence and physical suffering. The 'bloody skirts' metaphor is equally harrowing. There is further evidence of the poet's overpowering weariness in the prominent use of broad vowel sounds, for example in 'exhausts', 'mouth' and 'bloodied'.

In the **fifth stanza**, Plath's disorientated state turns to a distracted longing for escape. Having failed to use the vibrancy of the poppies to distract her from her pain, she now craves the feeling of oblivion or unconsciousness. But although she desires the dulling effects of drugs derived from the poppies, her **tone is hopelessly cynical** as she describes the 'fumes that I cannot touch'.

The mood becomes even more distraught in **lines 11–12**, with the poet begging for any alternative to her anguished state. 'If I could bleed, or sleep!' is an emphatic plea for release. It is her final attempt to retain some control of her life in the face of an overwhelming sense of powerlessness. Plath's **growing alienation** seems so unbearably intense at this point that it directly draws the reader's sympathy.

The **last three lines** record the poet's surrender, perhaps a kind of death wish. Worn down by her inner demons and the bright colours of the poppies, Plath lets herself become resigned to a 'colorless' world of nothingness. Her **complete passivity** and helplessness are emphasised by the dreamlike quality of the phrase 'Dulling and stilling'. As she drifts into a death-like 'colorless' private hell, there remains a terrible sense of betrayal, as if she is still being haunted by the bright red flowers. The ending of 'Poppies in July' is so dark and joyless that it is easy to understand why the poem is often seen as a desperate cry for help.

ANALYSIS

'Poppies in July' is one of Plath's most disturbing poems. What aspects of the poem affected you most?

Sample Paragraph

'Poppies in July' was written at a time when Plath was struggling with the fact that her husband had deserted her. This affected her deeply and it is clear that the poppies are a symbol of this excruciating time. Everything about the poem is negative. The images of the poppies are nearly all associated with fire and blood. Plath's language is alarming when she compares the poppies to 'little hell flames' and also 'the skin of a mouth'. The most disturbing aspect is Plath's own unstable mind. She seems to be in a kind of trance, obsessed by the red colours of the poppies, which remind her of blood. I got the impression that she was nearly going insane in the end. She seems suicidal – 'If I could bleed'. For me, this is the most disturbing moment in the poem. I can get some idea of her troubled mind. Plath cannot stand reality and seeks a way out through drugs or death. The last image is of Plath sinking into a dull state of drowsiness, unable to cope with the world around her.

Examiner's Comment

Overall, a solid middle-grade response which responds personally to the question. While some focus is placed on the disturbing thought in the poem, there could have been a more thorough exploration of Plath's style and how it enhances her theme of depression.

N.B. Access your ebook for additional sample paragraphs and a list of useful quotes with commentary.

CLASS/HOMEWORK EXERCISES

1. Would you agree that loneliness and pain are the central themes of 'Poppies in July'? Refer to the text of the poem when writing your response.

2. Discuss how the poet uses vivid description in this poem to explore her negative feelings. Support your answer with reference to the text.

SUMMARY POINTS

- Desire to escape into oblivion.
- Personal aspect, engaged in struggle with threatening force beyond self.
- Upsetting imagery, intense mood of despair.
- Despairing mood conveyed in downward motion of poem.
- Contrast between dynamic, vivid flowers, a symbol of vibrancy of life, and longed-for dullness of oblivion.

[handwritten top margin: ceremony. / significant / important - expectation]

[handwritten top margin: structured / frantic & noisy - chaotic / Place of work / Danger - frightening. / Container]

9 THE ARRIVAL OF THE BEE BOX

[handwritten: control] *[handwritten: mask]*

[handwritten: can be eroded if not taken care of - like your brain.]

I ordered this, this clean wood box *[handwritten: - damaged? - rigidity natural]*
Square as a chair and almost too heavy to lift. *[handwritten: - burden, pressure]*
I would say it was the coffin of a midget *[handwritten: - abstract - distortion]*
Or a square baby *[handwritten: dosent fit in with society - abnormal - rigid]*
Were there not such a din in it.   5

The box is locked, it is dangerous.   *[handwritten: - trapped - trapped inside a body - suffocation]*
I have to live with it overnight
And I can't keep away from it.
There are no windows, so I can't see what is in there. *[handwritten: no light, no escape]* *[handwritten: trapped inside her.]*
There is only a little grid, no exit. *[handwritten: trapped inside her - something stuck inside her.]*   10

I put my eye to the grid.
It is dark, dark,
With the swarmy feeling of African hands *[handwritten: enslaved.]*
Minute and shrunk for export,
Black on black, angrily clambering.   15

How can I let them out? *[handwritten: needs help.]*
It is the noise that appalls me most of all,
The unintelligible syllables.
It is like a Roman mob,
Small, taken one by one, but my god, together!   20

I lay my ear to furious Latin.
I am not a Caesar.
I have simply ordered a box of maniacs.
They can be sent back.
They can die, I need feed them nothing, I am the owner.   25

I wonder how hungry they are.
I wonder if they would forget me
If I just undid the locks and stood back and turned into a tree.
There is the laburnum, its blond colonnades,
And the petticoats of the cherry.   30

They might ignore me immediately
In my moon suit and funeral veil.
I am no source of honey
So why should they turn on me?
Tomorrow I will be sweet God, I will set them free.   35

The box is only temporary.

'It is the noise that appalls me'

Glossary

10	*grid*: wire network.
13	*swarmy*: like a large group of bees.
22	*Caesar*: famous Roman ruler.
29	*laburnum*: tree with yellow hanging flowers.

29	*colonnades*: long groups of flowers arranged in a row of columns.
32	*moon suit*: protective clothing worn by beekeepers; all-in-one suit.

INITIAL RESPONSE

1. How would you describe the poet's reaction to the bee box – fear or fascination, or a mixture of both? Write a paragraph for your response, referring to the poem.

2. Select two surreal images from the poem and comment on the effectiveness of each.

3. Would you describe this poem as exploring and overcoming one's fears and anxieties? Is the ending optimistic or pessimistic, in your opinion?

STUDY NOTES

'The Arrival of the Bee Box' was written in 1962, shortly after Plath's separation from her husband. Her father, who died when she was a child, had been a bee expert and Plath had recently taken up beekeeping. She explores order, power, control, confinement and freedom in this deeply personal poem.

The poem opens with a simple statement: 'I ordered this'. Straightaway, the emphasis is on order and control. The poet's tone in **stanza one** seems both matter-of-fact and surprised, as if thinking: 'Yes, I was the one who ordered this' and also 'Did I really order this?' **This drama has only one character, Plath herself.** We observe her responses and reactions to the arrival of the bee box. Notice the extensive use of the personal pronoun 'I'. We both see and hear the event.

The box is described as being made of 'clean wood' and given a homely quality with the simile 'Square as a chair'. But then a surreal, dreamlike metaphor, 'the coffin of a midget/Or a square baby', brings us into a nightmare world. The abnormal is suggested by the use of 'midget' and deformity by 'square baby'. The coffin conveys not only death, but also entrapment and confinement, preoccupations of the poet. The box has now become a sinister object. A witty sound effect closes the first stanza, as 'din in it' mimics the sound of the bees. They are like badly behaved children.

Stanza two explores the poet's ambivalent attitude to the box. She is fascinated by it, as she is curious to see inside ('I can't keep away from it'). Yet she is also frightened by it, as she describes the box as 'dangerous'. She peers in. The **third stanza** becomes claustrophobic and oppressive with the repetition of 'dark' and the grotesque image of 'the swarmy feeling of African hands/Minute and shrunk for export'. The milling of the bees/slaves is vividly captured as they heave around in the heat amid an atmosphere of menace and oppression, hopelessly desperate.

We hear the bees in **stanza four**. The metaphor of a Roman mob is used to show how if they are let loose they will create chaos and danger if they are let loose. The assonance of 'appalls' and 'all' underlines the poet's terror. The phrase 'unintelligible syllables', with its onomatopoeia and its difficult pronunciation, lets us hear the angry buzzing. Plath is awestruck at their collective force and energy: 'but my god, together!'

In **stanza five** the poet tries to listen, but only hears 'furious Latin' she does not understand. She doubts her capacity to control them, stating that she is 'not a Caesar', the powerful ruler of the Romans. She regards them as 'maniacs'. Then she realises that if she has ordered them, she can return them: 'They can be sent back'. She has some control of this situation. Plath can even decide their fate, whether they live or die: 'I need feed them nothing'. She has now redefined the situation as she realises that she is 'the owner'. They belong to her.

The poet's feminine, nurturing side of her now emerges as she wonders 'how hungry they are'. The stereotype of the pretty woman surfaces in the description of the bees' natural habitat of trees in **stanza six**. Plath thinks if she releases them, they would go back to the trees, 'laburnum' and 'cherry'. She herself would then merge into the landscape and become a tree. This is a reference to a Greek myth where Daphne was being pursued by Apollo. After begging the gods to be saved, they turned her into a tree.

Now she refers to herself in her beekeeping outfit of veil and boiler suit in **stanza seven**. She rhetorically asks why the bees would attack her, as she can offer no sustenance ('I am no source of honey'). She decides to be compassionate: 'Tomorrow I will be sweet God, I will set them free'. She realises that they are imprisoned for the time being: 'The box is only temporary'.

This poem can also be read on another level. The box could represent the poet's attempt to be what others expect, the typical 1950s woman – pretty, compliant, nurturing. The bees could represent the dark side of her personality, which both fascinated and terrified Plath. The box is like Pandora's box: safe when locked, but full of danger when opened. Although she finds this disturbing, she also feels she must explore it in the interests of developing as a poet. The references to the doomed character of Daphne and the 'funeral veil' echo chillingly. Would these dark thoughts, if given their freedom, drive her to suicide? The form of this poem is seven stanzas of five lines. One line stands alone, free like the bees or her dark thoughts. If the box represents Plath's outside appearance or body, it is mortal, it is temporary.

ANALYSIS

How does this poem address the themes of order and power? Write a paragraph in response. Support your views with reference to the text.

Sample Paragraph

The poem opens with a reference to order, 'I ordered this'. It is an assertion of power, a deliberate act by 'I'. Throughout the poem the repetition of 'I' suggests a person who consciously chooses to act in a certain way. 'I put my eye to the grid', 'I lay my ear to furious Latin'. It is as if the poet wishes to confront and control her fears over the contents of the box. This box contains live, buzzing bees, whose well-being lies in the hands of the poet. 'I need feed them nothing, I am the owner'. The box metaphor suggests constriction and a lack of freedom – 'locks', 'little grid' enhance this atmosphere of claustrophobic control. Although she realises that she is not 'Caesar', the mighty Roman ruler, she can choose to be 'sweet God'. She alone has the power to release the bees, 'The box is only temporary'. This poem can also be read as referring to the control a person exercises when confronting their innermost fears and desires. These thoughts can be ignored or faced. The person owns these thoughts and can choose to contain them or confront them. Plath feared her own dark side, but felt it should be explored to enable her to progress as a poet. For her 'The box is only temporary'.

Examiner's Comment

This is an assured top-grade response which focuses well on the central themes of order and power. Apt and accurate quotations are used effectively. The opening point on Plath's use of the personal pronoun is particularly impressive.

N.B. Access your ebook for additional sample paragraphs and a list of useful quotes with commentary.

CLASS/HOMEWORK EXERCISES

1. How does Plath create a dramatic atmosphere in 'The Arrival of the Bee Box'?

2. Plath examines repression in the poem, 'The Arrival of the Bee Box'. Why do you think she fears a loss of control? In your response, refer to both the subject matter and stylistic techniques evident in the poem.

SUMMARY POINTS

- Central themes include power, control, freedom, self-expression.
- Innovative use of metaphor, contrasting moods.
- Unusual personification, startling images.
- Clever word-play, witty sound-effects, internal rhyme.
- Disconcerting ending emphasised by single stand-alone line.

universal – no restrictions – not scripted.

10 CHILD – *easily sculpted.*

Why only one eye

Certainty

Your clear eye is the one absolutely beautiful thing. *uncontaminated open to experience.*

I want to fill it with color and ducks, *simple – open to new experience.*

The zoo of the new – *diversity – menggerie – mixture.*

everything new is exotic

Whose name you meditate –

April snowdrop, Indian pipe, *– names – stories*   5

Little

Stalk without wrinkle, *not exposed yet – no worries.*

Pool in which images

Should be grand and classical – *impressive, exciting sights – growth.*

inspirational – nothing boring.

Not this troublous   10

Wringing of hands, this dark *inner agitation. – conflict.*

limitations. Ceiling without a star. *– lost without stars – no direction.*

'The zoo of the new'

Glossary

4   *meditate*: reflect.
5   *Indian pipe*: American woodland flower.
7   *Stalk*: plant stem.

9   *classical*: impressive, enduring.
10 *troublous*: disturbed.

INITIAL RESPONSE

1. What was your own immediate reaction after reading 'Child'? Refer to the text in your answer.

2. Which images in the poem are most effective in contrasting the world of the child and the world of the adult?

3. Plath uses various sound effects to enhance her themes in 'Child'. Comment briefly on two interesting examples.

STUDY NOTES

Sylvia Plath's son was born in January 1962. A year later, not long before the poet's own death, she wrote 'Child', a short poem that reflects her intense feelings about motherhood.

The opening line of **stanza one** shows the **poet's emphatic appreciation of childhood** innocence: 'Your clear eye is the one absolutely beautiful thing'. The tone at first is hopeful. Her love for the new child is generous and unconditional: 'I want to fill it with color'. The childlike language is lively and playful. Plath plans to give her child the happiest of times, filled with 'color and ducks'. The vigorous rhythm and animated internal rhyme in the phrase 'The zoo of the new' are imaginative, capturing the sense of youthful wonder.

In **stanza two**, the poet continues to associate her child with all that is best about the natural world. The baby is like the most fragile of flowers, the 'April snowdrop'. The assonance in this phrase has a musical effect, like a soft lullaby. Yet her own fascination appears to mask a deeper concern. Plath feels that such a perfect childhood experience is unlikely to last very long. Despite all her positive sentiments, what she wants for the vulnerable child seems directly at odds with what is possible in a flawed world.

Run-on lines are a recurring feature of the poem and these add to the feeling of freedom and innocent intensity. **Stanza three** includes two effective comparisons, again taken from nature. Plath sees the child as an unblemished 'Stalk' that should grow perfectly. A second quality of childhood's pure innocence is found in the 'Pool' metaphor. We are reminded of the opening image – the child's 'clear eye', always trusting and sincere.

The poet would love to provide a magical future for her young child, so that the pool would reflect 'grand and classical' images. However, as a loving mother, she is trapped between her **idealism** – the joy she wants for her child – and a **distressing reality** – an awareness that the child's life will not be perfectly happy. This shocking realisation becomes clear in **stanza four** and overshadows her hopes completely. The final images are stark and powerful – the pathetic 'Wringing of hands' giving emphasis to her helplessness. The last line poignantly portrays the paradox of the tension between Plath's dreams for the child in the face of the despair she feels about the oppressive world: this 'Ceiling without a star'. The intensely dark mood is in sharp contrast with the rest of the poem. The early celebration has been replaced by anguish and an overwhelming sense of failure.

ANALYSIS

Do you think 'Child' is a positive or negative poem? Refer to the text in explaining your response.

Sample Paragraph

Plath's poem, 'Child', is essentially about a mother's inadequacy. The poet wants the best for her innocent son. Although the first half of the poem focuses on her wishes to protect him, this changes at the end. Plath starts off by wanting to fill the boy's life with happy experiences (bright colours and toys) and keep him close to nature. There are numerous references to nature right through the poem and Plath compares her son to an 'April snowdrop'. This tender image gave me a very positive feeling. Everything about the child is wonderful at first. He is 'absolutely beautiful'. This all changes at the end of the poem. The mood turns negative. Plath talks of being confined in a darkened room which has a 'Ceiling without a star'. This is in total contrast with the images early on which were of the bright outdoors. The poet was positive at the start. This has been replaced with negative feelings. The ending is dark and 'troublous' because Plath knows that her child will grow up and experience pain just as she has.

Examiner's Comment

This paragraph addresses the question well and offers a clear response. There is some good personal engagement which effectively illustrates the changing mood from optimism to pessimism and uses apt quotations in support. A mid-grade response. The style of writing is a little note-like and pedestrian. Fresher expression and more development of points would have raised the standard from its present average middle grade.

N.B. Access your ebook for additional sample paragraphs and a list of useful quotes with commentary.

CLASS/HOMEWORK EXERCISES

1. Write a paragraph comparing 'Child' with 'Morning Song'. Refer to theme and style in both poems.

2. 'Plath explores the changing nature of parental love in her poem, 'Child'. How does she reveal her sense of inadequacy in providing for her child? Support your response by reference to the poem.

SUMMARY POINTS

- One of several poems about children, moving from tenderness to anxiety.
- Lullaby, easy flowing movement, images of light and darkness.
- Contrast between love of child and poet's own depression.
- Appropriate style, clear, simple language.
- Juxtaposition of joyful, colourful world of child and dark despair of poet.

LEAVING CERT SAMPLE ESSAY

'Plath's disturbed and anguished poetic voice conveys her startlingly honest insights into life.' To what extent do you agree with this view? Support your answer with reference to both the themes and language use in the poetry of Sylvia Plath on your course.

Marking Scheme Guidelines

Candidates are free to agree and/or disagree with the statement. The key terms ('poetic voice' and 'insights into life') should both be addressed, though not necessarily equally. Reward responses that show clear evidence of personal engagement with the poems. Allow for a wide range of approaches in the answering.

Indicative material:

- Intense expressions of mother-child relationships emphasised by striking imagery.
- Surreal scenes heighten feelings and illustrate penetrating insights into life.
- Introspective moments of fear, trauma and joy conveyed through metaphor/simile.
- Preoccupation with life's darker side shown through sinister/dramatic language.
- Honest explorations of recurring themes of nature, transience, identity, etc.

Sample Essay

(Plath's disturbed voice conveys startlingly honest insight)

1. *Plath's personal poetry often reflects her intense feelings of entrapment, her pre-occupation with old age and fear for the future. Poems such as 'The Times are Tidy', 'Mirror', 'The Arrival of the Bee Box', 'Elm' and 'Child' provide the reader with a searing awareness of the human condition.*

2. *In her criticism of complacent 1950s America, Plath reflects on the death of the spirit of adventure. No longer does a hero ride 'against the lizard'. The poet laments the current lack of honour and courage which existed in the feisty medieval times of knights in armour. She describes today's organised society in her neat rhymes, ('record', 'accord'; 'lizard', 'hazard'). She is disturbed by the unproductive, automated evidence of easy living shown by the sterile images of the 'stuck record' and 'the mayor's rotisserie'. All move but go nowhere. Is this how Plath is feeling, that she is moving in accordance with the expectations of the times but achieving nothing? She is seething at the purposeless circling and lack of opportunities in this over-indulgent era. She sneers at a modern world of plenty with its 'cream an inch thick'. Her voice rips through the social restrictions on individuals, 'Unlucky the hero born/In this province'.*

3. *Plath's anguished voice expresses her unceasing search for identity in the poem 'Mirror'. Here, she adopts the cool critical tone of the mirror, 'the eye of a little god, four-cornered'. Sinister personification portrays the mirror as a being who has an almost claustrophobic relationship with the woman, scrutinising her 'day after day'. It announces that it is 'silver and exact' with 'no preconceptions', 'unmisted by love or dislike'. Yet in the chilling metaphor, 'I am a lake', I sense danger for the woman. She is dissatisfied with the image of herself reflected 'faithfully' in the mirror, standing 'with tears and an agitation of the hands'. This period of America placed enormous pressure on young women to conform to a stereotype of prettiness and to assume the conventional roles of wife, mother and homemaker. Plath shows with scrupulous honesty how there is no escape from this life with its terrible march of time, 'Each morning'. I feel Plath is using the personification of the mirror to show how her society cruelly views women, as worthless once their youth is spent.*

4. *'Elm' also effectively uses this technique of terrifying personification to present the poet's view of the dark side of life of being thrust by its pressures to the edge of insanity. A series of horrific experiences linked with madness is dramatised by the fearful voice of the tree which is also being pushed to its limits, 'Scorched to the root', 'Her radiance scathes me'. Plath explores dark feelings of despair through the confessional lines, 'I am terrified by this dark thing/that sleeps in me'. She expresses it as a malignant growth quietly and ominously increasing inside, 'all day I feel its soft, feathery turnings'. As in 'Mirror', there is a suffocating sense of confinement. Even an event like the birth of her baby is shrouded in shadow when she describes the new parents standing 'round blankly as walls'.*

5. In 'The Times are Tidy', Plath criticised society for its emphasis on control and order, now she herself assumes this role in 'The Arrival of the Bee Box'. She 'ordered this' so now she is in charge of the fate of the bees. She focuses on their confinement through a series of stifling images which mirror her own experience in society. She likens the bees to African slaves, 'the swarmy feeling of African hands ... Black on black, angrily clambering'. The innovative use of the adjective 'swarmy' conveyed to me the sweltering conditions of the bee-box and a slave ship. She evokes the clamour of the trapped bees, 'the unintelligible syllables,/it is like a Roman mob'. Her seeking for perfection is shown by her desperate wish to do what is right for them. She vows 'Tomorrow I will be sweet god, I will set them free'.

6. This feeling of doing right is also explored in 'Child'. Plath wants to give her infant child a sense of the wonder of the world, filling his eye with 'color and ducks'. But she is trapped by the distressing reality of this imperfect world. In a harrowing tone, she paints yet another picture. Of captivity. In a darkened room which has a 'ceiling without a star'. She is tortured by the idea that her child will experience pain. Disappointment in this oppressive world, 'this troublous wringing of hands'.

7. Plath's sensuous voice expresses a view of a brutal world. She struggles with her idealism, her deep desire to do her very best in everything, 'There is a voice within me/That will not be still', and the stressful reality of the human condition. Her poetry shows her escape, she dared to put her thoughts on record and her poems honestly confront the contradictions of life.

(approx. 830 words)

Examiner's Comment

This is a very well-focused and perceptive response which shows close engagement with Plath's poetry. A wide range of accurate quotations are used confidently to support various discussion points and there is some effective cross-reference. Expression is very assured – apart from some note-like comments in Paragraph 6.

MARKING
SCHEME
GRADE: H1
P = 15/15
C = 13/15
L = 13/15
M = 5/5
Total = 46/50

N.B. Access your ebook for additional sample paragraphs and a list of useful quotes with commentary.

SAMPLE LEAVING CERT QUESTIONS ON PLATH'S POETRY

(45–50 MINUTES)

1. 'Sylvia Plath effectively uses language to explore her personal experience of suffering and to reveal occasional moments of the redemptive power of love.' Discuss this statement, supporting your answer with reference to both the themes and language in the poetry of Plath on your course.

2. 'Although Sylvia Plath's poetry deals with intense experiences, her skill with language ensures that she is always in control of her subject matter.' Discuss this view, supporting your points with the aid of suitable reference to the poems by Plath on your course.

3. 'Sylvia Plath's poetry is often characterised by moments of intense introspection and heightened drama.' To what extent do you agree with this statement? Write a response, supporting your points with reference to the poems by Plath that you have studied.

Sample Essay Plan (Q2)

'Although Sylvia Plath's poetry deals with intense experiences, her skill with language ensures that she is always in control of her subject matter.' Discuss this view, supporting your points with the aid of suitable reference to the poems by Plath on your course.

- Intro: Identify the elements to be addressed – Plath's intensely disturbing themes and her innovative use of language.

- Point 1: Inner torment of 'Elm' presented through complex imagery and unsettling symbolism, allowing the reader to appreciate a nightmare world.

- Point 2: Contrast is effectively used in 'Poppies in July'. The speaker's deep yearning to escape is highlighted by the startling imagery of the flowers.

- Point 3: The depression in 'Black Rook in Rainy Weather' is also emphasised by conflicting images from nature and religion.

- Point 4: 'Child' and 'Morning Song' express strong themes about intense relationships through her mastery of language.

- Conclusion: Many poems deal with extreme emotional states, but Plath's poetic technique never lapses.

Sample Essay Plan (Q2)

Develop one of the above points into a paragraph.

Sample Paragraph: Point 2

'Poppies in July' is an intense poem about Plath's desperation to escape from her unhappy world. It begins on a disturbing note. The speaker is troubled by the sight of poppies, which she calls 'little hell flames'. The references to Hell and fire are developed through the rest of the poem, suggesting an extremely disturbed mind. The image of the red flames is both dramatic and terrifying – and typical of Plath's intense poetry. Readers can sense a standoff between the poppies and Plath herself. The flowers almost seem to mock the poet: 'You flicker. I cannot touch you'. Other images in the poem add to our understanding of the poet's deep pain – 'A mouth just bloodied' and 'fumes that I cannot touch'. Plath describes the poppies in a way that reveals her own troubled mental state. She is exhausted, almost beyond despair. We see her control of language when she contrasts the colour of the poppies with her own lifeless mood. We are left with a genuine sense of Plath's anguish. Unlike the blazing red flowers, the poet herself is 'colorless'.

Examiner's Comment

This is an impressive top-grade answer that concentrates on Plath's ability to use language in an inventive and controlled fashion. The contrast between the vivid appearance of the poppies and the poet's own bleak mood is well illustrated. There is also a sense of engagement with the feelings expressed in the poem.

N.B. Access your ebook for additional sample paragraphs and a list of useful quotes with commentary.

SAMPLE LEAVING CERT QUESTIONS ON PLATH'S POETRY

'Her poems have that heart-breaking quality about them.'

Joyce Carol Oates

'Artists are a special breed. They are passionate and temperamental. Their feelings flow into the work they create.'

J. Timothy King

'I am a genius of a writer; I have it in me. I am writing the best poems of my life.'

Sylvia Plath

W. B. YEATS

1865–1939

'I have spread my
dreams under your feet.'

William Butler Yeats was born in Dublin in 1865. The son of a well-known Irish painter, John Butler Yeats, he spent much of his childhood in Co. Sligo. As a young writer, Yeats became involved with the Celtic Revival, a movement against the cultural influences of English rule in Ireland that sought to promote the spirit of our native heritage. His writing drew extensively from Irish mythology and folklore. Another great influence was the Irish revolutionary Maud Gonne, a woman as famous for her passionate nationalist politics as for her beauty. She rejected Yeats, who eventually married another woman, Georgie Hyde Lees. However, Maud Gonne remained a powerful figure in Yeats's writing. Over the years, Yeats became deeply involved in Irish politics and despite independence from England, his work reflected a pessimism about the political situation here. He also had a lifelong interest in mysticism and the occult. Appointed a senator of the Irish Free State in 1922, he is remembered as an important cultural leader, as a major playwright (he was one of the founders of Dublin's Abbey Theatre) and as one of the greatest 20th-century poets. Yeats was awarded the Nobel Prize in 1923 and died in 1939 at the age of seventy-three.

INVESTIGATE FURTHER

To find out more about W. B. Yeats, or to hear readings of his poems, you could search some useful websites, such as YouTube, poetryarchive.org or bbc.co.uk. Also view the additional material available in your ebook.

Prescribed Poems

* The poems marked with an asterisk are also prescribed for the Ordinary Level course.

1 THE LAKE ISLE OF INNISFREE

I will arise and go now, and go to Innisfree,
And a small cabin build there, of clay and wattles made:
Nine bean-rows will I have there, a hive for the honey-bee,
And live alone in the bee-loud glade.

And I shall have some peace there, for peace comes dropping slow,   5
Dropping from the veils of the morning to where the cricket sings;
There midnight's all a glimmer, and noon a purple glow,
And evening full of the linnet's wings.

I will arise and go now, for always night and day
I hear lake water lapping with low sounds by the shore;   10
While I stand on the roadway, or on the pavements grey,
I hear it in the deep heart's core.

'I hear lake water lapping with low sounds by the shore'

Glossary

Innisfree: island of heather.

2 *clay and wattles*: rods and mud were used to build small houses.

7 *midnight's all a glimmer*: stars are shining very brightly in the countryside.

8 *linnet*: songbird.

10 *lapping*: gentle sounds made by water at the edge of a shore.

12 *heart's core*: essential part; the centre of the poet's being.

INITIAL RESPONSE

1. This poem was voted number one in an *Irish Times* poll of the top 100 poems. Why do you think it appeals to so many readers?

2. What does the poem reveal to you about Yeats's own state of mind? Use reference to the text in your response.

3. How does the second stanza describe the rhythm of the passing day? Use quotations to illustrate your response.

STUDY NOTES

'The Lake Isle of Innisfree' was written in 1890. Yeats was in London, looking in a shop window at a little toy fountain. He was feeling very homesick. He said the sound of the 'tinkle of water' reminded him of 'lake water'. He was longing to escape from the grind of everyday life and he wrote an 'old daydream of mine'.

This timeless poem has long been a favourite with exiles everywhere, as it **expresses a longing for a place of deep peace**. The tone in **stanza one** is deliberate, not casual, as the poet announces his decision to go. There are biblical overtones here: 'I will arise and go to my father,' the prodigal son announces. This lends the occasion solemnity. Then the poet describes the idyllic life of self-sufficiency: 'Nine bean-rows' and 'a hive for the honey-bee'. These details give the poem a timeless quality as the poet lives 'alone in the beeloud glade'.

Stanza two describes Innisfree so vividly that the future tense of 'I will arise' gives way to the present: 'There midnight's all a glimmer'. The **repetition** of 'peace' and 'dropping' suits the subject, as it lulls us into this tranquil place to which we all aspire to go at some point in our lives. Beautiful imagery brings us through the day, from the gentle white mists of the morning that lie like carelessly thrown veils over the lake to the blazing purple of the heather under the midday sun. The starry night, which can only be seen in the clear skies of the countryside, is vividly described as 'midnight's all a glimmer', with slender vowel sounds suggesting the sharp light of the stars. The soft 'l', 'm' and 'p' sounds in this stanza create a gentle and magical mood.

The **third stanza** repeats the opening, giving the air of a solemn ritual taking place. The **verbal music** in this stanza is striking, as the broad vowel sounds slow down the line 'I hear lake water lapping with low sounds by the shore', emphasising peace and tranquility. Notice the alliteration of 'l' and the assonance of 'o' all adding to the serene calm of the scene. The only **contemporary detail** in the poem is 'pavements grey', suggesting the relentless concrete of the city. The exile's awareness of what he loves is eloquently expressed as he declares he hears the sound 'in the deep heart's core'. Notice the monosyllabic ending, which drums home how much he longs for this place. Regular end rhyme (*abab*) and the regular four beats in each fourth line reinforce the harmony of this peaceful place.

ANALYSIS

'W. B. Yeats writes dramatic poetry that addresses the human desire for harmony and fulfilment.' Discuss this statement with reference to 'The Lake Isle of Innisfree'.

Sample Paragraph

The poem that is most associated with Yeats's heart's desire, 'The Lake Isle of Innisfree', depicts a tranquil refuge from the stress of modern living, 'And I shall have some peace there'. A dramatic opening statement, 'I will arise and go now, and go to Innisfree', declares his intention in a tone heightened by the repetition of the single syllable verb. In this idyllic place, time stands still. The steady end-rhyme ('Innisfree', 'honeybee') and long broad vowel sounds ('alone in the bee-loud glade') conjure up an alluring vision of tranquillity. A change of tense from the future to the present ('I will', 'peace comes') brings both the reader and poet to this wonderful paradise. The intensely hypnotic description weaves its magic, suggesting quietness and security. The use of slender vowel sounds mimics the dance of the moonlight on the dark lake, 'There midnight's all a glimmer'. The verbal music of alliteration and assonance ('I hear lake water lapping with low sounds by the shore') enables us to experience this perfectly calm atmosphere, even though Yeats is still stranded 'on the roadway, or on the pavement grey'. The poet's dream is a universal one, simply because we all long for peace. In the end, Yeats succeeds in implanting this vision 'in the deep heart's core'. The powerful monosyllabic four beats strike out the achievement of the poet's opening wish.

Examiner's Comment

This is a focused top-grade response that addresses the question effectively and shows good engagement with the poem. Ideas are considered closely, clearly expressed and aptly supported by accurate quotes. The sustained focus on sound effects is particularly impressive. Language use throughout is well controlled, with phrases such as 'intensely hypnotic' conveying the poet's dramatic style.

N.B. Access your ebook for additional sample paragraphs and a list of useful quotes with commentary.

CLASS/HOMEWORK EXERCISES

1. 'Yeats is a perceptive and subtle poet, both in terms of his universal themes and lyrical style'. Discuss this view with reference to 'The Lake Isle of Innisfree'.

2. 'Yeats's poems are often defined by a tension between the real world in which the poet lives and an ideal world that he imagines.' Discuss this view with reference to 'The Lake Isle of Innisfree'.

SUMMARY POINTS

- Poetic vision of longing and desire for utopian escape.
- Formal opening and repetition give the sense of a solemn ritual.
- Romantic details and sensual images place the poem out of time while concrete description produces a realistic experience for readers.
- Verbal music (assonance, alliteration, onomatopoeia) heighten the reader's involvement.
- Traditional rhyming structure and the steady beats of the concluding line of each quatrain add a sense of stability and security.

2 SEPTEMBER 1913

What need you, being come to sense,
But fumble in a greasy till
And add the halfpence to the pence
And prayer to shivering prayer, until
You have dried the marrow from the bone?   5
For men were born to pray and save:
Romantic Ireland's dead and gone,
It's with O'Leary in the grave.

Yet they were of a different kind,
The names that stilled your childish play,   10
They have gone about the world like wind,
But little time had they to pray
For whom the hangman's rope was spun,
And what, God help us, could they save?
Romantic Ireland's dead and gone,   15
It's with O'Leary in the grave.

Was it for this the wild geese spread
The grey wing upon every tide;
For this that all that blood was shed,
For this Edward Fitzgerald died,   20
And Robert Emmet and Wolfe Tone,
All that delirium of the brave?
Romantic Ireland's dead and gone,
It's with O'Leary in the grave.

Yet could we turn the years again,   25
And call those exiles as they were
In all their loneliness and pain,
You'd cry, 'Some woman's yellow hair
Has maddened every mother's son':
They weighed so lightly what they gave.   30
But let them be, they're dead and gone,
They're with O'Leary in the grave.

'Romantic Ireland's dead and gone'

Glossary

1   *you*: merchants and business people.
8   *O'Leary*: John O'Leary, Fenian leader, one of Yeats's heroes.
9   *they*: the selfless Irish patriots.
17 *the wild geese*: Irish Independence soldiers forced into exile in Europe after 1690.

20 *Edward Fitzgerald*: 18th-century Irish aristocrat and revolutionary.
21 *Robert Emmet and Wolfe Tone*: Irish rebel leaders. Emmet was hanged in 1803. Tone committed suicide in prison after being sentenced to death in 1798.

INITIAL RESPONSE

1. Comment on the effectiveness of the images used in the first five lines of the poem.

2. How would you describe the tone of this poem? Is it bitter, sad, ironic, angry, etc.? Refer closely to the text in your answer.

3. Were the patriots named in the poem heroes or fools? Write a paragraph in response to Yeats's views.

STUDY NOTES

'September 1913' is typical of Yeats's hard-hitting political poems. Both the content and tone are harsh as the poet airs his views on public issues, contrasting the idealism of Ireland's heroic past with the uncultured present.

Yeats had been a great supporter of Sir Hugh Lane, who had offered his extensive art collection to the city of Dublin, provided the paintings would be on show in a suitable gallery. When the authorities failed to arrange this, Lane withdrew his offer. The controversy infuriated Yeats, who criticised Dublin Corporation for being miserly and anti-cultural. For him, it represented **a new low in the country's drift into vulgarity and crass commercialism**. The year 1913 was also a year of great hardship, partly because of a general strike and lock-out of workers. Poverty and deprivation were widespread at the time, particularly in Dublin's tenements.

The **first stanza** begins with a derisive **attack on a materialistic society** that Yeats sees as being both greedy and hypocritical. Ireland's middle classes are preoccupied with making money and slavish religious devotion. The rhetorical opening is sharply sarcastic, as the poet depicts the petty, penny-pinching shopkeepers who 'fumble in a greasy till'. Yeats's tone is as angry as it is ironic: 'For men were born to pray and save'. Images of the dried bone and 'shivering prayer' are equally forceful – the poor are exploited by ruthless employers and a domineering Church. This disturbing picture leads the poet to regret the loss of 'Romantic Ireland' in the concluding refrain.

Stanza two develops the contrast between past and present as Yeats considers the **heroism and generosity of an earlier era**. Ireland's patriots – 'names that stilled' earlier generations of children – could hardly have been more unlike the present middle class. Yeats clearly relates to the self-sacrifice of idealistic Irish freedom fighters: 'And what, God help us, could they save?' These disdainful words echo the fearful prayers referred to at the start of the poem. The heroes of the past were so selfless that they did not even concern themselves with saving their own lives.

The wistful and nostalgic tone of **stanza three** is obvious in the rhetorical question about all those Irish soldiers who had been exiled in the late 17th century. Yeats's high regard for these men is evoked by comparing them to 'wild geese', a plaintive metaphor reflecting their nobility. Yet the poet's admiration for past idealism is diminished by the fact that **such heroic dedication was all for nothing**. The repetition of 'for this' hammers home Yeats's contempt for the pious materialists of his own imperfect age. In listing a roll of honour, he singles out the most impressive patriots of his own class, the Anglo-Irish Ascendancy. For the poet, Fitzgerald, Emmet and Tone are among the most admirable Irishmen. In using the phrase 'All that delirium of the brave', Yeats suggests that their passionate dedication to Irish freedom bordered on a frenzied or misplaced sense of daring.

This romanticised appreciation continues into the **final stanza**, where the poet imagines the 'loneliness and pain' of the heroic dead. His empathy towards them is underpinned by an **even more vicious portrayal of the new middle class**. He argues that the establishment figures of his own time would be unable to comprehend anything about the values and dreams of 'Romantic Ireland'. At best, they would be confused by the ludicrous self-sacrifice of the past. At worst, the present generation would accuse the patriots of being insane or of trying to impress friends or lovers. Perhaps Yeats is illustrating the cynical thinking of his time, when many politicians courted national popularity. 'Some woman's yellow hair' might well refer to the traditional symbol of Ireland as a beautiful woman.

The poet's disgust on behalf of the patriots is rounded off in the last two lines: 'But let them be, they're dead and gone'. The refrain has been changed slightly, adding further emphasis and a **sense of finality**. After reading this savage satire, we are left with a deep sense of Yeats's bitter disillusionment towards his contemporaries. The extreme feelings expressed in the poem offer a dispirited vision of an unworthy country. It isn't surprising that some critics have accused Yeats of over-romanticising the heroism of Ireland's past, of being narrow minded and even elitist. At any rate, the poem challenges us to examine the values of the state we are in, our understanding of Irish history and the meaning of heroism.

ANALYSIS

'W. B. Yeats often makes uses of contrasting images of self-interest and selflessness to communicate powerful feelings.' Discuss this statement in relation to 'September 1913'.

Sample Paragraph

Contrast plays a central role in 'September 1913'. The poem's angry opening lines are aimed at the greedy merchants and landlords who 'fumble in a greasy till'. Their mean-spirited behaviour is reflected by such vivid, concrete imagery. These materialistic individuals exploit ordinary people and could not be more unlike the Irish patriots who were prepared to die for the freedom of others – 'names that stilled your childish play'. This startling image stops us in our tracks. We can imagine how children used to hold men like Wolfe Tone and Robert Emmet in such great respect. Yeats also uses the beautiful image of the wild geese spreading 'the grey wing upon every tide' to describe the dignified flight of Irish soldiers who refused to accept colonial rule. The poet's simple imagery is taken from the world of nature and has a vibrant quality that makes us aware of Yeats's high opinion of those heroes who would willingly give up everything for their ideals. The poet's strength of feeling is evident in his graphically violent description of the materialistic society of his own time – and especially those who have 'dried the marrow from the bone'. Stark contrasts carry the argument throughout the poem and leave a deep impression on readers.

Examiner's Comment

Well focused on how the poet's imagery patterns convey deeply felt views. This top-grade response is also effectively supported by suitable reference and accurate quotation. Informed discussion covers a range of contrasting images (such as greed, natural beauty and violence). There is evidence throughout of close interaction with the poem. Expression is controlled, and the paragraph is rounded off with a succinct concluding sentence.

N.B. Access your ebook for additional sample paragraphs and a list of useful quotes with commentary.

CLASS/HOMEWORK EXERCISES

1. 'W. B. Yeats manages to create a series of powerfully compelling moods throughout "September 1913".' Discuss this statement with reference to both the subject matter and style of the poem.

2. 'Yeats frequently addresses political themes in poems that are filled with tension and drama.' Discuss this view with reference to 'September 1913'.

SUMMARY POINTS

- Central contrast between the materialistic present and the romanticised past.
- The heroic patriots were idealistic, unlike the self-serving middle classes of 1913.
- Various tones – disillusionment, irony, admiration, resignation.
- Effective use of repetition, vivid imagery, colloquial language.
- Refrain emphasises Yeats's deep sense of disenchantment with Ireland's cynical establishment.

③ THE WILD SWANS AT COOLE

The trees are in their autumn beauty,
The woodland paths are dry,
Under the October twilight the water
Mirrors a still sky;
Upon the brimming water among the stones   5
Are nine-and-fifty swans.

The nineteenth autumn has come upon me
Since I first made my count;
I saw, before I had well finished,
All suddenly mount   10
And scatter wheeling in great broken rings
Upon their clamorous wings.

I have looked upon those brilliant creatures,
And now my heart is sore.
All's changed since I, hearing at twilight,   15
The first time on this shore,
The bell-beat of their wings above my head,
Trod with a lighter tread.

Unwearied still, lover by lover,
They paddle in the cold   20
Companionable streams or climb the air;
Their hearts have not grown old;
Passion or conquest, wander where they will,
Attend upon them still.

But now they drift on the still water,   25
Mysterious, beautiful;
Among what rushes will they build,
By what lake's edge or pool
Delight men's eyes when I awake some day
To find they have flown away?   30

'The bell-beat of their wings above my head'

Glossary

5	*brimming*: filled to the very top or edge.
12	*clamorous*: loud, confused noise.
18	*Trod ... tread*: walked lightly; carefree.

19	*lover by lover*: swans mate for life; this highlights Yeats's loneliness.
21	*Companionable*: friendly.
24	*Attend upon them still*: waits on them yet.

INITIAL RESPONSE

1. Why do you think the poet chose the season of autumn as his setting? What changes occur at this time of year? Where are these referred to in the poem?

2. In your opinion, what are the main contrasts between the swans and the poet? Describe two, using close reference to the text.

3. What do you think the final stanza means? Consider the phrase 'I awake'. What does the poet awake from?

STUDY NOTES

'The Wild Swans at Coole' was written in 1916. Yeats loved spending time in the West, especially at Coole, the home of Lady Gregory, his friend and patron. He was fifty-one when he wrote this poem, which contrasts the swans' beauty and apparent seeming immortality with Yeats's ageing, mortal self.

The poem opens with a tranquil, serene scene of **autumnal beauty** in the park of Lady Gregory's home in Galway. This romantic image is described in great detail: the 'woodland paths are dry'. It is evening, 'October twilight'. The water is 'brimming'. The swans are carefully counted, 'nine-and-fifty'. The use of the soft letters 'l', 'm' and 's' emphasise the calm of the scene in **stanza one**.

In **stanza two**, the poem moves to the personal as he recalls that it is nineteen years since he first counted the swans. The word 'count' links the two stanzas. The poet's counting is interrupted as these mysterious creatures all suddenly rise into the sky. Run-through lines suggest the flowing movement of the rising swans.

Strong verbs ('mount', 'scatter') reinforce this elemental action. The great beating wings of the swans are captured in the onomatopoeic 'clamorous wings'. They are independent and refuse to be restrained. The ring is a symbol of eternity. The swans are making the same patterns as they have always made; they are unchanging. **Stanza two** is linked to **stanza three** by the phrases 'I saw' and 'I have looked'. Now the poet tells us his 'heart is sore'. He has taken stock and is **dissatisfied with his**

emotional situation. He is fifty-one, alone and unmarried and concerned that his poetic powers are lessening: '**All's changed**'. All humans want things to remain as they are, but life is full of change. He has lost the great love of his life, the beautiful Irish activist, Maud Gonne. He also laments the loss of his youth, when he 'Trod with a lighter tread'. Nineteen years earlier, he was much more carefree. The noise of the beating wings of the swans is effectively captured in the compound word 'bell-beat'. The alliterative 'b' reinforces the steady, flapping sound. The poet is using his intense personal experiences to express universal truths.

The swans in **stanza four** are **symbols of eternity**, ageless, 'Unwearied still'. They are united, 'lover by lover'. They experience life together ('Companionable streams'), not on their own, like the poet. He envies them their defiance of time: 'Their hearts have not grown old'. They do what they want, when they want. They are full of 'Passion or conquest'. By contrast, he is indirectly telling us, he feels old and worn out. The **spiral imagery** of the 'great broken rings' is reminiscent of the spirals seen in ancient carvings representing eternity. Yeats believed there was a cyclical pattern behind all things. The swans can live in two elements, water and air, thus linking these elements together. They are living, vital, immortal, unlike their surroundings. The trees are yellowing ('autumn beauty') and the dry 'woodland paths' suggest the lack of creative force which the poet is experiencing. Yeats is heartbroken and weary. Only the swans transcend time.

Stanza five explores a **philosophy of life**, linked to the previous stanza by the repetition of 'still'. The swans have returned to the water, 'Mysterious, beautiful'. The poem ends on a speculative note as the poet asks where they will 'Delight men's eyes'. Is he referring to the fact that **they will continue to be a source of pleasure to someone else** long after he is dead? The swans appear immortal, a continuing source of happiness as they practise their patterns, whereas the poet is not able to continue improving his own writing, as he is mortal. The poet is slipping into the cruel season of winter while the swans infinitely 'drift on the still water'.

ANALYSIS

'W. B. Yeats makes effective use of rich, dramatic symbols to address themes of transience and mortality.' Discuss this view with reference to 'The Wild Swans at Coole'.

Sample Paragraph

Two contrasting symbols are used by Yeats in 'The Wild Swans at Coole'. The swans represent youthful vigour and passion while autumn symbolises the mysterious sadness and decay of ageing. Through his imaginative symbolism, Yeats is presenting the view that life, in all its wonder, is fragile. The swans epitomise the simple, unchanging world of nature where renewal is possible. They are 'Wild', free, undomesticated, as seen in the verbs and adjectives associated with them, 'mount', 'scatter', 'clamorous'. The poet's frank confession, 'And now my heart is sore', engages the reader in accepting the profound truth that humanity cannot conquer time. Assonance ('now', 'sore') adds a note of melancholy to this stark acceptance. Unlike the poet, the strong, elegant swans 'drift on the still water,/ Mysterious, beautiful', but they are not subject to time's destructive powers. Yeats is connected to the decay of autumn, 'October twilight' where 'The woodland paths are dry', all of which signify advancing age. In considering these symbols, Yeats is led to ask a penetrating question about the transience of beauty and the failing of creative energy, 'when I awake some day/To find they have flown away?' I particularly liked the poignant final rhyme which trails off faintly into the distance – just like the 'brilliant creatures'.

Examiner's Comment

A perceptive high-grade response to the question. Informed discussion based on the poet's awareness of key symbols (the swans and the natural world). Effective supporting reference and accurate quotations throughout. Expression is also very good ('accepting the profound truth', 'penetrating question') and the paragraph is rounded off with an impressive personal comment.

N.B. Access your ebook for additional sample paragraphs and a list of useful quotes with commentary.

CLASS/HOMEWORK EXERCISES

1. 'W. B. Yeats frequently uses personal aspects of his own life to evocatively explore universal truths.' Discuss this view with reference to 'The Wild Swans at Coole'.

2. 'Yeats often draws on the beauty and stillness of the natural world to convey a deep sense of loss.' Discuss this statement with reference to 'The Wild Swans at Coole'.

SUMMARY POINTS

- Intense personal meditation on the search for lasting beauty in a transient world.
- Sad tone reflects concerns about ageing, romantic rejection, political upheaval, fading creativity.
- Slow rhythm conveys the poet's meditative mood.
- Vivid visual descriptive details portray places and creatures.
- Dynamic verbs, compound words and onomatopoeia capture the energy of the swans.
- Use of contrast highlights the gap between mortality and eternity.
- Poem ends on an optimistic note.

④ AN IRISH AIRMAN FORESEES HIS DEATH

I know that I shall meet my fate
Somewhere among the clouds above;
Those that I fight I do not hate,
Those that I guard I do not love;
My country is Kiltartan Cross,   5
My countrymen Kiltartan's poor,
No likely end could bring them loss
Or leave them happier than before.
Nor law, nor duty bade me fight,
Nor public men, nor cheering crowds,   10
A lonely impulse of delight
Drove to this tumult in the clouds;
I balanced all, brought all to mind,
The years to come seemed waste of breath,
A waste of breath the years behind   15
In balance with this life, this death.

'I balanced all'

Glossary

The Irish airman in this poem is Major Robert Gregory (1881–1918), son of Yeats's close friend, Lady Gregory. He was shot down and killed while on service in northern Italy.

3   *Those that I fight*: the Germans.

4   *Those that I guard*: Allied countries, such as England and France.

5   *Kiltartan*: townland near the Gregory estate in Co. Galway.

7   *likely end*: outcome.

12   *tumult*: turmoil; confusion.

INITIAL RESPONSE

1. 'This poem is not just an elegy or lament in memory of the dead airman. It is also an insight into the excitement and exhilaration of warfare.' Write your response to this statement, using close reference to the text.

2. Write a paragraph on Yeats's use of repetition throughout the poem. Refer to the text in your answer.

3. In your opinion, what is the central or dominant mood in the poem? Refer to the text in your answer.

STUDY NOTES

Thousands of Irishmen fought and died in the British armed forces during the First World War. Robert Gregory was killed in Italy at the age of thirty-seven. The airman's death had a lasting effect on Yeats, who wrote several poems about him.

Is it right to assume anything about young men who fight for their countries? Why do they enlist? Do they always know what they are fighting for? In this poem, Yeats expresses what he believes is the airman's viewpoint as he comes face to face with death. This **fatalistic attitude** is prevalent in the emphatic **opening line**. The poem's title also leads us to believe that the speaker has an intuitive sense that his death is about to happen. But despite this premonition, he seems strangely resigned to risking his life.

In **lines 3-4**, he makes it clear that he neither hates his German enemies nor loves the British and their allies. His thoughts are with the people he knows best back in Kiltartan, Co. Galway. Major Gregory recognises the irony of their detachment from the war. The ordinary people of his homeland are unlikely to be affected at all by whatever happens on the killing fields of mainland Europe. Does he feel that he is abandoning his fellow countrymen? What is the dominant tone of **lines 7-8**? Is there an underlying bitterness?

In **line 9**, the speaker takes time to reflect on why he joined the air force and immediately dismisses the obvious reasons of conscription ('law') or patriotism ('duty'). As a volunteer, Gregory is more openly cynical of the 'public men' and 'cheering crowds' he mentions in **line 10**. Like many in the military who have experienced the realities of warfare, **he is suspicious of hollow patriotism** and has no time for political leaders and popular adulation. So why did Robert Gregory choose to endanger his life by going to war? The answer lies in the key comments 'A lonely impulse of delight' (**line 11**) and 'I balanced all' (**line 13**). The first phrase is paradoxical. The airman experiences not just the excitement, but also the isolation of flying. At the same time, his 'impulse' to enlist as a fighter pilot reflects both his **desire for adventure** as well as his regret.

The **last four lines** explain the real reason behind his decision. It was neither rash nor emotional, but simply a question of balance. Having examined his life closely, Gregory has chosen the heroism of a self-sacrificing death. It is as though he only feels truly alive during the 'tumult' of battle. Yeats's language is particularly evocative at this point. Awesome air battles are effectively echoed in such dynamic phrasing as 'impulse of delight' and 'tumult in the clouds'. This **sense of freedom and power** is repeatedly contrasted with the dreary and predictable security of life away from the war – dismissed out of hand as a 'waste of breath'. From the airman's perspective, as a man of action, dying in battle is in keeping with 'this life' that he has chosen. Such a death would be his final adventurous exploit.

Some commentators have criticised Yeats's poem for glorifying war and pointless risk-taking. Others have suggested that the poet successfully highlights Anglo-Irish attitudes, neither exclusively Irish nor English. The poet certainly raises interesting questions about national identity and ways of thinking about war. However, in elegising Robert Gregory, he emphasises the **airman's daring solitude**. Perhaps this same thrill lies at the heart of other important choices in life, including the creative activity of artists. Is there a sense that the poet and the pilot are alike, both of them taking calculated risks in what they do?

ANALYSIS

'Some of Yeats's most poignant poems have a tragic vision, a sense that life is meaningless and has to be endured.' Discuss this view, with particular reference to 'An Irish Airman Foresees his Death'.

Sample Paragraph

The title itself obviously introduces the idea of warfare and death. However, the 'Irish Airman' in this touching poem is courageous in the face of danger. Although the word 'fate' suggests an inevitable destiny, the poem is dominated by a strong mood of resignation. The calm tone – 'I know that I shall meet my fate' – and slow repetitive rhythm is like a chant or a prayer. While the pilot is realistic about his chances in war, he seems to have distanced himself from everything and everyone. I believe that he simply accepts the reality of war and is prepared for anything. He also admits the truth about his passion for adventure – 'A lonely impulse of delight' – and this might well signify that he views life as something beyond his control. The poem's ending is certainly pessimistic, and he repeats the phrase 'waste of breath' to emphasise the sheer absurdity of life. Overall, the speaker in the poem is caught between realism and pessimism. The subtle concluding line sums this up perfectly – 'In balance with this life, this death' – and leaves me with a powerful sense of his tragic dilemma.

Examiner's Comment

An insightful, focused response to the question. Perceptive discussion engages with the airman's fatalistic attitude. Apt, accurate quotations are integrated effectively into the commentary. Expression is well controlled and vocabulary is also impressive ('inevitable destiny', 'sheer absurdity of life', 'subtle concluding line'). A solid, high-grade standard.

N.B. Access your ebook for additional sample paragraphs and a list of useful quotes with commentary.

CLASS/HOMEWORK EXERCISES

1. 'W. B. Yeats's evocative poems can raise interesting questions about national identity.' Discuss this statement with reference to 'An Irish Airman Foresees his Death'.

2. 'Yeats's poetry often explores fatalistic themes with tragic acceptance.' Discuss this view with reference to 'An Irish Airman Foresees his Death'.

SUMMARY POINTS

- Yeats adopts the persona of Major Robert Gregory who died in 1918.
- Dramatic monologue form engages the sympathy of readers.
- Contrasting attitudes and tones: passion, detachment, resignation, courage, joy, loneliness.
- Effective use of repetition, rhyme and contrast.

5 EASTER 1916

I have met them at close of day
Coming with vivid faces
From counter or desk among grey
Eighteenth-century houses.
I have passed with a nod of the head   5
Or polite meaningless words,
Or have lingered awhile and said
Polite meaningless words,
And thought before I had done
Of a mocking tale or a gibe   10
To please a companion
Around the fire at the club,
Being certain that they and I
But lived where motley is worn:
All changed, changed utterly: 15
A terrible beauty is born.

That woman's days were spent
In ignorant good-will,
Her nights in argument
Until her voice grew shrill.   20
What voice more sweet than hers
When, young and beautiful,
She rode to harriers?
This man had kept a school
And rode our wingèd horse;   25
This other his helper and friend
Was coming into his force;
He might have won fame in the end,
So sensitive his nature seemed,
So daring and sweet his thought.   30
This other man I had dreamed
A drunken, vainglorious lout.
He had done most bitter wrong
To some who are near my heart,
Yet I number him in the song;   35
He, too, has resigned his part
In the casual comedy;

He, too, has been changed in his turn,
Transformed utterly:
A terrible beauty is born.   40

Hearts with one purpose alone
Through summer and winter seem
Enchanted to a stone
To trouble the living stream.
The horse that comes from the road,   45
The rider, the birds that range
From cloud to tumbling cloud,
Minute by minute they change;
A shadow of cloud on the stream
Changes minute by minute;   50
A horse-hoof slides on the brim,
And a horse plashes within it;
The long-legged moor-hens dive,
And hens to moor-cocks call;
Minute by minute they live: 55
The stone's in the midst of all.

Too long a sacrifice
Can make a stone of the heart.
O when may it suffice?
That is Heaven's part, our part   60
To murmur name upon name,
As a mother names her child
When sleep at last has come
On limbs that had run wild.
What is it but nightfall?   65
No, no, not night but death;
Was it needless death after all?
For England may keep faith
For all that is done and said.
We know their dream; enough   70
To know they dreamed and are dead;
And what if excess of love
Bewildered them till they died?
I write it out in a verse –
MacDonagh and MacBride   75

And Connolly and Pearse
Now and in time to be,
Wherever green is worn,
Are changed, changed utterly:
A terrible beauty is born.   80

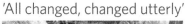

'All changed, changed utterly'

Glossary

Title: On 24 April 1916, Easter Monday, about 700 Irish Republicans took over several key buildings in Dublin. These included the Four Courts, Bolands Mills, the Royal College of Surgeons and the General Post Office. The rebellion lasted six days and was followed by the execution of its leaders. The Rising was a pivotal event in modern Irish history.

1   *them*: the rebels involved in the Rising.

14   *motley*: ridiculous clothing.

17   *That woman*: Countess Markiewicz, friend of Yeats and a committed nationalist.

24   *This man*: Padraig Pearse, poet and teacher, was shot as a leader of the Rising.

25   *wingèd horse*: Pegasus, the mythical white horse that flies across the sky, was a symbol of poetic inspiration.

26   *This other*: Thomas MacDonagh, writer and teacher, executed in 1916.

31   *This other man*: Major John MacBride was also executed for his part in the rebellion. He was the husband of Maud Gonne.

33   *most bitter wrong*: there were recurring rumours that MacBride had mistreated Maud Gonne.

67   *needless death*: Yeats asks if the Rising was a waste of life, since the British were already considering independence for Ireland.

76   *Connolly*: Trade union leader and revolutionary, executed in 1916.

INITIAL RESPONSE

1. Describe the atmosphere in the opening stanza of the poem. Refer closely to the text in your answer.

2. 'Easter 1916' has many striking images. Choose two that you find particularly interesting and briefly explain their effectiveness.

3. On balance, does Yeats approve or disapprove of the Easter Rising? Refer to the text in your answer.

STUDY NOTES

Yeats, who was in London at the time of the Rising, had mixed feelings about what had happened. He was clearly fascinated but also troubled by this heroic and yet in some ways pointless sacrifice. He did not publish the poem until 1920.

In the **opening stanza**, Yeats recalls how he used to meet some of the people who were later involved in the Easter Rising. He was unimpressed by their 'vivid faces' and he remembers routinely dismissing them with 'Polite meaningless words'. His admission that he **misjudged these insignificant Republicans** as subjects for 'a mocking tale or a gibe' among his clever friends is a reminder of his derisive attitude in 'September 1913'. Before 1916, Yeats had considered Ireland a ridiculous place, a circus 'where motley is worn'. But the poet confesses that the Rising transformed everything – including his own condescending apathy. In the stanza's final lines, Yeats introduces what becomes an ambivalent refrain ending in 'A terrible beauty is born'.

This sense of shock and the need to completely re-evaluate his views is developed in **stanza two**. The poet singles out individual martyrs killed or imprisoned for their activities, among them his close friend Countess Markiewicz. He also mentions Major John MacBride, husband of Maud Gonne, who had refused Yeats's proposal of marriage. Although he had always considered MacBride as little more than a 'drunken, vainglorious lout', Yeats now acknowledges that he too has been distinguished by his bravery and heroism. The poet wonders about the usefulness of all the passion that sparked the rebels to make such a bold move, but his emphasis is on the fact that **the people as well as the whole atmosphere have changed**. Even MacBride, whom he held in utter contempt, has grown in stature.

In **stanza three**, Yeats takes powerful images from nature and uses them to explore the meaning of Irish heroism. The metaphor of the stubborn stone in the stream might represent the defiance of the revolutionaries towards all the forces around them. **The poet evokes the constant energy and dynamism of the natural world**, focusing on the changes that happen 'minute by minute'. Image after dazzling image conjures up a vivid picture of unpredictable movement and seasonal regeneration (as 'hens to moor-cocks call') and skies change 'From cloud to tumbling cloud'.

For the poet, the Rising presented many contradictions, as he weighs the success of the revolt against the shocking costs. In contrasting the inflexibility of the revolutionaries with the 'living stream', he **indicates a reluctant admiration for the rebels' dedication**. Does Yeats suggest that the rebels risked the loss of their own humanity, allowing their hearts to harden to stone? Or is he also thinking of Maud Gonne and blaming her cold-hearted rejection of him on her fanatical political views?

In the **final stanza**, the poet returns to the metaphor of the unmoving stone in a flowing stream to warn of the dangers of fanaticism. The rhetorical questions about the significance of the rebellion reveal his **continuing struggle to understand** what happened. Then he asks the single most important question about the Rising: 'Was it needless death after all', particularly as 'England may keep faith' and allow Ireland its independence, all of which would prompt a more disturbing conclusion, i.e. that the insurgents died in vain.

Yeats quickly abandons essentially unanswerable questions about the value of the Irish struggle for freedom. Instead, he simply pays tribute to the fallen patriots by naming them tenderly, 'As a mother names her child'. The final assertive lines commemorate the 1916 leaders in dramatic style. Setting aside his earlier ambivalence, Yeats acknowledges that these patriots died for their dreams. The hushed tone is reverential, almost sacred. The rebels have been transformed into martyrs who will be remembered for their selfless heroism 'Wherever green is worn'. The insistent final refrain has a stirring and increasingly disquieting quality. The poem's central paradox, 'A terrible beauty is born', concludes that **all the heroic achievements of the 1916 Rising were at the tragic expense of human life**.

ANALYSIS

'W. B. Yeats's public poetry responds to particular situations in ambivalent contradictory terms.' Discuss this view with reference to both the subject matter and style of 'Easter 1916'.

Sample Paragraph

Yeats seems to have written 'Easter 1916' out of a quarrel with himself. He admired, yet was troubled by the 1916 Rising. He places himself centre stage in the opening anecdote, 'I have met them'. The formal rhyme scheme is dignified and the insistent drumbeat of the resonating refrain, 'All changed, changed utterly', adds a solemn funereal note. Yet Yeats also honestly debates the wisdom of the uprising, asking 'Was it needless death after all?' The potent image of the heart as a stone reflects the poet's own torn emotions because it not only suggests the fierce determination of those rebels involved, but also underlines the inflexibility of their narrow-minded thinking. The poem concludes with a list of the fallen rebel leaders and the grim realisation that the implacable stone in the midst of the 'living stream' does change the flow. These famous Irish names had changed history by their deeds – and also Yeats's opinion of them. They no longer wore the 'motley' of the clown but the 'green' of their country. The paradoxical statement, 'A terrible beauty is born', reflects the poet's romantic admiration of the rebels' sacrifice and also his shocked reaction to the bloody events they unleashed.

Examiner's Comment

A focused, top-grade response that addresses the question directly. The commentary throughout shows a very good understanding of Yeats's divided views. Points are aptly supported with accurate quotation. Some perceptive discussion regarding the poet's use of the stone symbol to illustrate his appreciation of how the 1916 Rising had changed Irish history. Expression ('resonating', 'inflexibility', 'implacable') is also impressive.

N.B. Access your ebook for additional sample paragraphs and a list of useful quotes with commentary.

CLASS/HOMEWORK EXERCISES

1. 'W. B. Yeats explores complex political themes in richly energetic language.' Discuss this statement with reference to 'Easter 1916'.

2. 'Yeats honestly reflects on change and immortality in his dynamic, lyrical poetry.' Discuss this view with reference to 'Easter 1916'.

SUMMARY POINTS

- Deeply felt elegy commemorating a controversial historical event.
- Effective contrast of formal structure with colloquial language.
- Ambivalent attitudes of admiration and shock.
- Formal rhyme scheme, rhythmic phrases, economy of language.
- Symbolism, repetition, antithesis and paradox all convey the poet's contradictory views.
- Thrilling refrain resonates with the consequence of change.

6 THE SECOND COMING

Turning and turning in the widening gyre
The falcon cannot hear the falconer;
Things fall apart; the centre cannot hold;
Mere anarchy is loosed upon the world,
The blood-dimmed tide is loosed, and everywhere   5
The ceremony of innocence is drowned;
The best lack all conviction, while the worst
Are full of passionate intensity.

Surely some revelation is at hand;
Surely the Second Coming is at hand.   10
The Second Coming! Hardly are those words out
When a vast image out of *Spiritus Mundi*
Troubles my sight: somewhere in sands of the desert
A shape with lion body and the head of a man,
A gaze blank and pitiless as the sun,   15
Is moving its slow thighs, while all about it
Reel shadows of the indignant desert birds.
The darkness drops again; but now I know
That twenty centuries of stony sleep
Were vexed to nightmare by a rocking cradle,   20
And what rough beast, its hour come round at last,
Slouches towards Bethlehem to be born?

'somewhere in sands of the desert/A shape with lion body and the head of a man'

Glossary

The Second Coming: This is a reference to the Bible. It is from Matthew and speaks of Christ's return to reward the good.

1 **in the widening gyre**: Yeats regarded a cycle of history as a gyre. He visualised these cycles as interconnecting cones that moved in a circular motion, widening outwards until they could not widen any further, then a new gyre or cone formed from the centre of the circle created. This spun in the opposite direction to the original cone. The Christian era was coming to a close and a new, disturbed time was coming into view. In summary, the gyre is a symbol of constant change.

2 **falcon**: a bird of prey, trained to hunt by the aristocracy.

2 **falconer**: the trainer of the falcon. If the bird flies too far away, it cannot be directed.

4 **Mere**: nothing more than; just; only.

4 **anarchy**: lack of government or order. Yeats believed that bloodshed and a worship of bloodshed were the end of an historical era.

5 **blood-dimmed**: made dark with blood.

12 **Spiritus Mundi**: Spirit of the World, the collective soul of the world.

14 **lion body and the head of a man**: famous statue in Egypt; an enigmatic person.

17 **desert birds**: birds of prey.

19 **twenty centuries**: Yeats believed that two thousand years was the length of a period in history.

20 **vexed**: annoyed; distressed.

20 **rocking cradle**: coming of the infant Jesus.

21 **rough beast**: the Anti-Christ.

22 **Bethlehem**: birthplace of Christ. It is usually associated with peace and innocence, and it is terrifying that the beast is going to be born there. The spiral has reversed its spinning. A savage god is coming.

INITIAL RESPONSE

1. This poem suggests that politics are not important. Does the poet convince you? Write a paragraph in response, with reference to the text.

2. Yeats uses symbols to express some of his most profound ideas. What symbols in this poem appeal to you? Use reference to the text in your response.

3. 'Yeats is yearning for order, and fearing anarchy.' Discuss two ways in which the poem illustrates this statement. Support your answer with reference to the text.

STUDY NOTES

'The Second Coming' is a terrifying, apocalyptic poem written in January 1919 against a background of the disintegration of three great European empires at the end of the First World War and against the catastrophic War of Independence in Ireland. These were bloody times. Yeats yearned for order and feared anarchy.

Sparked off by both disgust at what was happening in Europe as well as his interest in the occult, Yeats explores, in **stanza one**, what he perceives to be the failure at the heart of society: 'Things fall apart'. In his opinion, **the whole world was disintegrating** into a bloody, chaotic mess. This break-up of civilisation is described in metaphorical language. For Yeats, the 'gyre' is a symbol representing an era. He believed contrary expanding and contracting forces influence people and cultures and that the

Christian era was nearing its end. Images of hunting show how the old world represented its failing – 'The falcon cannot hear the falconer'. We have lost touch with Christ, just as the falcon loses touch with the falconer as he swings into ever-increasing circles. This bird was trained to fly in circles to catch its prey. The circular imagery, with the repetitive '-ing', describes the continuous, swirling movement. Civilisation is also 'Turning and turning in the widening gyre' as it buckles and fragments.

The **tension** is reflected in a list of contrasts: 'centre' and 'fall apart', 'falcon' and 'falconer', 'lack all conviction' and 'intensity', 'innocence' and 'anarchy'. The strain is too much: 'the centre cannot hold'. The verbs also graphically describe this chaotic world: 'Turning and turning', 'loosed', 'drowned', 'fall apart'. Humans are changing amidst the chaos: 'innocence is drowned'. **Anarchy** is described in terms of a great tidal wave, 'the blood-dimmed tide', which sweeps everything before it. The compound word reinforces the overwhelming nature of the water. Yeats feels that the 'best', the leaders and thinkers, have no energy; they are indifferent and 'lack all conviction'. On the other hand, the 'worst', the cynics and fanatics, are consumed with hatred and violence, 'full of passionate intensity'.

Disillusioned, Yeats thinks **a new order has to be emerging**. He imagines a Second Coming. He repeats the word 'Surely' in a tone of both belief and fear in **stanza two**. The Second Coming is usually thought of as a time when Christ will return to reward the good, but the image Yeats presents us with is terrifying. **A blank, pitiless creature emerges.** It is straight from the Book of Revelations: 'And I saw a beast rising out of the sea'. This was regarded as a sign that the end of the world was near. Such an unnatural hybrid of human and animal is the Anti-Christ, the opposite force of the gentle infant Jesus who signalled the end of the Greek and Roman Empires. The 'gaze blank' suggests its lack of intelligence. The phrase 'pitiless as the sun' tells us the creature has no empathy or compassion. It 'Slouches'. It is a brutish, graceless monstrosity.

The **hostile environment** is a nightmare scenario of blazing desert sun, shifting sands and circling predatory birds. The verbs suggest everything is out of focus: 'Reel', 'rocking', 'Slouches'. 'The darkness drops again' shows how disorder, disconnectedness and the 'widening gyre' have brought us to nihilism. This seems to be a prophetic statement, as fascism was to sweep the world in the mid-20th century. Then Yeats has a moment of epiphany: 'but now I know'. Other eras have been destroyed before. The baby in the 'rocking cradle' created an upheaval that resulted in the end of 'twenty centuries of stony sleep'.

Yeats believed that a **cycle of history** lasted two thousand years in a single evolution of birth, growth, decline and death. All change causes upheaval. The Christian era, with its qualities of innocence, order, maternal love and goodness, is at an end. The new era of the 'rough beast' is about to start. It is pitiless, destructive, violent and murderous. This new era has already begun: 'its hour come round at last'. It is a savage god who is coming, uninvited. The spiral has reversed its motion and is now spinning in the opposite direction. The lack of end rhyme mirrors a world of chaos. Yeats looks back over thousands of years. We are given a thrilling and terrifying prospect from a vast perspective of millennia.

ANALYSIS

'Yeats frequently uses powerful and disturbing imagery to express a dark vision of the future.' Discuss this view with reference to 'The Second Coming'.

Sample Paragraph

The contrasting themes of stability and chaos are central to 'The Second Coming'. From the opening line, 'Turning and turning in the widening gyre', Yeats presents the disturbing image of the falcon spinning out of control. The sense of disintegration continues and the language becomes more violent – 'The blood-dimmed tide is loosed'. Dramatic details create a dark vision of life – 'anarchy is loosed', 'innocence is drowned'. There is great irony in the poet's prophecy of a new saviour ('The Second Coming'). Unlike the first Christian Messiah, the next one will be a 'rough beast' bringing unknown horrors – 'A shape with lion body'. Yeats believed that Christianity was about to end to be replaced by a nightmarish world where evil would triumph. The image of the sinister beast, with its 'gaze blank and pitiless as the sun' was particularly chilling. For me, it summed up the poet's distracted terror and his despairing vision of what lies ahead.

Examiner's Comment

A clear, insightful response to the question. Informed points focused directly on how Yeats's imagery conveyed his pessimistic prophecy. Good choice of accurate quotations provided support throughout. Expression is impressive also: varied sentence length, wide-ranging vocabulary ('sense of disintegration', 'distracted terror') and good control of syntax. A high-grade standard.

N.B. Access your ebook for additional sample paragraphs and a list of useful quotes with commentary.

CLASS/HOMEWORK EXERCISES

1. 'W. B. Yeats's political poems are remarkable for their forceful language and sensuous imagery.' Discuss this statement with reference to 'The Second Coming'.

2. 'Yeats often presents a dramatic tension between order and disorder.' Discuss this view with reference to 'The Second Coming'.

SUMMARY POINTS

- The poem's title has obvious biblical associations.
- Scenes of anarchy and disorder lead to an apocalyptical vision of the future.
- Variety of tones/moods: foreboding, disillusionment, fear, despair.
- Effective use of contrast, dramatic imagery, symbols, striking comparisons.

❼ SAILING TO BYZANTIUM

I

That is no country for old men. The young
In one another's arms, birds in the trees
– Those dying generations – at their song,
The salmon-falls, the mackerel-crowded seas,
Fish, flesh, or fowl, commend all summer long   5
Whatever is begotten, born, and dies.
Caught in that sensual music all neglect
Monuments of unageing intellect.

II

An aged man is but a paltry thing,
A tattered coat upon a stick, unless   10
Soul clap its hands and sing, and louder sing
For every tatter in its mortal dress,
Nor is there singing school but studying
Monuments of its own magnificence;
And therefore I have sailed the seas and come   15
To the holy city of Byzantium.

III

O sages standing in God's holy fire
As in the gold mosaic of a wall,
Come from the holy fire, perne in a gyre,
And be the singing-masters of my soul.   20
Consume my heart away; sick with desire
And fastened to a dying animal
It knows not what it is; and gather me
Into the artifice of eternity.

IV

Once out of nature I shall never take   25
My bodily form from any natural thing,
But such a form as Grecian goldsmiths make
Of hammered gold and gold enamelling
To keep a drowsy Emperor awake;
Or set upon a golden bough to sing   30
To lords and ladies of Byzantium
Of what is past, or passing, or to come.

'the holy city of Byzantium'

Glossary

Sailing to Byzantium: for Yeats, this voyage would be one taken to find perfection. This country only exists in the mind. It is an ideal. The original old city of Byzantium was famous as a centre of religion, art and architecture.

1   *That*: Ireland – all who live there are subject to ageing, decay and death.

3   *dying generations*: opposites are linked to show that in the midst of life is death.

7   *sensual music*: the young are living life to the full through their senses and are neglecting the inner spiritual life of the soul.

9   *paltry thing*: worthless, of no importance. Old age is not valued in Ireland.

10   *tattered coat*: an old man is as worthless as a scarecrow.

10-11 *unless/Soul clap its hands and sing*: man can only break free if he allows his spirit the freedom to express itself.

13-14 *Nor is there ... own magnificence*: all schools of art should study the discipline they teach, while the soul should study the immortal art of previous generations.

17   *O sages*: wise men, cleansed by the holy fire of God.

19-24 *Come ... artifice of eternity*: Yeats asks the sages to teach him the wonders of Byzantium and gather his soul into the perfection of art.

19   *perne in a gyre*: spinning; turning very fast.

22   *fastened to a dying animal*: the soul trapped in a decaying body.

32   *past, or passing, or to come*: in eternity, the golden bird sings of transience (passing time).

INITIAL RESPONSE

1. This poem tries to offer a form of escape from old age. Does it succeed? Write a paragraph in response, with support from the text.

2. Why are the 'Monuments of unageing intellect' of such importance to the poet? What does this imply about Yeats's Ireland?

3. The poem is defiant in its exploration of eternity. Discuss, using reference or quotation.

STUDY NOTES

'Sailing to Byzantium' confronts the universal issue of old age. There is no easy solution to this problem. Yeats found the idea of advancing age repulsive and longed to escape. Here he imagines an ideal place, Byzantium, which allowed all to enjoy eternal works of art. He celebrates what man can create and he bitterly condemns the mortality to which man is subject.

Yeats wrote, 'When Irishmen were illuminating the Book of Kells … Byzantium was the centre of European civilization … so I symbolise the search for the spiritual life by a journey to that city.'

The poet declares the theme in the **first stanza** as he confidently declaims that the world of the senses is not for the old – they must seek another way which is timeless, **a life of the spirit and intellect**. The word 'That' tells us he is looking back, as he has already started his journey. But he is looking back wistfully at the world of the lovers ('The young/In one another's arms') and the world of teeming nature ('The salmon-falls, the mackerel-crowded seas'). The compound words emphasise the dynamism and fertility of the life of the senses, even though he admits the flaw in this wonderful life of plenty is mortality ('Those dying generations'). The life of the senses and nature is governed by the harsh cycle of procreation, life and death.

The poet asserts in the **second stanza** that **what gives meaning to a person is the soul**, 'unless/ Soul clap its hands and sing'. Otherwise an elderly man is worthless, 'a paltry thing'. We are given a chilling image of the thin, wasting frame of an old man as a scarecrow in tattered clothes. In contrast, we are shown the wonders of the intellect as the poet tells us that all schools of art study what they compose, what they produce – 'Monuments of unageing intellect'. These works of art are timeless; unlike the body, they are not subject to decay. Thus, music schools study great music and art schools study great paintings. The life of the intellect and spirit must take precedence over the life of the senses. Yeats will no longer listen to the 'sensual music' that is appropriate only for the young, but will study the carefully composed 'music' of classic art.

In Byzantium, the buildings had beautiful mosaics, pictures made with little tiles and inlaid with gold. One of these had a picture of martyrs being burned. Yeats addresses these wise men ('sages') in **stanza three**. He wants them to whirl through time ('perne in a gyre') and come to **teach his soul how to 'sing'**, how to live the life of the spirit. His soul craves this ('sick with desire'), **but it is trapped in the decaying, mortal body** ('fastened to a dying animal'). This is a horrendous image of old age. The soul has lost its identity: 'It knows not what it is'.

He pleads to be saved from this using two interesting verbs, 'Consume' and 'gather'. Both suggest a desire to be taken away. A fire consumes what is put into it and changes the form of the substance. Yeats wants a new body. He pleads to be embraced like a child coming home: 'gather me'. But where will he go? He will journey into the cold world of art, 'the artifice of eternity'. 'Artifice' refers to the skill of those who have created the greatest works of art, but it also means artificial, not real. Is the poet suggesting that eternity also has a flaw?

The **fourth stanza** starts confidently as Yeats declares that 'Once out of nature', he will be transformed into the ageless perfect work of art, the **golden bird**. This is the new body for his soul. Now he will sing to the court. But is the court listening? The word 'drowsy' suggests not. Isn't he singing about transience, the passing of time: 'what is past, or passing, or to come'? Has this any relevance in eternity? Is there a perfect solution to the dilemma of old age?

Yeats raises these questions for our consideration. He has explored this problem by contrasting the abundant life of the young with the 'tattered coat' of old age. He has shown us the golden bird of immortality in opposition to the 'dying animal' of the decaying body. The poet has lulled us with end-rhymes and half-rhymes. He has used groups of threes – 'Fish, flesh, or fowl', 'begotten, born, and dies', 'past, or passing, or to come' – to argue his case. At the end of the poem, do we feel that Yeats genuinely longs for the warm, teeming life of the senses with all its imperfections, rather than the cold, disinterested world of the 'artifice of eternity'?

ANALYSIS

'W. B. Yeats frequently uses vigorous language to denounce transience and old age.' Discuss this view with reference to 'Sailing to Byzantium'.

Sample Paragraph

In 'Sailing to Byzantium', Yeats confronts the physical limitations that old age imposes. A grotesque image of an old man as a scarecrow, 'A tattered coat upon a stick', is presented. The figure is unable to move forward, graphically illustrating the dilemma of old age. The vivid adjective 'tattered' suggests the physical wear and tear that elderly people endure. Yeats longed to escape this fate, through a passionate appeal to the 'sages' to 'Consume my heart away'. Thinking of time's decay, he is 'sick with desire' just as in his poem, 'The Wild Swans at Coole' – 'And now my heart is sore'.

So Yeats decides to reinvent himself, to shed the 'dying animal' of his ageing body and change into a golden bird, a precious, eternal immortal work of art, the 'artifice of eternity'. In this way, the poet challenges physical decline with imaginative intensity. However, the painted scene seems static and lifeless. Ironically, the bird's function is reduced to keeping a 'drowsy Emperor awake' while, like the scarecrow, it is tethered to one spot, 'set upon a golden bough'. I feel that it is the allure of 'The young/ In one another's arms' that Yeats really craves. His rich dynamic description of youthful exuberance is achieved through compound words ('salmon-falls, the mackerel-crowded seas'), alliteration ('Fish, flesh, fowl') and rushing enjambment. He longs to be young again. But in the end, his blunt admission in the opening line, 'That is no country for old men', denies him that choice. Sadly, the aged poet can only look back, unable to reverse the effects of time.

Examiner's Comment

A very successful top-grade response that focuses on both aspects of the question. Points are developed and aptly illustrated with accurate quotation. Impressive discussion regarding the poet's robust, vigorous style ('graphically illustrating', 'passionate appeal', 'rich dynamic description'). Some insightful personal response and cross-referencing show close engagement with Yeats's poems. Expression throughout is very well controlled.

N.B. Access your ebook for additional sample paragraphs and a list of useful quotes with commentary.

CLASS/HOMEWORK EXERCISES

1. 'Yeats's search for truth serves to highlight the intense fury and disillusionment expressed in his poetry.' Discuss this view with reference to 'Sailing to Byzantium'.

2. 'W. B. Yeats makes effective use of imagery and symbolism to communicate thought-provoking insights about life.' Discuss this statement with reference to 'Sailing to Byzantium'.

SUMMARY POINTS

- Central themes include transience, old age and the timeless world of art.
- Rich symbols, metaphors, imagery and similes communicate the complexity of man's struggle with transience and decay.
- Balance, contrast and paradox reveal the complexity of the problem of old age.
- Compound words, onomatopoeia, intriguing use of verbs lend energy and passion to the argument.

8 *from* MEDITATIONS IN TIME OF CIVIL WAR:
THE STARE'S NEST BY MY WINDOW

The bees build in the crevices
Of loosening masonry, and there
The mother birds bring grubs and flies.
My wall is loosening; honey-bees,
Come build in the empty house of the stare.   5

We are closed in, and the key is turned
On our uncertainty; somewhere
A man is killed, or a house burned,
Yet no clear fact to be discerned:
Come build in the empty house of the stare.   10

A barricade of stone or of wood;
Some fourteen days of civil war;
Last night they trundled down the road
That dead young soldier in his blood:
Come build in the empty house of the stare.   15

We had fed the heart on fantasies,
The heart's grown brutal from the fare;
More substance in our enmities
Than in our love; O honey-bees,
Come build in the empty house of the stare.   20

'days of civil war'

Glossary

Stare is another name for the starling, a bird with distinctive dark brown or greenish-black feathers.

3   *grubs*: larvae of insects.

12   *civil war*: the Irish Civil War (1922–23) between Republicans who fought for full independence and supporters of the Anglo-Irish Treaty.

13   *trundled*: rolled.

17   *fare*: diet (of dreams).

18   *enmities*: disputes; hatred.

INITIAL RESPONSE

1. Comment on how Yeats creates an atmosphere of concern and insecurity in stanzas two and three.

2. In your opinion, how effective is the symbol of the bees as a civilising force amid all the destruction of war? Support your answer with close reference to the poem.

3.   How would you describe the dominant mood of the poem? Is it positive or negative? Refer closely to the text in your answer.

STUDY NOTES

The Irish Civil War prompted Yeats to consider the brutality and insecurity caused by conflict. It also made him reflect on his own identity as part of the Anglo-Irish Ascendancy. The poet wrote elsewhere that he had been shocked and depressed by the fighting during the first months of hostilities, yet he was determined not to grow bitter or to lose sight of the beauty of nature. He wrote this poem after seeing a stare building its nest in a hole beside his window.

Much of the poem is dominated by the images of building and collapse. **Stanza one** introduces this tension between creativity ('bees build') and disintegration ('loosening'). In responding to the bitter civil war, Yeats finds suitable **symbols in the nurturing natural world** to express his own hopes. Addressing the bees, he asks that they 'build in the empty house of the stare'. He is desperately conscious of the political vacuum being presently filled by bloodshed. His desperate cry for help seems heartfelt in tone. There is also a possibility that the poet is addressing himself – he will have to revise his own attitudes to the changing political realities caused by the war.

In **stanza two**, Yeats expresses a sense of being **threatened by the conflict** around him: 'We are closed in'. The use of the plural pronoun suggests a community under siege. He is fearful of the future: 'our uncertainty'. Is the poet reflecting on the threat to his own immediate household or to the once powerful Anglo-Irish ruling class? The constant rumours of everyday violence are highlighted in the stark descriptions: 'A man is killed, or a house burned'. Such occurrences almost seem routine in the grim reality of war.

    Stanza three opens with a **haunting image**, the 'barricade of stone', an enduring symbol of division and hostility. The vehemence and inhumanity of the times is driven home by the stark report of soldiers who 'trundled down the road' and left one 'dead young soldier in his blood'. Such atrocities add greater depth to the plaintive refrain for regeneration: 'Come build in the empty house of the stare'.

    In the **final stanza**, Yeats faces up to the root causes of war: 'We had fed the heart on fantasies'. Dreams of achieving independence have led to even greater hatred ('enmities') and intransigence than could have been imagined. It is a tragic irony that the Irish nation has become more divided than ever before. The poet seems despairing as he accepts the failure represented by civil conflict: 'The heart's grown brutal'. It is as though he is reprimanding himself for daring to imagine a brave new world. His **final plea for healing** and reconstruction is strengthened by an emphatic 'O' to show Yeats's depth of feeling: 'O honeybees,/Come build in the empty house of the stare'.

ANALYSIS

'Yeats's poetic vision is one of darkness and disappointment, balanced by moments of insight and optimism.' Discuss this view with reference to '*from* Meditations In Time Of Civil War: The Stare's Nest By My Window'.

Sample Paragraph

    In 'The Stare's Nest By My Window', Yeats reveals his personal views on the Irish Civil War. Throughout the entire poem, there are recurring images of decay and destruction. Observing the bees outside his window, he is surprised to see something purposeful going on within the 'loosening masonry'. Although the crumbling building suggests the break-up of the Irish nation, there is also an ironic recognition of something new happening among the ruins. This is typical of the poet's ambivalent attitude – similar to his view of Easter 1916 as a 'terrible beauty'. The positive image of the bees is symbolic of recovery emerging from the recent divisive conflict. This is a key theme in the poem and shows that Yeats – who has been deeply shocked by the Civil War violence – now finds some hope in the world of nature. The poet's use of symbolism contrasts the two forces of devastation and regeneration when he urges the bees to 'build in the empty house'. However, there are several dark images that show the poet's realism, e.g. the 'house burned' and the tragic life of the 'young soldier in his blood'. These are stark reminders of human loss – the reality of conflict. But in the end, Yeats seems to argue that we can learn from nature. He hopes that just as the birds take care of their young, Ireland will recover from warfare. In the future there will be renewal after all the ruin.

Examiner's Comment

A well-written top-grade response. Informed discussion focused throughout on the balance between Yeats's positive and negative attitudes Accurate quotations provided good support. Cross-referencing shows engagement with the poet's complex views. Expression throughout is very well controlled ('recurring images', 'ironic recognition', 'stark reminders of human loss').

N.B. Access your ebook for additional sample paragraphs and a list of useful quotes with commentary.

CLASS/HOMEWORK EXERCISES

1. 'W. B. Yeats often uses startling language and imagery to raise key questions about Irish nationalism.' Discuss this statement referring both to the subject matter and style of 'The Stare's Nest By My Window'.

2. 'Yeats's poems frequently address serious issues in a fresh and accessible style.' Discuss this view with reference to 'The Stare's Nest By My Window'.

SUMMARY POINTS

- Another of Yeats's political poems expressing his personal views on Irish history.
- Central themes: Civil War violence and destruction; the natural world.
- Effective use of repetition, varying tones (dismay, hopelessness, acceptance, yearning).
- Contrasting images of destruction ('loosening masonry') and renewal ('bees build').

9 IN MEMORY OF EVA GORE-BOOTH AND CON MARKIEWICZ

The light of evening, Lissadell,
Great windows open to the south,
Two girls in silk kimonos, both
Beautiful, one a gazelle.
But a raving autumn shears   5
Blossom from the summer's wreath;
The older is condemned to death,
Pardoned, drags out lonely years
Conspiring among the ignorant.
I know not what the younger dreams –   10
Some vague Utopia – and she seems,
When withered old and skeleton-gaunt,
An image of such politics.
Many a time I think to seek
One or the other out and speak   15
Of that old Georgian mansion, mix
Pictures of the mind, recall
That table and the talk of youth,
Two girls in silk kimonos, both
Beautiful, one a gazelle.   20

Dear shadows, now you know it all,
All the folly of a fight
With a common wrong or right.
The innocent and the beautiful
Have no enemy but time;   25
Arise and bid me strike a match
And strike another till time catch;
Should the conflagration climb,
Run till all the sages know.
We the great gazebo built,   30
They convicted us of guilt;
Bid me strike a match and blow.

'that old Georgian mansion'

Glossary

1	*Lissadell*: the Gore-Booth family home in Co. Sligo.
3	*kimonos*: traditional Japanese robes.
4	*gazelle*: graceful antelope.
5	*shears*: cuts.
9	*Conspiring*: plotting; scheming.
11	*Utopia*: a perfect world.

22	*folly*: foolishness.
28	*conflagration*: blazing inferno.
29	*sages*: philosophers.
30	*gazebo*: ornamental summer house, sometimes seen as a sign of extravagance.

INITIAL RESPONSE

1. What mood does Yeats create in the first four lines of the poem? Explain how he achieves this mood.

2. Would you agree that this is a poem of contrasts? How does Yeats use contrasts to express his thoughts and feelings? Support your points with relevant reference.

3. What picture of Yeats himself emerges from this poem? Use close reference to the text to support the points you make.

STUDY NOTES

Yeats wrote this poem about the two Gore-Booth sisters shortly after their deaths. He was sixty-two at the time. Eva was a noted campaigner for women's rights and Constance was a revolutionary who took part in the 1916 Rising. She later became the first woman elected to the British House of Commons at Westminster. The poet had once been fascinated by their youthful grace and beauty, but he became increasingly opposed to their political activism. Although the poem is a memorial to the two women, it also reveals Yeats's own views about the changes that had occurred in Ireland over his lifetime.

Stanza one begins on a nostalgic note, with Yeats recalling a magical summer's evening in the company of the Gore-Booth sisters. The details he remembers suggest a **world of elegance and privilege** in the girls' family home, Lissadell House, overlooking Sligo Bay. 'Great windows' are a reminder of the grandeur to be found in the Anglo-Irish 'Big House'. Eva and Constance are portrayed as being delicately beautiful, their elusive femininity indicated by the exotic 'silk kimonos' they wear. The poet compares one of the girls to 'a gazelle', stylishly poised and graceful.

The abrupt contrast of mood in **line 5** disrupts the tranquil scene. Yeats considers the harsh effects of time and how it changes everything. He describes autumn (personified as an overenthusiastic gardener) as 'raving' and uncontrollable. The metaphor illustrates the way **time destroys** ('shears') the simple perfection of youth ('Blossom'). Typically, Yeats chooses images from the natural world to express his own retrospective outlook.

In **lines 7–13**, the poet shows his **deep contempt** for the involvement of both the Gore-Booth sisters in revolutionary politics. As far as Yeats is concerned, their activism 'among the ignorant' was a great mistake. These beautiful young women wasted their lives for a 'vague Utopia'. The graphic image of one of the girls growing 'withered old and skeleton-gaunt' is also used to symbolise the unattractive political developments of the era. Repulsed by the idea, Yeats retreats into the more sophisticated world of Lissadell's 'old Georgian mansion'.

The **second stanza** is in marked contrast to the first. Yeats addresses the spirits ('shadows') of Eva and Constance. The tone of voice is unclear. It appears to be compassionate, but there is an undertone of weariness as well. He goes on to scold the two women for wasting their lives on 'folly'. Yeats seems angry that their innocence and beauty have been sacrificed for nothing. It is as though he feels **they have betrayed both their own femininity and their social class**. If they had only known it, their one and only enemy was time.

In the **final lines** of the poem, Yeats dramatises his feelings by turning all his **resentment against time** itself. He associates the failed lives of the women with the decay of the Anglo-Irish Ascendancy. The energetic rhythm and repetition reflect his fury as he imagines striking match after match ('And strike another till time catch') and is consumed in a great 'conflagration'. The poet imagines that the significance of this inferno will eventually be understood by those who are wise, the 'sages'. In the last sentence, Yeats considers how 'They' (the enemies of the Anglo-Irish Ascendancy) hastened the end of a grand cultural era in Ireland. The 'great gazebo' is a symbol of the fine houses and gracious living that were slowly disappearing. The poem ends on a defiant note ('Bid me strike a match and blow'), with Yeats inviting the ghosts of Eva and Constance to help him resist the devastating effects of time.

ANALYSIS

'Many of Yeats's most evocative poems lament the loss of youth and beauty.' Discuss this view with reference to 'In Memory of Eva Gore-Booth and Con Markiewicz'.

Sample Paragraph

'In Memory of Eva Gore-Booth and Con Markiewicz' is largely focused on the effects of time as a destructive force. Yeats begins by describing the beautiful aristocratic sisters as 'Two girls in silk kimonos', the gentle sibilant sounds suggesting their elegance. The poem is really an elegy for the past and Yeats's nostalgic portrayal of the time he shared with the young women at Lissadell is filled with regret. The tone becomes more wistful as he remembers summer evenings relaxing together 'and the talk of youth'. Yeats illustrates the effects of age when he contrasts the beautiful girls in their graceful refinement with the way they were in their later years – 'withered old and skeleton-gaunt'. The image is startling, evidence of how he views the ravages of time. It is all the more shocking when compared with the exquisite kimonos – symbols of lost beauty. It's obvious that Yeats is also regretful of his own lost youth – similar to how he felt in 'Sailing to Byzantium'. At the end of the poem, he shows his deep anger at the ageing process and argues that youth has 'no enemy but time'.

Examiner's Comment

A well-focused high-grade standard which directly addresses the question. Good discussion of the poem's mood of regret ('nostalgic portrayal', 'tone becomes more wistful'). Excellent use of contrasting images to illustrate the poet's theme. The references and quotes are carefully chosen and show clear engagement with the poem. Expression is also impressive.

N.B. Access your ebook for additional sample paragraphs and a list of useful quotes with commentary.

CLASS/HOMEWORK EXERCISES

1. 'W. B. Yeats makes effective use of contrasting moods and atmospheres to express his strongly held ideas and heartfelt feelings.' Discuss this statement with reference to 'In Memory of Eva Gore-Booth and Con Markiewicz'.

2. 'Yeats frequently combines both a sensitive romantic nature and a fiercely critical voice.' Discuss this view with reference to both to the subject matter and style of 'In Memory of Eva Gore-Booth and Con Markiewicz'.

SUMMARY POINTS

- Elegy for a lost world of great beauty, style and sophistication.
- The poem reveals Yeats's own attitudes to the two sisters.
- Life's transience sharply contrasted with the longevity of art.
- Various tones – nostalgic, reflective, scornful, critical.
- Striking imagery of light and shade and seasonal change.

10 SWIFT'S EPITAPH

Swift has sailed into his rest;
Savage indignation there
Cannot lacerate his breast.
Imitate him if you dare,
World-besotted traveller; he   5
Served human liberty.

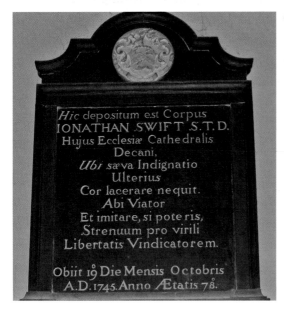

'Swift's Epitaph'

Glossary

Swift: Jonathan Swift, satirist and clergyman, author of *Gulliver's Travels* and dean of St Patrick's Cathedral. The original inscription in Latin is on his memorial in the cathedral. Yeats liked to spend time there.

Epitaph: inscription for a tomb or memorial.

1   **his rest**: suggestion of afterlife; death is not an end.

2   **Savage indignation**: the driving force of Swift's satirical work. He believed in a society where wrong was punished and good rewarded.

3   **lacerate**: cut; tear.

5   **World-besotted**: obsessed with travelling or with material concerns rather than spiritual matters.

5–6 **he /Served human liberty**: Yeats believed Swift served the liberty of the intellect, not liberty for the common people. Yeats associated democracy with organised mobs of ignorant people.

INITIAL RESPONSE

1. How would you describe the tone of this poem?

2. Comment on the poet's use of the verb 'lacerate'. What do you think Yeats is trying to convey?

STUDY NOTES

'Swift's Epitaph' is a translation from the original Latin epitaph composed by Swift for himself. Yeats adds a new first line to the original. He regarded this epitaph as the 'greatest ... in history'.

   W. B. Yeats admired Swift, who was proud and solitary and belonged to the Anglo-Irish tradition, as did Yeats himself. He regarded the Anglo-Irish as superior. He once said, 'We have created most of the modern literature of this country. We have created the best of its political intelligence.' **Yeats's additional first line** to the epitaph conveys a dignified sailing into the spiritual afterlife by the deceased Swift. The rest of the poem is a **translation** from the Latin original. Swift is now free from all the negative reactions he was subjected to when alive: 'Savage indignation there/Cannot lacerate his breast.' Swift's self-portrait conveys the impression of a man of fierce **independence and pride**. 'Imitate him if you dare' is the challenge thrown down like a gauntlet to the reader to try to be like him. 'World-besotted traveller' can be read as a man who has travelled extensively in his imagination as well as in reality. His contribution to humanity is summed up in the final sentence: 'he/Served human liberty'. **He freed the artist** from the masses so that the artist could 'make liberty visible'. The tone of this short, compressed poem is proud and defiant, like Swift.

ANALYSIS

'W. B. Yeats frequently confronts the painful reality of death in fierce, challenging poetry.' Discuss this view with particular reference to 'Swift's Epitaph'.

Sample Paragraph

   Yeats wrote two provocative epitaphs – his own in 'Under Ben Bulben' and this translation of Swift's self-composed epitaph in Latin. Both show a cool disregard for life as a permanent end in itself. Yeats reveals a fearless, confident Swift departing this life for the next in the easeful sibilant line, 'Swift has sailed into his rest'. The metaphor highlights the natural progression of the soul returning to its eternal rest. Death provides a sanctuary from the toil and trouble of this world. Death is a natural reality of life's circle. Swift's 'Savage indignation' was directed at the two great evils of contemporary society, starvation and emigration. But 'there', in paradise, he is able to leave aside his life's work and all the criticism he received. The verb 'lacerate' suggests the backlash he suffered as a result. Yeats challenges readers, asking if we are brave enough to stand up (like him) for what is right, 'Imitate him if you dare'. The enjambment of the final lines suggests the extensive imaginary journeys undertaken by his fictional heroes – particularly in his book, *Gulliver's Travels*. The powerful final comment – that he 'Served human liberty' – asks us to join him in demanding a world where good is rewarded and wickedness punished.

Examiner's Comment

A top-grade response that shows very good engagement with Yeats's poetry. This focused paragraph examines the poet's philosophy in some detail – and particularly his belief that what matters is the legacy an individual leaves behind after death. Several excellent discussion points are effectively supported with suitable quotation and there is fluent control of language throughout.

N.B. Access your ebook for additional sample paragraphs and a list of useful quotes with commentary.

CLASS/HOMEWORK EXERCISES

1. 'Yeats uses dramatic and forceful language to express his spirited views on ageing and the passing of time.' Discuss this statement with reference to 'Swift's Epitaph'.

2. 'W. B. Yeats often chooses confrontation when exploring universal themes in thought-provoking poetry.' Discuss this view with reference to 'Swift's Epitaph'.

SUMMARY POINTS

- The satirist Jonathan Swift has made a strong impact on Yeats's imagination.
- Sibilant metaphor of sailing suggests the ease of passage from this life to the next.
- Emphatic language highlights Swift's efforts to improve the human condition and the resulting response.
- Poem offers a direct provocative challenge to readers.

11 AN ACRE OF GRASS

Picture and book remain,
An acre of green grass
For air and exercise,
Now strength and body goes;
Midnight, an old house   5
Where nothing stirs but a mouse.

My temptation is quiet.
Here at life's end
Neither loose imagination,
Nor the mill of the mind   10
Consuming its rag and bone,
Can make the truth known.

Grant me an old man's frenzy,
Myself must I remake
Till I am Timon and Lear   15
Or that William Blake
Who beat upon the wall
Till Truth obeyed his call;

A mind Michael Angelo knew
That can pierce the clouds,   20
Or inspired by frenzy
Shake the dead in their shrouds;
Forgotten else by mankind,
An old man's eagle mind.

'An acre of green grass'

Glossary

2   *acre*: the secluded garden of Yeats's home, where he spent his final years.

5   *an old house*: the house was in Rathfarnham, Co. Dublin.

9   *loose imagination*: vague, unfocused ideas.

13   *frenzy*: wildly excited state.

15   *Timon and Lear*: two of Shakespeare's elderly tragic heroes, both of whom raged against the world.

16   *William Blake*: English visionary poet and painter (1757–1827).

19   *Michael Angelo*: Michelangelo, Italian Renaissance artist (1475–1564).

22   *shrouds*: burial garments.

INITIAL RESPONSE

1. How does Yeats create a mood of calm and serenity in the opening stanza?

2. Briefly explain the change of tone in stanza three.

STUDY NOTES

Written in 1936 when Yeats was seventy-one, the poet expresses his resentment towards ageing gracefully. Instead, he will dedicate himself to seeking wisdom through frenzied creativity. People sometimes take a narrow view of the elderly and consider them completely redundant. In Yeats's case, he is determined not to let old age crush his spirit.

Stanza one paints a picture of retirement as a surrender to death. Yeats's life has been reduced to suit his basic needs. 'Picture and book' might refer to the poet's memories. Physically weak, he feels like a prisoner whose enclosed garden area is for 'air and exercise'. There is an underlying **feeling of alienation and inactivity**: 'nothing stirs'.

In **stanza two**, the poet says that it would be easy to give in to the stereotypical image of placid contentment: 'My temptation is quiet', especially since old age ('life's end') has weakened his creative powers. **Yeats admits that his 'loose imagination' is not as sharp as it was when he was in his prime.** He no longer finds immediate inspiration ('truth') in everyday experiences, which he compares to life's 'rag and bone'.

The **third stanza** opens on a much more dramatic and forceful note as the poet confronts his fears: 'Grant me an old man's frenzy'. Yeats's personal prayer is totally lacking in meekness. Instead, he urges himself to focus enthusiastically on his own creative purpose – 'frenzy'. **He pledges to 'remake' himself** in the image of such heroic figures as Timon, Lear and William Blake. The passionate tone and run-on lines add to his sense of commitment to his art.

In **stanza four**, Yeats develops **his spirited pursuit of meaningful old age** by reflecting on 'A mind Michael Angelo knew'. The poet is stimulated and encouraged to follow the great artist's example and 'pierce the clouds'. The image suggests the daring power of imagination to lift the spirit in the search for truth and beauty. The final lines build to a climax as Yeats imagines the joys of 'An old man's eagle mind'. Such intense creativity can 'Shake the dead' and allow the poet to continue experiencing life to its fullest.

ANALYSIS

'W. B. Yeats uses powerful language and imagery to express his personal views.' Discuss this statement with reference to 'An Acre of Grass'.

Sample Paragraph

Yeats takes a highly unusual approach to ageing in 'An Acre of Grass'. To begin with, his subdued tone seems to suggest that he is happy to sit reading in his quiet 'acre of green grass'. Everything seems to be very organised, yet a little too organised for his liking. In the first few lines, we get a picture of someone close to second childhood, engrossed in his 'picture and book'. Late at night, he is awake and feels that 'nothing stirs but a mouse'. Acutely aware of his advancing years, he resents being at 'life's end' and is quick to rebel against it. Clearly, he still yearns for renewed energy and inspiration. The irony of returning to childhood and lacking 'loose imagination' appals him. His forceful language emerges in the second half of the poem when he demands 'an old man's frenzy'. His need to be creative again is illustrated by the references to Lear (the tragic heroic king in Shakespeare's play who fought to the bitter end) and to William Blake and Michelangelo. Like them, Yeats wants to live a productive life to the full – with an 'eagle mind'. The dramatic metaphor typifies his startling imagery. In these final lines, his tone is fierce and defiant. He will not fade away on his small acre of grass.

Examiner's Comment

There is some very good discussion in this paragraph and a clear sense of engagement. Informed points focused on the subdued tone and irony in the early stanzas. Accurate quotations are integrated effectively into the commentary. Expression is impressive also: varied sentence length, ranging vocabulary ('yearns for renewed energy and inspiration', 'dramatic metaphor typifies his startling imagery') and good control of syntax. A high grade standard.

N.B. Access your ebook for additional sample paragraphs and a list of useful quotes with commentary.

CLASS/HOMEWORK EXERCISES

1. 'Some of Yeats's most thought-provoking poems combine his personal concerns with public issues.' Discuss this view with reference to 'An Acre of Grass'.

2. 'Yeats uses simple and direct language in exploring his concerns about ageing and death.' Discuss this statement with reference to 'An Acre of Grass'.

SUMMARY POINTS

- Confessional poem addresses familiar themes of old age and artistic revitalisation.
- Striking contrast between his initial acceptance of age and his final determination to renew himself.
- Effective use of imagery to show that the house has also been engulfed by old age.
- References to Blake, Timon of Athens and King Lear focus on Yeats's desired poetic-frenzy.

12 *from* UNDER BEN BULBEN

V

Irish poets, learn your trade,
Sing whatever is well made,
Scorn the sort now growing up
All out of shape from toe to top,
Their unremembering hearts and heads   5
Base-born products of base beds.
Sing the peasantry, and then
Hard-riding country gentlemen,
The holiness of monks, and after
Porter-drinkers' randy laughter;   10
Sing the lords and ladies gay
That were beaten into the clay
Through seven heroic centuries;
Cast your mind on other days
That we in coming days may be   15
Still the indomitable Irishry.

VI

Under bare Ben Bulben's head
In Drumcliff churchyard Yeats is laid,
An ancestor was rector there
Long years ago, a church stands near,   20
By the road an ancient cross.
No marble, no conventional phrase;
On limestone quarried near the spot
By his command these words are cut:
    Cast a cold eye   25
    On life, on death.
    Horseman, pass by!

'Under bare Ben Bulben's head'

Glossary

2   *whatever is well made*: great art.
6   *base*: low; unworthy.
16 *indomitable*: invincible; unbeatable.
17 *Under bare Ben Bulben's head*: defiant symbol of the famous mountain.

19 *ancestor*: the poet's great-grandfather.
27 *Horseman*: possibly a symbolic figure from local folklore; or possibly any passer-by.

INITIAL RESPONSE

1. Comment on the tone used by Yeats in giving advice to other writers. Refer to the text in your answer.

2. From your reading of the poem, explain the kind of 'Irishry' that Yeats wishes to see celebrated in poetry. Support the points you make with reference or quotation.

3. Describe the mood of Drumcliff churchyard as visualised by the poet. Use close reference to the text to show how Yeats uses language to create this mood.

STUDY NOTES

This was one of Yeats's last poems. Sections V and VI of the elegy sum up his personal views on the future of Irish poetry and also include the enigmatic epitaph he composed for his own gravestone. Using art as a gateway to spiritual fulfilment is characteristic of the poet.

Section V is a hard-hitting address by Yeats to his contemporaries and all the poets who will come after him. He encourages them to set the highest 'well made' standards for their work. His uncompromisingly negative view of contemporary writing ('out of shape from toe to top') is quickly clarified. The reason why modern literature is in such a state of confusion is that the poets' 'unremembering hearts and heads' **have lost touch with tradition**. The formality and discipline of great classic poetry have been replaced by unstructured writing and free verse. The authoritative tone becomes even more scathing as Yeats castigates the inferiority of his peers as 'Base-born products'.

It is not only intellectual artistic tradition that the poet admires; he finds another valuable tradition in the legends and myths of old Ireland. Yeats urges his fellow writers to 'Sing the peasantry'. But he also advises them to **absorb other cultural traditions**. Here he includes the 'Hard-riding country gentlemen' of his own Anglo-Irish class and the 'holiness of monks' – those who seek truth through ascetic or spiritual means. Even the more sensuous 'randy laughter' of 'Porter-drinkers' can be inspirational. For Yeats, the peasant and aristocratic traditions are equally worth celebrating. Irish history is marked by a combination of joy, heroism, defeat and resilience. Yet despite (or perhaps because of) his harsh criticism of the present generation, there is little doubt about the poet's passionate desire to encourage new writing that would reflect the true greatness of 'indomitable Irishry'.

Section VI is a great deal less dogmatic. Writing in the third person, Yeats describes his final resting place in Drumcliff. The voice is **detached and dignified**. Using a series of unadorned images, he takes us to the simple churchyard at the foot of Ben Bulben. The mountain stands as a proud symbol of how our unchanging silent origins outlive human tragedy. It is to his Irish roots that the poet ultimately wants to return. His wishes are modest but curt – 'No marble'. Keen to avoid the well-worn headstone inscriptions, Yeats provides his own incisive epitaph. The three short lines are enigmatic and balance opposing views, typical of so much of his poetry. The poet's last warning ('Cast a cold eye') reminds us to live measured lives based on a realistic understanding of the cycle of life and death. The beautiful Christian setting, subdued tone and measured rhythm all contribute to the quiet dignity of Yeats's final farewell.

ANALYSIS

'W. B. Yeats's inspired poetry gives expression to the spirit of a whole nation through his mastery of form.' Discuss this view with reference to 'Under Ben Bulben'.

Sample Paragraph

W. B. Yeats was seventy-three when he wrote his epitaph, 'Under Ben Bulben'. The poem addresses themes close to Yeats's heart – the perfection of art, Irish nationalism and the reality of death. The poet's own views are evident throughout – always expressed in an imperative voice: 'Irish poets, learn your trade'. Yeats believed strongly in the value of traditional forms of verse, spending long hours shaping a poem. He is bitterly opposed to the type of free verse of contemporary poets, 'Scorn the sort now growing up/All out of shape from toe to top'. His use of enjambed lines and the inverted phrase ('toe to top') mimics the ugliness of modern poetry. Instead he offers readers the crafted perfection of heroic couplets and a succinct three-line conclusion, 'Cast a cold eye/On life, on death./Horseman, pass by!' He also makes being Irish something to be desired, a race, unbowed after years of oppression, 'Still the indomitable Irishry', even inventing a new word to express our unique culture and history. The modern poets he is addressing are urged to remember this, 'Cast your minds on other days'. Yeats's inspired poetry actually practises what he preaches, presenting a 'well-made' poem with a vision of what it means to be Irish. His moving epitaph not only shows great control of traditional verse, but a poet who speaks in a colloquial voice for us all.

Examiner's Comment

A high-grade response that explores the form and structure of the poem alongside the central theme of Irishness. Points are aptly illustrated with accurate quotation. Some impressive discussion regarding the poet's critical tone in mocking aspects of contemporary poetry. Expression throughout is clear and well controlled.

N.B. Access your ebook for additional sample paragraphs and a list of useful quotes with commentary.

CLASS/HOMEWORK EXERCISES

1. 'W. B. Yeats has remarked that his poetry is generally written out of despair.' Discuss this statement referring to both the subject matter and style of 'Under Ben Bulben'.

2. 'Yeats's forceful language and vivid imagery convey his intense vision of life and death.' Discuss this view with reference to 'Under Ben Bulben'.

SUMMARY POINTS

- Self-epitaph achieving his aim 'to hammer my thoughts into unity'.
- Formal vision of integrated spiritual reality, natural cycle of life and death.
- Revitalised use of traditional rhyme scheme and metered poetry (strict four-beat rhythm).
- Use of colloquial language. Short lines give a modern quality to the poem.
- Distinctive poetic voice, authoritative, compelling, direct and exhilarating.

⑬ POLITICS

'In our time the destiny of man presents its meanings in political terms.'
Thomas Mann

How can I, that girl standing there,
My attention fix
On Roman or on Russian
Or on Spanish politics?
Yet here's a travelled man that knows   5
What he talks about,
And there's a politician
That has read and thought,
And maybe what they say is true
Of war and war's alarms,   10
But O that I were young again
And held her in my arms.

'But O that I were young again/And held her in my arms'

Glossary

Politics: winning and using power to govern society. Thomas Mann was a German novelist who argued that the future of man was determined by states and governments.

3-4 *On Roman or on Russian/Or on Spanish politics*: a reference to the political upheavals of Europe in the 1930s.

INITIAL RESPONSE

1. This poem suggests that politics are not important. Does the poet convince you? Write a paragraph in response, with reference to the text.

2. Where does the language used in the poem convey a sense of deep longing? How effective is this?

STUDY NOTES

'Politics' is a satire written in 1939, when Yeats was seventy-three, in response to a magazine article. He said it was based on 'a moment of meditation'.

A **satire** uses ridicule to expose foolishness. A magazine article praised Yeats for his 'public' work. The poet was delighted with this word, as one of his aims had always been to 'move the common people'. However, the article went on to say that Yeats should have used this 'public' voice to address public issues such as politics. Yeats disagreed, as he had always regarded politics as dishonest and superficial. He thought professional politicians manipulated through 'false news'. This is evident from the ironic comment, 'And maybe what they say is true'. Here we see the poet's indifference to these matters.

This poem addresses **real truths**, the proper material for poems, the universal experience of **human relationships**, not the infinite abstractions that occupied politicians ('war and war's alarms'). Big public events, Yeats is suggesting, are not as important as love. The girl in the poem is more important than all the politics in the world: 'How can I ... My attention fix/On Roman or on Russian/Or on Spanish politics'? So Yeats is overthrowing the epigraph at the beginning of the poem, where the novelist Thomas Mann is stating that people should be concerned with political matters. Politics is the winning and using of power to govern the state. Yeats is adopting the persona of the distracted lover who is unable to focus on the tangled web of European politics in the 1930s. This poem was to be placed in his last poetry collection, almost like a farewell, as he states again that what he desires is youth and love.

But this poem can also give another view. Is the 'she' in the poem Ireland? Yeats has addressed public issues in poems such as 'Easter 1916' and 'September 1913' and he was already a senator in the Irish government. As usual, he leaves us with questions as he draws us through this deceptively simple poem with its **ever-changing tones** that range from the questioning opening to mockery, doubt and finally longing. The **steady rhyme** (the second line rhymes with the fourth and so on) drives the poem forward to its emphatic **closing wish**, the cry of an old man who wishes to recapture his youth and lost love.

ANALYSIS

'Yeats's final poems are particularly poignant because all that matters to him is youth and love.' Discuss this view with reference to 'Politics'.

Sample Paragraph

It's thought that 'Politics' is probably Yeats's last poem – and it expresses his belief in the importance of emotions over everything else. Although written in 1938 when Europe was edging towards war, the poet is unable to focus on public affairs – 'Roman or on Russian/Or on Spanish politics'. Instead, he is much more interested in a beautiful girl who is nearby. His tone is tender and filled with longing – 'O that I were young again/ And held her in my arms'. As in 'Sailing to Byzantium', he is well aware of the impossibility of reversing time – and that is what makes the poem so moving. The exclamation 'O' is all the more touching because the poet understands how hopeless his desires are. The sad reality is that he can never regain his youth or experience true love with a young woman again. For me, this old man's bittersweet realisation makes 'Politics' one of Yeats's most poignant poems.

Examiner's Comment

A short but insightful high-grade response that engages loosely with the poem. Points are clearly focused on Yeats's reluctant acceptance that youth and love can only be memories. Good focus on the poet's mood and tone ('tender', 'touching', 'bittersweet'). The cross-reference broadens the discussion and expression is well controlled throughout.

N.B. Access your ebook for additional sample paragraphs and a list of useful quotes with commentary.

CLASS/HOMEWORK EXERCISES

1. 'W. B. Yeats frequently writes simple but beautiful poems that have universal significance.' Discuss this statement with reference to 'Politics'.

2. 'Despite his intense disappointment with reality, Yeats can often find hope in his imagination.' Discuss this view with reference to 'Politics'.

SUMMARY POINTS

- Central focus on the poet's nostalgia for his younger days.
- Yeats is preoccupied with private human interaction rather than public or political situations.
- The poet expresses little optimism or even interest in the future.
- Various tones – reflective, sceptical, ironic, nostalgic, resigned.
- Effective use of contrasts: intellect and emotion, age and youth, male and female.

LEAVING CERT SAMPLE ESSAY

'Yeats addresses a range of personal and public themes through the use of powerfully evocative language.'
Discuss this statement, supporting your answer with reference to the poetry of W. B. Yeats on your course.

Marking Scheme Guidelines
Candidates are free to agree and/or disagree with the statement. However, the key terms ('range of personal and public themes' and 'use of powerfully evocative language') should be addressed. Reward evidence of genuine engagement with the poems.

Indicative material:
- Personal/public reflections conveyed through images/symbols and descriptive details.
- Formal/informal approach to key themes, e.g. Irish politics, nature, transience, art and beauty.
- Wide-ranging references and allusions reflect the public/personal dimensions of the poetry.
- Conflict and a desire to escape from reality are central concerns for the poet.
- Effective use of dramatic language, rhetoric, paradoxes, contrasting moods/tones, etc.

Sample Essay

(Yeats addresses personal and public themes using powerfully evocative language)

1. W. B. Yeats writes subjective poetry, arising from deep personal feelings. But he is also concerned with wider political and social issues which impact on his world. This poet communicates his personal thoughts and public views in the poems, 'The Lake Isle of Innisfree', 'September 1913' and 'Easter 1916', using vivid, lyrical language which resonates in the mind of the reader. His poetic technique is an impressive display of the use of imagery, symbolism, sound effects and contrast.

2. Yeats expresses subjective feelings in 'The Lake Isle of Innisfree'. As an exile in London, he longs for peace in the midst of the bustling city, 'While I stand on the roadway or on the pavement grey'. This homesick desire to escape is intense: 'I will arise and go now, and go to Innisfree'. Yet although this poem is very personal, it has a public dimension, relating to all those who are away from their homeland. His strong sentiments are conveyed through memorable language. Strikingly beautiful imagery is used to paint a picture of Innisfree as an idyllic place. The morning mist is described as a carelessly thrown veil, 'Dropping from the veils of the morning to where the cricket sings'. The fierce heat of midday is captured in the 'purple glow' as though the heather was on fire in the intense noonday sunlight. He suggests the light of the reflected stars in the moving lake water through slender vowel sounds, 'midnight's all a glimmer'. At the same time, broad assonant sounds slow the pace of the poem, 'rows', 'loud', 'alone', 'slow'. In this way, Yeats conjures up the magical serenity and tranquility longed for by poet and emigrant alike.

3. In contrast to this private longing, Yeats creates a hard-hitting political and social poem in 'September 1913'. I found the beginning of the poem to be a derisive attack on his materialistic contemporaries who spend their time adding 'the half-pence to the pence'. These merchant classes have a slavish attitude to religion as they add 'prayer to shivering prayer' to their judgemental God in an action straight from the world of exploitation. Yeats contrasts the grasping shopkeepers and landlords of Dublin with the idealistic men who took part in the Fenian Rising. His contempt for these self-interested men is evident in his use of the verb 'fumble' to portray these furtive underhand individuals. His ironic statement, 'For men were born to pray and save', also shows his disdain for these selfish hypocrites.

4. By contrast, natural imagery portrays the free-spirited rebels who went 'about the world like wind'. The simile's subtle alliteration echoes the idealistic patriotism of these great Irish heroes who travelled widely in the interest of national freedom. Yeats uses his refrain emphatically, 'Romantic Ireland's dead and gone/It's with O' Leary in the grave'. I felt that Yeats really hammered home this message through the repetition at the end of each stanza. A slight change to this refrain occurs at the end of the poem.

Yeats warns people not to dare judge these men, 'But let them be'. He defends these men who had so little time to 'pray and save'. His contemporaries have not the same breadth of vision to even understand what motivated these patriots, dismissing their vision as madness, the 'delirium' of the brave.

5. 'Easter 1916' is another tough political poem which deals with Yeats's ambivalent personal feelings about the significance of the Rising. The poem opens with an honest account of the poet's critical attitude to these rebels with whom he exchanged 'Polite, meaningless words'. He regarded Ireland as a land of fools 'where motley is worn'. But after the Rising, everything 'changed, changed utterly'. Yeats realises that 'A terrible beauty is born'. The conflicting words convey his concern. He was against the use of violence to achieve Irish independence. He uses this contradictory phrase as a device to pull the poem's conflicting viewpoints together and to emphasise his own personal attitude. He also uses the metaphor of a stone to convey his doubts about fanatic rebels who can only see one side of an argument. He feels that this narrow focus on an ideal, 'Too long a sacrifice/ Can make a stone of the heart'. Yet the poet leaves that thought aside and finally recognises the martyrs with a solemn roll of honour, 'MacDonagh and MacBride/And Connolly and Pearse'.

6. Yeats's poetry expresses the deep longing of the emigrant. It also criticises money-grabbing businessmen and asks questions about the price of freedom. His personal concerns are often universal ones, e.g. his deep fear for the future and the longing of an old man for lost youth. Yeats's themes are all the more engaging because of his technical skill as a poet, through his use of imagery, sound effects, repetition contrast and memorable refrains.

(approx. 800 words)

Examiner's Comment

A successful high-grade response showing very good engagement with Yeats's poetry. The opening provides a clear overview, mentioning the poems that will be discussed. Focus is well sustained on both the personal and wider public themes while detailed analysis of the poet's language use is to be commended. Expression is impressive throughout – particularly the controlled syntax, varied sentence length and vocabulary ('public dimension', 'contemporaries have not the same breadth of vision', 'ambivalent personal feelings').

MARKING SCHEME GRADE: H1
P = 15/15
C = 15/15
L = 15/15
M = 5/5
Total = 50/50

N.B. Access your ebook for additional sample paragraphs and a list of useful quotes with commentary.

(45–50 MINUTES)

1. 'Yeats's most engaging poems are defined by the contrast between the real world in which the poet lives and the ideal world.' Discuss this statement, supporting your answer with reference to the poems by W. B. Yeats on your course.

2. 'W. B. Yeats frequently examines the relationship between nature and art through his use of symbolism and dramatic language.' Discuss this view with reference to both the style and subject matter of the poetry of Yeats on your course.

3. 'Yeats's passionate poetic voice often confronts the reality of old age fearlessly and with deep regret'. Discuss this statement with reference to the poetry of W. B. Yeats on your course.

Sample Essay Plan (Q1)

'Yeats's most engaging poems are defined by the contrast between the real world in which the poet lives and the ideal world.' Discuss this statement, supporting your answer with close reference to the poems by W. B. Yeats on your course.

- Intro: Clear evidence of contrast is required; mention both themes and style in the response. Public and personal poems provide grounds of the conflict between reality and the ideal.

- Point 1: 'September 1913' – political poem, accusatory. Note the changing refrain, rhetorical questions, bitter tone, nostalgic view of Irish history. Savage contrast between the selfish society he saw and the ideal world which no longer exists.

- Point 2: 'Easter 1916' – another political poem, an attempt to answer questions raised by the 1916 Rising. All had changed. Yeats admits he was wrong.

- Point 3: The Wild Swans at Coole' – autumnal retrospection as the poet realises how his life had changed over the years. Laments loss of youth, passion and love. Compares human transience with the immortality of the swans.

- Point 4: 'Sailing to Byzantium' – theme of ageing, use of contrast to convey theme; repetition, declamatory opening, uncertainty a sign of his humanity.

- Conclusion: Yeats – ideal past contrasted with unsatisfactory present, attitude to Irish patriotism, escape, ageing. Raises questions, rather than providing answers.

Sample Essay Plan (Q1)

Develop one of the above points into a paragraph.

Sample Paragraph: Point 4

'Sailing to Byzantium' is an intriguing poem. Yeats hated the weaknesses brought on by old age: 'An aged man is but a paltry thing'. Yet he defies time, 'Once out of nature I shall never take/My bodily form from any natural thing'. The strong rhythm conveys the natural harmony of youth, 'Fish, flesh, fowl'. This is the lively energetic world that Yeats wants to experience, 'The young in one another's arms'. But, sadly, that is not possible anymore. He presents us with the contrasting truth for an older man such as himself: 'That is no country for old men.' Again, the difference is shown as the beauty of 'the gold mosaic of a wall' in contrast to the brutal reality of his soul 'fastened to a dying animal.' The poet explores the dilemma of ageing, which everyone faces, even though at eighteen, it seems very remote to me. I was also interested in Yeats's discovery of a flaw in the so-called perfect world of art. Now, Yeats is immortal as his soul has now taken the bodily form of a golden bird, 'such a form as Grecian goldsmiths make.' However, the audience for such art, the Emperor, is 'drowsy' and not paying attention. Yeats is now raising the question of who will listen as he himself writes poems 'Of what is past, or passing, or to come'. In his role as a poet, he is forced to raise such deep questions about our very existence for us all to consider.

Examiner's Comment

As part of a full essay answer, this is a very competent high-grade standard which offers a good personal response firmly rooted in the text of the poem. The paragraph focuses well on the use of contrast used by Yeats to explore ageing, and both style and content are examined effectively. Expression is impressive and discussion points based on high order analysis are very well supported by suitable quotation.

N.B. Access your ebook for additional sample paragraphs and a list of useful quotes with commentary.

LAST WORDS "

'Yeats's poetry is simple and eloquent to the heart.'

Robert Louis Stevenson

'He had this marvellous gift of beating the scrap metal of the day-to-day life into a ringing bell.'

Seamus Heaney

'All that is beautiful in art is laboured over.'

W. B. Yeats

Glossary of Common Literary Terms

alliteration: the use of the same letter at the beginning of each word or stressed syllable in a line of verse, e.g. 'boilers bursting'.

assonance: the use of the same vowel sound in a group of words, e.g. 'bleared, smeared with toil'.

aubade: a celebratory morning song, sometimes lamenting the parting of lovers.

blank verse: unrhymed iambic pentameter, e.g. 'These waters, rolling from their mountain-springs'.

conceit: an elaborate image or far-fetched comparison, e.g. 'This flea is you and I, and this/Our marriage bed'.

couplet: two successive lines of verse, usually rhymed and of the same metre, e.g. 'So long as men can breathe or eyes can see,/So long lives this, and this gives life to thee'.

elegy: a mournful poem, usually for the dead, e.g. 'Sleep in a world your final sleep has woken'.

emotive language: language designed to arouse an emotional response in the reader, e.g. 'For this that all that blood was shed?'

enjambment: the continuation of a sentence without a pause beyond the end of a line, couplet or stanza.

epiphany: a moment of insight or understanding, e.g. 'Somebody loves us all'.

free verse: unrhymed and unmetred poetry, often used by modern poets, e.g. 'but the words are shadows and you cannot hear me./You walk away and I cannot follow'.

imagery: descriptive language or word-pictures, especially appealing to the senses, e.g. 'He was speckled with barnacles,/fine rosettes of lime'.

irony: when one thing is said and the opposite is meant, e.g. 'For men were born to pray and save'.

lyric: short musical poem expressing feeling.

metaphor: image that compares two things without using the words 'like' or 'as', e.g. 'I am gall, I am heartburn'.

onomatopoeia: the sound of the word imitates or echoes the sound being described, e.g. 'The murmurous haunt of flies on summer eves'.

paradox: a statement that on the surface appears self-contradictory, e.g. 'I shall have written him one/poem maybe as cold/And passionate as the dawn'.

persona: the speaker or voice in the poem. This is not always the poet, e.g. 'I know that I shall meet my fate/Somewhere among the clouds above'.

personification: where the characteristics of an animate or living being are given to something inanimate, e.g. 'The yellow fog that rubs its back upon the window panes'.

rhyme: identical sound of words, usually at the end of lines of verse, e.g. 'I get down on my knees and do what must be done/And kiss Achilles' hand, the killer of my son'.

rhythm: the beat or movement of words, the arrangement of stressed and unstressed, short and long syllables in a line of poetry, e.g. 'I will arise and go now, and go to Innisfree'.

sestina: a complex 39-line verse form which can be traced back to twelfth-century France. The sestina relies on end-word repetition in place of rhyme. It consists of six sestets (6-line stanzas) followed by a concluding tercet (3-line stanza). The six words at the end of each of the lines of the first stanza are repeated in a different order at the end of lines in the subsequent stanzas. These six words are also included in the closing tercet.

sibilance: the whispering, hissing 's' sound, e.g. 'Singest of summer in full-throated ease'.

sonnet: a 14-line poem. The Petrarchan or Italian sonnet is divided into eight lines (octave), which present a problem or situation. The remaining six lines (sestet) resolve the problem or present another view of the situation. The Shakespearean sonnet is divided into three quatrains and concludes with a rhyming couplet, either summing up what preceded or reversing it.

symbol: a word or phrase representing something other than itself, e.g. 'A tattered coat upon a stick'.

theme: the central idea or message in a poem.

tone: the type of voice or attitude used by the poet towards his or her subject, e.g. 'O but it is dirty'.

villanelle: a five-stanza poem of three lines each, with a concluding quatrain, using only two end rhyming words throughout, e.g. 'I am just going outside and may be some time,/At the heart of the ridiculous, the sublime'.

Critical Analysis Checklist

Leaving Certificate examination questions in the Prescribed Poetry section usually refer to the poet's subject matter and style. You will be rewarded for showing genuine engagement with the poetry.

When discussing a poem, you will be expected to demonstrate an understanding of the poet's themes or ideas. Some poems reveal the poet's personal views or concerns.

It is also important to interact with the language in the poem. The poet's distinctive style refers to how language is used to communicate themes and ideas.

SUBJECT MATTER (What the poem is about)

Look beyond the surface meaning of the poem and remember that there is no 'perfect' or 'correct' meaning. However, your interpretation must always be rooted in the text of the poem.

When examiners read your responses, they will be assessing your own use of language and will reward fluent and controlled expression as well as fresh, insightful ideas.

Useful critical phrases include:

> The poet is suggesting ...
>
> This stanza indicates ...
>
> The reference reveals that ...
>
> The poet's final lines hint at ...
>
> This might well signify ...

STYLISTIC TECHNIQUES

Look closely at the language used in conveying the poet's meaning. Nouns, adjectives, verbs, adverbs, etc., are all chosen for a purpose. Consider why the poet preferred that word, and why it was selected. Is the poet using contrast, exaggeration, modern/archaic terms, personification, alliteration, similes, imagery, metaphors, assonance, onomatopoeia, etc.? What is the effect? Does a particular image engage you? Why?

OTHER USEFUL QUESTIONS

- Does the poet use repetition, lists, short/long sentences, commands, questions, etc.? Why?
- Is the poem written from a particular viewpoint (first, second, third person)? Why?
- Is it written in free verse? Or is rhyme used?
- Is there a definite rhythm? Or contrasting rhythms?
- Does the poet use end-stopped or enjambed lines?
- Is a particular form used (e.g. sonnet)?
- Is a line placed apart from the main body of the poem? Why?
- How does the poem start? How does it conclude?
- In all cases, consider why the poet has decided on that particular language technique.

Acknowledgements

The authors and publisher are grateful to the following for permission to reproduce copyrighted material:

'The Fish', 'The Bight', 'At the Fishhouses', 'The Prodigal', 'Questions of Travel', 'The Armadillo', 'Sestina', 'First Death in Nova Scotia', 'Filling Station', 'In the Waiting Room' by Elizabeth Bishop, from *Poems*, published by Chatto & Windus, reprinted with permission of The Random House Group Limited;

'The Forge', 'Bogland', 'The Tollund Man', 'Sunlight', 'A Constable Calls', 'The Skunk', 'The Harvest Bow', 'The Underground', 'Postscript', 'A Call', 'Tate's Avenue', 'The Pitchfork', 'Lightenings viii' by Seamus Heaney, from *Opened Ground*, reprinted with kind permission of Faber and Faber Ltd;

'Begin', 'Bread', '"Dear Autumn Girl"', 'Poem from a Three Year Old', 'Oliver to His Brother', 'I See You Dancing, Father', 'A Cry for Art O'Leary', 'Things I Might Do', 'A Great Day', 'Fragments', 'The soul's loneliness', 'St Brigid's Prayer' by Brendan Kennelly, from *Familiar Strangers: New and Selected Poems 1960–2004* (Bloodaxe Books, 2004), reprinted with permission of Bloodaxe Books;

'Black Rook in Rainy Weather', 'The Times Are Tidy', 'Morning Song', 'Finisterre', 'Mirror', 'Pheasant', 'Elm', 'Poppies in July', 'The Arrival of the Bee Box', 'Child' by Sylvia Plath, from *Collected Poems*, reprinted with kind permission of Faber and Faber Ltd;

'Lucina Schynning in Silence of the Nicht', 'The Second Voyage', 'Deaths and Engines', 'Street', 'Fireman's Lift', 'All for You', 'Following', 'Kilcash', 'Translation', 'The Bend in the Road', 'On Lacking the Killer Instinct', 'To Niall Woods and Xenya Ostrovskaia, Married in Dublin on 9 September 2009' by Eiléan Ní Chuilleanáin, from *Selected Poems* (2008) and *The Sunfish* (2009), reprinted with kind permission of the author and The Gallery Press, Loughcrew, Oldcastle, County Meath, Ireland.

The authors and publisher have made every effort to trace all copyright holders, but if any has been inadvertently overlooked we would be pleased to make the necessary arrangement at the first opportunity.